STUDIES

Editors

RALPH A. GRIFFITHS   CHRIS WILLIAMS
ERYN M. WHITE

5

POLITICAL POWER IN MEDIEVAL GWYNEDD

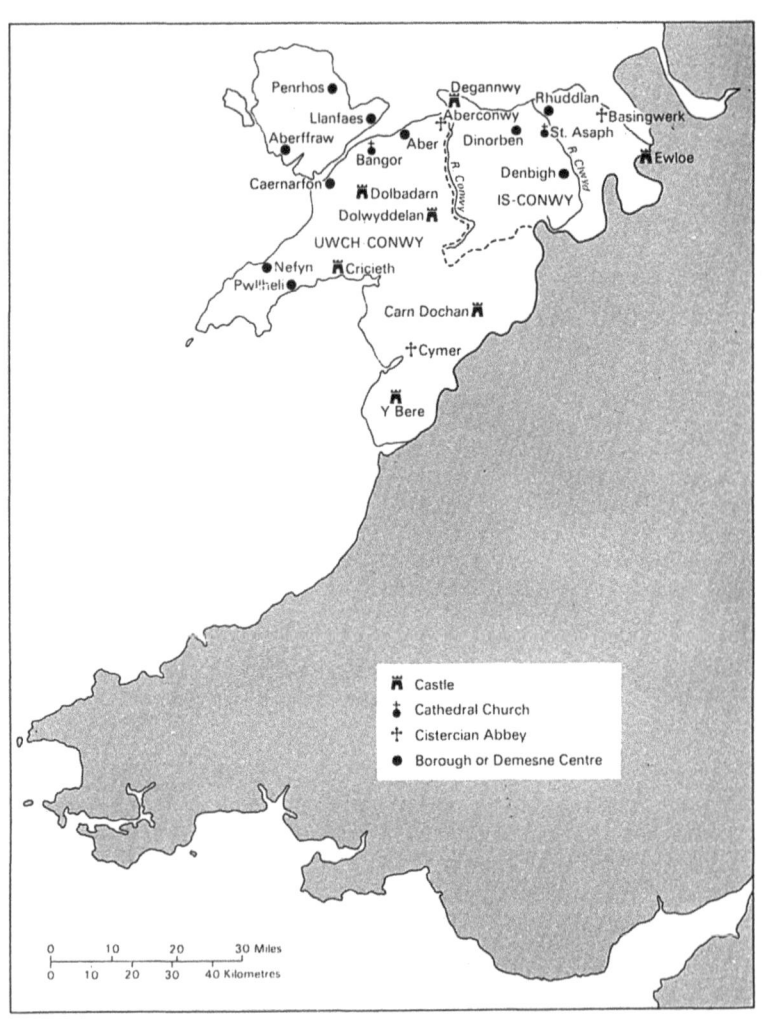

Gwynedd: some sites associated with the Princes' governance

POLITICAL POWER IN MEDIEVAL GWYNEDD

GOVERNANCE AND THE WELSH PRINCES

by

DAVID STEPHENSON

*Published on behalf of
the University of Wales*

**CARDIFF
UNIVERSITY OF WALES PRESS**

© David Stephenson, 1984

Second edition 2014

All rights reserved. No part of this book may be reproduced in any material form (including photocopying or storing it in any medium by electronic means and whether or not transiently or incidentally to some other use of this publication) without the written permission of the copyright owner. Applications for the copyright owner's written permission to reproduce any part of this publication should be addressed to the University of Wales Press, 10 Columbus Walk, Brigantine Place, Cardiff CF10 4UP.

www.uwp.co.uk

British Library CIP Data
A catalogue record for this book is available from the British Library

ISBN 978-1-7831-6004-4

The right of David Stephenson to be identified as author of this work has been asserted in accordance with sections 77 and 79 of the Copyright, Designs and Patents Act 1988.

Printed by CPI Antony Rowe, Chippenham

SERIES EDITORS' FOREWORD

Since the foundation of the series in 1977, the study of Wales's history has attracted growing attention among historians internationally and continues to enjoy a vigorous popularity. Not only are approaches, both traditional and new, to the study of history in general being successfully applied in a Welsh context, but Wales's historical experience is increasingly appreciated by writers on British, European and world history. These advances have been especially marked in the university institutions in Wales itself.

In order to make more widely available the conclusions of original research, much of it of limited accessibility in postgraduate dissertations and theses, in 1977 the History and Law Committee of the Board of Celtic Studies inaugurated this series of monographs, Studies in Welsh History. It was anticipated that many of the volumes would originate in research conducted in the University of Wales or under the auspices of the Board of Celtic Studies, and so it proved. Although the Board of Celtic Studies no longer exists, the University of Wales continues to sponsor this series. It seeks to publish significant contributions made by researchers in Wales and elsewhere. Its primary aim is to serve historical scholarship and to encourage the study of Welsh history.

PREFACE TO THE FIRST EDITION

At one stage or another in its evolution first as a thesis then as a book, this work has benefited from the criticism of Sir Idris Foster, Dr Thomas Charles-Edwards, Mr J. Beverley Smith, Professor Ralph Griffiths, Professor Glanmor Williams, and in particular of Professor Rees Davies without whose prompting and encouragement the thesis would have been much the poorer and the book quite probably non-existent. I doubt whether the result will fully satisfy any of them, but I am pleased and proud to record their help. They cannot be held responsible for the errors in which I have persisted. I also owe much to Mr Alun Treharne of the University of Wales Press who has dealt patiently but firmly with an infuriatingly dilatory author.

PREFACE TO THE SECOND EDITION

The decision of the University of Wales Press to re-issue this book gives me an opportunity to restate my gratitude to the late Sir Rees Davies, my doctoral supervisor and mentor. It was a privilege to have his support, criticism and encouragement. For nearly two decades after the book's publication in 1984 my career took me away from work on medieval Welsh history; when I was able to return to that subject, it was no less of a privilege to be able to contribute to the biennial Bangor colloquium on medieval Wales, where my perceptions have been challenged and sharpened by talking and listening to fellow workers in the field. The stimulus that they have provided is reflected, albeit inadequately, in the new introduction. My thanks are also due to Professor Ralph Griffiths, who suggested that the book should be re-issued, and to Charlotte Austin and Steven Goundrey of the University of Wales Press, for their help and advice. No one has supported my return to the full-time study of medieval Wales more effectively than my wife Jan, to whom I owe a great debt.

CONTENTS

SERIES EDITORS' FOREWORD		v
PREFACE TO THE FIRST EDITION		vi
PREFACE TO THE SECOND EDITION		vii
ABBREVIATIONS		xi
INTRODUCTION		xiii
INTRODUCTION TO THE SECOND EDITION		xliii
Part 1	The Structure of Governance	
I	THE PRINCE AND HIS COUNCIL	1
II	OFFICIALS OF THE PRINCE'S CURIA	11
III	THE PRINCE'S CLERKS	26
IV	LOCAL OFFICIALS	40
	CONCLUSION	52
Part 2	The Prince's Dues	
	INTRODUCTION: THE PROBLEM OF QUANTIFICATION	55
V	DEMESNE EXPLOITATION	57
VI	RENDERS AND DUES	64
	CONCLUSION	94
Part 3	The Personnel of Administration	
VII	RECRUITMENT AND REWARDS	95
Part 4	The Problems of Political Control	
VIII	THE PRINCES AND THE LORDS OF THE PRINCELY HOUSE	138
IX	PRINCES, BISHOPS AND ABBOTS	166
X	THE STATE AND KINSHIP GROUPS	186
Part 5	Assessment	193
APPENDIX I	A Check-list of Charters issued by the Thirteenth-century Rulers of Gwynedd	199
APPENDIX II	A Biographical Gazetteer of Laymen in the Service of the Thirteenth-century Princes	205

APPENDIX III	A Biographical Gazetteer of Clerical Servants of the Thirteenth-century Princes	222
APPENDIX IV	Llywelyn ap Gruffydd and the Opposition to David ap Llywelyn	229
APPENDIX V	The Itinerant Court, July 1273–January 1277	233
APPENDIX VI	Two Edwardian Extents: Dating and Significance	235
APPENDIX VII	Eiryoes	238

LIST OF ILLUSTRATIONS

Map of Gwynedd	*frontispiece*
Opening section of *Llyfr Iorwerth*	240
Charter granted by Llywelyn ap Gruffydd to Einion ap Maredudd	241
BIBLIOGRAPHY	243
INDEX	251

ABBREVIATIONS

A.L.	Aneurin Owen (ed.), *Ancient Laws and Institutes of Wales*, 2 vols., 8vo. (Record Commission, London, 1841)
Annales Cambriae	John Williams ab Ithel (ed.), *Annales Cambriae*, Rolls Series (London, 1860)
Arch. Camb.	*Archaeologia Cambrensis*
Aspects of Welsh History	*Aspects of Welsh History: Selected papers of the late Glyn Roberts* (Cardiff, 1969)
B.B.C.S.	*Bulletin of the Board of Celtic Studies*
BT, Pen. 20	Thomas Jones (gol.), *Brut y Tywysogyon (Peniarth MS. 20)* (Caerdydd, 1941)
BT, Pen. 20 Tr.	Thomas Jones (ed.), *Brut y Tywysogyon or the Chronicle of the Princes (Peniarth MS. 20 Version)* (Cardiff, 1952)
BT, R.B.H.	Thomas Jones (ed.), *Brut y Tywysogyon or the Chronicle of the Princes (Red Book of Hergest Version)* (Cardiff, 1955)
Cal. Anc. Corr.	J. G. Edwards (ed.), *Calendar of Ancient Correspondence concerning Wales* (Cardiff, 1935)
Cal. Anc. Pet.	William Rees (ed.), *Calendar of Ancient Petitions relating to Wales* (Cardiff, 1975)
C. Chanc. R., Various	*Calendar of Chancery Rolls, Various, 1277–1326*
C. Charter R.	*Calendar of Charter Rolls*
C. Close R.	*Calendar of Close Rolls*
C. Fine R.	*Calendar of Fine Rolls*
C. Inq. Misc.	*Calendar of Inquisitions Miscellaneous*
C. Inq. P.M.	*Calendar of Inquisitions Post Mortem*
C. Lib. R.	*Calendar of Liberate Rolls*
C. Pat. R.	*Calendar of Patent Rolls*
Cronica de Wallia	Thomas Jones (ed.), *Cronica de Wallia and other documents from Exeter Cathedral Library MS. 3514* (reprinted from the *Bulletin of the Board of Celtic Studies*, XII, 1948) n.d.
Dugdale, *Monasticon*	William Dugdale, *Monasticon Anglicanum*, ed. J. Cayley, H. Ellis and B. Bandinel, 8 parts (London, 1817–30)
Down, *Heraldic Visitations*	Lewys Dwnn, *Heraldic Visitations of Wales*, ed. S. R. Meyrick, 2 vols. (Llandovery, 1846)
Haddan and Stubbs, *Councils*	A. W. Haddan and W. Stubbs, *Councils and Ecclesiastical Documents relating to Great Britain and Ireland*, I (Oxford, 1869)
Jnl. Mer. Hist. Soc.	*Journal of the Merioneth Historical and Record Society*
L.T.W.L.	H. D. Emmanuel (ed.), *The Latin Texts of the Welsh Laws* (Cardiff, 1967)
Littere Wallie	J. G. Edwards (ed.), *Littere Wallie preserved in Liber A in the Public Record Office* (Cardiff, 1940)
Lloyd, *Hist. Wales*	J. E. Lloyd, *A History of Wales from the Earliest Times to the Edwardian Conquest*, 2 vols. (London, 1911)

Llyfr Blegywryd (or *Bleg.*)[1]	S. J. Williams a J. E. Powell (gol.), *Cyfreithiau Hywel Dda yn ôl Llyfr Blegywryd* (Caerdydd, 1942)
Llyfr Colan (or *Col.*)[1]	Dafydd Jenkins (gol.), *Llyfr Colan, y Gyfraith Gymreig yn ol hanner cyntaf Llawysgrif Peniarth 30* (Caerdydd, 1963)
Llyfr Iorwerth (or *Ior.*)[1]	A. R. William, *Llyfr Iorwerth, A Critical Text of the Venedotian Code of Medieval Welsh Law* (Cardiff, 1960)
Medieval Welsh Society	*Medieval Welsh Society: Selected Essays by T. Jones Pierce*, ed. J. B. Smith (Cardiff, 1972)
Mont. Coll.	*Montgomeryshire Collections*
NLW	National Library of Wales
N.L.W.J.	*National Library of Wales Journal*
PRO	Public Record Office
Rec. Caern.	Henry Ellis (ed.), *Registrum Vulgariter Nuncupatum the Record of Caernarvon*, Record Commission (London, 1838)
Rot. Chart.	*Rotuli Chartarum, 1199–1216*, ed. T. D. Hardy (Record Commission, London, 1837)
Rot. Claus.	*Rotuli litterarum clausarum, 1204–1227*, ed. T. D. Hardy, 2 vols. (Record Commission, London, 1833–44)
Rot. Pat.	*Rotuli litterarum patentium, 1201–1216*, ed. T. D. Hardy, Record Commission (London, 1833)
Seebohm, *Tribal System*	Frederic Seebohm, *The Tribal System in Wales* (London, 1895)
S.D.	P. Vinogradoff and F. Morgan (eds.), *Survey of the Honour of Denbigh, 1334* (London, 1914)
T.R.H.S.	*Transactions of the Royal Historical Society*
Trans. Angl. Ant. Soc.	*Transactions of the Anglesey Antiquarian Society*
Trans. Caerns. Hist. Soc.	*Transactions of the Caernarvonshire Historical Society*
Trans. Cymmr.	*Transactions of the Honourable Society of Cymmrodorion*
Trans. Denb. Hist. Soc.	*Transactions of the Denbighshire Historical Society*
W.H.R.	*Welsh History Review*
W.M.L.	A. W. Wade-Evans (ed.), *Welsh Medieval Law* (Oxford, 1909)
Welsh Assize Roll	J. C. Davies (ed.), *The Welsh Assize Roll, 1277–1284* (Cardiff, 1940)
Wynn, *Gwydir Family*	Sir John Wynn, *The History of the Gwydir Family*, ed. J. Ballinger (Cardiff, 1927)

[1] The following convention will be adopted in the citation of certain editions of legal texts: the texts themselves will be referred to as *Col.*, *Bleg.* and *Ior.*, the first by numbered sentences, the second by page and line number, and the third by section and line number. When editorial commentary or notes are cited, reference will be made to *Llyfr Colan*, *Llyfr Blegywryd* or *Llyfr Iorwerth*.

INTRODUCTION: GWYNEDD AND ITS SOURCES

In the course of the century before 1282 the descendants of an obscure lord of a petty domain in the Conwy valley contrived to raise themselves up to be the princes of the whole of Gwynedd and, sporadically, of most of Wales. Though attended by periodic defeats and humiliations, and fated to end in disaster, theirs was a story as heroic as any in the history of medieval Europe. The achievements of the princes, Llywelyn ab Iorwerth, David ap Llywelyn and Llywelyn ap Gruffydd, were not the product of mere chance, but of their efforts to harness to their will the resources of the lands under their control. To investigate these efforts and their consequences is the object of the present book.

Regarded in the thirteenth century as one of the main geopolitical blocs in that area of Wales still in the hands of native Welsh rulers, Gwynedd was an area of somewhat elastic boundaries, but it can be described roughly as the land to the north-west of a line connecting the mouths of the Dee and the Dyfi. The geography of this area, particularly its military aspects, has been the subject of extensive and important studies by Professor Glanville Jones,[1] but it will be convenient to give here a brief outline of some of its more salient features.

Gwynedd, occupying the north-west portion of Wales, confronted English territory around Chester to the east, the land of Powys to the south-east, and to the south was cut off by the Dyfi estuary from another part of *pura Wallia*, Ceredigion. Against hostile incursions from any of these quarters Gwynedd was well protected by natural barriers, most notable of which were three concentric rings of upland. The outer wall was formed by the Cader Idris, Berwyn and Clwydian ranges, a chain completed and reinforced in its central section by Llywelyn ab Iorwerth's seizure, in 1202, of Penllyn from a representative of the house of Powys. The second wall consisted

---

[1] See in particular G. R. J. Jones, 'The Military Geography of Gwynedd in the Thirteenth Century', University of Wales M.A. thesis, 1949; *idem*, 'The Defences of Gwynedd in the Thirteenth Century', *Trans. Caerns. Hist. Soc.*, 1969, pp. 29–43.

of the uplands of Hiraethog and Migneint, and the inner ring was formed by the Snowdon massif. The areas protected by these mountain barriers were the grain-producing territories of the Llŷn peninsula and the island of Anglesey. These fertile lands were the productive nucleus of Gwynedd.

At three points between the south-western corner of Gwynedd and the point at which the Llŷn peninsula juts out into the sea, the coast is deeply indented, in the south by the Dyfi estuary, about twelve miles farther north by the Mawddach estuary, and at the north of this stretch of coast by the twin arms of the sea at Traeth Bychan and Traeth Mawr. In a similar fashion, northern Gwynedd is effectively cut into two by the river Conwy, which flows into the sea about half-way along the northern coastline. The area to the west is designated as Gwynedd Uwch Conwy (above Conwy), and that to the east as Gwynedd Is Conwy (below Conwy) or the Perfeddwlad (middle country). The coastal indentations noticed here accentuated the obstacles to easy movement offered by the mountain barriers, as did the Menai Strait cutting off Anglesey from the mainland.[2]

Such terrain presented a daunting aspect to the stranger, as we know from the description of one of the most articulate observers of the age, Gerald of Wales, who toured the land preaching the crusade with Archbishop Baldwin in 1188.[3] Gerald's journey through Gwynedd began with the crossing of the Dyfi from Ceredigion into Meirionydd, where he followed the coast, stopping a night at Tywyn. From here the party moved on into Ardudwy, crossing the sea at Traeth Bychan and Traeth Mawr into Eifionydd. Another night was spent at Nefyn, on the northern coast of the Llŷn peninsula, whence the route lay north-east, through Caernarfon and Bangor, to Anglesey. After a brief stay on the island, Gerald and his companions moved eastward along the coastal road, crossing the Conwy at

---

[2] In rugged or thickly-wooded areas river-carriage might offer a better means of transport than did carriage by land; see E. A. Lewis, 'The Development of Industry and Commerce in Wales during the Middle Ages', *T.R.H.S.*, N.S., XVII (1903), p. 141.

[3] The *Itinerarium Kambriae* is printed in J. F. Dimock (ed.), *Giraldi Cambrensis Opera*, Vol. VI, Rolls Series, London, 1868. Lewis Thorpe provides a recent translation in *Gerald of Wales: The Journey through Wales and the Description of Wales*, (Harmondsworth, 1978), though the notes and introduction to this volume do not fully take into account modern scholarship.

its mouth and continuing to Rhuddlan and St. Asaph. The final stages of the journey took them through Basingwerk to the point where they crossed the Dee into English territory near Chester.

Gerald tells us much about the lands through which he passed—though his silences are often as significant as his observations. For example, he notes some of the stone castles which were beginning to dot the terrain of Gwynedd, but he says nothing of the ordinary court buildings of the local rulers, even though he must have passed by some of them, as at Nefyn or Caernarfon. They were mainly wooden structures, and were evidently not considered by Gerald to be noteworthy.[4] Again, we know that primitive trading boroughs existed in Gwynedd in the thirteenth century, and at Nefyn at least we find burgesses before 1200.[5] But Gerald says nothing of any nascent boroughs: if any existed in 1188 they cannot have impressed him.

Indeed, it was not the works of man that absorbed Gerald in Gwynedd, but the awesome nature of the land itself. The mountains were particularly impressive. Those of Meirionydd, 'the rudest and roughest of all the Welsh districts', are recorded as being very high, and characterised by narrow ridges and numerous sharp peaks 'all jumbled together in confusion'. The mountains of Snowdonia itself, seen from Anglesey, seemed to Gerald 'to rear their lofty summits right up to the clouds', and he recalls a saying that if all the herds of Wales were gathered together, the mountains of Snowdonia could supply them with pasture.

Anglesey could not boast of mountains, but this 'arid, stony land' was none the less remarkable for that. In the first place it was marvellously fertile, for 'when crops have failed in all other regions, this island, from the richness of its soil and its abundant produce, has been able to supply all Wales'. It was, moreover, an island of mysteries, and Gerald could not forebear from recounting a few of the strange stories that he had heard: a great stone reputed to return to its site if carried away; a breed of tail-less dogs; the Listener's Rock, so called in irony,

---

[4] See however pp. 4–5 below for a discussion of some impressive sculptured stones at the court of Aberffraw, which was probably not visited by Gerald.
[5] See below, p. 197.

for if two people stood on opposite sides of it and shouted, they could not hear each other.

In the gentler country further east, beyond the Conwy and the vale of Clwyd, Gerald noted a great quicksand, and the densely forested region around Coleshill, where the sons of Owain Gwynedd had inflicted a severe reverse upon Henry II in 1157.

Throughout Gerald's narrative are reports of the river and sea crossings which broke up the journey. In some places, fords may have existed, but Gerald notes the crossing by boat of the Dyfi, the Mawddach, the Menai and the Conwy. At each of these points there were probably already organised ferries under the control of the princes.[6] Indeed, the river-crossings must have seemed small obstacles in comparison with much of the land through which Gerald passed. Near Caernarfon the party encountered a valley 'with many steep climbs up and down', which seemed to them as bad as anything which they might encounter en route to Jerusalem, and left them all exhausted.

Difficult enough for peaceful travellers, the terrain made progress slow and dangerous for any aggressor. When Henry II had launched a great assault on the north in 1165, his army had been bogged down and all but washed away as it became trapped in storms in the Berwyn mountains, so that Henry was forced to turn back before he had even encountered a major Welsh force. But these same obstacles to the stranger served to make internal communications a difficult undertaking for the native ruler. If Gwynedd was a difficult territory to attack, its geographical segments also made it a land which was not easily welded into a coherent polity.

THE POLITICAL BACKGROUND
In a work devoted largely to the study of forms of government, political history need not be set out in detail, except in so far as it helps to explain, or forms the basis of, institutional developments. The main outlines of the complex political history of Wales in the thirteenth century have been brilliantly established by Sir John Edward Lloyd, whose *History of Wales from the*

---

[6] See below, p. 79.

Earliest Times to the Edwardian Conquest, though it has been subject to piecemeal additions and corrections, contains a still indispensable narrative. Detailed additions will be made in the course of the present work, but all that will be undertaken at this point is a survey of the political fortunes of the princes of Gwynedd.[7]

The dominant theme of the political history of early medieval Wales is the chronic instability of a land divided between the territories of numerous petty lords. The areas which they ruled, the commotes or *cantrefi*, or agglomerations of these units, were often smaller than a modestly-sized English country. And in order to control these attenuated domains, the rulers had to struggle against the murderous plans of their kin and occasionally of their *uchelwyr*, their leading freemen. The story of these struggles, recorded in the Welsh chronicles, makes a doleful history of killing interspersed with blinding and emasculation.[8]

Should one of the Welsh lords succeed in establishing, by luck, cunning, or main force, a more ample domain, extending perhaps over all Gwynedd, or Deheubarth in the south, his pride in this achievement had perforce to be tempered by the knowledge that it was unlikely to last, for on his death a ruler's territory was usually subject to division amongst his sons.[9] Such had been the case with Owain Gwynedd, who had managed in the central decades of the twelfth century to attain control over most parts of Gwynedd above and below Conwy. Even during his lifetime, however, he had been troubled by the sporadic challenges of his brother, Cadwaladr, and upon his death in 1170 his 'kingdom' of Gwynedd was torn apart for a generation, as his sons and grandsons struggled for shares or, depending on their ambitions, for supremacy.

The shifting patterns of power and fortune in these years were kaleidoscopic, and have yet to be mapped out with accuracy. But the principal participants can be established clearly

---

[7] For what follows, see Lloyd, *Hist. Wales*, II, pp. 573–764. Attention will be drawn in the notes only to the works in which substantial additions or corrections of Lloyd's narrative of thirteenth-century events are to be found.

[8] Wales was by no means unique in this respect. If anything, the methods of political elimination employed there were, by contemporary European standards, unimaginative.

[9] For discussion see below, pp. 138–9.

enough. In the late 1180s Gerald of Wales found Gruffydd and Maredudd, the sons of Cynan ab Owain, ensconced in the south-west—in Meirionydd, Ardudwy and Eifionydd; Llŷn he vaguely attributed to the sons of Owain;[10] Rhodri ab Owain held Anglesey, and Dafydd ab Owain was lord below the Conwy. Yet already another force was making itself felt in the politics of Gwynedd: one of Owain's grandsons, Llywelyn ab Iorwerth, though a mere youth, was beginning to cause his uncles Dafydd and Rhodri some trouble.

Llywelyn had been born in 1173, the son of Iorwerth Drwyndwn (flat-nose), who was probably the ruler of Nant Conwy until he died soon after the birth of his son. Until he began his campaign against his uncles in 1188, Llywelyn was probably brought up beyond Gwynedd, amongst his maternal kin: his mother was Margaret, daughter of Madog ap Maredudd, lord of Powys. We know nothing of his initial moves against Dafydd and Rhodri, but it seems that by the mid-1190s he had obtained the help of the sons of Cynan, and had driven out both of his uncles.[11] Rhodri died in 1195, and Dafydd was finally driven into exile in England in 1197. The later 1190s saw his allies Gruffydd and Maredudd ap Cynan ruling in the south-west of Gwynedd and in Llŷn, and their power may have caused Llywelyn some anxiety. But Gruffydd died in 1200, and Maredudd was expelled by Llywelyn from Llŷn in 1201, and then lost Meirionydd from which he was driven by Gruffydd's son, Hywel, in 1202.

By 1202 Llywelyn was thus in direct control of almost all of Gwynedd, to which he added Penllyn, seized from his uncle Elise ap Madog. In Meirionydd, Hywel ap Gruffydd remained generally loyal to Llywelyn except for a brief period in 1211, but even if Hywel posed any threat to Llywelyn, it was removed by his death in 1216.[12] From that date Llywelyn was the

---

[10] Following Lloyd, *Hist. Wales*, II, p. 613 n. 5, it is generally considered that Rhodri is meant by this phrase to have held Llŷn, as he is alleged to have driven Dafydd from the whole of Gwynedd Uwch Conwy in 1175. But see a charter issued by Dafydd to Haughmond abbey, apparently granting lands in Nefyn, in Shrewsbury Public Library MS.1, f.149. This grant would seem to have been made in or after 1177, for one of the witnesses is Gwion, bishop of Bangor; Gwion was not consecrated until 1177: see Haddan and Stubbs, *Councils*, I. p. 385.

[11] See below, pp. 199–200.

[12] The political situation in south-west Gwynedd is very obscure in the first two decades of the century; one of the sons of Maredudd ap Cynan may have held some of his father's former lands: see below pp. 142–3.

effective master of Gwynedd until his death in 1240, and thus was able to use the resources of that land to further his wider ambitions in Wales.

In 1204 Llywelyn's determination to play more than a parochial part in the politics of his day was underlined by his marriage to Joan, the daughter of King John. From the first years of the century he had begun to make threatening moves towards southern Powys, which was then under the rule of its ambitious lord, Gwenwynwyn. When the latter fell under King John's displeasure in 1208, Llywelyn took the opportunity to overrun his lands, whence he began to interfere in the affairs of Ceredigion. Before two years were out, however, Llywelyn himself had incurred John's anger, and in 1210 English forces attacked Gwynedd, whilst others drove back the prince's allies in the south. In 1211, John personally joined the attack on Llywelyn, who was forced to cede Gwynedd Is Conwy to the king and to deliver up hostages. His allies in Ceredigion were also defeated, and at Aberystwyth a royal castle began to rise.

On the surface, John had humbled Llywelyn and crushed his rising influence in Wales, but this was at the cost of provoking widespread suspicion amongst the minor Welsh lords. Welsh rulers were generally quite prepared to accept the exercise by the English kings of a nebulous overlordship,[13] but they tended to become extremely agitated if the kings threatened to play a more active part in Welsh affairs. Now Llywelyn was to profit from just such a bout of collective agitation, whilst he also showed his vision and resourcefulness by negotiating for an alliance with King Philip of France in 1212.[14]

In any case, the gathering storm of baronial discontent in England was soon to curtail John's capacity to intervene in Welsh politics. Llywelyn was thus able to sweep rapidly back through Gwynedd Is Conwy, and in 1215 to lead the Welsh lords of northern and central Wales into the south, where he displayed his military prowess by capturing royal and baronial

---

[13] For a general survey see A. J. Roderick, 'The Feudal Relations between the English Crown and the Welsh Princes', *History*, XXXVII (1952), pp. 201–12.

[14] R. F. Treharne, 'The Franco-Welsh Treaty of Alliance in 1212', *B.B.C.S.*, XVIII (1958), pp. 60–75.

castles almost with ease. So powerful a demonstration of Llywelyn's power was this, that in the following year he was to preside over an assembly of Welsh magnates at Aberdyfi, at which he partitioned Deheubarth amongst the descendants of its former lord, Rhys ap Gruffydd.

It may have been in the course of the preparations for the 1215 expedition that Gwenwynwyn of Powys, once more restored to his lands by John, agreed to do homage to Llywelyn, and to hand over hostages as pledges of his fidelity. But in 1216 Gwenwynwyn went over to the side of the king, thus providing Llywelyn with the occasion to expel him once again from southern Powys. It was to be the final encounter between the two, for later in the year Gwenwynwyn died, at about the same time as did King John.

The opening of the reign of Henry III thus saw Llywelyn ab Iorwerth prince of all Gwynedd, lord of southern Powys and overlord of Deheubarth. This, broadly speaking, was the situation which was formalized in the Treaty of Worcester between Llywelyn and the English government in 1218. But if the young king's councillors had thought that concession would dampen Llywelyn's spirit, they had miscalculated. He roamed the borders of his domains, now raiding the lands of the earl of Pembroke, now destroying potentially hostile castles in Shropshire, whilst strengthening his hand in 1222 by marrying his daughter, Helen, to the son of Earl Ranulf of Chester.

In 1223, however, Llywelyn's turbulence brought retribution: he was attacked by a combination of royal and baronial forces, losing Montgomery to the king and the castles of Cardigan and Carmarthen, the custody of which he had been granted in 1218, to the earl of Pembroke. These setbacks, however, were the product of a rare interlude in which the English crown and the marcher lords demonstrated a unity of purpose. They taught Llywelyn not to be too reckless, but this presaged no great English onslaught, and the mid-1220s were years of relative calm, with Llywelyn's practical authority in Wales hardly in doubt. Thus, when the great justiciar, Hubert de Burgh, engineered an invasion of mid-Wales in 1228, Llywelyn was able to beat it off without great difficulty, and capitalized on his successes by securing a renewal of royal recognition of his younger son, David, as his successor. This plan had much to recommend it to the English government, as David was the son of Joan and, hence, the king's brother-in-law, whereas the elder son, Gruffydd, to whom he was preferred by Llywelyn was the offspring of an earlier liaison with a Welsh woman, Tangwystl Goch.

David's future was further consolidated by arrangements for his marriage to Isabella, offspring of the great marcher family of de Braose. These arrangements even survived the hanging by Llywelyn in 1230 of Isabella's father, William, who had been rash enough to embark on an affair with Princess Joan. But if Llywelyn's domestic life was troubled in 1230, his political standing had never been more secure. It was now that he discarded his former title of prince of north Wales, in favour of the style of prince of Aberffraw and lord of Snowdon. Aberffraw, on the western coast of Anglesey, was the chief seat of the rulers of Gwynedd, and its lord had a shadowy claim to supremacy over all other Welsh rulers. Llywelyn's new title was thus a highly significant one.

There was to be one final storm to test the stability of Llywelyn's authority: a second struggle with Hubert de Burgh. In 1231 Llywelyn apparently resolved to exploit the power vacuum created by the recent death of several leading marchers, including William de Braose and William Marshall, earl of Pembroke.[15] Accordingly, he launched an attack on the southern march. The royal grant of custody of the Braose lands to Hubert de Burgh failed to halt Llywelyn's assault, and may indeed have merely angered him, for his onslaught grew fiercer and more widespread, culminating in the capture of Cardigan castle. No great counter-attack came; Hubert's efforts were expended on building a fortress at Painscastle in Elfael. Indeed, the English court was soon absorbed by the internal struggles between Hubert and the growing band of his enemies. After the fall of the justiciar, a new conflict between Peter de Rivaux and the earl of Pembroke served to distract attention from Llywelyn. The prince even contrived to join in the attack on de Rivaux, who had succeeded to most of Hubert de Burgh's Welsh interests.

[15] R. F. Walker, 'Hubert de Burgh and Wales', *E.H.R.*, LXXXVII (1972), pp. 465–94.

With the fall of Peter de Rivaux in 1234, the way was open for a settlement with the English government, which was effected in the Pact of Middle. Llywelyn was to retain the gains of 1231: effectively this implied recognition of his supremacy in Wales. For his last six years the prince was at peace. He seems to have suffered a paralytic stroke in 1237, and from that date it may be that his son, David, took over effective control of the principality, issuing confirmation charters to monastic houses,[16] taking oaths of fealty from the Welsh magnates, and depriving his brother, Gruffydd, of most of the territories assigned to him by Llywelyn.

On Llywelyn's death in 1240, however, there occurred precisely what he had striven hard to avoid: discord between his two sons. This was clearly the result in large part of David's determination not only to establish himself as the head of the principality which Llywelyn had created, but also to deny his half-brother any part of the lands accumulated by their father.[17] For the moment, however, David lacked Llywelyn's authority, and the opening years of his principate were little short of disastrous. Facing trouble from the supporters of Gruffydd, David was obliged to buy English recognition, in the Treaty of Gloucester of 1240, by renouncing the homage of the Welsh lords and submitting the fate of Llywelyn's acquisitions beyond Gwynedd to arbitration. At once, the whole future of the wider principality which Llywelyn had created in central and southern Wales was thrown into the gravest doubt.

David's not unnatural reluctance to implement the Gloucester settlement led in 1241 to armed conflict with the king, and a further decline in his position. English military advances through Gwynedd Is Conwy forced him to accept the Treaty of Gwern Eigron, whereby Gruffydd ap Llywelyn was delivered from David's prison into the custody of Henry, who undertook to investigate Gruffydd's right to a part of the patrimony.[18] In addition, Llywelyn's conquests beyond Gwynedd were to be given up, and parts of Gwynedd itself were lost: Meirionydd

---

[16] See Appendix I below, nos. 17 and 18.
[17] G. A. Williams. 'The Succession to Gwynedd, 1238-1247', *B.B.C.S.*, XX (1962-4), pp. 393-413.
[18] For Gruffydd's subsequent detention by Henry, see below, p. 154.

went to representatives of the line of Maredudd ap Cynan, and Tegeingl, the easternmost of the four *cantrefi* of Gwynedd Is Conwy, was lost to the crown.

The fortunes of the ruler of Gwynedd were thus at a lower ebb than at any time since the days of John's attack in 1211. But just as John's success had produced a reaction amongst the Welsh, so Henry's triumph brought the lesser Welsh lords to David's side. Suspicions rose amongst those who had allied with the king—such as Gruffydd ap Madog of northern Powys—that Henry meant to impose new laws and customs upon them. Then, on St David's Day 1244, Gruffydd ap Llywelyn was killed in a fall from the Tower of London as he tried to escape from royal custody. The way was clear for David to renew the fight, for Gruffydd's death not only gave him a pretext for action but also removed the danger that Henry might set up his half-brother as an alternative ruler.

It was probably at this time that David assumed the title of prince of Wales,[19] for he now stood at the head of a widespread reaction against Henry's power. He also called for, and for a few months obtained, papal support. The year 1245 was marked by fierce fighting centred on Henry's advance to Degannwy, at the mouth of the Conwy, where he built a great castle in the face of constant Welsh raids. But early in 1246, during the lull in operations caused by the winter, David died, leaving no children.

There were two principal claimants to the principality: Llywelyn and Owain, two of the four sons of Gruffydd ap Llywelyn. Owain, the eldest of the sons, had been maintained by the royal government in Chester, but on his uncle's death he hastened into Wales to stake his claim to Gwynedd. Llywelyn's background was rather different: for a time in the early 1240s he had been established in Gwynedd Is Conwy, apparently in opposition to David, and probably with royal connivance.[20] He had, however, gone over to the prince by 1245, and was thus the nearer of the two claimants to hand when David died.

---

[19] *C.A.C.*, pp. 50–1. See also Michael Richter, 'David ap Llywelyn, the first Prince of Wales,' *W.H.R.*, V (1971), pp. 205–19.

[20] See below, Appendix IV.

A struggle between the two brothers seemed inevitable, but they were persuaded by the magnates of the land to partition Gwynedd between them.[21] This partition was not, however, the end of their problems, for the two brothers were in no state to maintain for long an effective resistance to Henry III's armies. Royal forces struck easily through Meirionydd, Ardudwy and the vale of Conwy to Degannwy. Below the Conwy all was in Henry's hands, and a hopeless struggle was ended with the Treaty of Woodstock in April 1247.[22] Owain and Llywelyn lost much; Gwynedd below Conwy was ceded to the crown; the rights of minor scions of the ruling dynasty were to be recognised in Meirionydd and Llŷn; and the obligations of the brothers to provide Henry with military service were set out in detail. Beyond Gwynedd, Gruffydd, son of Gwenwynwyn, for some years a royal partisan, was by now firmly established in his father's lands of southern Powys, thus barring the way to the south and the middle march from Gwynedd.

The following years were marked by apparently conflicting tendencies. On the one hand, the fragmentation of Gwynedd increased as a third son of Gruffydd, Dafydd, arrived on the scene and was granted the lordship of Cymydmaen in Llŷn. The fourth son, Rhodri, was also approaching the age at which some provision might have to be made for him. On the other hand, Owain and Llywelyn, and particularly the latter, began to negotiate alliances with other Welsh lords, which suggest that they were growing restless at their confinement to but a part of the ancestral lands.[23] The mid-1250s saw these manifold tensions resolved in violent fashion: first, Llywelyn and two of his brothers, Owain and Dafydd, came to blows over the division of territory between them. At the battle of Bryn Derwin in 1255 Llywelyn was victorious: Owain and Dafydd were consigned to his prison. The next year brought Llywelyn out of the lands to which he and Owain had been restricted in 1247.

His initial drive took him over the Conwy into the Perfeddwlad, which had been in the hands of Henry's son Edward since

---

[21] See below, pp. 156–8 for an attempt to establish the form of partition.
[22] C. W. Lewis, 'The Treaty of Woodstock, 1247: its background and significance', *W.H.R.*, II (1964), pp. 37–65.
[23] *Littere Wallie*, pp. 148, 160.

1254. There was little opposition, and in all Gwynedd Is Conwy only the castles of Diserth and Degannwy remained to be reduced later. Llywelyn now released his brother Dafydd (Owain he probably thought irreconcilable) and established him in part of the newly-won territory. His next move was to chase out of Meirionydd and Llŷn those lesser members of the ruling house who had held the area since the 1240s.[24]

Thus, by the end of 1256 the full principality of Gwynedd had been reconstituted. There is, however, no evidence that Llywelyn hastened to adopt the title of prince of north Wales: his ambition clearly ran beyond this, and so he employed, for the moment, no title at all. It was in 1257 that Llywelyn began to assert himself beyond Gwynedd, raiding almost at will in southern Powys, and then in Ystrad Tywi, Dyfed and Glamorgan, and finally returning to Gwynedd to beat off a half-hearted attempt at invasion by King Henry. Already such a run of successes had begun to attract the adherence to Llywelyn of some of the Welsh lords of the south, and of Gruffydd ap Madog, the greatest lord of northern Powys.

Still greater triumphs lay ahead, as the English king became totally absorbed by the baronial unrest which dominated English politics for most of the next decade. The preoccupations of Henry and the marcher lords, who were also to feature prominently in the English crises, allowed Llywelyn first to consolidate and then to enhance his position. Consolidation took the spectacular form of an assembly of Welsh lords early in 1258 which included every Welsh ruler of note except Gruffydd ap Gwenwynwyn; there they rendered homage and fealty to Llywelyn. It was perhaps at this assembly that negotiations were put in train which resulted in an agreement in March 1258 between Llywelyn and the Welsh lords, on on one hand, and the Scottish magnates led by the earl of Menteith, on the other. The Scots pledged themselves not to aid Henry III against the Welsh, and, more constructively, to encourage trade between Wales and Scotland. Perhaps more important was Llywelyn's designation as prince of Wales in the record of the agreement: here was the dignity towards which he had been aspiring. The implications of this status and of the homage and oaths of fealty, which Llywelyn

---

[24] See below, pp. 144–51.

had exacted from the Welsh lords, were demonstrated in 1259, when Maredudd ap Rhys of Ystrad Tywi, greatest of the southern magnates, in a council held in Arwystli, was formally convicted of treason against his lord, and imprisoned by Llywelyn. He was released only on the surrender of his eldest son, Rhys, as a hostage, and the cession to Llywelyn of lands and castles, including Dinefwr, the chief seat of Deheubarth.

In the course of the next five years, the new prince of Wales occupied himself in negotiating truces with the English government and in sporadic harrying and annexation of the lands which bordered his principality. The year 1260 saw the capture of Builth from Roger Mortimer and the submission of Elfael. In 1262 Maelienydd and Brecon also fell to Llywelyn's forces, whilst in the following year the defection to the English of his brother Dafydd was amply balanced by the submission to Llywelyn of Gruffydd ap Gwenwynwyn of southern Powys.

During these years Llywelyn entered into the shifting pattern of alliances that constituted English politics; by 1264 he was giving his help to Simon de Montfort, and was thus ranged against the majority of the marcher lords, who supported the cause of Henry III. From Simon de Montfort Llywelyn doubtless expected recognition of his paramount position in Wales. His need at this time was for an English government sufficiently strong and stable for its recognition of his status to be worth having, yet not so strong that it might be tempted to withhold recognition and humble him by force.

An attempt to achieve a lasting settlement was made with Earl Simon in 1265. By the agreement reached at Pipton, Llywelyn's status as prince of Wales, the suzerain of all the Welsh lords, was to be recognised. But the régime of the earl was already tottering to its eventual downfall at Evesham later in the year. The Welsh troops sent by Llywelyn to help Simon were of little use: a pitched battle was not their style of warfare. Even with his ally overthrown, however, Llywelyn was still able to hold his own in conditions more congenial to his warriors: in 1266 he continued to enjoy success against royal and marcher armies.

It was in these circumstances that the government of Henry III, intent upon the work of reconstruction that followed such a long period of turmoil, resolved to come to terms with

Llywelyn. In the Treaty of Montgomery of 1267 Llywelyn received the acknowledgement that he sought. He was to have the homage of all the Welsh lords, except that of Maredudd ap Rhys of Ystrad Tywi, who was to remain the king's vassal. He was to hold not only his gains in the Perfeddwlad, but virtually all those in the middle March. In return, he was to restore Dafydd to a suitable portion of Gwynedd, and, most importantly, he was to pay the king 25,000 marks in instalments. He might, in addition, be allowed to purchase the homage of Maredudd ap Rhys for a further payment of 5,000 marks.

On the surface, Montgomery marks a great triumph for Llywelyn. It was, however, a costly one: the cash render due from so small and rugged a principality was heavy; the restoration of Dafydd might cause problems; and Llywelyn's accumulation in the March of territories under his own immediate lordship was likely to rouse the envy and hostility not only of the marcher lords, many of whom had lost lands to him, but also of his new vassals, the lesser Welsh magnates. Indeed, once the initial euphoria of his achievement had passed, Llywelyn can have known little peace of mind. With the lords of northern Powys, it is true, he experienced few problems. But elsewhere the prince either found or created trouble with disconcerting regularity. In 1270 he contracted to pay to Henry the extra 5,000 marks that brought him the homage of Maredudd ap Rhys of Ystrad Tywi. It was a debt which Llywelyn might have spared himself: Maredudd was to die the next year, and his son, Rhys, never bore his subordination to Llywelyn easily and deserted him at the first crisis.

In the south-east Llywelyn maintained his hold on the lordship of Brecon only in the face of the attacks of Humphrey de Bohun. Again, in spite of the prince's agreement in 1268 to a settlement with Gilbert de Clare, earl of Gloucester, the decade after 1267 was marked by constant hostility between them, much of it focused on the great castle which Gilbert began to build at Caerphilly. Llywelyn succeeded in destroying the new fortress in 1270,[25] only for Gilbert to begin its construction anew, and on an even more ambitious scale.

[25] F. M. Powicke, *King Henry III and the Lord Edward* (Oxford, 1966), pp. 578–82, has a good summary of the struggle over Caerphilly.

It was southern Powys, however, which posed the most serious problems, for it was the seed-bed of a formidable plot on Llywelyn's life in 1274.[26] The plot involved his brother, Dafydd, and the lord of southern Powys, Gruffydd ap Gwenwynwyn, together with Gruffydd's son, Owain, and wife, Hawise. The actual killing was to have been done by Owain, after he had made his way secretly to Llywelyn's court, where Dafydd would admit him. Bad weather foiled the stratagem, and gradually the prince's suspicions were aroused. For a while he lacked sufficient proof, but he secured Owain in prison and continued his probing, with the result that Dafydd, Gruffydd and Hawise fled to England. The prince responded to the defections by taking over the territories of the fugitives. But Dafydd and Gruffydd, safe in English territory, began an irritating series of raids on Llywelyn's lands, and thus contributed to the most portentous of all the quarrels in which the prince became involved—that with his feudal lord, the king of England.

The alleged failure of the English government to keep to the bargain struck at Montgomery elicited complaints from Llywelyn as early as 1270, and the complaints increased in urgency after Edward I's government persisted in harbouring the fugitives, Dafydd and Gruffydd. It was what he perceived as a refusal to honour solemn obligations that prompted Llywelyn to withhold payment of the money due under the terms of the Treaty of Montgomery, and to persist in his refusal to swear fealty and perform homage to the new king.[27]

A further cause of conflict developed in 1275, when Edward imprisoned Llywelyn's bride, Eleanor, the daughter of Simon de Montfort, after the ship carrying her from France to Wales was intercepted by English vessels. So attitudes hardened on both sides, and in 1276 Edward resolved to bring the rebellious prince to heel. In spite of last-minute attempts at conciliation by Llywelyn,[28] Edward duly launched against him a massive and costly army.

---

[26] The best discussion of these events is to be found in J. G. Edward's introduction to *Littere Wallie*, pp. liii–lv.
[27] See ibid., pp. lvi–lx.
[28] J. B. Smith, 'Offra Principis Wallie Domino Regi'. *B.B.C.S.*, XXIV (1966), pp. 362–7.

In the face of Edward's onslaught, the principality crumbled. Most of the Welsh lords went over to the king—some, like Rhys ap Maredudd, doing so with an alacrity that betrays their relief at Llywelyn's downfall. By late 1277, Llywelyn was prepared to accept terms, and hard terms they were. By the Treaty of Conwy, Llywelyn was to retain the title of prince of Wales, but his principality was spectacularly reduced in size, so that it constituted little more than Gwynedd Uwch Conwy. All else was lost: some areas, such as parts of the Perfeddwlad, to the crown, some to the marcher lords, and, most galling of all, some to the conspirators of 1274. Even within Gwynedd Uwch Conwy, Llywelyn was obliged to make provision for his brother, Owain, now released from his prison, and for one of the latter's few remaining supporters amongst the minor lords, Rhys Fychan, who had been driven out of his own lands in Ceredigion.

It had been a signal defeat, and Llywelyn had to show that he accepted it. For the next five years he appears on the surface as a model vassal of Edward, dutiful and respectful. In turn the king was benevolent, and the delayed wedding to Eleanor de Montfort was allowed to go ahead in 1278 at Worcester. Yet there are signs that Llywelyn was all the time planning to push beyond the bounds within which he had been confined. He fought a long and frustrating legal battle with Gruffydd ap Gwenwynwyn for control of Arwystli and Cyfeiliog.[29] Possibly in an attempt to gain his ends by other means, he concluded an agreement with Roger Mortimer, one of Gruffydd's neighbours in the March,[30] and another with Gruffydd's steward, himself a man of Cyfeiliog, who stated his readiness to return to 'unity' with the prince.[31] It may be that Llywelyn had still not abandoned hope of a rapid resurgence.

Ironically, it was Dafydd ap Gruffydd who precipitated the final crisis. Dissatisfied, so it seems, with his share of the spoils in 1277, Dafydd put himself at the head of all those Welsh

---

[29] J. C. Davies discusses most aspects of this struggle in his long introduction to *W.A.R.*, but his treatment of the matter is virtually an apologia for Llywelyn and an indictment of the prince's enemies, real or imagined. F. M. Powicke, op. cit., pp. 669–76, is more balanced, as is J. E. Lloyd, 'Edward I's Commission of Enquiry of 1281', in *Y Cymmrodor*, XXV (1915).

[30] J. B. Smith, 'The Middle March in the Thirteenth Century', *B.B.C.S.*, XXIV (1970), pp. 77–92.

[31] *Littere Wallie*, p. 34.

who were resentful of the exactions and arrogance of royal officials in and near the areas seized by Edward in that year. On Palm Sunday 1282 he attacked and captured the castle of Hawarden, and in the following week many of the lords of the south also rose, directing their attacks at royal castles. If Llywelyn was to retain his pride of place amongst Welsh rulers, he could do little but assume leadership of the movement.[32]

Though theirs was far from being a national movement, with Rhys ap Maredudd and Gruffydd ap Gwenwynwyn conspicuous among those who held aloof, the element of surprise enabled Llywelyn and Dafydd to make headway. Their allies amongst the minor lords enjoyed some success in the south, whilst a royal force which had landed in Anglesey was overwhelmed whilst trying to cross the Menai Straits. His early success tempted Llywelyn to reject offers of mediation, and, leaving Dafydd in charge in the north, he sent his steward to raise support in Brycheiniog, whilst he turned to Builth to organize the campaign in that March. It was in Builth that Llywelyn met his end: in a battle at Irfon Bridge on 11 December 1282, the prince was killed. Resistance was continued for some months by Dafydd,[33] but after his capture and execution in 1283 the principality of Wales was finally brought under English control.

It is clear from this survey that Gwynedd served periodically as the power-base on which a much wider principality was constructed. The careful use by Llywelyn ab Iorwerth and Llywelyn ap Gruffydd of the title 'lord of Snowdon' alongside their more far-reaching titles of, respectively, prince of Aberffraw and prince of Wales, underlines the point. It is possible to discern three periods of expansion within and beyond Gwynedd: the years between about 1190 and 1210, between 1212 and 1234, and between 1255 and 1266. There were also, however, periods of contraction, when the princes were driven back within the fortresses of Gwynedd, as in 1210–12, 1240–55 and

---

[32] This is the interpretation of Llywelyn's involvement in the rising given by J. G. Edwards, *Littere Wallie*, pp. lxviii–lxix.
[33] Ralph Maud, 'David, the last Prince of Wales', *Trans. Cymmr.*, 1968, pp. 43–62.

1277–83. Finally, we find periods of apparently settled greatness, in 1234–40 and 1267–76.

Each phase of political development imposed its own forms of stress upon the structure of governance in Gwynedd. Implicit in a period of contraction was a political weakness which might, for instance, force a prince to accede to the demands of other members of the ruling house for a share, or a greater share, of the lands of Gwynedd. The military effort attending periods of expansion involved the raising and, perhaps, the payment of large numbers of troops,[34] and the construction of castles. The retention of an expanded principality necessitated a search for trustworthy ministers and lieutenants, whose loyalty was best strengthened by material rewards.[35] Most ominous of all is the fact that the attempts of the princes to extend, or even maintain their power, repeatedly forced them to make large payments, mainly but not exclusively to the English kings, whether as diplomatic *douceurs* or by way of formal tribute or indemnity.

It is possible that as early as 1208 Llywelyn ab Iorwerth bought off the wrath of King John, which had been aroused by the prince's seizure of the lands of Gwenwynwyn. At the close of the year, John announced his willingness to forgive Llywelyn, *ex quo ipse inde fecerit quod se facturum nobis mandavit, iuxta tenorem literarum suarum . . .*[36] Twenty years later, at the close of the campaign of 1228, Llywelyn contracted to pay Henry III £2,000 as an indemnity and in return for the dismantling of the castle which Hubert de Burgh had begun to build in Ceri. This obligation was, however, neatly balanced by Llywelyn's receipt of a like sum as ransom for William de Braose.[37]

The year 1241 saw a promise by Senena, wife of the disinherited Gruffydd ap Llywelyn, to pay Henry III 600 marks if the king would secure her husband's re-establishment in Gwynedd. Senena further pledged an annual payment of 300 marks, one third in cash and the remainder in cattle and horses, if Gruffydd were accorded his share of the patrimony.[38] Three years later,

---

[34] See below, pp. 89–93.
[35] See below, pp. 95–102.
[36] *Foedera*, I, p. 151.
[37] Lloyd, *Hist. Wales*, II, p. 670.
[38] *Littere Wallie*, pp. 52–3. It seems that David actually paid three hundred marks to the king in order to secure his hold on Gwynedd: *Close Rolls, 1237–42*, p. 427, and ibid., *1242–7*, p. 71.

David's efforts to secure papal support against the king were backed up with gifts,[39] as were Llywelyn ap Gruffydd's endeavours in the mid-1250s to persuade Henry III to accept his overthrow of Owain and Dafydd.[40]

With Llywelyn ap Gruffydd's attempts in the late 1250s and afterwards to achieve a secure settlement with the English government, the scale of actual or projected payments rose steeply. He offered 1,500 marks in 1257 for a seven-year truce.[41] This was rejected, as was an offer of 4,500 marks for a permanent peace.[42] Accordingly, this was increased by Llywelyn in 1259 to an offer of £16,000, payable over eighty years in annual instalments of £200;[43] in return, Llywelyn sought recognition as lord of all the territories which had been held by Llywelyn ab Iorwerth. Here we have a series of bids for a settlement on something like easy terms: if we compare Senena's pledge of £200 per year, to be raised, presumably, from rather less than half of Gwynedd, we gain some idea of the level of tribute which the northern principality might comfortably bear around the middle years of the century. It is clear, however, that these offers were totally inadequate, even derisory; something much more substantial would be required if a settlement were to be reached.

After sundry relatively small payments for short truces, Llywelyn offered 30,000 marks to Simon de Montfort in 1265 for a permanent peace in which his right to rule the principality of Wales would be acknowledged. After the earl's death, the prince made a very similar offer, now to the victorious royal party, in 1267.[44] The arrangement made at Montgomery was that Llywelyn would pay a tribute of 25,000 marks, to be discharged in annual payments of 3,000 marks. Initially, the homage of Maredudd ap Rhys of Deheubarth was to be withheld from Llywelyn, but might be purchased by him at a further cost of 5,000 marks. It is true that this burden fell upon more extensive territories than had been controlled by

---

[39] *Matthaei Parisiensis ... Chronica Majora*, ed. H. R. Luard, R.S., IV, p. 401.
[40] *Close Rolls, 1256–9*, p. 104.
[41] *C.A.C.*, pp. 50–1.
[42] *M. Paris*, V, p. 727.
[43] *Close Rolls, 1259–61*, p. 4.
[44] For the offer of 1265, see W. W. Shirley (ed.), *Royal Letters ... Henry III*, II (1866), pp. 284–6, and for the terms agreed in 1267, *Littere Wallie*, pp. 3–4.

Llywelyn in 1259, but nevertheless it represents a level of obligation which goes far beyond anything contemplated in the past. So great was the financial commitment entered into at Montgomery that it seems to cast grave doubts on Llywelyn's grasp of reality. In his most able analysis of the situation,[45] Keith Williams-Jones has written of the prince's 'overweening ambition and ill-conceived policies', and concludes bluntly that 'intention outran capacity'. It is a powerful argument, but it cannot be accepted, for it seems to involve an untested assumption about the nature of the prince's government. This assumption is revealed in the statement that 'the machinery at Llywelyn's disposal for raising revenue cannot possibly have been as sophisticated or as well-lubricated as the crown's'.[46] Now this statement may be true, as far as it goes; but it does not mean that the prince did not dispose of flexible and highly effective means of raising revenue. Sophistication and an excess of machinery, however well-lubricated, are not necessarily the best guarantees of effectiveness.

Indeed, Llywelyn shows signs of being able to meet the obligations imposed at Montgomery, if he wished to do so. He even increased his debt in 1270 by purchasing the homage of Maredudd ap Rhys. It is true that he was falling behind with his payments after 1270, but this may have been because he was dissatisfied with the way in which the treaty was being observed.[47] In the five years after the Treaty of Montgomery, Llywelyn paid over some 15,000 marks, or half of the total debt.[48] When payments did cease, at the end of 1272, it is noteworthy that the prince showed few signs of financial exhaustion. He was already engaged in strenuous fighting in the south,

[45] Keith Williams-Jones (ed.), *The Merioneth Lay Subsidy Roll, 1292–93* (Cardiff, 1976), Introduction, pp. xvii–xx.

[46] Ibid., p. xviii.

[47] As early as the autumn of 1270 Llywelyn was threatening that he might have to ignore the treaty if it were not better observed: see *Close Rolls, 1268–72*, pp. 234–6.

[48] The documents cited in Lloyd, *Hist. Wales*, II, p. 755 n. 198 seem amply to bear out Edwards's cautious suggestion, *Littere Wallie*, p. li n. 1, that only 2,000 marks were owing at the end of the reign of Henry III, by which date 17,000 marks should have been paid. On the other hand, it would seem that Llywelyn had not paid the 5,000 marks for the homage of Maredudd ap Rhys, for in 1277 he offered that sum for the homage of Maredudd's son and successor: see J. B. Smith, 'Offra Principis Wallie Domino Regi', *B.B.C.S.*, XXIV (1966), p. 366.

against Gilbert de Clare and Humphrey de Bohun. Again, it was apparently in 1273 that he began to build Dolforwyn castle: as well as the expenditure on building works, it was estimated by Edward I's captains in 1277 that it would require something like 1,000 marks per year to garrison Dolforwyn.[49] Llywelyn's ideas of a garrison may not have been so ambitious or so thorough, but obviously the enterprise would not be cheap. Furthermore, shortly after beginning the building of Dolforwyn, the prince was rumoured to be planning yet another new castle, in the region of Clun.[50] Finally, we should remember that after the flight of Dafydd and Gruffydd ap Gwenwynwyn in 1274, the prince greatly increased the territory, and hence the resources, under his direct control.

To these points may be added Llywelyn's own statements, for what they are worth, of his readiness to meet, and even to increase, his obligations. In 1274 he claimed that he was prepared to pay off all arrears of tribute,[51] whilst at the beginning of 1277, under very heavy pressure, he offered Edward the resumption of annual payments, the cash for the homage of Rhys ap Maredudd, and an additional 6,000 marks.[52] This last offer was made *pro vexatione et interesse domini regis, ac pro confirmatione pacis inter eos dudum facte et eius suplecione; necnon pro restitutione domini Alienore uxoris sue et sue comitive.*

The contributions which Gwynedd made to the financial effort of the years after 1267 cannot be calculated with any certainty. But it is perhaps of some importance in this context that after the Treaty of Conwy in 1277, Llywelyn was burdened with annual payments of 500 marks, as well as being obliged to pay off a debt of nearly 1,000 marks, to his brother Rhodri.[53] These payments were to be raised from only a part of Gwynedd Uwch Conwy, for Llywelyn was also obliged to make territorial provision for his elder brother Owain, whom he apparently settled in Llŷn.[54] It is also noteworthy that when Archbishop Peckham was trying to induce Llywelyn to come to the king's peace in 1282, he held out

---

[49] *C.A.C.*, pp. 30–1.
[50] Ibid., p. 49.
[51] Ibid., p. 93.
[52] J. B. Smith, art. cit.
[53] *C. Close R., 1272–79*, p. 374.
[54] *B. T. (R.B.H.)*, p. 268.

the offer, in exchange for the truncated principality, of English estates worth £1,000 a year.[55] In the circumstances, the offer may be assumed not to have been over-generous. Interestingly enough, the sum of £1,000 does not fall very far short of the total valuation put upon the rents and services due to the prince in the early post-conquest extents of Gwynedd Uwch Conwy.[56] The extents' total of a little over £1,000 does not, however, take into account the bulk of the profits of justice or the proceeds of extraordinary taxation. It is perhaps not unreasonable to assume, in the light of this evidence, that the fully extended Gwynedd of the decade after 1267 was probably capable of bearing the major share of the day-to-day maintenance of Llywelyn and his entourage,[57] and of contributing between one third and one half of the annual sums demanded under the terms of the Treaty of Montgomery.

Such contributions were not made painlessly: it may, for instance, have been necessary to delay the castle-building programme until payments were suspended, whilst the devices employed to raise money rapidly undoubtedly strained the loyalty of all manner of Llywelyn's subjects. It is indeed a point of difficulty to decide which impresses most: the magnitude and complexity of the problems faced by the thirteenth-century princes, or the vigour and resourcefulness with which those problems were tackled for so long.

THE EVIDENCE

If the exercise of governance was beset with difficulties, so too is its analysis, not least because of the paucity of the evidence. It should be stressed that neither the quantity nor

---

[55] C. T. Martin (ed.), *Registrum epistolarum Johannis Peckham, archiepiscopi Cantuariensis*, Rolls Series (London, 1882–5), II, p. 467.
[56] This total is obtained by adding the sums given by T. Jones Pierce, *Medieval Welsh Society*, p. 118, for the commotes of Gwynedd Uwch Conwy, to those for the demesne centres and associated lands in the same area, which are to be found in Seebohm, *Tribal System*, Appendix A (Anglesey); M. C. J. (ed.), 'Extent of Merionethshire *temp.* Edward I', *Archaeologia Cambrensis*, 3rd Ser., XIII (1867), pp. 153–66: T. Jones Pierce and J. Griffiths, 'Documents relating to the early history of the borough of Caernarvon', *B.B.C.S.*, IX (1939), pp. 236–46; T. Jones Pierce, 'Lleyn Ministers' Accounts, 1350–51', ibid., VI (1933), pp. 255–75; 'Aber Gwyn Gregin' *Trans. Caerns. Hist. Soc.*, 1962, pp. 37–43. The last four articles are based on P.R.O., S.C. 6/1171/7, which supplies additional details for Caernarvonshire.
[57] See Appendix V below.

the quality of evidence available to the student of governance in the territories of Welsh rulers is at all comparable with that available to anyone investigating English royal, or even seigneurial, administration of the same period. Indeed, the sources available for work on thirteenth-century Gwynedd are not entirely dissimilar to those which exist for the study of Anglo-Saxon institutions and society in the tenth and eleventh centuries.[58]

There are some thirteenth-century, pre-conquest records of Venedotian origin, which often bear directly on problems of governance, but they are not numerous. The bulk of them is to be found in the charters listed in Appendix I, in the relevant sections of two volumes edited by J. G. Edwards, *Littere Wallie* and the *Calendar of Ancient Correspondence concerning Wales*, and in some very illuminating copies of pre-conquest documents from Llyfr Coch Asaph.[59] Beyond these sources, much material can be extracted from the rolls compiled by the contemporary English royal administration: in most cases Welsh material is scattered thinly throughout these records, but notable exceptions are the Welsh Rolls of 1277–94[60] and the *Welsh Assize Roll* of 1277–84. The letters and reports of dignitaries who negotiated with the princes of Gwynedd form another useful source; the letters of Archbishop Peckham are of particular interest.[61]

Amongst records of later date, the series of Ministers' Accounts, relating to areas which were administered by royal officials or those of the princes of Wales, provides some valuable information, as do the court rolls of the lordship of Dyffryn Clwyd, or Ruthin. One of the most important aspects of the

---

[58] This is not, of course, to say that Anglo-Saxon institutions themselves necessarily provide a close parallel to the institutions of thirteenth-century Gwynedd.

[59] Some of these documents are printed in Haddan and Stubbs, *Councils*, I. A full text with introduction is provided by O. E. Jones, '*Llyfr Coch Asaph:* A Textual and Historical Study', University of Wales M.A. thesis, 1968.

[60] The Welsh Rolls are to be found, in calendared form, in *C. Chanc. R., Various*. Two notable additions to the corpus of material readily available to historians of medieval Wales which should be mentioned here are N. M. Fryde (ed.), *List of Welsh Entries in the Memoranda Rolls* (Cardiff, 1974), and W. Rees (ed.), *Calendar of Ancient Petitions relating to Wales* (Cardiff, 1975). Both are primarily of interest to the student of post-conquest Wales but nevertheless contain much information of value for the study of the pre-conquest period.

[61] *Registrum epistolarum Johannis Peckham;* see especially vol. II, pp. 435–78.

Ministers' Accounts for the county of Caernarvon is that they refer to, and so can be used to reconstruct, a lost extent or survey of that county made soon after the Edwardian conquest.[62] The post-conquest extents are indeed of the greatest value for the study of governance under the native princes, because they frequently contain references to the institutions or social arrangements of the pre-conquest period. Very informative surveys were made of Anglesey and Caernarvonshire in 1352,[63] and of the honour of Denbigh, covering the western half of the Perfeddwlad, in 1334.[64] A rather less useful (for present purposes) survey was made of the lordship of Dyffryn Clwyd in 1324.[65] Extents of Merionethshire were made shortly after the Edwardian conquest[66] and again in the fifteenth century,[67] the former being of much greater value. An extent of the episcopal lands of the see of Bangor, made in 1306,[68] is of some use in establishing the nature of obligations, primarily military ones, under the native princes. Finally, one survey, that of Anglesey, printed by Frederic Seebohm in an appendix to his work on *The Tribal System in Wales*,[69] deserves special notice. It is of greater importance than has previously been assumed, firstly because it should be dated to 1284 rather than 1294, and can thus be taken with greater confidence to reflect pre-conquest conditions, and secondly because it contains an extent of the

---

[62] For the Ministers' Accounts, see in particular John Griffiths, 'Two Early Ministers' Accounts for North Wales', *B.B.C.S.*, IX (1939), pp. 50–70, and *idem*, 'Early Accounts relating to North Wales *temp.* Edward I', ibid., XIV (1952); XV (1954); XVI (1955). The very important Caernarvonshire accounts for 1350–51, embodying an early post-conquest extent, are to be found in P.R.O., S.C. 6/1171/7. The sections relating to Llŷn have been published by T. Jones Pierce, 'Lleyn Ministers' Accounts, 1350–51' *B.B.C.S.*, VI (1933), pp. 255–75. See also *idem*, 'Documents relating to the early history of the borough of Caernarvon', ibid., IX (1939), pp. 236–46. The surviving Ruthin court rolls of the early post-conquest period are printed or summarized in R. A. Roberts (ed.), *The Court Rolls of the Lordship of Ruthin or Dyffryn Clwyd of the reign of King Edward the First*, (Cymmrodorion Record Series No. 2, London, 1893).
[63] *Rec. Caern.*, pp. 1–89.
[64] *S.D.*, pp. 1–323.
[65] R. I. Jack, 'Records of Denbighshire Lordships. II. The Lordship of Dyffryn Clwyd in 1324', *Trans. Denb. Hist. Soc.*, XVII (1968), pp. 7–53.
[66] 'Extent of Merionethshire, *temp.* Edward I, ed. M. C. J., *Arch. Camb.*, 3rd Ser., XIII (1867), 184ff. (henceforth, Extent of Merionethshire).
[67] *Rec. Caern.*, pp. 261–92.
[68] Ibid., pp. 92–115. See Appendix VI below for the date.
[69] Seebohm, *Tribal System*, Appendix, pp. 3–25. See Appendix VI below for the date.

vill of Penrhos which is the only survey known to have been made by a native of Gwynedd drawn from the circle of families closely connected with the princes' administration. The general problems raised by the records of English or post-conquest origin are obvious enough. References to pre-conquest conditions in a fourteenth-century extent or court roll may be the product of a confused or imperfectly understood tradition. Again, many documents of pre-conquest Venedotian origin survive only in copies, and are thus possibly subject to textual inaccuracies or omissions: the risk is greater when the copies were made by English clerks unfamiliar with the subject matter of the texts. In a similar way, incidental references to Welsh institutions or conditions in contemporary English rolls or other sources may reveal more about the assumptions of the clerks or of, say, the English government than about the matters to which they purport to relate.[70]

The evidence to be derived from chronicles is not plentiful. English chroniclers, most notably Matthew Paris,[71] supply some information on Welsh affairs, but it is frequently incidental and sometimes distorted. The Welsh chronicles prove to be of more value, though their usefulness is restricted by the fact that, with one relatively insignificant exception, their principal connections were not with Gwynedd.[72]

The work of the court poets of the princes[73] provides another body of information upon which it is possible to draw; but archaism and hyperbole abound in their poetry, which can thus be used only with extreme caution in the context of institutional or political history.

---

[70] To some extent, the requests to be found in *Cal. Anc. Pet.* avoid this problem, as they emanate more directly from local sources.

[71] The importance of Paris's testimony is underlined by G. A. Williams, art. cit.

[72] On the provenance of *Brut y Tywysogyon* and related texts, see *BT, R.B.H.*, pp. lii–liii; *BT, Pen. 20 tr.*, pp. lxii–lxiii; J. B. Smith, ' "The Cronica de Wallia" and the Dynasty of Dinefwr: A Textual and Historical Study', *B.B.C.S.*, XX (1963), pp. 261–82, and Kathleen Hughes, 'The Welsh Latin Chronicles: *Annales Cambriae* and Related Texts', *Proc. British Academy*, LIX (1973), and separately printed. The only chronicle undoubtedly produced in Gwynedd is the sketchy and inaccurate chronicle associated with Aberconwy abbey, for which see H. Ellis (ed.) *Register and Chronicle of the Abbey of Aberconway, Camden Miscellany*, I (London, Camden Society, 1843). See also R. W. Hays, *The History of the Abbey of Aberconwy, 1186–1537* (Cardiff, 1963), pp. 144–53.

[73] The best single collection of texts is *Llawysgrif Hendregadredd*, gol. John Morris-Jones a T. H. Parry-Williams (Caerdydd, 1971).

In the discussions of the personnel of government, it is frequently necessary to make use of the genealogies.[74] These are abundant, but of uncertain reliability. Sometimes the information which they contain is obviously wrong, but, where checking by comparison with record sources is possible, the accuracy of the genealogies is generally impressive. Such comparison often reveals, however, that the genealogies are incomplete. This is not surprising, for the manuscripts in which they survive are often no earlier than the fifteenth or sixteenth centuries, and the recording of the descent of a family prominent at a much earlier period was largely dependent on its survival, and continuing success, to the later date: there is a large measure of truth in Sir John Wynn's statement that 'povertie soone forgett whence it be discended'.[75] Consequently, genealogical deductions have sometimes to be made from the evidence of record sources, for which the pedigrees provide no support: such deductions are not *ipso facto* any less valid.

There remains the problem of the Welsh lawbooks, with which a student of almost any aspect of life in thirteenth-century Wales must come to terms. The difficulties are well known, and can be stated briefly. The codification of Welsh law was, traditionally, held to have been the achievement of the early tenth-century ruler Hywel Dda,[76] though the earliest manuscript of the laws, a Latin version, comes from the mid-thirteenth century.[77] Their usefulness to the historian is marred chiefly by what T. Jones Pierce called 'the persistent delineation of law and custom against an antiquated background'.[78] It is clear that an understanding of the lawbooks' treatment of a subject frequently involves the ability to distinguish what was current practice at any one time from a mixture of chronologically undifferentiated material. Moreover, the laws do not take the form of pronouncements by kings or princes, though they

---

[74] The work of Mr P. C. Bartrum has made the task of using the genealogies much easier. The culmination of his efforts is his *Welsh Genealogies, AD 300–1400*, 8 vols. (Cardiff, 1974), in which hundreds of pedigrees are given in tabular form, with exhaustive indices.
[75] Wynn, *Gwydir Family*, p. 36.
[76] J. G. Edwards, *Hywel Dda and the Welsh Lawbooks* (Bangor, 1928).
[77] Daniel Huws, 'Leges Howelda at Canterbury', *N.L.W.J.*, XIX (1975–76), pp. 340–4.
[78] *Medieval Welsh Society*, p. 356.

sometimes refer to these; instead they are commentaries on the law, made by jurists, some of whose names are known, and with some of whom groups of texts representing distinct redactions are associated, as in the books of Iorwerth, Cyfnerth, or Colan.[79] The texts may thus reflect the idiosyncrasies of their compilers, and may represent the jurists' ideal constructs rather than attempts to deal with real situations: this is particularly likely in one section of the laws of particular interest to the student of governance, that is, the tractate on the laws of the court, in which highly formalized and obviously archaic elements abound.[80]

Of the various redactions, the books of Iorwerth and Colan are of most immediate interest to the student of thirteenth-century Gwynedd. *Llyfr Cyfnerth* represents in part an earlier stage of legal development, though its alleged redactor, Cyfnerth ap Morgenau, was of the same stock as Iorwerth ap Madog, redactor of *Llyfr Iorwerth*.[81] *Llyfr Blegywryd* seems to be a translation of a Latin text closely associated with southern Wales.[82] Iorwerth ap Madog, the jurist particularly associated with *Llyfr Iorwerth*, apparently flourished in Gwynedd in the first third of the thirteenth century.[83] It is, however, hard to sustain the suggestion that *Llyfr Iorwerth* represents 'the product of juristic activity in the court of Llywelyn the Great',[84] for neither Iorwerth ap Madog nor any other known Venedotian jurist can be identified in the entourage of Llywelyn ab Iorwerth or in that of any of his successors. Thus, it is unknown how far such men as Iorwerth ap Madog reflected in their work the interpretations of, or attitudes to, the law which were prevalent in the princes' court. Whether they were the inspiration behind changes in the field of law or merely recognized them in their compilations can only be a matter for speculation. Finally, *Llyfr Colan* would seem

---

[79] See Dafydd Jenkins, *Cyfraith Hywel* (Llandysul, 1970), pp. 5–12.
[80] Ibid., p. 25, where Professor Jenkins comments that: *Yr oedd rhannau o'r adran hon (sc. cyfreithiau llys) yn hollol farw yn y drydedd ganrif ar ddeg.*
[81] On the genealogical connections of some of the Gwynedd jurists of the thirteenth century and earlier, see Dafydd Jenkins, 'Iorwerth ap Madog', *N.L.W.J.*, VIII (1953), pp. 164–70, and *idem*, 'Yr Ynad Coch', *B.B.C.S.*, XXII (1968), pp. 345–46.
[82] See *L.T.W.L.*, pp. 520–2.
[83] See note 81 above.
[84] *Medieval Welsh Society*, p. 296; cf. Lloyd, *Hist. Wales*, I, p. 355.

to be an 'edited' version of *Llyfr Iorwerth*,[85] though not, unfortunately, a complete one, for the surviving text lacks in particular the laws of the court.

Aids in solving the problems presented are few. Sometimes statements in the laws can be related to developments known to have taken place from other sources, and thus the chronology of the pronouncements of the lawbooks can be roughly fixed. Where such extra-legal sources do not exist, it is sometimes possible to work out the sequence of statements on textual grounds, though in such a case dating may not be possible. A further problem should be noted at this stage. J. G. Edwards pointed out that 'the Welsh lawbooks took for granted that there was a great mass of Welsh law which lay outside their pages'.[86] The novel appearance of a point of law or custom in a manuscript is therefore not necessarily an indication of the date of its appearance in practice. Indeed, if, as is quite conceivable, the compiler took the point from an older, lost manuscript, there is no certainty even that it represented current practice at the time of its later insertion into a text.

The general difficulties in the way of interpreting the lawbooks which have been outlined here will take specific form at many points of the discussion which follows, and each one must clearly be considered in its context. But the remarks made here will perhaps explain a general attitude which has been adopted throughout. That is to say, although the lawbooks may elucidate or complement the evidence obtained from other sources, no attempt should be made to force such evidence into a framework created by reference to the lawbooks alone.

Finally, it should be stressed that the evidence is of very uneven distribution. There is, for example, far more information available on most aspects of the principate of Llywelyn ap Gruffydd than on the corresponding aspects of the principate of Llywelyn ab Iorwerth, whilst there is more evidence relating to the latter's governance than to that of his mid- and late twelfth-century predecessors. It is thus very difficult in most cases to establish a pattern of institutional development: apparent

---

[85] See Dafydd Jenkins, *Cyfraith Hywel*, p. 8, for an excellent *stemma* showing the relationship between the various books.

[86] J. G. Edwards, 'The Historical Study of the Welsh Lawbooks', *T.R.H.S.*, 5th Series, XII (1962), p. 152.

innovations by, say, Llywelyn ap Gruffydd may simply be the product of the lack of evidence for previous rulers' methods of governance. An additional problem lies in the fact that in order to reconstruct certain institutions or structures of governance it is sometimes necessary to combine references relating to different periods within, or even beyond, the thirteenth century; hence there arises the danger that the resulting picture may not actually represent the institution or structure as it existed at any one time.

INTRODUCTION TO THE SECOND EDITION

A re-issue of this book provides an opportunity for a review and in some cases a critical assessment of the more important work that has been done in the three decades since its first appearance. In that period our understanding of the history and culture of thirteenth-century Gwynedd has been greatly aided by the publication of some excellently edited collections of record sources and literary materials. In the former category, Huw Pryce's edition of the *acta* of Welsh rulers of the period 1120–1283, produced with the assistance of Charles Insley, is a quite outstanding piece of work, providing not only thoroughly reliable texts but also critical discussion of, for example, the development of rulers' styles and seals as well as of the milieux within which their documents were produced.[1] In the second category, the seven-volume edition of the work of all the known Welsh court poets of the twelfth and thirteenth centuries by a team of scholars working under the auspices of the Centre for Advanced Welsh and Celtic Studies, Aberystwyth, represents a monumental achievement.[2] The impact of this major enterprise on the wider world of scholarship has been limited by the fact that all introductory material and notes, as well as the texts, are in Welsh; but a useful and important survey in English is provided by Rhian Andrews in her edition and discussion of a selection of the court poetry.[3]

Both of the above projects have stimulated significant analytical studies that relate to the political history of Gwynedd and to the

---

[1] Huw Pryce (ed., with the assistance of Charles Insley), *The Acts of Welsh Rulers, 1120–1283* (Cardiff, 2005).

[2] These volumes, in series order, are:
Gwaith Meilyr Brydydd a'i Ddisgynyddion, goln J. E. Caerwyn Williams et al. (Caerdydd, 1994);
Gwaith Llywelyn Fardd I ac Eraill o Feirdd y Ddeuddegfed Ganrif, goln Kathleen Anne Bramley et al. (Caerdydd, 1994);
Gwaith Cynddelw Brydydd Mawr I, goln Nerys Ann Jones ac Ann Parry Owen (Caerdydd, 1991);
Gwaith Cynddelw Brydydd Mawr II, goln Nerys Ann Jones ac Ann Parry Owen (Caerdydd, 1995);
Gwaith Llywarch ap Llywelyn 'Prydydd y Moch' gol. Elin M. Jones (Caerdydd, 1991);
Gwaith Dafydd Benfras Fardd ac Eraill o Feirdd Hanner Cyntaf y Drydedd Ganrif ar Ddeg, goln N. G. Costigan et al. (Caerdydd, 1995);
Gwaith Bleddyn Fardd a Beirdd Eraill Ail Hanner y Drydedd Ganrif ar Ddeg, goln Rhian M. Andrews et al. (Caerdydd, 1996).

[3] Rhian M. Andrews (ed.), *Welsh Court Poems* (Cardiff, 2007).

governance of the princes. Charles Insley's work on the *acta* of the princes formed the basis of an important paper that relates to the Aberconwy charters of Llywelyn ab Iorwerth.[4] It is clear, as a result of his studies, that we can no longer regard the dispositive clauses in these charters as a reliable basis for commenting on the governmental structures of the late twelfth century. On the other hand, Insley's derived argument that the period before 1200 represents 'the wilderness years' of Llywelyn ab Iorwerth is perhaps a step too far.[5] He pictures Gruffudd ap Cynan ab Owain Gwynedd as the dominant figure in Gwynedd until his death in 1200, with Llywelyn 'hanging on' in the Perfeddwlad 'in quite a precarious position'.[6] This is not the place for a detailed examination of the situation in and beyond Gwynedd in the last decade of the twelfth century, but a few observations will perhaps help to reestablish the case for Llywelyn's prominence east and indeed west of the Conwy in the years 1194–9. A key passage in the Chester annals is translated by Insley as follows:

> Many nobles of all *Norwallia* were slain, and Llywelyn's men in particular were killed or scattered to a man, and Mold castle was besieged and captured from Llywelyn on the day of the Lord's Epiphany.[7]

The mention of the killing of the nobles of north Wales and of Llywelyn's men refers to the events at Painscastle in Elfael in the summer of 1198; this itself indicates the prominence of Llywelyn's forces in an army, organised by Gwenwynwyn of Powys, that was drawn from many parts of Wales; but this section of the text has nothing to do with the events at Mold in January 1199.[8] The

---

[4] C. L. G. Insley, 'Fact and Fiction in Thirteenth-Century Gwynedd: the Aberconwy Charters', *Studia Celtica*, 33 (1999), 235–50.

[5] Charles Insley, 'The Wilderness Years of Llywelyn the Great', in Michael Prestwich, Richard Britnell and Robin Frame (eds), *Thirteenth-Century England IX, Proceedings of the Durham Conference 2001* (Woodbridge, 2003), pp. 163–73.

[6] Ibid., p. 172.

[7] Ibid., p. 168.

[8] This is made clear by the immediately preceding words: *mcxcviij Infinitus numerus Walensium ut dicunt ad quatuor milia ije idus Augusti a Francis apud castellum Paui* [where *Paui* is to be read as *Pain*]: 'An infinite number of Welsh, up to four thousand, they say, [were killed] by the French on the second of the Ides of August at Painscastle'. In the original work of 1984 that follows, I have used 'Gruffydd' rather than the now standardized 'Gruffudd' (which I use here in my introduction to the second edition).

INTRODUCTION TO THE SECOND EDITION   xlv

notion that Mold castle was captured from Llywelyn assumes that we should so translate the words *et obsessum est castellum Moald et captum in die epiphanie domini a Lewelini*. But it is clear that the Chester annalist consistently uses Latin *a/ab* in its agency sense, that is 'by': among many examples, see entries under 1185, 1189, 1192, 1194 and 1196.[9] That Llywelyn's men were victorious at Mold supports the claim of Prydydd y Moch that Llywelyn's forces won two battles on the same day, one in Bro Alun (that is Mold), and the other deep in Gwynedd uwch Conwy, in Arfon.[10] It thus seems that Llywelyn was operating on both sides of the Conwy significantly before Gruffudd ap Cynan's death. Again, Insley argues that it is inconsistent to use 'the poetry of Cynddelw Brydydd Mawr as a source for a battle (Coedanau) unattested by any other source, but [to reject] the authority of Prydydd y Moch when the poet speaks of Gruffudd ap Cynan's overlordship of Gwynedd'.[11] This overlooks important points. There is surely a difference between a reference to a specific event – that is a battle, in a named place – and the implication that a patron enjoyed overlordship, which might contain an element of flattery or exaggeration, and may be based on recent history rather than current reality. As to Coedanau, it is in fact attested by another source, the chronology known as *O Oes Gwrtheyrn Gwrthenau*.[12] Other evidence, not explicitly considered by Insley, needs to be brought into play, including the testimony of Gerald of Wales, in a passage added to the Itinerary in *c*.1197, that Llywelyn had driven his uncles, Dafydd and Rhodri, from almost all of Gwynedd. Material contained in the English Pipe Rolls supplements the evidence of the *Brut* that Llywelyn and his allies defeated Dafydd in 1194, leaving him only three castles, and that Llywelyn captured him in 1197. Gerald emphasises that Llywelyn left Dafydd with some lands through his mercy and the advice of his counsellors. It appears that Llywelyn, far from 'hanging on' east of the Conwy, was chiefly responsible for driving his uncle Dafydd

---

[9] R. C. Christie (ed.), *Annales Cestrienses* (Lancashire and Cheshire Record Society, 1887), pp. 34–5, 40–5. It is thus unnecessary to 'emend' the text to read 'by Llywelyn', as Insley, 'Wilderness Years', p. 168, suggests that some scholars have done.
[10] *Gwaith Llywarch ap Llywelyn, Prydydd y Moch*, 23.78–82.
[11] Insley, 'Wilderness Years', p. 170.
[12] Noted by J. E. Lloyd, *A History of Wales from the Earliest Times to the Edwardian Conquest*, 3rd edition (London, 1939), p. 589, n. 72.

out of Gwynedd.[13] Insley's analysis of the 1190s cannot therefore be accepted in its entirety, though his emphasis on the importance of Gruffudd ap Cynan must eventually be incorporated in any comprehensive study of the generation between the death of Owain Gwynedd and the ascendancy of Llywelyn ab Iorwerth. It seems likely that we may have to envisage a military/political environment in late twelfth century Gwynedd in which a ruler's presence in an area did not necessarily imply political mastery or enduring political control over it. In 1196 it seems certain that Gruffudd ap Cynan was present at the head of forces from Gwynedd allied to the English in an attack on southern Powys; it is possible that Gruffudd had made his way into southern Powys through parts of Gwynedd is Conwy, at a time when Llywelyn ab Iorwerth was preoccupied with dealing with the last strongholds of Dafydd ab Owain in that region.[14] By the same token, the presence of Llywelyn ab Iorwerth west of the Conwy in the mid- and later-1190s is difficult to deny. If we allow for the possibility that Llywelyn's spurious charters to Aberconwy may incorporate parts of an authentic grant of 7 January 1199, including the witness-list, it would seem that by that date Llywelyn had acquired the support of Gwyn ab Ednywain, a man of Gwynedd uwch Conwy who had apparently served Gruffudd ap Cynan.[15] It seems certain that, in Insley's phrase, the 1190s were

---

[13] Llywelyn's prominence in the events of 1194–7 can be established by reference to *BT, RBH*, pp. 174–5, 180–1; and by *Giraldi Cambrensis Opera*, VI, p. 134. *Pipe Roll 7 Richard I*, p. 244, and *Pipe Roll 8 Richard I*, p. 42, show English government expenditure in 1195–6 at a castle at Denbigh, presumably one of the three castles left to Dafydd. English concern may have been prompted by the fact that Dafydd was married to Emma, aunt of Richard I; *Gwaith Llywarch ap Llywelyn*, 23. 167, notes Llywelyn's assault on Denbigh, surely describing events in 1196–7. See *Feet of Fines 9 Richard I* (Pipe Roll Society, 1898), p. 79, for the mission of Archbishop Hubert to negotiate the liberation of the captive Dafydd; *BT, RBH*, pp. 186–7 shows that Llywelyn was Dafydd's captor; *Pipe Roll 10 Richard I*, p. 167, for Dafydd's presence in London in 1198. He does not reappear in Gwynedd. That one of the castellans of Denbigh had lost horses there (*Pipe Roll 8 Richard I*, p. 42) suggests military conflict in 1196.

[14] Gruffudd ap Cynan's presence at Welshpool is established by *Gwaith Llywarch ap Llywelyn*, 10. 60–1, to be read in conjunction with *BT, RBH*, pp. 176–7, which records the attack on the castle of Welshpool by the English in 1196, 'along with all the princes of Gwynedd'.

[15] See *Acts of Welsh Rulers* pp. 360–3, where Pryce notes that the Aberconwy charter 'cannot be accepted as an authentic act issued by the prince on 7 January 1199', but does not rule out the possibility that parts of it may reflect an authentic grant. The very uniqueness of Llywelyn's designation as *totius Norwallie princeps*, regarded by Pryce as suspect, may actually be an indication of an early and 'bombastic' style on which Llywelyn insisted in the immediate aftermath of an important military victory. Another of the witnesses, Madog ab Iarddur, was probably a man of Gwynedd uwch Conwy: see pp. 99–100 below.

characterized by 'a kaleidoscope of shifting alliances and loyalties' and we have to confront the possibility that the pattern of political control was similarly kaleidoscopic, a situation to which Llywelyn himself contributed significantly. We should picture Llywelyn neither as succeeding in 1200 to a well-established supremacy exercised by Gruffudd ap Cynan, nor as enduring a marginalised existence on the fringes of Gwynedd Is Conwy. The political situation of the 1190s, in which he had been a key element, had been tumultuous and fast-changing, but in large parts of Gwynedd his advance had been steady and substantial. By 1200 Llywelyn ab Iorwerth was an experienced ruler and a warrior and negotiator of proven ability and considerable prominence. Here was the perfect apprenticeship for one who would develop the mechanisms of governance and political control in his principality.

The editing of the entire corpus of Welsh court poetry in the twelfth and thirteenth centuries has allowed and encouraged the production of significant studies that draw upon the work of the *Gogynfeirdd*. Most notable of those that relate to the political culture of Wales in that period has been Rhian Andrews's study of the nomenclature of kingship that was employed by the court poets.[16] By careful categorisation and analysis of the political nomenclature applied to rulers by their poets she is able to inject much new thinking into the reconstruction of political structures and events. Thus, to take just one example, something of the pomp of the courts of Llywelyn ab Iorwerth and Llywelyn ap Gruffudd is conveyed by their poets' occasional application to them of rare and exalted terms such as *amherawdr/ymherodr* or *arbennig wledig*. On the other hand, Andrews suggests that the poets were very cautious in their application to the Llywelyns of terms such as *brenin Cymry*, involving a claim to be the ruler of Wales, noting that 'despite Llywelyn ab Iorwerth's supreme position among the rulers of Wales from 1216 onwards, none of the poems datable to the following years contains this style' and that, in the case of the relatively late application of such terms to Llywelyn ap Gruffudd, the apparent reluctance of the poets to style the prince *brenin Cymry* 'is in contrast to written, and thus more private, documents in which Llywelyn

---

[16] Rhian M. Andrews, 'The Nomenclature of Kingship in Welsh Court Poetry, 1100–1300. Part I: The Terms', *Studia Celtica*, 44 (2010), 79–109; *eadem*, 'The Nomenclature of Kingship in Welsh Court Poetry, 1100–1300. Part II: The Rulers', *Studia Celtica*, 45 (2011), 53–82.

appears as *princeps Wallie*, first in 1258 and regularly from late 1262 onwards'. It is possible that this caution was intended to avoid embarrassing leading lordly (and in poetic terms royal) supporters of those princes.[17]

Among other studies that have underscored the importance of the poets as political commentators is an ambitious attempt by Kathryn Hurlock to chart both changes in the composition of those who advised the princes of Gwynedd, and the role of the poets as part of the machinery of decision-making.[18] In this paper Hurlock confronts two important issues: first, she suggests that the thirteenth century saw a shift, within an emergent Welsh polity, from discussions of policy by a confederacy of Welsh rulers to formulation of policy in a 'council' of leading officials and dignitaries from Gwynedd; second, she discusses the influence of the court poets on the princes of Gwynedd/Aberffraw/Wales. Referring specifically to the question of whether Wales should come under the leadership of a single ruler, Hurlock notes that 'the crux here is whether the poetry reflected the change or encouraged it in the first place'.[19] Unfortunately, it is at present very unlikely that this question can be answered satisfactorily. No document exists in which a Welsh ruler accepts that he adopted a policy as a result of the urging of a poet. And except in rare cases, we cannot date the poetry of the *Gogynfeirdd* with any precision. We can sometimes establish a *terminus post quem*, because the poem refers to an event that can be dated; we can sometimes postulate a *terminus ante quem* because a poem does not mention a datable event that we believe it should/would have done if it post-dated that event; and sometimes, but rarely, it is possible to establish both. But even if we can give an approximate date to a poem that appears to advocate a policy, and if we can then establish that a similar policy was implemented, it is still not

---

[17] Andrews, 'The Nomenclature . . . Part II: The Rulers', pp. 69, 72–4.

[18] Kathryn Hurlock, 'Counselling the Prince: Advice and Counsel in Thirteenth-Century Welsh Society', *History*, 94 (2009), 20–35.

[19] Ibid., p. 28. Hurlock's related argument that the rulers of Gwynedd moved from taking 'advice from a confederacy of princes' to reliance on 'advice from men of the prince's land and household' (ibid., pp. 21–2) is problematic. The composition of the groups that counselled princes is only rarely noticed in record sources, and the chronology suggested by Hurlock is sometimes manifestly faulty: her comment that 'the last time Llywelyn ap Gruffudd consulted the other Welsh princes was in 1258' (ibid., p.33) seems to conflict with her earlier comments (p. 22) and ignores, *inter alia*, the Arwystli assembly of 1259 (for which, see *Annales Cambriae*, p. 97).

INTRODUCTION TO THE SECOND EDITION   xlix

possible to establish whether the poet prompted the policy, or contributed in some measure to its implementation, or whether he merely composed a poem that he was required to produce in order to mark the adoption of the policy. It is clear that the poets, if suitably rewarded, constituted a potent source of propaganda on behalf of the rulers who patronised them. The fact remains that we catch hardly a glimpse of the poets in the records of the magnates and important functionaries of the courts, and it is thus difficult to estimate their impact on policy.[20] And where poets appear critical of the decisions or approaches of the princes, it is noticeable that their warnings seem to have been rejected or to have gone unheeded.[21] At present it is wise to note Rhian Andrews's careful conclusion that 'as the modern practitioners of an ancient craft [the poets] reflected contemporary changes in the balance of power within Wales by judicious use of the vocabulary that they had inherited'.[22]

Closely connected to the poets were the lawyers and jurists, and major developments in the study of the Welsh laws since 1984 include the publication of one volume that relates very directly to the nature of the princes' governance, and the attitudes to it of the compilers of the lawbooks.[23] This is a collection of essays focusing on what the law-texts and related materials tell us about the ruler and his court. Publication of this volume was prompted in part by the contrast between the ruler's court as it appears in the present study and the court depicted in the lawbooks.[24] One contributor described reading the tractate on the Laws of court side by side with the present book as 'a highly disorientating experience'.[25] Many of the contributions to *The Welsh King and his Court* explore

---

[20] One of the poets, Einion ap Gwalchmai, does appear in the records that list members of the entourage of Llywelyn ab Iorwerth: see below, Appendix II and, for Einion's poetry, *Gwaith Meilir Brydydd a'i Ddisgynyddion*, pp. 427–503. But Einion almost certainly appears in the records in his capacity as an administrator and diplomat.

[21] See, for example, Hywel Foel's poem requesting the freeing of Owain ap Gruffudd (though Hurlock, 'Counselling', p. 25, mis-identifies Llywelyn ab Iorwerth, rather than Llywelyn ap Gruffudd, as Owain's captor): *Gwaith Bleddyn Fardd ac Eraill*, poems 22 and 23.

[22] Andrews, 'The Nomenclature . . . Part II: The Rulers', p. 81.

[23] T. M. Charles-Edwards, Morfydd E. Owen and Paul Russell (eds), *The Welsh King and his Court* (Cardiff, 2000).

[24] Ibid., pp. 1–2.

[25] Robin Chapman Stacey, 'King, Queen and *Edling* in the Laws of Court', ibid., pp. 29–62, at p. 29.

1   INTRODUCTION TO THE SECOND EDITION

the thirteenth-century 'relevance' of what often seem formulaic and archaic rules and depictions. Exploration of aspects of court ceremony is particularly fruitful. That ceremonial activity seems to have been particularly pronounced and important at the three principal feasts of Christmas, Easter and Whitsun, usually, it seems, to the exclusion of those processes of governance that feature prominently in the record sources.[26] At times the law-texts seem to strike a note of criticism of current developments of which their compilers disapproved; in discussing the 'pointedly political' treatment of the queen in the thirteenth-century Gwynedd 'Iorwerth' redaction, Robin C. Stacey portrays the redactor's depiction of the queen as enjoying considerable luxury and elevated status while moving within a restricted domestic, and therefore private, sphere as a commentary on the emergence of Joan, wife of Llywelyn ab Iorwerth, as a powerful political force in the principality.[27] Other contributions emphasise the equally 'political' emphasis of the Laws of Court on aspects of ceremonial that symbolise, and so promote, the unity of the political establishment. Formal gifts of clothing from one officer of the court to another might have a particular symbolic significance: thus, when the laws of court prescribe that the *distain* should receive the clothing of the *penteulu* at the three principal feasts, this serves to symbolise the binding together of the head of the military wing of the household and the head of the domestic side.[28] Ceremony as a promoter of unity within the court must have been of particular importance in periods of political transition, when some officers were inherited from a previous ruler, or when rival factions were present in the court.[29] Other papers in the same volume draw attention to different characteristics of the

---

[26] David Stephenson, 'The Laws of Court: Past Reality or Present Ideal?', ibid., pp. 400–14.

[27] Stacey, 'King, Queen and *Edling*', pp. 53–62.

[28] T. M. Charles-Edwards, 'Food, Drink and Clothing in the Laws of Court', ibid., pp. 319–37, at p. 335. See also for development of this point, Robin Chapman Stacey, 'Clothes Talk from Medieval Wales', ibid., pp. 338–46, at pp. 344–5.

[29] Tensions must have existed in Llywelyn ab Iorwerth's court when Dafydd ap Llywelyn and his half-brother and rival Gruffudd had their supporters (in the original work of 1984 that follows, I have used 'David' throughout rather than the now standardized 'Dafydd', primarliy to underline the Anglo-Welsh parentage of Dafydd ap Llywelyn). Gruffudd was clearly a talented military leader, as he showed in his campaign of 1223 against William Marshall, and may have acted as *penteulu*; but it seems that Llywelyn's *distain*, Ednyfed Fychan, remained loyal to the cause of Dafydd, whom he also served as *distain*. See below Appendix II, sub Gruffudd ab Ednyfed, and Appendix IV.

courts of the princes, including the blend of entertainment and political content in the work of the court poets,[30] and the physical environment of the *llys*.[31]

The work of Glanville R. J. Jones on the court and its associated lands can now be read in conjunction with the fruits of archaeological research. A major project, '*Llys* and *Maerdref*', undertaken by Gwynedd Archaeological Trust, probing the location and nature of the courts and associated complexes of the thirteenth-century princes, has significantly deepened our knowledge of the physical environment within which the rulers functioned and which sustained their entourage and projected their power and authority. Papers embodying the results of this project have been published by both David Longley and Neil Johnstone.[32] They chart the distribution of the courts and associated *maerdrefi*. Work at the Anglesey *llys* of Rhosyr has revealed the complexity and the substantial nature of that court's construction, and similar conclusions can be drawn from the investigations at Aber on the mainland. Johnstone has noted that some *llysoedd* were characterised by the presence of an earthwork castle,[33] though this was not the case on Anglesey. Longley has emphasised that the stone castles of the late twelfth and thirteenth centuries 'were predominantly on new sites which came to usurp the functions of the *maerdrefi* while they continued to exploit their resources ... Demesne lands continued to be exploited for the maintenance of the court at some traditional *maerdrefi*, but in some instances services had been transferred for the support of castles'.[34]

Among works of interpretation that have appeared since 1984, pride of place must be given to the exceptionally important study of

---

[30] Peredur I. Lynch, 'Court Poetry, Power and Politics', *The Welsh King and his Court*, pp. 167–90.
[31] Glanville R. J. Jones, 'Llys and Maerdref', ibid., pp. 296–318.
[32] N. Johnstone, *Llys and Maerdref: An Investigation into the Location of the Royal Courts of the Princes of Gwynedd* (Bangor, Gwynedd Archaeological Trust, Report 167, 1995); idem, 'Llys and Maerdref: The Royal Courts of the Princes of Gwynedd', *Studia Celtica*, 34 (2000), 167–210; David Longley 'The Royal Courts of the Welsh Princes in Gwynedd, AD 400–1283', and Neil Johnstone, 'An Investigation into the Locations of the Royal Courts of Thirteenth-Century Gwynedd', in Nancy Edwards (ed.), *Landscape and Settlement in Medieval Wales* (Oxford, 1997), pp. 41–54 and 55–69.
[33] Johnstone, 'An Investigation', p. 67.
[34] Longley, 'The Royal Courts', p. 53.

Llywelyn ap Gruffudd by J. Beverley Smith.³⁵ This major work presents a careful narrative of Llywelyn ap Gruffudd's career, and explores the nature of his government in considerable depth. It takes account of an important paper by Llinos Beverley Smith setting out complaints against the governance of the dead Llywelyn by representatives of the community of Gwynedd that were made at an assembly before the bishop of Bangor at Nancall in 1283.³⁶ Those complaints 'describe a harsh lordship exercised by a prince who made heavy demands upon his people'.³⁷ Much valuable material relative to the mechanisms, processes and problems of government has been made available in extensive studies on the Welsh Church, the role and structures of kinship and a substantial volume on the south-western region of Gwynedd.³⁸ Several volumes containing collections of essays include papers relevant to an understanding of the exercise of governance in Gwynedd and the factors that conditioned it.³⁹

Among works of synthesis, the examination of the history of Wales between 1063 and 1415 by Sir Rees Davies is outstanding, and helps to set the subject considered in the present book in a broader context.⁴⁰ Indeed, it is no longer necessary or helpful to study governance in thirteenth century Gwynedd in a vacuum. Detailed studies that help to set this work within a broader framework of developments in Wales are now numerous. Paul Russell's brilliant

---

³⁵ J. Beverley Smith, *Llywelyn ap Gruffudd, Prince of Wales* (Cardiff, 1998); this book was preceded by a less comprehensive Welsh-language volume by the same author, *Llywelyn ap Gruffudd, Tywysog Cymru* (Cardiff, 1986). Llywelyn ab Iorwerth lacks a comparable biography; Roger Turvey, *Llywelyn the Great* (Llandysul, 2007), provides a succinct survey.

³⁶ Llinos B. Smith, 'The Gravamina of the Community of Gwynedd against Llywelyn ap Gruffudd', *Bulletin of the Board of Celtic Studies*, 31 (1984), 158–76.

³⁷ Smith, *Llywelyn ap Gruffudd*, p. 193. But subsequently (ibid., p. 271) Smith rather modified this verdict, when he pointed out that 'the document compiled at Nancall may be read as a forthright condemnation of the prince but it calls both for a broader historical perspective and a proper appreciation of the ambivalences of those now placed in an entirely new contingency'.

³⁸ Huw Pryce, *Native Law and the Church in Medieval Wales* (Oxford, 1993); T. M. Charles-Edwards, *Early Irish and Welsh Kinship* (Oxford, 1993); J. Beverley Smith and Llinos Beverley Smith (eds), *History of Merioneth II: the Middle Ages* (Cardiff, 2001).

³⁹ See, for examples, David Stephenson, 'From Llywelyn ap Gruffudd to Edward I: Expansionist Rulers and Welsh Society in Thirteenth-Century Gwynedd'; David Longley, 'Gwynedd Before and After the Conquest'; and Lawrence Butler, 'The Castles of the Princes of Gwynedd', in Diane M. Williams and John R. Kenyon (eds), *The Impact of the Edwardian Castles on Wales* (Oxford, 2010), pp. 9–15, 16–26 and 27–36; David Stephenson, 'The Rulers of Gwynedd and Powys', in Janet Burton and Karen Stöber (eds), *Monastic Wales: New Approaches* (Cardiff, 2013), pp. 89–102.

⁴⁰ R. R. Davies, *Conquest, Coexistence and Change* (Oxford, 1987).

INTRODUCTION TO THE SECOND EDITION   liii

reconstruction of the twelfth-century Latin original text of the *Vita Griffini filii Conani*[41] adds a crucial new dimension to the understanding of developments in Gwynedd in the century before the birth of Llywelyn ab Iorwerth – already probed in a volume of essays on the life of the effective founder of the dynasty of the Llywelyns.[42] Beyond Gwynedd, significant work has been done on the Lord Rhys, greatest of the rulers of Deheubarth in the twelfth century.[43]

Recent work has thus clarified many previously obscure aspects of political development that forms the essential context for studies of institutional change and continuity. We understand more of the political environment out of which the dominance of Llywelyn ab Iorwerth emerged, and we have a much surer grasp of the problems that faced Llywelyn ap Gruffudd. Significant advances have been made in our understanding of the immediate environments in which the princes exercised political leadership. We can appreciate the impact that the court made on observers and visitors as it progressed from place to place, establishing itself at castles, monastic granges and *llysoedd*; we can grasp more of the way in which the court poets supplied not just entertainment, important though that was, but also strove to emphasise the majesty of their princely and lordly patrons, at times acting as their critics, but more usually encouraging and proclaiming to important audiences of notables the rightness of their political ambitions and policies. The princely court as a focal point of politically charged ceremony, and of displays of generosity, as well as a hub of political management has come more clearly into focus. The proliferation of stone castles proclaimed the power and resources of the princes.[44] The tensions

---

[41] Paul Russell (ed.), *Vita Griffini filii Conani. The Medieval Latin Life of Gruffudd ap Cynan* (Cardiff, 2006).
[42] K. L. Maund (ed.), *Gruffudd ap Cynan; A Collaborative Biography* (Woodbridge, 1996).
[43] Nerys Ann Jones a Huw Pryce (goln), *Yr Arglwydd Rhys* (Cardiff, 1996); Roger Turvey, *The Lord Rhys: Prince of Deheubarth* (Llandysul, 1997).
[44] The various studies of the courts and castles sometimes reveal divergences in interpretation. Compare Longley's comment (note 34 above) with Smith, *Llywelyn ap Gruffudd*, p. 252: 'the services of the bond and free communities was [*sic*] directed to the courts rather than to the castles which had been constructed within the ambit of some of the courts'. There is also divergence in identification, as between the stone castles mapped by Butler, 'The Castles', p. 28 fig. 4.1, and by Longley 'The Royal Courts', p. 44 fig. 4.2: Butler, surely correctly, gives Prysor as a stone castle, whereas Longley does not; Longley counts only one of the fortifications at Dolwyddelan as stone, whereas Butler records both; Longley marks Ty'n y Twr, Bethesda, as a 'possible' stone castle: it is omitted by Butler. Such uncertainties continue to stimulate enquiry.

liv   INTRODUCTION TO THE SECOND EDITION

within Gwynedd – and beyond – generated by the ambitions of the thirteenth-century princes, and the sometimes veiled criticisms from within important classes of society have been made more apparent. Central to the processes of political control are the mechanisms and contexts of governance, and the associated personnel, that are explored in the present book.[45]

---

[45] In one area the evidence for Gwynedd has become less clear that it seemed to be in 1984: the statement at xxxviii n. 72, above, that the so-called Chronicle of the Abbey of Aberconway was 'undoubtedly produced in Gwynedd' can no longer be regarded as valid. On this, see David Stephenson, *The Aberconwy Chronicle* (Kathleen Hughes Memorial Lectures 2, Cambridge, 2002).

Part I
The Structure of Governance

I
THE PRINCE AND HIS COUNCIL

At the apex of the structure of government in thirteenth-century Gwynedd stood the prince. The comment of *Llyfr Cyfnerth* that a prevaricating lord was one of the three things which might lead a country to ruin,[1] though it may have originated in a more distant age, nevertheless expresses a truism in the context of the thirteenth century.

Perhaps the main political task facing a prince was that of securing the loyalty of his leading subjects, a task in which much depended on the personalities of the parties involved. The qualities of the truly successful ruler are graphically expressed in the encomium of the Lord Rhys of Deheubarth in *Brut y Tywysogyon*, where Rhys is said to have been 'the glory of battles, the shield of warriors, the defence of his land, the splendour of arms, the arm of prowess, the hand of generosity, the eye of reason, the light of worthiness, the height of magnanimity, the substance of might'.[2] Of the vigour and personality possessed by Llywelyn ab Iorwerth and Llywelyn ap Gruffydd there can be no doubt: they were both the dominant figures of their time in the political life of Wales. Even David ap Llywelyn, in his short and troubled principate, showed signs of the drive which characterized the two Llywelyns. These rulers had their faults, but the neglect of governance was not one of them.

The prince's task of ensuring loyalty was probably most difficult at the outset of his rule. A well-known feature of medieval governmental instability is the disruption caused within polities by the death of rulers. In an attempt to combat this problem, there was widely adopted the practice of

[1] *W.M.L.*, p. 281.
[2] *BT, R.B.H.*, p. 178.

designating a successor, often from the ruler's near kin, and 'associating' him with the ruler during the latter's lifetime.[3] A practice of this sort seems to have been of ancient origin in Wales, where the designated successor to the ruler was commonly called in the lawbooks the *edling*, a word derived from the Anglo-Saxon *aepeling*, and largely replacing the still older term *gwrthrych*.[4] The lawbooks state that the *edling* was to be one of the ruler's near relations; he would be the most kingly, *brenhinolaf*,[5] of these, the one to whom the king gave hope and expectation, *gobeyth a gwrthrych*.[6] Nor, apparently, were these statements entirely divorced from reality: David ap Llywelyn was quite clearly the designated successor of his father, Llywelyn ab Iorwerth, who passed over his older, but illegitimate, son, Gruffydd.

Llywelyn obtained recognition of David as his heir by the English government in 1220, by the pope in 1222, and by the magnates of Wales in 1226.[7] One of these moves, that of 1222, was probably connected with the dispossession of Gruffydd, who had been driven out of Meirionydd and Ardudwy by his father in 1221;[8] but there is nothing to indicate that the others involved anything more than the recognition of the 'most princely' of Llywelyn's near kin. In 1238, Llywelyn attempted to strengthen David's position still more, by exacting an oath of fealty to him from a gathering of Welsh chiefs at Strata Florida.[9] Llywelyn's designation of David as his successor, though by no means wholly successful, should not be dismissed as a failure: despite the fact that the principality which he had constructed beyond Gwynedd collapsed rapidly after his death, in Gwynedd itself David, though he met opposition, seems to have retained a large measure of control. This point will be examined in greater detail below.[10]

---

[3] *Cf.* A. L. Poole, *Domesday Book to Magna Carta* (Oxford, 1951), p. 2.
[4] For discussions of the relationship between the terms *edling* and *gwrthrych* or *gwrthrychiad*, see D. A. Binchy, *Celtic and Anglo-Saxon Kingship* (Oxford, 1970), and below pp. 138–9 and references there cited.
[5] *Bleg.*, 5.15 has *breinholaf*, but some texts have *brenhinolaf*: see *Llyfr Blegywryd*, p. 134.
[6] *Ior.*, 4. 16–17.
[7] See below, pp. 152–3.
[8] *BT*, *R.B.H.*, p. 220.
[9] For a discussion of this episode, see G. A. Williams, 'The Succession to Gwynedd, 1238–47', *B.B.C.S.*, XX (1963), pp. 395–6.
[10] See below, pp. 154–5.

The circumstances of the succession to David in 1246 and to Llywelyn ap Gruffydd in 1282 were much more difficult than those which faced David in 1240: in neither case is it evident that the dead prince had designated a successor, and in both cases English armies were striking at Gwynedd when the prince's death occurred. In 1282, Dafydd ap Gruffydd was probably the natural leader of the Welsh against Edward I's armies, but his authority within Gwynedd, as within the lands beyond that area, was fatally undermined by the vigour of Edward's onslaught. In 1246 there was no natural leader against Henry III, and the result was partition of Gwynedd and nearly a decade of political weakness.

The prince's authority, then, rested not only on his own personality, but on the care with which his succession had been prepared for by his predecessor, and on the political conditions in which the principality changed hands. Beyond these factors, the princes of Gwynedd seem not to have laid great claims to supernatural or mystical sanctions for their rule. None of them is known to have claimed to rule by the grace of God.[11] In the eighteenth century, Thomas Pennant wrote of an anointing ceremony at the accession of the twelfth-century rulers of Gwynedd, at which the bishop of Bangor supposedly officiated,[12] but it is unknown whether the story had any basis in fact. On the other hand, some form of coronation may have been normal in the thirteenth century, for David ap Llywelyn apparently wore a coronet symbolic of his rank when he did homage to Henry III at Gloucester in

---

[11] This point is made by Keith Williams-Jones, 'Llywelyn's Charter to Cymer Abbey in 1209', *Jnl. Mer. Hist. Soc.*, 1957, p. 51. It is noteworthy in this context that those texts of the Welsh laws which are definitely associated with thirteenth-century Gwynedd (i.e. *Llyfr Iorwerth* and associated texts) omit the phrase *o rad Duw* (= *Dei gratia*) from the title given to Hywel Dda in the prologues. There may be one exception to the regular omission of the phrase *Dei gratia* from the styles adopted by the princes: the letters of protection for Ratlingcope priory, Shropshire, issued by Llywelyn ab Iorwerth and printed in Dugdale, *Monasticon*, VI, p. 496, have *Lewelinus filius Gervasii Dei gratia princeps Norwalliae*. The original of this document has not come to hand, but a seventeenth-century copy, by Sir Roger Wiliems, N.L.W., Peniarth MS. no. 225 p. 128, omits the phrase *Dei gratia*. However, written near to the *intitulatio* in an early modern hand are the words 'It is otherwise in ye originall'.

[12] Thomas Pennant, *Tours in Wales*, ed. John Rhys (Caernarvon, 1883), III, p. 428.

1240,[13] and the *talaith* or coronet makes significant appearances in the work of the court poets.[14]

Once the initial establishment of a prince's authority had been achieved, however, the mode of governance, which was dependent for its effectiveness upon the vigour of the prince, tended to emphasize his importance and, hence, to buttress his position. With their itinerant court,[15] moving from one to another of the princely residences and sometimes stopping at favoured ecclesiastical centres, the rulers came into frequent, and probably fairly regular, contact with most parts of Gwynedd. The power of the prince was symbolized by the impressive construction or ornamentation of some of the *llysoedd* and castles at which the court rested. Amongst the stone castles[16] were some rudimentary enough structures, such as the tower at Dinas Emrys or the late-twelfth-century fortress at Carn Fadryn, which was possibly a dry-stone building. Even these, however, were much more formidable than structures of wood and earth. Other castles represent more sophisticated examples of the art of fortification, as at Dolbadarn, Dolwyddelan, Ewloe and Castell y Bere. At Castell y Bere, in particular, the standard of ornamentation was high,[17] indicating an emphasis on display as well as military functionalism.

Some of the old demesne-centres were also fortified, as was the case at Aber, Caernarfon and Nefyn, whilst the recent discovery and examination of some large sculptured stones of the early thirteenth century relating to the court complex at Aberffraw suggests that we should not dismiss the demesne-centres as mere collections of makeshift huts.[18] The Aberffraw stones took the form of heads looking out from a central core;

---

[13] For the description by the Tewkesbury annalist of David's wearing of the coronet, see H. R. Luard (ed.), *Annales Monastici*, (Rolls Series, London, 1864), I, p. 115.

[14] See a reference to Llywelyn ap Gruffydd as *taleithawc* by Llygad Gwr in *Llawysgrif Hendregadredd*, gol. John Morris-Jones a T. H. Parry-Williams (Caerdydd, 1971), p. 218.

[15] See Appendix V below.

[16] See A. H. A. Hogg and D. J. C. King, 'Masonry Castles in Wales and the Marches: a List', *Arch. Camb.*, CXIV (1967), pp. 71–132.

[17] L. A. S. Butler, 'Medieval Finds from Castell y Bere, Merioneth', ibid., CXXIII (1974), pp. 78–112.

[18] R. B. White, 'Sculptured Stone Heads from Aberffraw, Anglesey', ibid., CXXVI (1977), pp. 140–5.

they may have been representations of the great figures of the princely house. If their original position was as suspended bosses from a complex roof, they clearly formed part of an elaborate scheme of ornamentation.

Yet structurally impressive or not, the resting-places of the court must always have been busy when the prince was at hand. His retinue was often large: Llywelyn ap Gruffydd took provender for five hundred men from the lands of Basingwerk abbey when he came to hunt in Penllyn each year.[19] As well as huntsmen and falconers, the prince's companions would normally include his *teulu*, or household guard, and a group of his leading ministers. There was indeed much work to be done: the princes may be seen occupied in such business as sending out orders to distant local officials,[20] conducting diplomatic negotiations,[21] and dispensing justice to their subjects.[22] To the majority of men living in Gwynedd the prince represented the highest source of justice, and wherever the court halted much time was doubtless spent in hearing and determining cases. Whilst the prince was absent from a commote, courts were certainly held in his name, but upon his arrival there would probably be an accumulation of cases, which were beyond the competence of the commote court, to be determined.[23] It is known, for example, that certain ecclesiastical bodies were privileged to have cases in which they were involved heard only in the court of the prince

---

[19] *C. Inq. Misc.*, I, no. 1357.

[20] See, for example, mandates by Llywelyn ab Iorwerth to his ministers of Maelienydd, in Dugdale, *Monasticon*, IV, p. 56; by David (ap Llywelyn?) to his bailiffs of Builth, in Edward Owen (ed.), *A Catalogue of the Manuscripts relating to Wales in the British Museum* (London, 1900–22), IV, p. 909; and by Llywelyn ap Gruffydd to his bailiffs of Builth, Brecon, Elfael and Gwerthrynion, in *Cal. Anc. Corr.*, pp. 53–4.

[21] See, for example, note 29 below. When, in the period before the decisive war of 1277, Archbishop Kilwardby sent messengers to Llywelyn, it was considered a grave insult that the prince did not deal with them in person, but rather left his ministers to treat with them: see *Littere Wallie*, p. 172.

[22] In many cases the prince dispensed *iusticia*, but did not give *iudicium*: he held the court but left judgement to appointed judges. See the procedural rules set out in *Ior.*, 73–8. But there are clear signs of the exercise by the prince of that *iudicium* by precept (as, for example, in the quashing of an action against the abbot of Aberconwy in 1281, for which see *Littere Wallie*, p. 25) which J. E. A. Jolliffe stressed in the activities of the Anglo-Norman and Angevin kings of England: see his *Angevin Kingship* (London, 2nd ed., 1963), especially ch. 2.

[23] For the local courts and their officials, see ch. IV below.

himself.[24] Records relating to the reign of Llywelyn ap Gruffydd often show him acting in a judicial capacity. By the nature of the records, the cases normally involve only magnates, though it is clear that more humble men also pleaded before the prince.[25] Probably closely connected with the prince's role as the dispenser of justice was his generally accepted capacity to institute changes in the law itself: he was acknowledged as law-giver in secular matters. The prince did not act in his capacity as law-giver entirely without constraint, however, for he was under the moral obligation to 'correct' the law, to change it for good.[26] In this weighty process the prudent prince would take counsel, as traditionally Hywel Dda had done when he reformed the law.[27]

Chronicles and other sources reveal a long tradition in Welsh polities, in common with others in western Europe, by which the leading men were taken into counsel by the ruler,[28] and the taking of counsel by the thirteenth-century princes of Gwynedd is well attested in record sources. More interestingly, references are found at this period not simply to counsellors, but

---

[24] S. W. Williams, *The Cistercian Abbey of Strata Florida* (London, 1889), Appendix xxxii, for a post-conquest (1293) claim by the abbot that *predictus abbas nec praedecessores seu placitare vel implacitare consueverunt de terris tenementis possessionibus sive placitis aliis hucusque nisi in Curia Principis Wallie per brevia ipsius Principis*. See also *Rec. Caern.*, p. 221, for a similar claim by the prior of the Hospital of St. John, Dolgynwal, in 1305.

[25] See *Montgomeryshire Collections*, LI (1949–50), pp. 182–3, for cases in Arwystli early in the century which involved men clearly below the magnate level, and which were heard before Maredudd ap Rhotpert of Cydewain acting *vice* Llywelyn ab Iorwerth.

[26] See the testimony of Gwion ap Madog of Tegeingl before Edward I's commission of inquiry into the operation of the law of Hywel in 1281, given in *C. Chanc. R. Various*, pp. 196–7, which includes the observation that the prince 'can amend the laws for the alleviation and not the aggrieving (of the country)'.

[27] The prologues to the laws generally mention the gathering of wise men or counsellors by Hywel in order to reform the laws: see, for example, *Ior.*, I, 1–4; *L.T.W.L.*, pp. 109, 276, 316, 434. For the operation in the thirteenth century of the tradition of counsel in the refashioning of laws, see the statement of Ithel ap Philip before the 1281 commission, that David ap Llywelyn and his council had abolished the law of *galanas* in north Wales: *C. Chanc. R., Various*, p. 199.

[28] There are many such references in the Mabinogion: see, for example, *Branwen verch Lyr*, ed. D. S. Thomson (Dublin, 1961), ll. 39, 44, 100. See also *BT, R.B.H.*, p. 136, for the decision of Rhys ap Gruffydd of Deheubarth to submit to Henry II in 1158, *gwedy mynet yg kygor ef ae wyrda* (after he had taken counsel with his leading men).

to a prince's council,[29] strongly suggesting that the tradition of counsel had crystallized into some institutional form by the thirteenth century. Perhaps owing to the nature of the records themselves, the prince is very often seen treating with his council in judicial matters.[30] On one occasion, the council apparently acted alone in a preliminary stage of judicial inquiry: in the course of the investigations into the conspiracy of 1274 against Llywelyn ap Gruffydd, his brother Dafydd was summoned to Rhuddlan by the prince, *et a principis consilio fuerat increpatus.*[31] The council was not, it seems, a mere cypher. Its standing in the first half of the century is particularly hard to ascertain, but a comment in a letter of Henry III to Llywelyn ab Iorwerth in 1228 may be significant, for it clearly refers to a previous letter sent by Llywelyn to the king: *super eo autem quod nuncios vestros pro premissis ad nos misissetis si consiliarii nostri nobiscum fuissent, vobis significamus quod numquam ita fuimus consilio destituti quin consilium nostrum ad maiora et difficiliora sufficeret.*[32] The

---

[29] See the following examples:
(a) Llywelyn ab Iorwerth to Philip of France in 1212 on their treaty of alliance: *Quod ut inviolabiliter observetur, Congregato procerum meorum consilio, et communi assensu cunctorum Vallie principum, quos omnes vobiscum in huius federis amicicie colligavi, Sigilli mei testimonio me vobis fidelem imperpetuum promitto.* The text is given in R. F. Treharne, 'The Franco-Welsh treaty of alliance in 1212', *B.B.C.S.*, XVIII (1958), pp. 74–5.
(b) The abbot of Vaudey writes in 1230 to Ralph Neville, chancellor of Henry III, to inform him that he had handed over certain letters to Llywelyn at Denbigh, *et consilio suo convocato et audito, nobis repondit . . . : Royal and other historical letters illustrative of the reign of Henry III,* ed. W. W. Shirley, (Rolls Series London, 1862–6), I, p. 366.
(c) The agreement between Llywelyn ap Gruffydd and Maredudd ap Rhys in 1261 contains the clause: *Si autem super obiecto vel obiectis eidem confessus fuerit vel convictus (sc.* Maredudd) *si poterit facere iusticiam de bonis vel de terris suis secundum qualitatem et quantitatem sui delicti ad provisionem proborum virorum de curia et consilio domini L(ewelini) ipse erit sine capcione et incarceracione.* See *Littere Wallie*, p. 105.
(d) In the crisis of 1277, Llywelyn ap Gruffydd's envoys presented his *offra* to Edward I, these proposals being described as *visa sibi (sc. Lewelino) et suo consilio sufficientia.* See the text in J. B. Smith, 'Offra Principis Wallie ad Dominum Regem', *B.B.C.S.*, XXI (1966), p. 367. See the following note.
[30] In 1279, Llywelyn wrote to Edward I concerning the dispute between Margaret of Bromfield and Gruffydd Fychan, and that Margaret had refused to produce her charters before him, *licet primo et secundo ac tertio super hoc monita coram nostro consilio . . . (Cal. Anc. Corr.,* p. 85). Again, in a plea before the Hopton commission at Oswestry in 1278, it was recalled that one Madog ap Gruffydd had offered Llywelyn ap Gruffydd a sum of money to enquire in his court regarding Madog's right to Cydewain, and that *dictus princeps cum suo consilio super hoc tractasset.* See *Welsh Assize Roll*, p. 255.
[31] *Littere Wallie*, p. 136.
[32] *Close Rolls, 1226–31,* p. 116.

reasoning behind Llywelyn's evident decision not to send his messengers until the king's councillors were with him is obscure: it may well be that he was simply attempting to gain time, or to calculate the balance of political power in England. On the other hand, his attitude may reflect his relationship with his own council. If so, then a strikingly similar attitude seems to underlie the letter of Llywelyn ap Gruffydd to Reginald de Grey in 1273, on being called to attend the coronation of Edward I: *set quia in receptione dictarum litterarum non habuimus nobiscum de consilio nostro preter solum David fratrem nostrum et D [recte A] dominum episcopum Bangor' qui attamen venit ad dictum ideo competenter ad dicta negotia non potuimus tam festinanter respondere.*[33] Llywelyn goes on to say that he will send a reply at Michaelmas when, presumably, a full formal council, drawn no doubt from the whole principality of Wales, would be assembled. Once again, the prince may have been using the need to have councillors with him as a delaying tactic: in 1273, after all, the English government was beginning to demand payment of the arrears of money due from Llywelyn under the terms of the 1267 Treaty of Montgomery.[34]

Even taken at their face value, such references as these may show little more than that the princes felt the need to consult as many as possible of their councillors on major issues. Of greater interest is an episode relating to the final crisis of Llywelyn's rule in 1282. Archbishop Peckham, in his final attempt at mediation between the prince and King Edward, thought it politic to divide into two groups the peace proposals which he made to Llywelyn. The first group was to be proposed to the prince *coram consilio suo*, but the second, extremely radical, set of proposals was to be set before him *in secreto*.[35] It was a significant commentary upon the respect which Llywelyn might be expected to show for the men who composed his council, by a man who had several years' experience of negotiating with the prince. In the event, the ploy failed: all of the proposals came before the council, and Llywelyn's reply to Peckham, when he no longer, perhaps, had need of diplo-

---

[33] *Foedera*, I, p. 505. Cf. *Cal. Anc. Corr.*, pp. 161–2.
[34] *Cal. Anc. Corr.*, p. 161.
[35] *Registrum epistolarum Johannis Peckham*, II, pp. 466–7.

matic artifice, is revealing: *nullo modo permittet consilium nostrum nos in eam consentire, si vellemus*.[36] There is little explicit evidence as to the identity of the princes' councillors, but this can be approximately established. In 1273 the bishop of Bangor and Dafydd ap Gruffydd, the prince's brother, were of the council.[37] These two may perhaps be taken as representative of two substantial groups amongst a prince's councillors, Dafydd representing the 'barons' of the principality and the bishop the leading ecclesiastics. Into a somewhat different category falls the group of officials which surrounded each prince: the presence of members of this group in the council is put beyond any doubt by the clause, in the Treaty of Conwy of 1277, by which Dafydd ab Einion and Goronwy ap Heilyn, both ministers of Llywelyn, swore *pro se et aliis de consilio eiusdem principis* to ensure that hostages were handed over to the king from Llywelyn's territories.[38] As the group which was undoubtedly in most regular contact with the prince, the officials may have formed the nucleus of a 'working council' as opposed to a larger formal body meeting only infrequently. There are, however, no grounds for supposing that any distinction was drawn between 'magnate' and 'official' groups in the council. Indeed, the members of the great official families discussed at a later stage[39] were sometimes territorial magnates of some standing, and it will be shown that many members of the princely house were absorbed into the ranks of the princes' ministers.[40] Such, then, seem to have been the types of men who formed the princes' councils. Their feelings were not to be lightly disregarded. Great clerics such as the bishops possessed the not inconsiderable powers of ecclesiastical censure, a weapon used against the princes of Gwynedd more than once in the thirteenth century. Members of the princely house were, in common with most of the Welsh 'barons', frequently difficult to control, and, because they sometimes held large territories within Gwynedd, their

---

[36] Ibid., II, p. 468.
[37] See note 33 above.
[38] *Littere Wallie*, p. 121.
[39] See below, chapter VII.
[40] See below, pp. 115–19, 147–50. It is worth noting, however, that in charters the names of dependent rulers almost always precede those of the princes' servants of non-royal descent: the integration of these groups was far from complete.

association with the princes' plans was a vital factor in the latter's success. And the ministerial group was one upon which the princes placed great reliance: important figures in their localities and experienced in the business of governance, they were *par excellence* the upright men *de curia et consilio domini Lewelini* mentioned in a treaty between Llywelyn ap Gruffydd and the southern magnate Maredudd ap Rhys in 1261.[41] It is to these curial officials and their responsibilities that we now turn.

---

[41] See note 29 (c) above.

II

OFFICIALS OF THE PRINCE'S CURIA

THE DISTAIN

The principal servant of the thirteenth-century princes was the officer called in Welsh *distain*, a title generally latinized in record sources as *senescallus*.[1] Much information about the role and status of the *distain* is preserved in the Welsh laws, though in several respects these are an inadequate foundation for the study of the office under Llywelyn ab Iorwerth and his successors. Some of the duties which the legal texts ascribe to the *distain* were clearly archaic, or at least nominal, by the thirteenth century: such almost certainly were the statements that he was in charge of the kitchens of the court, and that it was his duty to hand round the 'supper-money'.[2] A corollary of the persistence of such archaic material is that the laws do not reflect the full range of the *distain's* activities in the thirteenth century, though information from the legal texts sometimes gives important support to the evidence of record and narrative sources. It is at least clear that the *distain* of the thirteenth century no longer corresponded to the domestic steward portrayed in the lawbooks. A measure of the disparity between the picture of the lawbooks and reality may be found in the fact that Latin redactions of the laws produced at this period do not translate *distain* as *senescallus*, but use instead *assecla*,[3] which appears to be a direct borrowing from classical Latin. The reason for this is by no means clear: it may simply represent a stylistic flourish, or it may have been intended to avoid the use of a title, *senescallus*, which was currently being

---

[1] As will be seen, the *distain* occasionally appears in records of Venedotian provenance as *justiciarius*; on the other hand, the designation *senescallus* is at times applied to officials who were almost certainly not *disteiniaid*: thus, in 1241, when Ednyfed Fychan was apparently *distain*, his son Tudur appears at the head of embassies from David ap Llywelyn to Henry III and is designated as *senescallus* by the prince: *Littere Wallie*, p. 18.
[2] *Ior.*, 8, 20–21, 40–50.
[3] *L.T.W.L.*, pp. 193 (Redaction B), 276 (Redaction C). R. E. Latham (ed.), *Revised Medieval Latin Word-List*, gives *assecla* only as a rendering of *dystein* (sic); the word does not appear in Du Cange's *Glossarium*.

adopted in official documents to describe a wider range of officials. It may, however, be that the archaism and vagueness of *assecla*, signifying a servant or follower, suited the compilers of the legal texts well, in that they were thereby able to convey the difference between the official so styled in their text and the contemporary *distain*.

It is difficult to form an impression of the routine duties of the thirteenth-century *distain:* the limited nature of the surviving evidence means that he is generally seen only when engaged on affairs of some moment. This problem should not be exaggerated, however, because it is possible that such important business absorbed most of the *distain's* energies. There are, for example, numerous indications that he was throughout the century the prince's closest regular adviser. This is evident from the frequency with which he appears working with the prince, witnessing his charters and other documents, and carrying out responsible diplomatic missions. In the lists of witnesses to charters or of diplomatic envoys the *distain* is almost invariably found at the head of the list of the prince's ministers, his name generally following those of ecclesiastical dignitaries, and of subject rulers.[4]

Especially noteworthy as evidence of the expansion of the *distain's* field of activity when compared with the functions accorded him in the laws are signs of the involvement of some holders of the office in judicial and military matters. The judicial eminence of *disteiniaid* need cause no surprise, for it belonged to the prince to dispense all manner of justice to his subjects, a task in which, as has been seen, he was frequently aided by the men of his council.[5] As one of the foremost of these, the *distain* may be expected to have worked closely with the prince in judicial as well as other matters, and to have

---

[4] See the entries under the names of *disteiniaid* such as Ednyfed Fychan, Goronwy ab Ednyfed and Tudur ab Ednyfed in Appendix II. See also the statement of *Ior.*, 6, 5–6, that the men of Gwynedd do not include the *penteulu*, or captain of the household troops, amongst the twenty-four officials under the *distain* (*y adan y dysteyn*). This seems to be at variance with the *distain's* traditional location, followed in the format of *Ior.*, as the third of the twenty-four court officials, and probably indicates that by the time of the compilation of *Llyfr Iorwerth*, in the early thirteenth century, the *distain* was recognized as the principal official of the court.

[5] See above, pp. 5–7

been an obvious choice should the prince need to appoint someone to do justice in his place.

In 1278 it was recalled[6] that two brothers, lords of Mechain, had pleaded before Ednyfed, 'then justice of the prince', in a dispute over lands which was settled by the law of Hywel Dda. Ednyfed was Ednyfed Fychan,[7] *distain* in turn to Llywelyn ab Iorwerth and David ap Llywelyn. Again, a charter of Madog ap Gruffydd Maelor,[8] dated 1234, records a dispute over lands in Llangollen between a group of laymen and the abbot and convent of Valle Crucis, in which a group of monks was chosen to arbitrate, *die vero ad hoc constituto a domino principe et suo senescaldo J. Paruuo*. The title *dominus princeps* sounds very much like a reference to Llywelyn ab Iorwerth, who exercised, at this time, suzerainty over Madog ap Gruffydd. If that is the case, then *J. Paruuo* will represent Ednyfed Fychan (*Fychan* = the small, generally 'junior'), whose name was often written Idneved, or some such rendering.[9]

For the holders of the office of *distain* after Ednyfed Fychan, no clear record of involvement in judicial administration survives, though it can probably be assumed on the *a priori* grounds already noted. The occasional use by Tudur ab Ednyfed,[10] *distain* to Llywelyn ap Gruffydd in the years 1268–78, of the title *justiciarius* would suggest that he was prominent in judicial matters. But of greater significance is the reply given to a petition from north Wales to Prince Edward in 1305, containing a reference to *sustentatio hospicii Principis vel Justiciarii sui qui est loco destein*.[11] The justice of north Wales was the principal administrative and judicial official of the post-conquest principality, and his equation here with the *distain* strongly suggests that the latter was assumed to have held a similar position under the last of the native princes.

---

[6] *C. Inq. Misc., 1219–1307*, p. 333.
[7] For the career of Ednyfed Fychan, probably the greatest of the thirteenth-century *disteiniaid*, see the entries under his name in Appendix II.
[8] *C. Chart. R., 1257–1300*, p. 458.
[9] The same document, however, refers to the arbitrators *jurantes coram J. senescaldo domini Madoci*. Again, in a charter of 1236, in *C. Chart. R., 1257–1300*, p. 459, given by Gruffydd ap Madog, who had by then succeeded his father, the grantor's steward is given as Gervase (= Jervasius, or Iorwerth). There is no evidence, however, that Iorwerth was known as *Parvus* or *Fychan*.
[10] See Appendix II *sub* Tudur ab Ednyfed.
[11] *Rec. Caern.*, p. 213.

The legal texts, however, ascribe special judicial eminence and responsibility, and the role of chief counsellor of the prince, to another official, the *ynad llys*, or judge of the court,[12] and there are faint signs that such an official may have been employed at least into the early-thirteenth century. In Anglesey early in the nineteenth century a tradition persisted that the poet Gwalchmai ap Meilir had been 'advocate to Owain Gwynedd'.[13] There are no firm grounds for supposing that Gwalchmai was Owain's *distain;* he may have combined the functions of *ynad llys* and *bardd teulu* (household poet). Equally interesting but inconclusive evidence exists to suggest that Gwalchmai's son, Einion, held a rather similar place in the court of Llywelyn ab Iorwerth. In 1281, Cynfrig Sais, one of the witnesses from Tegeingl in Edward I's inquiry into the use of the law of Hywel Dda, said that his father had told him of a plea between Llywelyn ab Iorwerth and Gwenwynwyn, lord of Powys (d. 1216), before the king's justices, in which *Eynon ap Walchmayn associatus fuit Justiciariis Domini Regis apud Westmonasterium et ipsi simul judicaverunt.*[14] Eynon ap Walchmayn is certainly to be identified as Einion ap Gwalchmai, himself of considerable renown as a poet and a man who appears several times in the service of Llywelyn ab Iorwerth in the second and third decades of the century.[15] He is not known to have been *distain:* Ednyfed Fychan is seen in that office from about 1216, and, before Ednyfed, the holder of the office was probably Gwyn ab Ednywain, who was certainly *distain* about 1209.[16] In the persons of Gwalchmai and his son Einion, then, we may see men who retained the functions and the eminence of the *ynad llys* of the legal texts. Even if this were so, however, the greatness of Ednyfed Fychan and his successors as *distain* soon obscured the situation.

As has been suggested above, military leadership was sometimes undertaken by the *distain*. Prowess in arms was

---

[12] See, for example, *L.T.W.L.*, p. 126 (Redaction A), for the rule that the court judge is necessary to the king *ad iudicandas causas et ad dandum consilium.*
[13] R. Fenton, *Tours in Wales (1804–1813)*, (Cambrian Archaeological Association, 1917), p. 306.
[14] *Cyfreithiau Hywel Dda ac Ereill seu Leges Wallicae*, ed. W. Wotton (London, 1730), p. 522, and cf. *C. Chanc. R. Various*, p. 195.
[15] See Appendix II and *D.W.B.*, *sub* Einion ap Gwalchmai.
[16] See Appendix II *sub* Gwyn ab Ednywain.

ascribed both to Ednyfed Fychan[17] and to his son, Goronwy ab Ednyfed, *distain* to Llywelyn ap Gruffydd, *c.* 1258–68,[18] though in Ednyfed's case his military reputation may have been gained before his rise to the office of *distain*. For later holders of the office there is more concrete evidence. Thus, in 1263 Peter de Montfort reported to Roger Bigod a Welsh attack on Gwent,[19] led by Goronwy ab Ednyfed with the princes Maredudd ap Rhys, Rhys Fychan, and Maredudd ab Owain, while it is recorded in *Brut y Tywysogyon* that in 1282 Llywelyn ap Gruffydd's last *distain* was sent to organize resistance in Brycheiniog to the forces of Edward I.[20] But these are the only clear references, and the evidence is not sufficient to warrant the assumption that military leadership was a formal responsibility attached to the office of *distain:* it was the sort of duty which might follow simply from prominence in the prince's service and from personal aptitude in military matters.

Professor Jones Pierce's comment[21] that the *distain* 'gradually supplanted the old military office of *penteulu*' may thus put the case for the *distain's* military role rather too strongly. Certainly, it would not be surprising to see the office of *penteulu* decline under the thirteenth-century princes, if only because it provided a power-base for potential dynastic rivals: the lawbooks state that the *penteulu*, the captain of the household troop, should be a near relation of the ruler.[22] As it had developed by the thirteenth century the *teulu* seems to have been a potent fighting force, equipped, for example, with siege engines.[23] It might, therefore, seem safer for the prince to entrust its leadership to a tried servant, rather than to a man whose lineage made him a possible rival. Yet there are signs that the office of *penteulu*, in something like its traditional

---

[17] See Lloyd, *Hist. Wales*, II, p. 684, for the story that Ednyfed fought in a campaign against Ranulf of Chester, possibly in 1210, and cut off the heads of three Englishmen.
[18] On Goronwy, see *BT, Pen. 20 Tr.*, p. 218, where he is called 'eminent in arms', and Bleddyn Fardd's elegy on Goronwy in *Llawysgrif Hendregadredd*, gol. John Morris-Jones a T. H. Parry-Williams (Caerdydd, 1971), pp. 75–6.
[19] *Cal. Anc. Corr.*, p. 52.
[20] *BT, Pen. 20*, p. 228.
[21] *Medieval Welsh Society*, p. 34.
[22] See, for example, *Ior.*, 6. 1–2.
[23] *BT, R.B.H.*, p. 174, has a reference to a late-twelfth-century *teulu*, that of Maelgwn ap Rhys of Deheubarth, which undertook siege operations with catapults.

form, did survive in the thirteenth century. The *Cronica de Wallia*, in its report of Llywelyn ap Gruffydd's battle with, and capture of, his brothers Owain Goch and Dafydd in 1255, refers to Dafydd as *dux familie sepe dicti Owini*.[24] Though captured in 1255, Dafydd was soon restored to a position of considerable influence, and the entry in *Annales Cambriae* under 1258 contains a passage[25] which suggests that Dafydd may have occupied a similar status under Llywelyn to that which he held under Owain, for he is here pictured leading troops on Llywelyn's behalf: *Praeterea David filius Grifini juvenis in armes splendidissimus et in equo fortissimus cum paucis de Nortwallia et Maredut filius Owini et Res Bethan cum magno exercitu per duos dies Maynour castrametati fuerunt*. In view of Dafydd's defection to the English in April 1263,[26] the appearance of Goronwy ab Ednyfed at the head of Venedotian forces in March of that year may indicate that Prince Llywelyn had already lost confidence in his brother over a month before he actually transferred his allegiance.

Professor Jones Pierce's claim that the *distain* sometimes appears as seneschal (*synysgal*) and constable (*cwnstabl*),[27] with the latter designation indicating his regular military functions, also presents problems. The only available reference in which the titles of seneschal and constable appear together, occurs in an entry in *Brut y Tywysogyon* under 1262[28] which notes an attack by the men of Maelienydd on Roger Mortimer's castle of Cefnllys: *A menegy hynny a wnaethant y synyscal a chwnystabyl yr Arglwyd Lywelin*. But the context makes it clear that two men are being referred to, and there are no grounds for supposing either to have been the *distain*: it is more likely that they were local officials, as was certainly the case with other ministers of the princes who appear as 'constables'.[29] Perhaps the only certain point which emerges from the facts set out above is that the *distain* was at least not excluded from military responsibilities by any rigid conception of the limits inherent in his office.

[24] *Cronica de Wallia*, p. 14.
[25] *Annales Cambriae*, pp. 96–7.
[26] Lloyd, *Hist. Wales*, II, p. 731.
[27] *Medieval Welsh Society*, pp. 33–4.
[28] *BT, R.B.H.*, p. 252.
[29] See below, pp. 216–17.

The evidence presented so far reveals little rigidity in the *distain's* relationship with the prince. The latter was free to use any of his servants to implement his wishes, the only practical restrictions on this freedom being the need to find men adequate to the burden of responsibility. The *disteiniaid* seem to have been employed more consistently over a wider field of activity than any other of the prince's servants, as indeed befitted their status as the principal amongst them. The comment of Stenton on the Anglo-Norman baronial *dapifer* of the early twelfth century is probably applicable to the thirteenth-century *distain*, namely that though the lord 'will generally use [him] when he is compelled to find a deputy, the office does not of itself make a man his lord's representative'.[30]

Lloyd stated that the *distain* held his office by hereditary right.[31] This deserves consideration in some detail, for the existence of a closely-defined hereditary right to an office of such prestige might have imposed a check on the prince's freedom of action. It is clear that any theory of hereditary tenure is difficult, if not impossible, to reconcile with the fact that the first two *disteiniaid* of the thirteenth century were Gwyn ab Ednywain of the 'tribe' of Collwyn ap Tango and Ednyfed Fychan of the 'tribe' of Edrud ap Marchudd, Ednyfed almost certainly being Gwyn's immediate successor. But it is well recognized that the office was held between 1258 and 1278 by two of Ednyfed's sons, first by Goronwy until his death in 1268, and then by Tudur. Tudur's successor in the office was probably drawn from a different stock, but Dafydd ap Gruffydd's *distain* in 1282–83 was Goronwy ap Heilyn,[32] Ednyfed Fychan's nephew, although the circle of Dafydd's adherents was probably too small to allow him much choice.

[30] F. M. Stenton, *The First Century of English Feudalism* (2nd ed., Oxford, 1961), p. 76.
[31] Lloyd, *Hist. Wales*, II, p. 622 and note 54. The passages in the legal texts cited by Lloyd in support of his statement are extremely difficult to interpret; but as the succession to the office in the thirteenth century can be worked out with some certainty, it seems possible to confine discussion to the discernible historical tendency and to omit theorizing based on the legal texts.
[32] For the suggestion that the office of *distain* may have been held between 1278 and 1282 by Dafydd ab Einion of the line of Gwalchmai, see below, pp. 107–8. For the career and ancestry of Goronwy ap Heilyn, see below, pp. 103–4 and Appendix II, *sub nomine*.

Ednyfed's tenure appears to have lasted until his death in 1246. It is usually assumed that he was followed immediately by his son Goronwy, but there are signs that this was not so; this does not, however, weaken the case for some form of hereditary succession during this period. The matter is complicated by the fact that Ednyfed died in the same year as Prince David ap Llywelyn, the sequel to whose death was the division of Gwynedd Uwch Conwy between his nephews Owain and Llywelyn ap Gruffydd. Consequently it is possible that there were two successors to Ednyfed, each serving one or other of the Venedotian rulers. Little is known of Owain's organization of his share of Gwynedd, but it seems probable that Llywelyn entrusted the office of *distain* within his dominions to Gruffydd ab Ednyfed Fychan.[33] A genealogical source contains the information that, among the sons of Ednyfed Fychan by the daughter of the Lord Rhys of Deheubarth, Gruffydd and Goronwy were *ambo disteyn principis*.[34] Two pieces of record evidence lend weight to this statement. In the first of these Gruffydd heads the witness-list to a charter granted by Llywelyn ap Gruffydd to Basingwerk abbey in 1247.[35] He is given no title, but he attests before such men as Tudur ap Madog and Iorwerth ap Gwrgunon, who had been prominent in Llywelyn's entourage even before he became joint ruler of Gwynedd Uwch Conwy.[36] Gruffydd's eminence clearly lasted into the mid-1250s for early in 1256 he headed a Venedotian embassy to England.[37] Thereafter, he is heard of no more.

The sequence of officials described above reveals, at the least, a hereditary tendency in the history of the *distain*'s office after the rise of Ednyfed Fychan. At the same time, it seems likely that the prince was able to control the descent of the office to accord with his best interests. This is most apparent in the exclusion from the highest office of Tudur ab Ednyfed until 1268. Apparently older than both Gruffydd and Goronwy, his appearance in a prominent and clearly responsible diplo-

---

[33] See Appendix II *sub* Gruffydd ab Ednyfed Fychan for details of his ministerial career.
[34] *Cronica de Wallia*, p. 16.
[35] See Appendix I, no. 23.
[36] See Appendix II *sub* Tudur ap Madog and Iorwerth ap Gwrgunon.
[37] *C. Pat. R., 1247–58*, p. 471.

matic role as early as 1241 can probably be taken as an indication that at that date he was recognised as the likely successor to his father's pre-eminence.[38] Yet in 1246 and again in 1256–8 he was passed over. On the first occasion, the reason is not far to seek: in the course of Henry III's attack on Gwynedd in 1245, Tudur had been captured and subsequently imprisoned in England. His captivity ruled him out as the direct successor to Ednyfed. He was apparently released in, or shortly after, September 1246, when the conflict with English forces was still being carried on by Owain and Llywelyn ap Gruffydd, but as a condition of his release Tudur had done homage to Henry III, swearing to do all in his power to aggrieve the king's foes, and had provided two of his sons as hostages. In the years after 1247, Tudur appears frequently as a royal pensioner, and was active in the royal service. He was still too much the king's man to be Gruffydd ab Ednyfed's successor in 1256–8, and there was chosen instead Goronwy, whose reputation for military valour and patriotism marks him out as a particularly appropriate choice in a period when Llywelyn was fighting to establish his supremacy in Wales.

It is perhaps significant that Tudur's son Heilyn,[39] was released by the English in 1263, and, after this, Tudur became far more prominent in the prince's service. By the time Goronwy ab Ednyfed died in 1268, Tudur's adherence to the prince was no longer in any doubt, and he was able to assume the office which, in different circumstances, he might have held for the previous twenty-two years.

Nearness in blood to Ednyfed was clearly a factor of great importance in the descent of the office of *distain* in Gwynedd, while valuable comparative evidence relating so the lordship of Gwynllŵg provides an example of the descent of the *disteiniaeth* from father to son through three generations in the

---

[38] See Appendix II *sub* Tudur ab Ednyfed Fychan. Tudur was not, apparently, one of the sons whom Ednyfed had by Gwenllian, who died in 1236: see *Cronica de Wallia*, p. 12 (for death of Gwenllian) and 16 (for a list of sons by Leucu *recte* Gwenllian); cf. Lloyd, *Hist. Wales*, II, p. 684. As Tudur is the first of the sons of Ednyfed to appear regularly in a ministerial role, it may be that he was the senior amongst them.

[39] See Appendix II *sub* Heilyn ap Tudur.

late-twelfth and early thirteenth-centuries.[40] Even if the hereditary tendency seen in Gwynedd and confirmed in Gwynllŵg were merely the product of chance, it is probable that the longer an office remained in the hands of one family the stronger became their prescriptive right to it.

FINANCIAL OFFICIALS

There is only a remote possibility that the *distain* of the thirteenth century continued to be responsible for household finances such as the 'supper-money', which the legal texts depict him as distributing to the ruler's leading servants. The functions of domestic stewardship, which the *distain* once exercised, seem by the thirteenth century to have devolved upon lesser officials, some of whom, as will be suggested, were attached to the local courts of commotes and *cantrefi* which were the frequent resting-places of the itinerant court and household of the prince. The thirteenth-century *disteiniaid* seem not to have taken a prominent part in the routine of financial administration; in so far as special responsibility for financial matters was vested in any single official, it lay, instead, with the chamberlain.

The chamberlain's duties were doubtless a logical development of his primitive function of guarding the king's bedchamber, in which many of the ruler's valuables were normally stored.[41] Thus, *Llyfr Iorwerth* assigns to the *gwas ystafell*, the *camerarius* of the Latin texts, the duty of keeping the king's treasure,[42] and a reference to Llywarch *gwas ystafell a thrysorier*, chamberlain and treasurer, to Gruffydd ap Llywelyn in the eleventh century, occurs in the *History of Gruffydd ap Cynan*.[43] It is difficult to assess the significance of this last reference in

---

[40] In Dugdale, *Monasticon*, IV, p. 634, is a charter of Hywel ab Iorwerth of Gwynllŵg, given during his father's lifetime (*assensu . . . patris mei*) to which one of the witnesses is *Cardoco* (i.e. Caradog) *senescallo*. C. *Charter R.*, *1226–57*, p. 294, provides the information that Adam ab Iorwerth ap Caradog was steward to Morgan, son of Hywel ap Iorwerth. J. A. Bradney, *A History of Monmouthshire* (London, 1904–33), III, p. 218, states on unknown authority that Iorwerth ap Caradog was steward to the lord of Gwynllŵg. For the succession in Gwynllŵg, see Lloyd, *Hist. Wales*, II, p. 771.

[41] *Ior.*, 12, 4–5.

[42] Ibid., 12. 12.

[43] Arthur Jones (ed.) *History of Gruffydd ap Cynan (1054–1137)* (Manchester, 1910), p. 112.

terms of its chronological location. The official in question lived in the mid-eleventh century, but the Welsh version of the *History* was written early in the thirteenth century and was in turn a close rendering of a (lost) original Latin text probably of the third quarter of the twelfth century.[44] It cannot be proven that *gwas ystafell a thrysorier* was a title actually borne by Llywarch during his lifetime, and it may be that the identification of the chamberlain as treasurer may relate to the late-twelfth or early thirteenth-century rather than to the eleventh.

Professor Jones Pierce appears, however, to reject this identification in a passage which, since it requires examination at several points, must be quoted at length:

> In the royal courts of Hywel's day, the *gwas ystafell* (chamberlain) was the keeper of the king's treasure. But such was not the way things were ordered in the court of Gwynedd during the age of the Llywelyns . . . The Prince's valet would no longer be competent to deal with revenue derived from so many different sources. During the century, we catch a glimpse of a new department of the prince's government dealing with fiscal business. The chief official in this department bore the same title as the head of the Anglo-Norman Exchequer—the Treasurer.[45]

It is true that a prince's valet would probably be incapable of handling the government finance of thirteenth-century Gwynedd. But it cannot be assumed that the officers called *camerarius* or *vice-camerarius* in thirteenth-century records relating to Gwynedd, and who could presumably have traced the descent of their offices from that of the *gwas ystafell* of the legal texts, should be classified as valets even if they retained the title of such. The scanty evidence relating to the chamberlain's activities in this period shows that he retained his financial functions. One member of several of the Venedotian embassies which paid to English receivers amounts due under the terms of the Treaty of Montgomery was Richard of Mold.[46] He was almost certainly the man referred to as Richard the

---

[44] See ibid., Introduction.
[45] *Medieval Welsh Society*, p. 33.
[46] See Appendix III *sub* Richard of Mold. Entries under this name include references not only to Richard of Mold *eo nomine*, but also to Richard the clerk, vice-chamberlain.

clerk who, as vice-chamberlain of the prince, handed over a loan of £20 from the prince to the dean and chapter of St. Asaph in 1266. Richard the clerk of Mold was amongst those handing money to the English in 1268, 1269 and again in 1270; on the last occasion he was designated *thesaurarius* of Llywelyn ap Gruffydd. It is not possible to establish whether this change of title indicates a change of status, or whether the vice-chamberlain might also be called treasurer, but at least it seems clear that the two titles were not unconnected.

The view that the treasurer was 'the chief official of a new department of the prince's government',[47] is hard to substantiate. The records of Llywelyn's embassies mentioned above provide some relevant evidence, since for the period 1268–72 they list the names of the Welsh envoys involved. Though there are signs of continuity of personnel over consecutive missions, there is little to suggest that the envoys, apart from Richard of Mold, were financial specialists. Thus, Cynfrig ab Ednyfed, who was prominent in the missions of 1268 and 1269, also appears in the prince's service in other contexts.[48] More important, he is known to have been with the court at Bach yr Anneleu in April 1274. Were he a member of a department responsible for financial administration, then his absence from a group of ministers who audited the account of the castellan of Dolforwyn at that date[49] would be hard to explain. Also to be found at least three, and possibly five, times amongst the envoys in the period 1269–72 is Roger the clerk of Rhuddlan.[50] But he, too, is absent from the auditors of 1274 (though in his case there is no evidence that he was with the court at that time) and his description in 1270 as *maiore de Rothelan* may suggest that he was a local official of some kind. The Einion ap Goronwy[51] who appears in the 1268–9 missions may be the Goronwy ab Einion, rector of Dineirth, of the 1270 mission if the inversion of forename and patronymic is regarded as a copyist's error. Nothing more is known of him. The other envoys seem only to have taken part

---

[47] *Medieval Welsh Society*, loc. cit.
[48] See Appendix II *sub* Cynfrig ab Ednyfed.
[49] *Littere Wallie*, pp. 23–4.
[50] See Appendix III *sub* Roger of Rhuddlan, under which heading are also located references to Roger the clerk, almost certainly the same man.
[51] See ibid., *sub* Einion ap Goronwy.

OFFICIALS OF THE PRINCE'S CURIA 23

in one mission each, and there is nothing to show that they were specially concerned with financial business. The audit of the account of the castellan of Dolforwyn on 22 April 1274 has already been mentioned. The composition of the group of auditors is of considerable interest as a pointer to the nature of the officials who were active in financial administration. The auditors are listed as Einion ap Caradog, Gruffydd Fychan, Pyll Goch, Mordic Ddu and David ab Ithel, prince's clerk. Of these, Einion ap Caradog[52] and Gruffydd Fychan[53] were both prominent in the prince's entourage, men whose activities in his service were wide-ranging. This is the only occasion on which they are seen engaged in financial business, though in view of the extreme paucity of relevant evidence not too much can be made of this. Pyll Goch and Mordic Ddu appear only in this record: they may have been local men. But David ab Ithel[54] was one of the prince's men who handed five hundred marks to Edward I's official at Rhuddlan in 1279: this may suggest that he was regularly concerned with finance. He, Owain the chamberlain (who appears early in the century),[55] and Richard of Mold are the only officials of whom this view may reasonably be held. In view of the fact that Richard of Mold is heard of no more after 1270, it may be that David ab Ithel had succeeded to his position by 1274. But though individual, and apparently non-contemporary, financial specialists may be distinguished, the evidence does not support the assumption that they formed part of a 'department of government'. They seem more likely

[52] See Appendix II *sub* Einion ap Caradog.
[53] Gruffydd Fychan was probably the lord of Iâl of that name who was with Llywelyn's court at this time: see his name amongst the witnesses to the agreement of 18 April 1274 in *Littere Wallie*, p. 99. On the other hand, the same document contains the name of a Gruffydd Fychan ab Iorwerth. But this latter man was probably from the lands of Gruffydd ap Gwenwynwyn: a Gruffydd ab Iorwerth ap Gruffydd attests another document (ibid., p. 110), issued by Gruffydd ap Gwenwynwyn in April 1274, which includes a list of that lord's men who are henceforth to owe homage to the prince of Wales. Amongst them is a Gruffydd ab Iorwerth of Deuddwr, probably the same man as the witness. Gruffydd Fychan of Iâl was amongst those minor lords who were gravitating to the group of ministers of the prince's court. For another example of his attendance at Llywelyn's court, see *Littere Wallie*, p. 46. Llywelyn also appointed Gruffydd as one of his attorneys before the Hopton commission in 1278: see *Welsh Assize Roll*, pp. 252, 259.
[54] See Appendix III *sub* Dafydd ab Ithel.
[55] See Appendix II *sub* Owain the chamberlain.

to have given direction to the work of non-specialized officials to whom financial duties had been delegated by the prince on an *ad hoc* basis.

UNSPECIALIZED OFFICIALS

It seems clear that the majority of the officials associated with the central *curia* were employed in any business for which their talents made them suitable, without any clear differentiation of function. This is apparent from the known careers of prominent ministers such as Einion ap Caradog, Iorwerth ap Gwrgunon and Tudur ap Madog. This argument is advanced with the reservation that the surviving documents relating to such men cover in general a limited range of situations, and so may not reflect accurately an official's typical activities in the service of the prince.

Perhaps more significant is the fact that records, emanating from Gwynedd in the thirteenth century, which record the names of prince's servants are characterized by the paucity of titles by which they may be distinguished. Putting aside references to local officials, only the following titles are found: *senescallus*, almost always referring to the *distain; justiciarius*, also applied to the *distain;*[56] *camerarius*, *vice-camerarius* and *thesaurarius*, all applied to financial officials;[57] *cancellarius* and *vice-cancellarius*, the application of which will be discussed below.[58] The great majority of the prince's servants associated with the itinerant court are never given titles, which suggests that they did not hold clearly differentiated offices, or, if they did, that these were largely nominal and bore little relation to their normal duties. The reasons for this situation may centre upon the pre-eminence of the thirteenth-century *disteiniaid*, for the existence throughout most of the century of an official capable of undertaking a wide variety of duties delegated by the prince clearly obviated the need for, and

---

[56] For the use of *senescallus*, see above, p. 11 and note 1. *Justiciarius* is occasionally applied to Tudur ab Ednyfed, once in 1271 (*Littere Wallie*, p. 26) and once in 1274 (ibid., p. 109). The Chester annalist, recording the death of Ednyfed Fychan in 1246, calls him *justiciarius*: see *Annales Cestrienses*, ed. R. C. Christie (Record Society for Lancashire and Cheshire, London, 1887) p. 66. It is highly unlikely, however, that this reflects Venedotian usage in mid-century.

[57] See above, pp. 20–3.

[58] See below, pp. 28–32.

OFFICIALS OF THE PRINCE'S CURIA 25

restricted the possibility of, the assumption by other ministers of specialized functions.

It is true that the sections of the Welsh lawbooks dealing with the organization of the ruler's court, *cyfreithiau llys*, describe a hierarchy of officials with precisely defined duties. But these duties, and the offices to which they relate, are largely concerned with the ruler's domestic establishment and leisure activities. Sometimes, as in the case of the *offeiriad teulu*, or household priest, the discussion in *Llyfr Iorwerth* shows signs of the intrusion into an archaic text of later material, which indicates that the post in question was evolving into one of the known specialized offices of the thirteenth century.[59] *Llyfr Iorwerth* and the other legal texts continue, however, to list amongst the leading offices of the court those which show no signs of such a development. Thus, considerable promineenc is given to officials such as the *penhebogydd* and the *pencynydd*.[60] There were undoubtedly servants in charge of the princes' falcons and hounds in the thirteenth century, but it is very doubtful that they enjoyed quite the prominence accorded to the *penhebogydd* and the *pencynydd* in the lawbooks, though it is possible that prominent ministers held posts such as these as sinecures, discharging only nominal duties, and enjoying perquisites attached to the offices in question.

---

[59] Ibid. See also the valuable discussion in J. G. Edwards, 'The Royal Household and the Welsh Lawbooks', *T.R.H.S.*, 5th series, XIII, pp. 163–76, which touches on several points developed in this and the following chapter.
[60] *Ior.*, 9 and 15.

III
THE PRINCE'S CLERKS

THE PROBLEMS OF THE 'CHANCERY'

It is sometimes assumed that the thirteenth-century princes of Gwynedd were served by a chancery,[1] but there seems to be little to support such an assumption. In the first place, the word 'chancery', or any other term signifying a writing department, is never found in documents emanating from Gwynedd in the thirteenth century. Certainly, each of the princes seems to have been able to call upon a small number of clerks, who appear fairly frequently in the ruler's entourage,[2] and who were undoubtedly capable of drafting documents, but in view of the fact that it cannot be determined what constituted the typical duties of these clerks, the use of an evocative term such as 'chancery' risks giving a false impression of the institutional maturity of this aspect of the princes' auministration. It is perhaps safest to assume that these clerks belonged to no definable department, but were employed in any task for which literacy and learning suited them. Indeed, it is not even certain that the clerks who appear most frequently in the prince's entourage normally drew up the prince's documents. It will be made clear that there was a strong link between the princes' administration and certain ecclesiastical centres in Gwynedd,[3] and it is likely that drafting work for the princes was frequently undertaken at such centres.

[1] See, for a particularly influential example, *Medieval Welsh Society*, p. 33, especially for the comment that 'a legal commentator can in fact refer quite casually to the fees charged by the chancery for letters patent dealing with real property and other important transactions'. This seems to relate to *Ior.*, 7. 10–11: *Ef (sc. yr offeiriad teulu) a dely pedeyr keynnyauc o pob ynseyl agoret a rodho e brenhyn am tyr a daear neu am negesseu mawr ereyll.* Of great value in a discussion of the office of chancellor, the passage cannot be used to argue the existence of a chancery. Dafydd Jenkins, '*Cynghellor* and Chancellor', *B.B.C.S.*, XXVII (1976), pp. 115–18, an otherwise extremely helpful discussion of the use of the words *cynghellor* and *cancellarius*, also makes the unsupported assumption that the thirteenth-century princes had a chancery.
[2] See, for example, the careers of Master Adam, David the clerk (servants of Llywelyn ab Iorwerth), Philip ab Ifor (servant to Llywelyn ab Iorwerth, David ap Llywelyn and Llywelyn ap Gruffydd), David ap William and Madog ap Magister (servants of Llywelyn ap Gruffydd) in Appendix III, *sub nn.*
[3] See below, pp. 33–7.

The documents issued in the name of the princes will not be subjected to a detailed diplomatic analysis, as it seems unlikely that this would help to elucidate the princes' secretarial arrangements. There are several reasons for this. First, and most obvious, is the fact that there are critical deficiencies in the sources: it is quite impossible to establish what proportion of the princes' *diplomata* is represented by the surviving documents; the charter evidence seems particularly unbalanced from a chronological point of view, for while charters are fairly numerous for the first half of the century, they are extremely sparse thereafter.[4] Moreover, the princes' charters, letters and other documents can often—in fact usually—only be studied in the form of copies, with all the attendant dangers of omissions or alterations. Secondly, such characteristics as may be discerned in the *diplomata* cannot safely be used to support any single theory regarding the existence of a secretariat. The princes' documents do indeed reveal a fairly high degree of consistency regarding some basic diplomatic forms. For example, the princely style of Llywelyn ab Iorwerth was generally *Princeps Northwallie* in the period before 1230, and for the next decade was *Princeps Aberffraw et dominus de Snowdon*. David ap Llywelyn reverted to *Princeps Northwallie* in his earlier rule, but he may later have adopted the title of *Princeps Wallie*. And Llywelyn ap Gruffydd consistently styled himself *Princeps Wallie et dominus de Snowdon* after 1267. Again, the princes generally referred to themselves in the first person plural after the first few years of the century, when the singular was used. In the case of both examples of diplomatic consistency given here, there are significant exceptions to the general tendency.[5] Even so, such consistency gives little indication of

[4] See Appendix I for a check-list of the princes' charters.
[5] Ibid., no. 8, is a charter of Llywelyn ab Iorwerth to the Hospital of St. John, Dolgynwal, apparently to be dated 1225, in which he is styled prince of Aberffraw and lord of Snowdon. In the matter of the use of the first person plural by the princes, it is to be noted that in a charter issued in the name of David ap Llywelyn to Basingwerk in 1240, for which see ibid., no. 19, the first person singular is employed. But the charter was so obviously produced by the beneficiaries, on the model of a previous grant from Llywelyn ab Iorwerth (ibid., no. 4), that it is misleading to say that David 'reverted to the singular', as does Keith Williams-Jones, 'Llywelyn's Charter to Cymer Abbey in 1209', *Jnl. Mer. Hist. Soc.* III (1957), p. 50, n. 30. The singular is also used very occasionally in letters of the princes after the first decade of the century: see for an example, *Royal and other historical letters . . . Henry III*, ed. W. W. Shirley, (2 vols., Rolls Series, London 1862–6), I, p. 369.

the circumstances in which the documents were drawn up: it may simply suggest that drafting was normally supervised by the princes or their representatives. A somewhat similar caveat applies also to such phraseological repetitions (normally confined within fairly narrow chronological limits) as are seen occasionally in the princes' *diplomata*.[6] Such repetitions may, alternatively, be signs of the work of a single, regularly employed clerk.

On the other hand, it cannot be proven that a chancery or writing office did not exist. The princes' documents sometimes show signs of being drawn up by men influenced by the drafting of ecclesiastical instruments,[7] but that does not necessarily mean that they could not have belonged to a writing office, which may have drawn its drafting traditions and practice from ecclesiastical rather than English royal models. If the existence or non-existence of a chancery cannot be proven, it is at least clear that the prince was served by a chancellor, for the study of whose office rather more satisfactory evidence survives.

THE CHANCELLOR AND OTHER *CLERICI PRINCIPIS*

There are occasional references in thirteenth-century records from Gwynedd to a *cancellarius*.[8] It seems that the origin of the office may be found in that of the *offeiriad teulu*, or household

---

[6] It is clear that in many cases phraseological repetitions occur only in documents relating to the same beneficiaries, thus suggesting not the work of a princes' chancery, but rather drafting by grantees, or by clerks about whose employment nothing should be assumed, working from models provided by previous grants. See, for example, the Basingwerk charters discussed in the previous note, and the charters granted to Einion ap Maredudd and his son Madog by Llywelyn and Dafydd ap Gruffydd respectively: Appendix I, nos. 21 and 25. Again, Llywelyn ab Iorwerth's charter to Strata Marcella (ibid., no. 2) is quite clearly heavily indebted in its terminology to earlier charters of other lords to the same house: compare particularly the charter of Cadwaladr ap Hywel printed in *N.L.W.J.*, V (1947), pp. 51-2. In contrast, there are few signs of any significant recurrences of diplomatic forms in documents issued by the princes to different and unconnected grantees or addressees.

[7] This is hardly surprising, however, in view of the prominence in the princes' governance of important ecclesiastical centres such as the abbeys of Aberconwy and Cymer, and of groups such as the canons of Bangor. See below, pp. 33-7. J. C. Davies, 'A Grant of David ap Gruffydd', *N.L.W.J.*, III (1943), p. 32, suggests that the charter in question was drawn up by someone familiar with clerical instruments, and suggests notarial influence. He is, however, quite wrong in his assertion that 'the [princes'] grants of lands and privileges were more commonly noted as witnessed by notaries rather than by clerks'.

[8] See below, pp. 31-2.

priest, described in the legal texts.⁹ *Llyfr Iorwerth* assigns to the *offeiriad teulu* four pence for every open seal issued by the king concerning land and other great matters.¹⁰ The passage suggests, as has been noted by Sir Goronwy Edwards, that 'by the early thirteenth century at any rate, the priest of the household was evidently responsible for the most typical of all functions performed by a chancellor—the function of sealing royal charters.'¹¹

The legal texts provide some further hints as to the duties of the thirteenth-century chancellor. Another text refers explicitly to the household priest as the person responsible for drafting the letters patent of the ruler,¹² and in what is almost certainly a reference to the *offeiriad teulu*, the Latin redactions mention the priest engaged in making or reading a charter before the king.¹³ Again, a late text makes it clear that the household priest was by tradition responsible for keeping the record of legal actions in the princes' court.¹⁴ That the household priest/chancellor had secretarial responsibilities, and that he was the ruler's principal clerical servant¹⁵ are points which emerge strongly from a survey of the lawbooks, and accord well, as will be seen, with the evidence of record sources.

The lawbooks also contain many references to an official designated as the *cynghellor*. It is quite clear that in most cases he is a local official, originally, perhaps, known as the *cymellawr*, or enforcer;¹⁶ but Professor Jones Pierce advanced the argument that some of the references are to the *cancellarius*

---

⁹ The benefice of *offeiriad teulu* is occasionally found in post-conquest records, as in *C. Chanc. R. Various*, p. 284. The chancellor's office was fairly clearly derived from that of *offeiriad teulu*, but that is not to say that after the emergence of the former the latter office was entirely assimilated to it. The office of *offeiriad teulu* may have retained its character as an ecclesiastical benefice quite distinct from the office of chancellor.
¹⁰ *Ior.*, 7. 10–11.
¹¹ J. G. Edwards, 'The Royal Household and the Welsh Lawbooks', *T.R.H.S.*, 5th Ser., XII (1963), p. 172.
¹² *A.L.*, XIV, xxi, 26.
¹³ *L.T.W.L.*, pp. 128 and 323.
¹⁴ Ibid., p. 323.
¹⁵ In addition, the *sacerdos placita scribens* was apparently a regular feature of the commote court, at least in the ideal constructions of the lawyers: *L.T.W.L.*, p. 332.
¹⁶ It is as *kymellawr*, or renderings thereof, that the office appears in Latin Redaction A of the laws: see, for example, *L.T.W.L.*, p. 120. In Latin Redaction C, *cynghellor* is glossed in a thirteenth-century hand as *compulsor(is)*: ibid., p. 288.

of thirteenth-century records,[17] and can therefore be used to elucidate the role and status of the latter. Perhaps the most significant of the references noticed by Jones Pierce is one, found in a fourteenth-century text, which states that 'it is the chancellor's duty to stand and be in the place of the king, in his presence and his absence, in everything, and when he is invested with office he receives from the king a gold ring, a harp and a chess-board'. The reference is easily identified as a passage from one of the books of so-called anomalous laws printed by Aneurin Owen. But it is closely related to a passage in *Llyfr Cyfnerth* which serves to clarify the situation:

> It is the duty of the *cynghellor* to hold the pleas of the king, in his presence and in his absence. It belongs to him to place a cross and restriction in every suit. The *cynghellor* sits on the left of the king at the three principal festivals, if the king be holding court in his *cynghellor*-ship. He receives, on entering into office, a gold ring, a harp and a chess-board from the king.[18]

There can be little doubt that the *cynghellor*-ship (*cynghelloriaeth*) mentioned in the above passage is a territorial unit and that the *cynghellor* is a local official. The placing of the cross of interdiction is especially noteworthy, as this was a duty associated with local officials in the thirteenth and fourteenth centuries.[19] As the passage in *Llyfr Cyfnerth* reads like an amplified version of the one commented on by Professor Jones Pierce, it is reasonable to assume that the *cynghellor* of the latter text was merely a local official. It is perhaps safest to forego efforts to see the chancellor of record sources in terms of the *cynghellor* of the legal texts.[20] References to a *cancellarius eo nomine* in the records of thirteenth-century Gwynedd are few, and the situation is clearer for the first half of the period under review than for the second. The earliest occurrence in record sources of a *cancellarius* is in a charter of the 1230s, where the title is given to one Instructus.

---

[17] *Medieval Welsh Society*, p. 32.
[18] *A.L.*, V, i, 1, and compare *W.M.L.*, 29, 7–12.
[19] See below, p. 44.
[20] That any attempt to relate references to the *cynghellor* in the legal texts to the chancellor of the thirteenth century must be rejected has been put beyond doubt by Dafydd Jenkins, '*Cynghellor* and Chancellor', *B.B.C.S.*, XXVII (1976), pp. 115–18. See also, on this article, note 1 above.

THE PRINCE'S CLERKS

A clerk, or clerks, called variously Ystrwyth, Ostrucius and Instructus, or variants thereof, appears as a very prominent servant of Llywelyn ab Iorwerth during the first third of the century.[21] It is possible that all of the references are to one man, though two similarly named men may have been involved. The problem is perhaps of little significance, for it is tolerably certain that even if there were two men concerned they held a similar position, that of the most prominent of the prince's clerical servants.

David *cancellarius* appears in records relating to diplomatic missions sent by David ap Llywelyn to Henry III in 1240-1. It seems clear that this is the same man as David, archdeacon of St. Asaph, who is seen several times in the 1230s engaged on similar missions, frequently being accompanied by the men who are seen with David the chancellor in 1240-1.[22] Since the archdeacon of St. Asaph was the most prominent of the prince's clerical servants from the mid-1230s, there being no certain reference to Instructus after that date, it is likely that David the archdeacon had succeeded to the chancellor-ship some years before he appears as *cancellarius*. The paucity of records relating to the later years of David ap Llywelyn's principate makes it impossible to determine how long he retained the office; he does not appear after 1241.

It is not possible to judge, from the circumstances in which the men discussed above appear, how far the chancellor was normally remote from scribal work, though for the bulk of the period it is at least clear that he was not the only clerk in princely service capable of drawing up the prince's documents: this work could presumably have been done by men such as Master Adam, David the clerk, servants of Llywelyn ab Iorwerth, and Master Philip ab Ifor, servant of Llywelyn ab Iorwerth, David ap Llywelyn and Llywelyn ap Gruffydd. Nor can it be shown whether the chancellor's control of the prince's seal, which may be inferred from *Llyfr Iorwerth*, was personal or indirect. The very frequent presence of the chancellors amongst the witnesses to the princes' charters may be indicative

---

[21] All of the references to a man or men of this name are grouped together *sub* Ystrwyth in Appendix III.
[22] For David as archdeacon and chancellor, see ibid., *sub* David archdeacon of St. Asaph.

of sealing duties. But the chancellor is absent from the witness-lists of several charters which the prince is known to have sealed.[23] It must also be remembered that the princes were not dependent upon a single seal for authenticating their documents: from very early in the century the existence of a secret seal is known.[24]

The status of the chancellor *vis-à-vis* that of other officials of the prince cannot of course be strictly defined: it was bound up with the personal qualities of the men involved. It is at least clear, however, that the chancellors of the first forty years of the century were men of great prominence, certainly paramount amongst clerical servants of the princes. For the period of Llywelyn ap Gruffydd's principate, the situation regarding the identity of the chancellors is far more obscure. No individual is referred to as *cancellarius*, though in 1277 a *vice-cancellarius* appears.[25] For some years after Llywelyn ap Gruffydd's seizure of power in Gwynedd in 1255, several clerics were prominent in his service, including the bishop of Bangor, the abbot of Aberconwy, David, archdeacon of Bangor, David ap William, official of Dyffryn Clwyd, and Master Madog ap Philip.[26] The bishop, who headed diplomatic missions to England in the period 1259–61, can probably be excluded as a possible chancellor. He showed too much inclination to fight for the rights of his see to be a leading servant of the prince; by the mid-1260s prince and bishop were in open conflict. The conclusion must be that he was probably a virtual figurehead on diplomatic missions. The chancellor, or whoever discharged functions similar to those of a chancellor, in Llywelyn ap Gruffydd's earlier principate is probably to be found amongst the other four clerics mentioned above. These figures have, however, a significance quite

[23] See, for example, the 1230 Rhos Fyneich charter of Llywelyn ab Iorwerth, cited in Appendix 1, no. 13. The witnesses do not include Ystrwyth/Instructus.
[24] For references to Llywelyn ab Iorwerth's secret seal, see R. F. Treharne, 'The Franco-Welsh Treaty of Alliance in 1212', *B.B.C.S.*, XVIII (1958), pp. 61–2, where its use in 1222 is discussed, and *Cal. Anc. Corr.*, pp. 24 (which refers to a privy seal) and 51. After his death in 1282, Llywelyn ap Gruffydd's 'privy seal' was found about his person: see *Registrum . . . Peckham*, II, p. 489.
[25] The vice-chancellor was Master Gervase, for whom see below, pp. 36–7, and Appendix III *sub nomine*.
[26] For Llywelyn ap Gruffydd's relations with the bishop of Bangor, see below, pp. 170–1; for those with the abbot of Aberconwy, see pp. 33–4. For the careers of the other men, see Appendix III *sub nominis*.

separate from, and greater than, the possibility that one of them was Llywelyn's chancellor, for they exemplify the prominence in Llywelyn's governmental arrangements of certain ecclesiastical centres in Gwynedd.

Perhaps the most interesting figure is the abbot of Aberconwy. Following the truce between Llywelyn and Henry III concluded by the abbot and Madog ap Philip in 1258, the two envoys agreed to ensure that letters patent of the prince were made to ratify it.[27] And after the extension of the truce negotiated by the abbot in 1262, he bound himself to ensure that the prince's seal would be affixed to the record.[28] It may plausibly be inferred that the abbot was able to exercise some control over the prince's diplomatic instruments. Certainly Aberconwy had a record of goodwill to the princes of Gwynedd,[29] and in 1258 an unidentified monk of the abbey was sent by Llywelyn as an envoy to Henry III.[30] Moreover, in the later years of Llywelyn ap Gruffydd's rule, there are significant references to the abbot of Aberconwy which suggest a continuing association with the prince's administration. In 1275 the abbots of Aberconwy and Strata Florida were sent by Llywelyn with a letter to the archbishops of Canterbury and York and their suffragans at a council in London.[31]

An *inspeximus*, which was clearly intended to further Llywelyn's interests, of the 1274 *causa accusacionum* against Gruffydd ap Gwenwynwyn and his fellow-conspirators, was made in 1278 by the abbot of Aberconwy and the dean of Arllechwedd at Arddau, a grange of the abbey.[32] Finally, in the course of the case between Prince Llywelyn and his brother Rhodri, held before Edward I at Rhuddlan in 1278, the prince

---

[27] *Littere Wallie*, p. 14.
[28] Ibid., p. 18.
[29] See generally R. W. Hays, *The History of the Abbey of Aberconwy, 1186–1537* (Cardiff, 1963), pp. 40–55; cf. ibid., pp. 27–31. Of particular importance is the episode in which the abbots of Aberconwy and Cymer were empowered as commissioners by the pope in 1244, following a petition by David ap Llywelyn, to call Henry III to defend himself against charges that he had deliberately chosen to go to war against David in 1241 rather than go through the process of arbitration. As this was clearly a political manoeuvre, they cannot have been chosen for their impartiality: *Matthaei Parisiensis monachi Sancti Albani Chronica Majora*, ed. H. R. Luard (Rolls Series, London, 1872–83), IV, pp. 398–400.
[30] *Close Rolls, 1254–9*, p. 320.
[31] Haddan and Stubbs, *Councils*, I, p. 508.
[32] *Littere Wallie*, p. 110.

proffered by the hand of the abbot of Aberconwy a deed under the seal of Rhodri.[33] The abbot, it seems, had access to, and may have acted as keeper of, the prince's records.

Another Cistercian abbey, that of Cymer, also seems to have figured in the prince's administrative arrangements. Like Aberconwy, Cymer had benefited from the favour of Llywelyn ab Iorwerth,[34] and also had a record of loyalty to the rulers of Gwynedd, most particularly to Llywelyn ap Gruffydd. When Gruffydd ap Gwenwynwyn fled from Llywelyn into England in 1274, the abbot and prior of Cymer were sent by the prince to go and order him to return and submit himself to justice.[35] The letters and other documents of Llywelyn ap Gruffydd were sometimes dated at granges of Cymer,[36] whilst the extent of Merioneth compiled shortly after the Edwardian conquest contains the following highly significant passage: *De catallis Principis dicunt quod Rogerus Extraneus cepit de Abbathia de Kymm. et de grangia de Aberthyon (sc. Aberyddon) mobilia Principis.*[37] The suggestion has been made that Aberconwy was used by Llywelyn ap Gruffydd as a record repository, as indeed Llywelyn ab Iorwerth had used ecclesiastical centres for similar purposes,[38] and it may be imagined that those abbeys favourable to the princes of Gwynedd proved valuable to them as safe storehouses.

It was not only monastic centres which provided servants and support for the princes, however. Leading members of the clerical hierarchy of the sees of St. Asaph and Bangor also took on such a role. It has been seen that David, archdeacon of St. Asaph, the chancellor of David ap Llywelyn, had risen to prominence in the service of Llywelyn ab Iorwerth in the 1230s. One of David's most regular companions in the prince's service was Master Philip ab Ifor, whose career may be of considerable significance. Master Philip is seen in the prince's service from the mid-1220s. He disappears from the records in

---

[33] *C. Close R., 1272-9*, p. 506.
[34] See Keith Williams-Jones, 'Llywelyn's Charter to Cymer Abbey in 1209', *Jnl. Mer. Hist. Soc.*, III (1957), pp. 45–78.
[35] *Littere Wallie*, p. 138.
[36] See for examples, Appendix V.
[37] 'Extent of Merionethshire *temp.* Edward I', ed. M. C. J., *Arch. Camb.*, 3rd Ser., XIII (1867), p. 185.
[38] R. F. Treharne, art. cit., pp. 74–5.

1241 until 1257, when he is seen undertaking a diplomatic mission for Llywelyn ap Gruffydd. The obvious inference is that Philip ab Ifor was a cleric of St. Asaph diocese, possibly a member of the cathedral chapter like his colleague David the archdeacon; his absence from the ranks of the prince's servants between 1241 and 1257 coincides exactly with the period in which the Perfeddwlad, including the church and much of the diocese of St. Asaph, was in the hands of the English. It may be that Philip's ecclesiastical role necessitated his remaining in English-occupied territory, and took precedence over his role as a servant of the princes.

The eminence of Master Philip ab Ifor and of David the archdeacon under Llywelyn ab Iorwerth and David ap Llywelyn coincides with a period in which relations between the princes and the bishops of St. Asaph were close. Abraham, bishop from 1225 to 1232, was a Cistercian,[39] and may have been the same man as the *pater Abraham de Aberthou* who attests one of Llywelyn ab Iorwerth's charters in 1221.[40] Hywel ab Ednyfed, bishop from 1240 to 1247, was probably a son of Ednyfed Fychan, and certainly appears several times in the entourage of David ap Llywelyn.[41]

It is the chapter of Bangor which seems to have developed the closest links with Llywelyn ap Gruffydd. The dean and chapter wrote to Archbishop Kilwardby what seems to be Llywelyn's 'official' account of the 1274 conspiracy against him.[42] And from the ranks of the clerks of Bangor emerged several of Llywelyn's servants. David ap William, official of Dyffryn Clwyd, appears in the service of Llywelyn ap Gruffydd in the early and middle years of his principate, as, to a lesser extent, does David, archdeacon of Bangor. Again, Llywelyn's envoy to the Scots, in the negotiations which produced the Scotto-Welsh agreement of 1258, was Gwion of Bangor, and whilst it is impossible to identify this man positively, there was a Guy (Latin *Guido*, Welsh *Gwion*) in the household of

---

[39] See R. W. Hays, op. cit., p. 37, where it is put beyond reasonable doubt that Abraham was a monk of Aberconwy.
[40] *C. Chart. R., 1257–1300*, p. 459. Aberyddon was a grange of Cymer.
[41] For David's relations with Hywel ab Ednyfed, see below, p. 170.
[42] *Littere Wallie*, pp. 136–8.

the bishop of Bangor at this period.[43] Nor are references lacking for Llywelyn's later years. One of the men who handed over money from Llywelyn to English receivers in 1279 was Madog Fychan, clerk,[44] and it is fairly certain that this was the Madog Parvus, canon of Bangor, recorded in Peckham's register as being accused that, in the 1282-3 war, *fuit incentor guerrae et quod impulit quemdam armigerum de equo suo, cujus impetus occasione fuerat interfectus.*[45] The evidence in a second case is more problematical. In January 1277 Llywelyn sent, as envoys to Edward I, Anian, bishop of Bangor, and Master Gervase, the prince's clerk and vice-chancellor.[46] This Master Gervase is almost certainly the man of the same name who witnessed the abbot of Cymer's quitclaim of lands in Cyfeiliog to Llywelyn in 1281. More significantly, it is probably to him that the following passage in the post-conquest extent of Merioneth refers: *De Magistro Gervasio Moel pro terra que fuit Gwyn Voyl quem tenet de dono Lewelini Principis x s. Idem Gervasius dicit quod nihil reddere debet.*[47] The land in question was in Ardudwy. There are two references to a clerk or clerks from Bangor who may be identified with Llywelyn's servant, Gervase. In 1267 a Master Gervase, canon of Bangor, went to Henry III with letters of his chapter announcing the death of Bishop Richard and obtaining licence to elect a new bishop.[48] Gervase is simply the Latin form of Iorwerth, one of the most common names of the period, but though the men in Gwynedd called Iorwerth must have been very numerous, there cannot have been many clerks of that name who had attained the status of *magister*. The fact that a Master Gervase appears both as Llywelyn's servant and as a canon of Bangor, given the favour shown by the chapter of Bangor to the prince's cause, creates a strong suspicion that the two are identical. Secondly, a Gervase of Llanfair appears as a member (apparently a junior member) of the bishop of Bangor's household in 1259.[49] It is

---

[43] See *C. Pat. R., 1258-60*, p. 57, for a list of members of the bishop's household. For Gwion of Bangor, see Appendix III *sub nomine.*
[44] See Appendix III *sub* Madog Fychan.
[45] *Registrum . . . Peckham*, III, p. 781.
[46] See Appendix III *sub* Master Gervase for references to his service to Llywelyn ap Gruffydd.
[47] 'Extent of Merionethshire *temp.* Edward I', pp. 190-1.
[48] *C. Pat. R., 1266-72*, p. 165.
[49] *C. Pat. R., 1258-66*, p. 57.

not clear from which Llanfair Gervase took his name, but it may have been Llanfair in Ardudwy, an area in which, as has been seen, Llywelyn's servant, Master Gervase, held land. A junior member of the bishop of Bangor's household in 1259 may well have become a prominent canon, with the rank of *magister*, by 1267, vice-chancellor of the prince a decade later, and by 1284 may have merited the epithet *moel*, the bald.

Master Gervase's title of vice-chancellor presents something of a problem. Professor Jones Pierce argued that in the course of the thirteenth century it became necessary to appoint an assistant minister—the vice-chancellor—to supervise the chancery staff—the *ysgolheigion* or clerics.[50] In view of the difficulties presented by the question of the chancery, discussed above, it should be stressed that there is no positive evidence as to the reason for Gervase's appointment as vice-chancellor. But neither is there any sign that Gervase worked under a chancellor who was regularly involved in the prince's business. It may well be that Gervase was vice-chancellor not in the sense of being charged with responsibility for some specific area of the chancellor's work, but rather in the sense of being a full replacement, either because there was no chancellor or because that official's responsibilities were largely nominal. It is not inconceivable that by Llywelyn ap Gruffydd's later years some dignitary such as the abbot of Aberconwy had virtually an *ex officio* claim, involving minimal duties, upon the post of chancellor.

The discussion of Master Gervase already contains many conjectures, but nevertheless it is tempting to add one more. Master Gervase Moel seems to have enjoyed royal favour after the Edwardian conquest: in 1291 he was described as king's clerk, and noted as receiving ten shillings per year as a royal pension.[51] If it was the case that Gervase had been a leading servant of Prince Llywelyn, the royal generosity may require some explanation, and one is reminded of the terse statement of *Brut y Tywysogyon*, that in 1282 there was effected 'the betrayal of Llywelyn, in the belfry of Bangor, by his own men'.[52]

[50] *Medieval Welsh Society*, p. 33.
[51] John Griffiths (ed.), 'Early accounts relating to North Wales *temp.* Edward I', *B.B.C.S.*, XV (1954), p. 308.
[52] *BT, Pen. 20*, p. 228.

Another of Llywelyn's clerks who appears not to have suffered greatly from the Edwardian conquest was William ap Daniel, who retained his hold on thirty acres of land in Aberffraw, granted to him by the prince, and also received a royal pension of forty shillings a year.[53] His career before 1282 is of interest in two respects. First, it illustrates something of the nature of the duties which a prince's clerk might undertake. In 1282, Friar William of Llanfaes wrote to Edward I regarding one of Llywelyn's grievances, namely, that he had been distrained upon to compel him to return goods belonging to Robert of Leicester and which he had taken as his rightful wreck. This, said the friar, altogether took away the prince's liberty, since no inquisition in that matter had yet been made in his land, as William of Llanfaes had already told the king, and as William Daniel, who was entrusted with making that inquisition, would declare to the king, as he was once ready to attest at Dunanmey. Here, apart from what appears to be a reference, in the final phrase, to the diplomatic duties frequently undertaken by clerks, is evidence of their involvement in the legal administration of Gwynedd. The prince's clerks, often with a legal training, sometimes acquired in England,[54] were obvious administrators of new methods of legal procedure, such as the use of the inquest,[55] which were being adopted by the princes.

In the second place, like those clerks who have already been discussed in the context of the financial officials of the prince, William ap Daniel represents the clerks in princely service who were not apparently members of any major ecclesiastical establishment, such as those of Bangor or Aberconwy. His name is never linked with any such centre, and in 1280, along with Madog, son of the Magister,[56] another of Llywelyn's prominent clerical servants, William was still,

---

[53] See Appendix III *sub* William ap Daniel.
[54] See *Rot. Claus.*, I, pp. 464, 511, for payments by Henry III in 1221 and 1222 to Ystrwyth, Llywelyn's clerk, *ad se sustentandum in scolis*.
[55] The 1281 inquiry into the operation of the law of Hywel Dda, reported in *C. Chanc. R. Various*, 196ff., contains many references to the move away from the use of the law of Hywel towards the use of the inquisition.
[56] See Appendix III *sub* Madog filius Magistri for details of his career.

THE PRINCE'S CLERKS

it seems, in minor orders.[57] This category of clerks was important to the prince. Their support freed him from complete dependence for clerical servants upon the major ecclesiastical centres. A man such as William ap Daniel was more completely a *clericus principis* than was an abbot of Aberconwy or of Cymer, a bishop or even a canon of Bangor, for William was dependent for his advancement upon the prince, and his interests, at least until 1282, were those of the prince, whereas the abbots, bishops and cathedral chapters had rights and privileges, proper to their houses and sees, to protect.[58] Co-operation with the princes was not always possible in such circumstances, and this aspect of their relations with the great ecclesiastics of Gwynedd has been examined in more detail below.

---

[57] Writing to Llywelyn *à propos* of Madog and William, Archbishop Peckham reminds the prince that *licet ad ordines ascendere minime compellantur, currit eis tamen tempus, nisi infra annum ascendant ad sacerdotium; et vacant eorum beneficia ipso iure.* See Haddan and Stubbs, *Councils*, I, 527.
[58] See ch. IX below.

IV
LOCAL OFFICIALS

Thus far, investigation has been centred on servants of the prince who were frequently, if not regularly, associated with the ruler's itinerant court. Beyond that fairly small group of officials, however, there is a much larger number of local officers who operated within the context of the administrative units of the commote and the *cantref*.[1]

The limitations inherent in a survey of the work of local officials should be established at the outset. Generalizations are hazardous, given the nature of the evidence. In the first place, the characteristics of offices, as of most aspects of government, certainly varied from one locality to another. Secondly, it is improbable that there existed in practice strict lines of demarcation between the duties of different officials. The evidence of the legal texts and the descriptions of post-conquest surveyors which tend to suggest that the work of local administration could be neatly categorized, with different areas allocated to specific officers, both represent in their own way an artificial construction of ideal types. The criteria which governed local administration in practice were the availability and personal competence of the officials. Where one officer was unavailable or incompetent, his nominal role had to be assumed by another of the prince's agents, otherwise the work went undone.

In the following discussion, therefore, the activities of the known holders of specified offices are outlined, but it must be stressed that such descriptions, often based on a few references widely scattered in terms of both time and locality, do not

---

[1] The *cantref* was the larger unit, generally consisting of two or three commotes. In the thirteenth century the commote seems to have been the basic unit of administration for most purposes and in most areas, although the *cantref* was by no means obsolete: in the Perfeddwlad the *rhaglaw* generally controlled a *cantref* rather than a commote, as was usually the practice in Gwynedd Uwch Conwy; again, some subordinate officers in the Perfeddwlad also operated in the *cantref* rather than the commote: see a reference to the woodward of Rhos in the 1270s in NLW Peniarth MS. no. 231, p. 80.

necessarily indicate 'normal' situations. In some cases the title of an office goes some way towards explaining some at least of its functions: such is the case with the *coedwr* or the *cais*. This does not necessarily imply that the obvious functions of such officers were their exclusive preserve, or that the officers themselves were to be found in every area. The following survey is intended therefore to demonstrate something of the scope of governance in the localities rather than to depict the situation in every commote or *cantref*.

A prefatory note on the sources is necessary. Though sources of thirteenth-century origin are hardly abundant, too much reliance should not be placed on the material relating to local administration in the fourteenth century and to be found in the extents and ministers' accounts emanating from royal and marcher government. A fair measure of continuity, most evident at the nominal level, can be detected between local administration in the pre-conquest and post-conquest periods, but this cannot justify the assumption that fourteenth-century conditions necessarily reflect those obtaining under the native princes. Evidence from fourteenth-century sources will thus be used only when it explicitly refers, or can be directly related, to pre-conquest conditions. Much is doubtless lost by establishing these criteria, but if the resulting picture is manifestly incomplete it may be hoped that it is reasonably free from undue distortion.

THE *RHAGLAW*

The legal texts portray the *maer* and the *cynghellor* as the leading local officials,[2] but it is fairly clear that by the thirteenth century their place had been taken by other officers, the chief of whom was the *rhaglaw*. This development may have involved more than a change of nomenclature, though that alone is significant: the designation *rhaglaw*, or lieutenant, marked out the official more surely than did that of *maer* or *cynghellor* as the prince's representative. The introduction of the title of *rhaglaw* may represent an attempt to assert the dependence upon

---

[2] See for example, *Ior.*, 91, *passim*.

princely authority of the foremost local official.[3] *Rhaglaw* was generally Latinized as *ballivus* in the thirteenth century, and often so in the fourteenth;[4] conversely, although *ballivus*, like *minister* and *serviens*, cannot be assumed to be a consistently employed term of art, it is fairly safe to suppose that it generally represents *rhaglaw*, except where it is clearly a generic description covering any officer.

The scope of the *rhaglaw's* authority reflected that of the prince. This is nowhere more clearly illustrated than in his paramount position in the administration of justice in the localities. Rare references to the *rhaglaw* in *Llyfr Iorwerth* illustrate this aspect of his work: he is mentioned as exercising discretion over awarding fines (*gobrau*) in legal cases to *uchelwyr*[5]—presumably those whose men were involved. Again, he is portrayed as supervising the laying of information by men too frightened to make public accusations.[6] Much additional evidence is supplied by the records relating to Llywelyn ap Gruffydd's relations with the bishops of Bangor and St. Asaph. In a list of evidences relating to the rights of the see of St. Asaph, collected by the bishop and chapter in 1274, there are repeated references to the *ballivus* (in the Latin text) or *rhaglaw* (in the Welsh text) apparently presiding over the *cantref* courts of Rhos, Rhufoniog and Tegeingl.[7] It is doubtless a reflection of the *rhaglaw's* role and powers under Llywelyn ap Gruffydd that the *ballivus* of Rhos in the period immediately after the Edwardian conquest of the Perfeddwlad in 1277, Goronwy ap Heilyn, apparently influenced the methods of trying cases relating to land in the *cantref*.[8] A clause

[3] The new title may thus represent rather more than a change of designation: it may reflect an attempt to introduce new personnel into the governance of the localities.
[4] For examples see note 7 below and also J. Griffiths (ed.), 'Two early ministers' accounts for North Wales', *B.B.C.S.*, IX (1939), p. 70, where there are the following references in a sheriff's account of 1291-2: *de ballivo et eius ringildo Cantredi de Aberffraw; de ballivo ringildo et portario de Talboleon et Kemmeys*. Here *ballivus* must represent *rhaglaw*. Note also in the case of Aberffraw that the *cantref* rather than the commote seems to be the basic administrative unit: cf. note 1 above.
[5] *Ior.*, 91. 22–3 and note 3 for the C. text reading.
[6] Ibid., 113. 9, 14.
[7] NLW Peniarth MS. no. 231, pp. 45–52, for the Latin text and pp. 116–25 for the Welsh text. For a discussion of the characteristics of these texts see below p. 119.
[8] *C. Chanc. R. Various*, p. 198, where Cynfrig ap Carwed (Kareweth) says that the men of Rhos think themselves contented with their laws, because their bailiff, Goronwy ap Heilyn, conducts himself well by encouraging them to enquire always the truth of the matter (i.e., as opposed to the use of the law of Hywel).

of the concordat between Llywelyn and the bishop of Bangor in 1261 provides a final illustration of the *rhaglaw's* role on judicial matters, and also suggests his authority over other local officials:

> Si qui servientes domini Lewelini vel suorum ballivorum vel aliorum iumenta hominum Episcopi sine ipsorum assensu ad sua negotia facienda rapiunt, nobis videtur, si eorum querimonia ad ballivum domini Lewelini venerit, et eis non satisfecerit, raptores rigide puniendo ut alii terreantur, quod dominus Lewelinus debet multare ballivum suum in XX solidos ad minus.[9]

The *rhaglaw's* role in judicial administration and in the supervision of lesser officials was paralleled by his responsibility for the raising of the prince's revenue. In the lordship of Bromfield and Yale in the fourteenth century, the *rhaglaw* was responsible for the collection of the lord's dues, a duty discharged through his subordinates, the *rhingylliaid*.[10] That this reflects thirteenth-century conditions in Gwynedd is suggested by the fact that when in 1242 Henry III granted a charter to the men of Englefield (Tegeingl), he charged them with payments of fifty pounds yearly, to be made by the hand of the *ballivus* of the *cantref*.[11] After the Edwardian conquest of the Perfeddwlad, as the office of *rhaglaw* in Englefield came to be regarded as a sinecure, the *rhingylliaid* themselves accounted for dues from the *cantref*.[12] Interesting light is shed upon the problem by an inquest of 1322 which revealed that two *rhaglawiaid* of Dinllaen, or equivalent officials, in the time of Llywelyn ab Iorwerth had imposed dues upon the lands in Nefyn of Haughmond abbey, and had apparently exercised a large measure of discretion in determining their severity.[13] The limited evidence suggests that the *rhaglaw's* powers were

---

[9] Haddan and Stubbs, *Councils*, I, p. 490.
[10] *Rec. Caern.*, p. xi and note.
[11] *C. Chart. R., 1226–57*, pp. 274–5.
[12] *Flintshire Ministers' Accounts, 1301–28*, ed. Arthur Jones, Flints. Hist. Soc., 1913, pp. 22–3.
[13] *C. Inq. Misc.*, II, p. 166, where an inquest of 1323, after recording the acquisition in the mid-twelfth century of lands in Nefyn by Haughmond abbey, notes that in the time of Llywelyn ab Iorwerth the keeper of the church and lands paid out of courtesy and not of debt 23s. 2½d. to Richard ap Cadwaladr, *rhaglaw* of the commote of *Dinllaen*. Later, in the time of the same Llywelyn, Philip ap Gilbert, *rhaglaw* of the said commote, yearly extorted the same sum from the Haughmond lands.

considerable, and that, especially in areas not often penetrated by the itinerant court of the prince, his practical autonomy may have been almost as great as that of many a subordinate chief.

THE *RHINGYLL*

The office of *rhingyll* provides an interesting example of nominal, and to some extent institutional, continuity between the legal texts and the record sources of the thirteenth and fourteenth centuries. In the legal texts he appears as the servant of the *cynghellor*,[14] and the post-conquest records show him as the servant of the *rhaglaw*, the successor to the *cynghellor*.

It appears from the descriptions in the legal texts that the original role of the *rhingyll* was primarily that of an officer of the courts of law over which the *cynghellor* presided: the *rhingyll* acted as apparitor or summoner and also kept order whilst the court was in session.[15] The record sources confirm that the *rhingyll* remained an agent of the courts of law in the thirteenth century. He was responsible, in some cases at least, for setting up the cross of interdiction, a preliminary to many cases relating to real property,[16] and a task with which he is associated, along with the *cynghellor*, in some legal texts.[17] Further information is contained in the record of the evidence presented to the St. Asaph diocesan assembly on episcopal rights of 1274. One of the cases cited[18] refers to a man found in possession of stolen property, and sentenced to suffer confiscation of all his goods. His domestic utensils were shared between the *sygynnabiaid* of the bishop, and the *rhingylliaid* of the prince: this perhaps suggests that those officers directed

---

[14] *L.T.W.L.*, p. 373 (Redaction D), gives *gwas kyghellawr* as one of the three names of the *rhingyll*. See for the relationship between *rhingyll* and *rhaglaw* the 1291-2 sheriff's account referred to in note 4 above, especially the phrase *de ballivo et eius ringildo*.

[15] *Ior.*, 34. 21-2; 73. 13, 16; 77. 10.

[16] E. A. Lewis, 'The Proceedings of the small hundred court of the commote of Ardudwy in the county of Merioneth from 8 October 1325 to 18 September 1326', *B.B.C.S.*, IV (1928), p. 162, has the following case: *Adaf ap Cad' convictus est per cognicionem suam ad sectam domini regis de eo quod ipse cepit crucem de manu Ringildi ad ponendum super terram suam, et illam non posuit*.

[17] See *A.L.*, XIV. XLI. 30.

[18] NLW Peniarth MS. no. 231, pp. 48, 117.

the process of distraint. There are indeed suggestions in the legal texts that the *rhingyll* undertook distraining duties.[19]

In other fields interesting developments of the *rhingyll*'s functions took place: such are his evolution as the steward of the commotal *llys*, and his acquisition of additional responsibilities in the sphere of revenue collection. Light is shed on both of these developments by an ingenious and very plausible suggestion by Professor Dafydd Jenkins that by the thirteenth century the office of *gostegwr*, or silentiary, described in the laws, had been subsumed within that of the *rhingyll*.[20] There is indeed considerable similarity between many of the functions of the two officers as described in the legal texts. As Professor Jenkins notes, the *rhingyll* is said in some texts to have called for silence at the start of judicial proceedings.[21] It may be added that the laws suggest that the *rhingyll* had developed the function of a silentiary in the court of the commote when the ruler was in residence. Thus, *Llyfr Iorwerth* contains the rule, relating to the *rhingyll*, that he should not strike the post on the king's side.[22] Striking one of the posts, or columns, of the court seems to have been the method of calling for silence: a very similar rule, expressed in a rather different fashion, is contained in the description of the *gostegwr* in the same source: it is his duty to serve and call for silence and strike the post above the head of the household priest.[23] Most important, it is stated in the laws that the *gostegwr* collected the *twnc* of the commote, [24] whereas there is evidence from the early post-conquest period that the *rhingyll* performed this task.[25]

These factors discussed above make it entirely credible that the *rhingyll* had assumed the functions of the *gostegwr* by or during the thirteenth century. It is thus interesting to note that *Llyfr Iorwerth*'s treatment of the *gostegwr* strongly suggests that this officer had developed into what may best be described as the steward of the local *llys*: he was to superintend the food

---

[19] See the rule found in some of the legal texts (for example *L.T.W.L.*, p. 324), by which the *rhingyll* is made responsible for distraining the *penhebogydd*.
[20] *Llyfr Colan*, p. 165.
[21] Ibid., and see *Ior.*, 77. 9–10: *guedy dangosser e guystlon, erchy e'r ryghyll dody gostec ar e maes*.
[22] *Ior.*, 34. 5–6.
[23] Ibid., 14. 6–7.
[24] Ibid., 90. 61.
[25] See note 12 above.

and drink under the *distain;* he was to receive sixty pence from the land-*maer* when the latter took office; and while there was no land-*maer* he was to keep (*gwarchadw*) the court, taking care of its furnishings and such of the king's goods as it might contain.²⁶ It would seem, therefore, from the evidence of the legal texts, that the *rhingyll* had by the thirteenth century acquired responsibility for the upkeep of the commotal *llys* in addition to his duties in connection with judicial and fiscal administration.

The *rhingyll* was the factotum of the commote. The wide range of his duties suggests that his presence made it possible for the importance of the office of *rhaglaw* to lie primarily in its value as a means of patronage and for its holder to become a dignitary rather than an active administrator.

PEACE-KEEPING OFFICIALS: THE *CAIS*

Peace-keeping, which largely consisted of activities with a deterrent effect such as retributory distraint, seems at one time to have been one of the duties of the *teulu*.²⁷ The plundering missions of the *teulu* referred to in the legal texts seem to relate sometimes to the process of distraint rather than to expeditions into a *gorwlad*, or neighbouring country.²⁸ It may be to the peace-keeping role of the *teulu* that Giraldus Cambrensis refers in his account²⁹ of an incident which took place in Anglesey, apparently in 1188. Giraldus tells of certain *iuvenes electi*, said to be *de familia Rotherici* (*sc.* Rhodri ab Owain Gwynedd), who undertook a disastrous pursuit of *praedones patriae*, presumably a band of robbers.

By the time of the Edwardian conquest, however, there had emerged a group of officials whose chief responsibility was the

---

²⁶ *Ior.*, 14. 5, 8–12. It is interesting to note that a unique reference in *Ior.* to the *estywart llys* would seem to relate more appropriately in this instance to the *gostegwr* than to the *distain*, the latter identification being the one suggested by Dr. Wiliam, *Llyfr Iorwerth*, p. 107. The passage in question, *Ior.*, 33, deals with the duties of the land-*maer* and states: *ef a dele guarchadu e llys en penhaf guedy er estywart llys*. Compare the following passage. *Ior.*, 14. 9–10, relating to the *gostegwr: Ef a dele, o'r pan dyotter e maer ene dotter arall, guarchadu e llys*.

²⁷ For the *teulu*, or household troops, see above, pp.

²⁸ See *L.T.W.L.*, p. 324, for the legal distraint of the *penhebogydd*, to be carried out by the *teulu* (*familia*) or the *rhingyll* (*preco*).

²⁹ *Giraldi Cambrensis Opera*, ed. J. S. Brewer et al., 8 vols. (Rolls Series, London, 1861–91), VI, p. 126.

suppression of wrongdoers: these were the local officers called variously the *ceisiaid, servientes pacis* or *satellites pacis*. Dr. Stewart-Brown has investigated the problems of the early history of the *cais* in north Wales, and concludes that it is doubtful whether the *ceisiaid* were employed under the native princes in any but the most easterly areas of Gwynedd.[30] He notes a reference to serjeants of the peace in Tegeingl in 1242, but, emphasizing the peculiar dependence of Tegeingl upon Chester in the early middle ages, concludes that 'it seems unlikely that the system, if an innovation, can have been extended further west into North Wales until the conquest by Edward I'.[31] Such a view is almost certainly false. It seems to be based on the assumption that the office of *cais* was an English importation into Gwynedd, and rules out the possibility that it represents a development of an indigenous office. To judge from the statements of the legal texts, there had indeed been officers charged with carrying out duties similar to those of the *cais*. The *maer* and the *cynghellor*, in particular, undertook the distraint of offenders, as is clearly implied by the regulation, given in one of the Latin redactions,[32] concerning distraint of the chief falconer: *Si iure exigente, id est, o gyvreith, depredatus fuerit, predam ipsius non capiet maer neque kyghellaur sed familia, id est, teulu, vel preco.*

By the thirteenth century the *maer* and the *cynghellor* seem to have been replaced as leading commotal officers, yet there are two curious early-fourteenth-century references to officials called *meiri cynghellorion* which deserve further investigation In 1305 a petition to Prince Edward by Tudur ap Goronwy complained that *quidam qui vocantur Meiri Getigelehoryon exigunt de hominibus dicti Tudur et terris suis diversas consuetudines quassatas per dominum Regem post conquestum per Statutum de Rothelan.*[33] And in 1315 John de Grey, justice of north Wales, was ordered 'to supersede the demands made upon . . . the free tenants of the commote of Ardudwy in the county of Merioneth, for twenty shillings for an office called *Meyryd Kynkellorion*, which office they used to have and from which they say that they

---

[30] R. Stewart-Brown, *The Serjeants of the Peace in Medieval England and Wales* (Manchester, 1936), pp. 35–44.
[31] Ibid.
[32] *L.T.W.L.*, p. 324.
[33] *Rec. Caern.*, p. 215.

have been amoved by the king's officers'.[34] The nature of the evidence will permit only speculation, but it may be that *meiri cynghellorion* were officers akin to *ceisiaid*, and perhaps identical with them;[35] the name may represent an archaic survival, betraying the office from which the *cais* evolved.

There is more positive evidence that the office of *cais* or something akin to it was to be found throughout Gwynedd during the thirteenth century. The existence of serjeants of this type seems to be a regular feature of areas of England and southern Scotland which retained strong traces of a Celtic socio-political organization.[36] A particularly significant passage in a charter of Llywelyn ab Iorwerth to Aberconwy abbey, dated 1198/9[37] and relating to the abbey's extensive lands in Gwynedd Uwch Conwy, strongly suggests that the *cais* operated in that area by the early-thirteenth century. Llywelyn states that *ad satillites et ministros meos qui ad custodiendam pacem sunt assignati pertinet latrones fures et malefactores investigare prosequi et capere*.[38] As has been seen, *satellites*, or *satellites pacis* were frequently-employed latinizations of *ceisiaid* in the post-conquest period.[39] The passage seems, then, to be a valuable summary of at least some of the functions of the *cais* in the early-thirteenth century.

Finally, three passages relating to the history and functions of the *cais* are found in an undated collection of documents which appears in the Record of Caernarvon, and which is stated to have been found *in recordis North Walliae*.[40] The first, alleged to have been abstracted from material *inter ordinacionem*

---

[34] *C. Close R., 1313–18*, p. 179.
[35] It is interesting that some legal texts refer to an office of *maer cynghellor*, apparently distinct from the offices of *maer* and *cynghellor*: see Dafydd Jenkins, '*Cynghellor* and Chancellor', *B.B.C.S.*, XXVII (1976), p. 118. This composite office may have been a development from the older ones of *maer* and *cynghellor*. In the Ardudwy reference given in the previous note, it is clearly stated that it is the *free* men who have been moved from the office of *meiri cynghellorion*. It should be noted in this context that the *maer* and *cynghellor* of the legal texts were generally burdensome not to the free community but to the ruler's bondmen: only, significantly enough, in their distraining activities would they come into frequent contact with freemen.
[36] See G. W. S. Barrow, 'The pattern of lordship and feudal settlement in Cumbria', *Journal of Medieval History*, I (1975), pp. 129–30.
[37] For the problem of dating see Appendix 1, no. 1.
[38] *Rec. Caern.*, p. 148.
[39] See above, p. 47.
[40] *Rec. Caern.*, pp. 131–2.

pro pace in North Wallia, states that the justice of north Wales had, at the request of the county of Merioneth, abolished the office of *cais* and substituted communal responsibility for peace-keeping. The third passage records that, following many homicides and robberies, the leading men of Caernarvonshire had come together with the justice, and ordained on behalf of themselves and the community to appoint *custodes pacis* in each commote who were to arrest thieves, homicides and breakers of the peace. Afterwards (*postea*) the community was fined 405 marks for not keeping the peace according to the ancient ordinance, and was charged as formerly with keeping the peace according to this ordinance. The Welsh communities of Merioneth and Anglesey were similarly fined and charged. The second passage, which looks rather like a gloss upon the first, is perhaps the most interesting of the three. It states that according to the ancient law of Wales, *antiquam legem Walliae*, the *keys* (i.e., *ceis*) were responsible for peace-keeping in north Wales (*custodirent patriam de malefactoribus et responderent de corporibus eorum et de eorum factis*); but as the community had felt itself burdened by the need to find puture for the *ceisiaid*, the latter had been abolished, and communal responsibility substituted. The account of the function of the *cais* given here complements and confirms that given in Llywelyn ab Iorwerth's charter to Aberconwy abbey.

The argument advanced in the edition of the survey of Denbigh by Vinogradoff and Morgan,[41] and quoted approvingly by Stewart-Brown,[42] that the statement, in the second passage, that the *cais* functioned according to the ancient law of Wales cannot be true because the surviving Welsh legal texts do not mention the *cais*, is hardly convincing: the princes are known to have made alterations to the law,[43] and whether these were incorporated in any of the lawbooks depended on the whims and intentions of the various redactors.

The terminology of the three passages summarized above is so vague as to prohibit the construction of a precise chronology of events. Nevertheless, some general, if tentative, deductions

---
[41] *S.D.*, p. lxxxiv.
[42] R. Stewart-Brown, op. cit., p. 40.
[43] See above, p. 6 and see *Ior.*, 82. 2.

can be made. Firstly, it seems, on the basis of the second passage, that the *ceisiaid* had operated in Gwynedd Uwch Conwy before the Edwardian conquest, but were shortly afterwards abolished. This explains the fact that the *ceisiaid* do not appear in the late-thirteenth- and fourteenth-century accounts and surveys of the northern principality, though they do appear in the marcher lordships of Perfeddwlad.[44] The evidence of the third passage implies that at some stage after the Edwardian settlement an attempt, apparently short-lived, was made to restore the old system of *ceisiaid*, or something closely akin to it.

Most significantly, it is clear from the background to the abolition of the *ceisiaid* after the conquest, given in the second and, probably, the first passage, that they had not been popular officials. The provision of puture, or *cylch*-dues, represented an unwelcome burden upon the population. The number of *ceisiaid* may have been formidable: a total of twenty-four serjeants was envisaged for Tegeingl in 1242,[45] a total of eight per commote, and they seem normally to have been sufficiently numerous to require organization under a *magister satellitum* or *pencais*.[46] It is doubtless a reflection of the way in which the *ceisiaid* generally carried out their duties that in middle Welsh (and in middle English in the loan-word *keys*) *cais* developed strong connotations of rapacity and violence.[47] The *ceisiaid* may well have been as burdensome upon the country as the malefactors whom they were intended to suppress.

OFFICERS OF THE DEMESNE

There are numerous references in the laws to officials charged with particular responsibility for the administration of the ruler's demesne and associated lands: the *maer* and *cynghellor*, assisted by the *rhingyll*, regulated the king's waste and the

---

[44] They also appear in south and west Wales: see note 47 below, and Myvanwy Rhys, *Ministers' Accounts for West Wales, 1277–1306* (Cymmrodorion Record Series, XIII, 1936), p. 77 n. 17.
[45] *C. Chart. R., 1226–57*, pp. 274–5.
[46] See Appendix II *sub* Gruffydd Gryg, and for Madog ap Maredudd see *Registrum . . . Peckham*, II, p. 450.
[47] See Joy Russell-Smith, 'Keys in Sawles Warde', *Medium Aevum*, XXII (1953), pp. 104–10.

majority of his bond-vills; the land-*maer* controlled the *maerdref*, in which dwelt the bondmen most closely linked with the *llys* and its associated mensal land or *tir bwrdd*, and he also supervised the king's summer pastures or *hafotiroedd;* the *porthawr* acted as *rhingyll* for the *maerdref* and took charge of the king's prisoners, while the *gostegwr* supervised the activities of the land-*maer*[48].

If this particular nexus of officials and responsibilities ever existed in practice, it certainly no longer did so by the thirteenth century. By then, as has been seen, the *maer* and *cynghellor* had been replaced by other officials, whilst significant changes had taken place in some areas in the structure of the *maerdref-tir bwrdd-hafotir* complex. In some commotes, particularly in Gwynedd Uwch Conwy, the *maerdref* itself had declined considerably in size, in places to the point of extinction.[49] In such areas the traditional role of the officers of the *llys*, *maerdref* and *tir bwrdd* would undergo considerable modification. Thus, the land-*maer's* responsibilities might be limited to care for the *hafotiroedd:* there are references in post-conquest sources relating to Gwynedd, above and below Conwy, to officials whose specific responsibility was the custody of *hafotiroedd* or vaccaries,[50] and the widespread nature of these references suggests that they may reflect pre-conquest institutions, which were developed in order to facilitate the exploitation of the pasture-lands. Again, the *porthawr* of a *llys* whose associated *maerdref* was in severe decline might become almost solely employed as a gaoler, though it is worth noting in this context that the keepers of the stone castles which were appearing in some areas of Gwynedd were probably taking over the task of guarding the more important prisoners, such as members of the princely house.[51]

---

[48] *Ior.*, 14, 33, 34, 35, 91.
[49] See below, pp. 58–9.
[50] There are, for example, references to wardens of vaccaries or *hafotiroedd* in the early post-conquest period in the Denbigh lordship (*S.D.*, p. lxxi), Dolwyddelan and Snowdon, for which see John Griffiths (ed.), 'Early accounts relating to North Wales *temp.* Edward I', *B.B.C.S.* XIV (1952), p. 312, and ibid., XV (1954), p. 128.
[51] In cases in which stone castles were built at old commotal centres the office of keeper might simply represent a development of that of *porthawr*. In such a castle, Cricieth, David ap Llywelyn imprisoned Gruffydd ap Llywelyn and Owain ap Gruffydd (*BT, R.B.H.*, p. 237) and Llywelyn ap Gruffydd imprisoned Maredudd ap Rhys (*Annales Cambriae*, s.a. 1259, MS. B reading).

It is possible that early post-conquest references to the *rhaglaw advocariorum*[52] may relate to an office developed under the native princes: the use of the native form *rhaglaw* suggests this, while there had certainly existed tenants equivalent to *advocarii*, settled on the prince's lands and subject to his special protection, in the pre-conquest period.[53]

Another class of specialized officials, which had certainly emerged before the conquest was that concerned with the prince's forest; *coedwr*, *wtwrt*, or *forestarius* are the terms generally used.[54] Little is known of the work of these officers, but they were clearly wardens, administering a forest law, for infractions of which they made arrests.[55]

There is, then, much that is obscure about the nature and number of the offices through which the princes attempted to exploit the lands and associated resources under their direct control. There are, however, some signs that the major development here was the development of offices concerned with specific resources, in an effort by the princes to maximize the exploitation of these, perhaps their most readily accessible sources of revenue.

CONCLUSION

The ministerial structure set out above was extremely flexible, well adapted to the political circumstances and requirements of the princes. Amongst the officials closely associated with the itinerant *curia*, specialization is found only in those concerned with secretarial activity and with financial administration, and in the latter case the extent of specialization would seem to have been minimal. Behind the lack of specialization lies the near omnicompetence of the prince and of his great servant, the *distain*, a condition facilitated by the compact nature of the territories under the prince's direct control.

---

[52] For the *rhaglaw advocarie* in Llysfaen and Penmaen see *S.D.* p. 318. See also J. Griffiths, 'Early accounts relating to North Wales *temp.* Edward I', *B.B.C.S.*, XIV (1952), p. 240, for a reference to the *rhaglaw advocariorum* of Arfon, Arllechwedd and Creuddyn in 1287.

[53] *Medieval Welsh Society*, pp. 355–6.

[54] For *coedwr*, see *S.D. passim;* for the *wtwrt* of Rhos in the early 1270s, see NLW Peniarth MS. no. 231, p. 80; for *forestarius* in the same period, see Haddan and Stubbs, *Councils*, I, p. 513.

[55] This may be inferred from the petition of the abbot of Bardsey in 1305, given in *Rec. Caern.*, p. 221, that *secundum antiquam libertatem suam . . . nullus Wodwardus intromittat se de aliquibus attachiamentis faciendis in terris aut in boscis eorum.*

The dependence on ecclesiastical centres in Gwynedd, which seem to have provided technical secretarial and diplomatic help as well as providing facilities as repositories for some of the prince's records and *mobilia*, merely reflects the more general value to the princes of the support of influential ecclesiastics for their cause.[1]

Though there is not sufficient evidence to permit the compilation of even a sketchy itinerary, except for very limited periods, it seems that the princes' court was a truly itinerant one, which did not remain for long periods at any one place.[2] The prince was thus in frequent contact with the localities, and in these circumstances there was no necessity for a unit of administration larger than the commote or *cantref* within Gwynedd nor for an official intermediate between the *rhaglaw* and the prince, such as the sheriff of the post-conquest period.[3] The contrast between the ministerial structure of the pre-conquest period and that set up after the Edwardian settlement should almost certainly not be interpreted in terms of different levels of ability or efficiency in those charged with governance: it reflects instead the different political circumstances of the two periods.

---

[1] See below, pp. 166-7.
[2] See Appendix V. It would seem that Llywelyn ap Gruffydd, even when in direct control of territories in the south and the Marches, rarely made expeditions beyond the borders of Gwynedd. This may lend significance to his reference in the period 1267-77 to his *senescallus de Ultra Berwyn*, who would appear, from his title, to have exercised authority over an area wider than that covered by a single *cantref*: see *Cal. Anc. Corr.*, p. 92.
[3] See the previous note.

Part 2
The Prince's Dues

INTRODUCTION:
THE PROBLEM OF QUANTIFICATION

It is the purpose of the following chapters to elucidate the range of revenues and services at the disposal of the princes. Because of the fragmentary nature of the evidence, it is not practicable to attempt to define in quantitative terms the relationships between various sources of revenue, or to chart their development during the century in anything but an impressionistic fashion.

In particular, it should be stressed that no realistic attempt can be made to establish the amount of cash revenue available to the princes. They clearly derived much of their income from sources, such as the profits of justice, which were of irregular incidence and amount.[1] An estimate of the cash income derived from fixed annual renders in the immediately pre-conquest period has been made for Gwynedd Uwch Conwy by Professor Jones Pierce,[2] but it is possible that such estimates may prove misleading. The fact that a render in kind or a service had been translated into cash terms by the time of the conquest does not necessarily indicate that the full cash value given to it was exacted every year. An inquisition of 1285[3] revealed that Llywelyn ap Gruffydd took puture for five hundred men, as well as taking two yearling foals, from the Penllyn lands of Basingwerk abbey when he came to hunt in that area each year. In years when he did not come to hunt, however, he took money in place of the puture and the foals. This implies that a render might be taken in kind even when a cash value had been fixed for it. Though this evidence relates to monastic lands, it is probably not entirely unrepresentative of the situation regarding the estates of laymen.

[1] See below, pp. 74–89.
[2] *Medieval Welsh Society*, pp. 103–25, esp. p. 118.
[3] *C. Inq. Misc.*, I, no. 1357.

A clause in the Bardsey concords of 1252,[4] one of the few pre-conquest sources to provide information about the development of commutation, states that the poorest class of *abadaeth* tenants must pay to the lord of Cymydmaen one penny per year, *aut eius valenciam*. Thus, the sums which appear in post-conquest extents as *redditus assise*, identified by Professor Jones Pierce as indices of pre-conquest commutation levels,[5] may only represent a maximum level rather than one which was regularly attained. Moreover, figures derived from such sources do not generally reveal anything about the rate of progression of commutation in the thirteenth century, since they record only the high-water mark of commutation in the period of native rule.

---

[4] *Rec. Caern.*, p. 252.
[5] *Medieval Welsh Society*, pp. 115–18. It may be that in some cases the figures given by Jones Pierce are a little too precise: for example, the extent of Porthaethwy (Seebohm, *Tribal System*, Appendix A, p. 5) seems to include *redditus assise,* customs and services in a composite total valuation of ten shillings.

V

DEMESNE EXPLOITATION

The princes possessed demesne lands in every commote, and it seems clear that these were being intensively exploited in the thirteenth century. The principal demesne lands were generally the arable areas located close to the commotal *llys* and, where one survived, the *maerdref*. Even in cases where the *maerdref* had been replaced by a borough, as at Llanfaes or Pwllheli, or had been greatly reduced in size, as at Neigwl, the associated demesne generally remained as the directly exploited resource of the princes.[1] These developments are discussed in more detail below.[2]

The size and value of the arable areas contiguous to the *llys* varied considerably from place to place, from the thirteen carucates at Llanfaes, assessed after the conquest at £20 10s. per year,[3] to the single carucate at Crogen in Penllyn valued at one pound per year.[4] There were other arable lands in demesne apart from those adjacent to the *llys*: in Penllyn, for example, the demesne arable was dispersed throughout commotes rather than being concentrated around *llysoedd*.[5] Moreover, the prince's demesne at any one time included lands which had come into his hands by escheat through default of

---

[1] For the decay of *maerdrefi* in Gwynedd Uwch Conwy, see *Medieval Welsh Society*, pp. 140, 278–80. Professor Jones Pierce assumed that all three carucates of arable demesne at Pwllheli were being leased out by the conquest, but the post-conquest extent, as reflected in the ministers' accounts, suggests that only one carucate, that held by Rhirid ap Cadwgan, was being leased, the others remaining in the princes' direct control. The accounts refer to forty shillings, *de ii carucatis terre dominice manerii de Porthelli*, without making the burgesses responsible for that amount, and later refer to sixty shillings *de i carucata terre dominice pertinente ad dictum manerium unde Ryrit ap Cad' magister vaccariarum solebat respondere*. For these references see T. Jones Pierce, 'Lleyn Ministers' Accounts 1350–51', *B.B.C.S.*, VI (1933), p. 265. Twenty or thirty shillings per carucate was the common value put upon land still in demesne by post-conquest surveyors whereas a valuation of sixty shillings per carucate was wholly exceptional.
[2] See below, pp. 59–62.
[3] Seebohm, *Tribal System*, Appendix A, p. 3.
[4] 'Extent of Merionethshire *temp*. Edward I', ed. M. C. J., *Arch. Camb.*, 3rd Ser., XIII (1867), p. 189.
[5] Ibid., pp. 187–9, and Glanville Jones, 'The Military Geography of Gwynedd in the Thirteenth Century' (University of Wales M.A. thesis, 1949) p. 67.

heirs or through failure of tenants to perform obligations. Such lands were scattered in random fashion and might in some circumstances be merely temporary additions to the demesne.[6]

The exploitation of the arable demesnes, and the utilization of their produce was based on a network of labour services covering both free and bond tenants. Labour services were subject to considerable local variation according to the needs of the rulers, the customs of the commote or *cantref*, and the level of commutation: it is intended here to give no more than a broad survey in order to demonstrate the various means by which the princes maintained demesne exploitation.

The agricultural services most generally rendered were ploughing, reaping and threshing. Labour services were also performed in the meadows appurtenant to the *llys*, so that mowing was common. Agricultural services were not, indeed, the only labour obligations performed at the commotal centre: the *llys* itself and its associated buildings were built and kept in good order by the men of the commote, work which seems in many cases to have been done by both bondmen and freemen, in contrast to the statement of the lawbooks that it was the bondmen who were responsible for constructing the court buildings.[7] We seem to have here a case, one of several, in which the needs of the rulers produced in practice a situation more complex than the neat social distinction and demarcation of roles often found in the legal texts.

The primary source of labour was usually the *maerdref* and its associated bond hamlets wherein dwelt the bondmen described by post-conquest surveyors as being 'of the manor'. In a number of cases, however, the *maerdrefi* had disappeared or declined, and thus the pattern of obligation to labour services was changed. At Llanfaes, where trading activity at the commotal centre had been formalised by the princes with the creation of a borough, which seems to have been formed

---

[6] Such lands appear in some sources, such as *S.D.*, as *tir diffyk*. Where lands escheated for non-performance of services or nonpayment of dues the laws stipulated that they should be restored once the service had been performed or the dues paid: *L.T.W.L.*, p. 230. For practical examples of land held in escheat by Llywelyn ap Gruffydd, see *C. Close R., 1327–30*, pp. 294–5.

[7] See for the obligation to repair court-buildings in Ceinmeirch, *S.D.*, pp. 8 (bondmen) and 45 (freemen), and in Rhufoniog Is Aled, ibid., p. 149 (both bond and freemen). For the pronouncement of one of the lawbooks on the obligation of the bondmen to construct the court, see *Ior.*, 93. 19–22.

out of the former *maerdref*, the princes continued to hold the burgesses responsible for the performance of works on the demesne.[8] In other cases of declining or disappearing *maerdrefi*, the princes had modified or permitted the modification of the old socio-economic structure to maintain the exploitation of the demesne. At Penrhos and Cemais in Anglesey, the *maerdrefi eo nomine* had disappeared by the conquest, but there remained groups of tenants, later distinguished as *gwŷr gwaith*, 'work men', whose obligations were dominated by labour services. At the same time, the distinction between *gwŷr gwaith*, *gwŷr mal* 'rent-paying men' and *gwŷr tir bwrdd* of the 1352 extent,[9] with the clear differentiation of roles implied by the first two terms, should not be read back to the period prior to the conquest. The *gwŷr tir bwrdd*, settlers on the demesne-land, emerged, it seems, as the result of demesne-leasing after the conquest,[10] and in the valuable extent of Penrhos made by Prior Llywelyn in 1284,[11] though an incipient group of *gwŷr mal* is visible, there are respects in which different types of obligations overlapped: the men who provided most of the labour on the demesnes were nevertheless required to give up food renders, and in this respect they resemble traditional *maerdref* tenants.[12] Outside Anglesey, Dolgellau provides an example of another adaptation of the traditional *maerdref* structure: a reference in the 1284 extent to *decem firmarii sub . . . villanis de Dolgellau* (the *firmarii* being responsible for works valued at 7*s*. 4*d*. per year), betrays the arrival of an adventitious element to supplement the traditional *maerdref* tenants.[13] The reference to the *firmarii*

---

[8] Seebohm, *Tribal System*, Appendix A, p. 4: *De operacionibus ville de Lammas, videlicet metendum, cariandum, et herciandum xxvjs. viijd.*
[9] *Rec. Caern.*, pp. 63–5, 70–2.
[10] Dafydd Jenkins, *Llyfr Colan*, pp. 173–4, fails to draw the clear distinction between men of the *maerdref* and men of the *tir bwrdd*: the latter represent, quite simply, tenants holding the former *tir bwrdd*. This is very well illustrated in the case of the *gwŷr tir bwrdd* of Penrhos: in 1352, the extent of Penrhos records no demesne land in the lord's hand, whilst the *gwŷr tir bwrdd* pay rent of £5 (seven and a half marks). The post-conquest extent had valued the demesne at Penrhos at £6 (Seebohm, *Tribal System*, Appendix A, p. 13), but from the early 1290s it is clear from the accounts that it was being leased at £5 per year: ibid., p. 26.
[11] For the date, see Appendix VI.
[12] The prototypes in 1284 of *gwŷr mal* are the tenants of the *gavelli de quibus dominus haberet redditus pecuniarios cum frumento*, for which see Seebohm, *Tribal System*, Appendix A, p. 24. The overlapping of obligations is shown by reference to renders from the community of the whole vill, ibid., p. 25.
[13] 'Extent of Merionethshire *temp.* Edward I', pp. 184–5. See also Glanville Jones, op. cit., pp. 28, 117.

as being *sub villanis* is interesting: it rouses the suspicion that the latter may have taken the initiative in the settlement of the *firmarii*.

As Professor Jones Pierce observed, however, the mainland *maerdrefi* of Gwynedd Uwch Conwy, with only a few exceptions such as Aber, were showing clear signs of decay by the end of Llywelyn ap Gruffydd's principate, at which time they generally consisted of only a few households apiece.[14] In the majority of cases there had been no obvious modification of the *maerdref*-structure, the princes having fallen back on a further source of labour, the *forinsec* bondmen of the commote. It is instructive in this context to look at two contrasting localities: the *cantref* of Aberffraw in which the centre at *llys* Aberffraw was supported by appurtenant *tir bwrdd* covering five carucates,[15] and the commote of Talybont, where the centre of Dolgellau contained two carucates of arable.[16] The balance of services was as follows: in Aberffraw, with a substantial nexus of *maerdref* and associated vills, the 'manorial' bondmen provided agricultural works valued at almost £8 5s. per year, while the *forinsec* bondmen, those of the *cantref*, rendered agricultural services worth £1 19s.[17] In Talybont, the *villani* and *firmarii* of Dolgellau gave services valued at £1 13s. 4d., while the works of the *forinsec* bondmen were surveyed at one pound exactly, if carriage works are excepted.[18] There is an obvious contrast of scale here, but more than that, it seems that even when the figures have been adjusted to compensate for the differences in size of the demesne areas, the arable of Aberffraw was being exploited more intensively than that of Dolgellau. This may reflect a difference in the level of bond

---

[14] T. Jones Pierce, 'Aber Gwyn Gregin', *Trans. Caerns. Hist. Soc.*, XXIII (1962), pp. 37–43.
[15] Seebohm, *Tribal System*, Appendix A, p. 5.
[16] 'Extent of Merionethshire *temp*. Edward I', pp. 184–5.
[17] The totals are obtained by adding the commutation values put on agricultural services in the 1284 extent, given in Seebohm, *Tribal System*, Appendix A, pp. 6–10. The extent, ibid., p. 7, gives a total value of 66s. 9d. to autumn works of three hundred men, found by the manorial bondmen, and of eighty men found by the *forinsec* bondmen: this sum has thus been apportioned between the two groups in the ratio 30 : 8. It has been assumed that the bulk of the *operaciones* mentioned, ibid., p. 6, were of an agricultural nature. It has likewise been assumed that the six hundred day-works *ad herciandum*, ibid., p. 7, were due from the manorial bondmen only.
[18] 'Extent of Merionethshire *temp*. Edward I', pp. 184–5.

population in the two areas, and even, in spite of the surveyors' valuation of a carucate of demesne land at thirty shillings per year at both centres, a difference in the quality of the arable. But it may also reflect the probability that commutation of renders was more advanced in Aberffraw *cantref* than in Talybont,[19] so that in the former area the prince may have depended heavily upon his demesne land for produce in kind. Finally, there is a clear difference between the balance of *intrinsec* and *forinsec* services in the two areas, which probably relates to the relative vigour of *maerdrefi* and related institutions, on the one hand, and the outlying bond vills, on the other. Whatever the expedients adopted to ensure cultivation, it remains clear that the great majority of the princes' demesne centres, or home-farms, were still directly exploited by them down to the conquest.

Valuable features of the demesne associated with arable farming were the princes' mills, for the bondmen of the commote, and such freemen as did not have mills of their own, were obliged to grind their grain at the prince's mill, and to pay for the privilege.[20] The mills, particularly numerous in areas of intensive agricultural activity such as Anglesey,[21] were kept in working order by the labour of the bond population.[22]

Pasture lands formed a highly significant part of the demesne, especially in the mountain commotes where arable land was sparse and the economy mainly pastoral. Though some were farmed out[23] by the time of the conquest, the vaccaries were mainly retained in the direct control of the princes. In this way, the ruler could stock them with his own herds and could exact rents for their occasional or seasonal use by his subjects:

[19] *Medieval Welsh Society*, p. 118.
[20] See the 1352 extent of Eifionydd, *Rec. Caern.*, p. 41, where it is recorded that in Rhwng Dwyfor a Dwyfach, the tenants of *gwely Wyrion Utot* claim the freedom to mill wherever they wish by grant of Llywelyn ab Iorwerth, former prince of Wales, because their ancestors once had their own mill. Llywelyn had built another mill downstream from theirs, which would have been useless had they not allowed the prince *cursum aque molendini eorum;* as a result of this the prince had granted them the privilege of grinding their corn freely wherever they wished.
[21] The renders associated with the many Anglesey mills are recorded in the 1284 extent: Seebohm, *Tribal System*, Appendix A, pp. 3 (Llanfaes), 5 (Aberffraw), 11 (Cemais), 13 (Penrhos), 17 (Rhosfair).
[22] See *S.D.*, *passim*, for references to *reparacio molendini* carried out by bondmen.
[23] See the 'Extent of Merionethshire *temp.* Edward I', p. 189, for references to *firmarii pasture* in Merioneth in 1284.

this may have been the basis for the bond render called *maeroniaeth* in the early post-conquest extents.[24] Professor Glanville Jones has pointed to the close relationship between the distribution of vaccaries and the siting of the mountain stone castles:[25] the two were indeed complementary institutions, with the castles giving protection to the vaccaries and the vaccaries providing provisions for the castles. It is significant that an examination of Llywelyn ap Gruffydd's itinerary in the period July 1273–January 1277,[26] for which evidence is fuller than at most other times, reveals that the court spent much of its time at centres associated with upland areas characterized by demesne pastures and lactic renders: the need to consume the typical products of such areas may have involved the frequent presence of the court.

One further important part of the demesne which deserves mention is the forest, which was a source of building material, firewood, pannage, sport by way of hunting, and meat from the animals and birds killed. Amongst the services of bondmen in some areas was the collection of eggs.[27] It is, moreover, clear that there was some form of forest law, enforced by *coedwyr*,[28] so that the forest constituted a special source for the profits of justice, a topic treated at greater length below. The exploitation of the non-arable demesne lands was facilitated by a further network of labour services involving the bond population: carriage-works were probably the most important and widespread, though these were not confined to non-arable demesne produce.[29]

---

[24] The render is mentioned throughout the 1284 Anglesey extent and occasionally in the Merioneth extent, but the best account of it is in Prior Llywelyn's survey of Penrhos (Seebohm, *Tribal System*, Appendix A, p. 25, and cf. below, Appendix VI), where it is described thus: *Item, pro maronia lactis predicte ville in estate et autumpno dimidii totius lactis dicioris* (sic) *hominis de villa et illud aliquando esset fructus iiii vaccarum et aliquando duarum, ille vacce in festo omnium sanctorum redirent ad suum possessorem.*
[25] Glanville Jones, op. cit., p. 109.
[26] See Appendix V.
[27] 'Extent of Merionethshire *temp.* Edward I', p. 189.
[28] See above, p. 52.
[29] See a reference in the Llŷn accounts to a payment of three shillings *de villanis tocius commoti pro victualibus domini Principis in montibus cariandis que cariagium vocatur Teythymyn.* See T. Jones Pierce, 'Lleyn Ministers' Accounts, 1350–51', *B.B.C.S.*, VI (1933), p. 269.

DEMESNE EXPLOITATION

The demesne lands, because they were frequently well sited in relation to the princes' *llysoedd* and castles, formed the primary means of provisioning these local centres of the princes' governance. Demesne produce was not, however, sufficient to support the whole of the large itinerant court of the princes, and even less were the demesnes able to provide adequate material foundations for the expansionist policies of the princes. For these purposes the rulers of Gwynedd had to look to a far wider range of renders and obligations.

VI

RENDERS AND DUES

CYLCH, TWNC AND CORNAGE

The lawbooks provide a simple outline picture of renders with which the subjects of a Welsh king might be frequently burdened. The free vills owed an entertainment render, *gwestfa*, which might be commuted into a cash payment, the so-called *twnc*-pound, levied on each *maenol* of four vills; the bond population, with the exception of *maerdref* bondmen, owed a twice-yearly food-gift, *dawnbwyd*. In addition, the same bondmen were obliged to supply provender to various royal officials on circuit or *cylch* through the localities, whilst the free were to support a great winter progress through the kingdom, undertaken by the *teulu*.[1]

Elements of continuity with such a system are visible in records relating to the thirteenth and fourteenth centuries, but these also make it clear that in most respects a wide gulf separates the situation depicted in the lawbooks from the reality of the thirteenth century. Professor Jones Pierce has gone a long way towards establishing the outlines of the latter, in particular in the course of a brilliant paper on the development of commutation in Gwynedd Uwch Conwy before the Edwardian conquest,[2] from which much of what follows is derived.

An initial contrast between the evidence of thirteenth- and fourteenth-century records and that of the lawbooks is that of nomenclature. *Cylch* is still found, but the terms *gwestfa* and *dawnbwyd* do not appear in records relating to Gwynedd, whilst *porthiant* (latinized as *procuratio* or *potura*), a term which occurs only infrequently in the lawbooks, is common.[3] Finally, the meaning of *twnc* had, it seems, become somewhat flexible by the mid-thirteenth century: there is evidence that it was used

---

[1] See *Ior.*, 96, for *gwestfa* and *dawnbwyd;* ibid., 90. 55-61 for *twnc*, and 92. 7 for the *cylch mawr teulu*.
[2] *Medieval Welsh Society*, pp. 103-26.
[3] For its occurrence in a legal text, see *L.T.W.L.*, p. 239.

to refer to both commuted and uncommuted *gwestfa* renders.⁴ The problem of commutation will be examined in greater detail below.

Considerable renders in kind survived in most parts of Gwynedd, and, where their composition can be ascertained, they betray none of the clearly artificial regularity of the *gwestfa* and *dawnbwyd* of the legal texts. Jones Pierce is surely correct in characterizing these latter as 'ideal standards of social obligation and not by any means . . . a universal reflection of actual conditions prevailing at any stage in the evolution of Welsh society'.⁵ In contrast, the Edwardian extents reveal that, as might be expected, renders in kind varied according to regional economic bias, with upland areas providing a higher proportion of meat and milk products than the lowland areas, where the renders reflect greater agricultural activity.⁶

Amongst the renders which in many localities had not become subject to commutation, and so capable of consolidation into a single cash total per area of assessment, the most prominent by the end of the thirteenth century was one latinized variously as *procuratio*, *potura* or *pastus*, the corresponding vernacular terms being *porthiant* or *cylch*. These renders sometimes correspond in some measure to the *cylchoedd* assigned to specific officials in the legal texts. For example, *Llyfr Iorwerth* assigns a *cylch* of this type to the *penhebogydd*, the chief falconer, the *pencynydd*, the chief huntsman, and to the local officials, the *maer* and *cynghellor*, each of these *cylchoedd* being provided by the bondmen exclusively.⁷ Post-conquest records reveal related *cylchoedd*: *cylch hebogyddion* or *potura falconum*, is found in Gwynedd Uwch Conwy,⁸ as is *potura venatorum*,⁹ whilst the *cylch rhaglaw*, *pastus ragloti*,¹⁰ relating to the official who stood

---

⁴ See a reference in the Bardsey concords of 1252, in *Rec. Caern.*, p. 252: *Tunc predicte ville sic est quod reddant annuatim xviijd. cum xij Gwyelyn ordei cum cumilo.*
⁵ *Medieval Welsh Society*, p. 115.
⁶ Ibid., p. 119. Compare the renders from the lowland areas of Anglesey given in the post-conquest extent, Seebohm, *Tribal System*, Appendix A, pp. 3–25, with those from the uplands of Merioneth, for the contemporary survey of which see 'The Extent of Merionethshire *temp.* Edward I', ed. M. C. J., *Arch. Camb.*, 3rd Ser., XIII (1867), 184ff.
⁷ *Ior.*, 9. 15–16; 15. 36–8; 96. 31–3.
⁸ *Rec. Caern.*, pp. 1–94 *passim*.
⁹ T. Jones Pierce, 'Lleyn Ministers' Accounts, 1350–51', *B.B.C.S.*, VI (1933), p. 273.
¹⁰ *Rec. Caern.*, pp. 1–94 *passim; S.D., passim.*

at the head of commotal administration in the thirteenth century, is found throughout most areas of Gwynedd. Other *cylchoedd* found in post-conquest records do not have such a readily distinguishable pedigree. Some of these reflect the development of local officials with apparently specific functions: such were the *pastus forestariorum*, and the *pastus satellitum* or *servientum, porthiant ceis*, found in the Perfeddwlad (and probably in Gwynedd Uwch Conwy before the Edwardian conquest).[11] Still others reflect more of the hunting activities of the court, an example being the *cylch dyfrgwn* (otterhounds),[12] or the importance to the prince of his horses: such are the *cylch greorion* (herdsmen), *cylch stalwyn* or *pastus stalonum*, and *pastus dextrarii*.[13]

It is not only the greater range of circuit-dues revealed in the records which forms a contrast with the information of the legal texts, but also the pattern of obligation. The lawbooks state quite clearly that freemen owe no *cylch* beyond the great winter circuit of the *teulu*,[14] which is yet to be discussed. But in the post-conquest records it is quite clear that the burdens of *cylch* had spread unevenly to freemen by the end of the period of native rule. In Gwynedd Uwch Conwy, free *gwelyau* are found, for example, paying *cylch stalwyn, cylch rhaglaw, cylch hebogyddion* and *cylch dyfrgwn*.[15] To take an example from the Perfeddwlad, both free and bond tenants in the commote of Cynmeirch rendered *pastus Stalonis et Garcionis, pastus Lucrarii* and *pastus Penmackew et Waission Bagheyn*.[16] Few of these or other circuit dues are traceable throughout Gwynedd, but again replacement of one *cylch* by another according to local conditions is surely to be expected.

The legal texts refer to another *cylch* which has not yet been examined: the great winter circuit of the *teulu*. This circuit probably provides the background to the *pastus principis* owed by freemen and the *pastus familie principis* owed by bondmen recorded in the 1334 Denbigh survey.[17] Corresponding to these

[11] Above, pp. 46–50.
[12] *Rec. Caern.*, pp. 30, 34, 36.
[13] Ibid., pp. 3, 4, 5, *et passim* (*stalwyn*); 39 (*greorion*); *S.D.*, pp. 8, 49 *et passim* (*dextrarii*).
[14] *Ior.*, 92. 7.
[15] See, for example, *Rec. Caern.*, pp. 53 (*gwely Wasteyniol*) and 59 (*gwely Conus*).
[16] See the common customs of Cynmeirch in *S.D.*, pp. 49–50.
[17] Ibid.

RENDERS AND DUES 67

pastus dues are the obligations to render *procuratio* or *potura* to large numbers of men, horses and dogs, which lay upon both bondmen and freemen in many areas of Gwynedd Uwch Conwy. (It is interesting to note in this context that the legal texts clearly imply that only freemen were burdened with the *cylch mawr* of the *teulu*.)[18]

It is these possible descendants of the *cylch mawr* that Jones Pierce calls *porthiant*, defining this as 'the obligation to billet the prince's men and horses for a specified period annually', and he further suggests that there is positive evidence that in the time of Llywelyn ab Iorwerth *porthiant* was only levied when the prince visited a district in person, and that it had only recently become stabilized through the action of Llywelyn ap Gruffydd.[19] The reference here is to a report of 1285 regarding the Penllyn lands of Basingwerk abbey, to the effect that Llywelyn ab Iorwerth and David his son, princes of Wales, were accustomed to have puture for three hundred men once a year when they came to hunt in Penllyn, namely, bread, butter, fish and cheese in the house of the abbot and convent of Basingwerk; they took nothing, however, in the years when they did not come to hunt. Llywelyn ap Gruffydd claimed such puture as his right, and took it once a year for five hundred men, along with two yearling foals, which previous princes never took; he also took money for the puture when he did not come.[20] Superficially, this account supports the general point made by Jones Pierce. But evidence relating to abbey lands may well be an unreliable guide to general conditions if used as a direct illustration of the latter. Indeed, the text quoted above implies that the princes had no right to the Basingwerk puture throughout the thirteenth century: it may have been rendered *de curialitate*.

It may not, then, be possible to fix with any certainty the chronology of the development of obligation where the *porthiant* of the court is concerned. In the same way the available evidence will not shed much light on the rate of development of commutation under the thirteenth-century princes: the highest level of commutation reached in the pre-conquest

[18] *Ior.*, 93. 1, *Ny dele meybyon eyllyon e brenhyn e porthy na porthy e teylu* . . .
[19] *Medieval Welsh Society*, p. 116, note 53; cf. ibid., p. 120.
[20] *C. Inq. Misc.*, I, no. 1357.

period can, however, be calculated for large areas of Gwynedd.[21] For Gwynedd Uwch Conwy, Professor Jones Pierce suggested very plausibly that the sums recorded in the Edwardian extents, drawn up shortly after the conquest, as *redditus assisae*, represent the cash values which had been set upon a proportion of the annual renders in each commote.[22] Jones Pierce notes fairly clear regional differences in the scale of commutation thus recorded. Almost everywhere, it is true, the scale of commutation among bondmen was low: with the demesne vills, the bond townships remained 'the principal economic resource in direct tribute and labour of the last rulers of Gwynedd'.[23] In terms of the commuted, or commutable, renders amongst the freemen, Jones Pierce distinguishes four regional groupings in Gwynedd Uwch Conwy, the first comprising Anglesey and the adjacent mainland commotet, the second Uwch Gwyrfai and Llŷn, the third the coastal tip of Merionethshire (Ystumanner and Talybont), and the last the mountain commotes around Snowdon. The scale of commutation was very high, in some cases comprehensive, in the first group, and progressively smaller in each of the following groups; in the fourth it was negligible.[24]

The reasons behind the regional distribution of commutation were probably matters partly of policy and partly of economic exigencies. The establishment before the Edwardian conquest of ports and trading centres in Anglesey and Llŷn is certainly important, for, as Jones Pierce comments, 'A definite relationship would . . . appear to exist between the volume of trade transacted in a given centre and the capacity of the neighbouring countryside to sustain a total or partial conversion of customary fiscal liabilities into cash charges'.[25] On the other hand, princely policy probably affected the rate of development, an assumption resting on the *a priori* grounds suggested by Jones Pierce that 'spontaneous adjustment of fiscal structure in response to a progressive expansion of trade is surely rare'.[26] But this may mean no more than that the

[21] See above, pp. 55–6.
[22] *Medieval Welsh Society*, p. 113.
[23] Ibid., p. 120.
[24] Ibid., pp. 118–19.
[25] Ibid., p. 123.
[26] Ibid.

princes needed money, and that those areas best fitted, by their economic structure, to disgorge money were pressed to do so.

In view of the financial commitments of the princes, however, (in particular those of Llywelyn ap Gruffydd after 1267), the money thus obtained from commuted renders was by no means adequate to meet demand. The cash revenues from renders subject to commutation, excluding those from the old *maerdrefi*, which were worked out by Jones Pierce for Gwynedd Uwch Conwy, the area most consistently under the control of the princes, total no more than £250 per annum by 1282.[27] Even with the addition of commuted renders from Gwynedd Is Conwy, the total cannot have been much above £400 per year as an outside estimate.[28]

It is clear that in order to meet the costs imposed by warfare, by the Treaty of Montgomery and other diplomatic efforts, and by the need to build and maintain castles, other sources of cash were heavily drawn upon. It will be seen that incidental revenues were probably heavily exploited,[29] but there is also evidence that at some stage a form of extraordinary taxation was developed by the princes. A letter written to Edward I by Anian, bishop of St. Asaph, possibly in 1275 or 1277, informed the king that upon his recent return from the March, Llywelyn ap Gruffydd made it known in his dominions that he had made peace with the king, and on that pretext had levied a tax of three pence per head of cattle and other animals, at pleasure, claiming that he would pay the money to the king.[30] It would

---

[27] See the table, ibid., p. 118.

[28] In 1242, for example, Henry III commuted most customs and services in the *cantref* of Tegeingl, whose links with Chester were well-established, for an annual sum of £50: *C. Chart. R., 1226–57*, pp. 274–5. The highest level of commutation reached in the *cantrefi* of Rhos and Rhufoniog was certainly not as great as this. The estimates of pre-conquest commutation levels in these *cantrefi* in D. H. Owen, 'Tenurial and Economic Developments in North Wales in the Twelfth and Thirteenth Centuries', *W.H.R.*, VI (1972), pp. 117–35, are too low, as they are based on the sums recorded as *tunc* in the 1334 extent. Dr. Owen's subsequent paper '*Treth* and *Ardreth:* Some Aspects of Commutation in North Wales in the Thirteenth Century', *B.B.C.S.*, XXV (1974), pp. 446–53, makes it clear that sums given as *treth* or *ardreth* in the 1334 extent may denote a secondary, but still pre-conquest, phase of commutation.

[29] See below, pp. 74–89.

[30] *Cal. Anc. Corr.*, p. 105. See also F. M. Powicke, *King Henry III and the Lord Edward* (Oxford, single volume edition, 1966), p. 638 note 3, for a discussion of the date.

be interesting to know whether this was the first time that such a tax had been raised. Anian's letter implies that the levy had caused much concern amongst Llywelyn's subjects, but this may have been provoked by the rate rather than the form of the tax.[31] It has been suggested that this tax was based upon the *commorth*, a tribute of cattle customary in south Wales,[32] but there is a suggestion in an entry on the Close Roll of 1256 that Llywelyn ab Iorwerth had exacted, apparently with some regularity, a cornage, or levy on horned cattle,[33] which may have formed the basis for the extraordinary taxation of Llywelyn ap Gruffydd. It may well be that extraordinary taxation, the form of which would not of course appear in post-conquest extents, and the fact of which might be taken for granted by post-conquest administrators, was resorted to more frequently in the pre-conquest period than one might assume from the paucity of the evidence. This might explain a reference in a statute of Edward II to the custom of Welsh princes of taxing the goods of villeins, *spadones*, and men of the advowry before those of freemen,[34] though this may relate to requisition of goods rather than to taxation.

ASSESSMENT

It is possible to form some impression of the various units of assessment of renders which were in use by the end of the principate of Llywelyn ap Gruffydd, though the evidence is far too sparse to allow analysis either of chronological development or of distribution within Gwynedd. Three bases of assessment

---

[31] Anian, of course, was a biased commentator, and by the mid-1270s an English partisan: see below pp. 174–7. He was thus likely to exaggerate to Edward the discontent caused by Llywelyn's tax. It is, however, interesting that Llywelyn is reported by Anian to have made an excuse in order to levy the tax: this may suggest that some form of justification was required before extraordinary taxation might be levied.

[32] F. M. Powicke, loc. cit. The comparison seems inadequate, as *commorth* was a tribute of cattle in kind, whereas Llywelyn's levy was a tax on cattle.

[33] *Close Rolls, 1254–56*, p. 301: *tallagium quod vex assidere fecit per Willelmum de Axemuth et socios suos super homines regis de novo conquestu regis in Wallia conversum fuit in cornagium per preceptum regis, quod quidem cornagium vel auxilium rex levari precepit annuatim . . . sicut levari consuevit tempore Leulini quondam principis Norwallie*. See also an important reference made in an inquiry at Denbigh in 1311 when it was recalled that the community of Rhos and Rhufoniog had rendered under the princes a certain *treth y gwartheg*, which seems to have been likened to a fifteenth levied in the period when Henry III controlled those *cantrefi*: NLW Peniarth MS. no. 231, pp. 90–1.

[34] Ivor Bowen, *The Statutes of Wales* (London, 1908), pp. 27–9.

are discernible. In the case of *twnc*, it is clearly implied in the legal texts that the unit of assessment was territorial: *twnc*-pound is said by *Llyfr Iorwerth* to be levied as follows:

> *A honno a rennyr try ugeynt ar pob tref o pedeyr tref a vyd en e vaenaul, ac evelly o petwareran buygylyd e rennyr ene el ar pob eru or tedyn e ran.*[35]

This picture is confirmed in the Bardsey concords of 1252, where *twnc* is clearly associated with the *rhandir*,[36] and also by the evidence of the 1334 Denbighland survey. This latter document records many instances of seizure of portions of *gwelyau* or *gafaelion* in the post-conquest period, by way of escheat:[37] in each case a proportionate part of the *twnc* associated with the holding ceased to be levied on the unescheated section. This seems to indicate that within the *gwely* or *gafael*, *twnc* was distributed on a territorial basis rather than, say, *per capita*.

In contrast, many *cylchoedd* were clearly levied on a fixed *per capita* basis amongst those holders of houses who, in theory, provided the officials or members of the court with provender. The list of common customs of Rhufoniog in 1334 includes the following:

> *Et sciendum quod tempore Principis solebat unus stalo et unus garcio Principis pasci ad domum cuiuslibet liberi non habentis tenentem aut eciam ad domum cuiuslibet tenentis liberorum et eciam ad domum cuiuslibet Nativi istius commoti, per unum diem et unam noctem, et valuit eorum pastus adinvicem per diem et noctem secundum quodreperitur in vetere extenta ii d. ob . . . et accidit iste pastus secundum maius et*

---

[35] *Ior.*, 90, 57–9. The sixty pence levied from each of the four *trefi* in a *maenol* was thus further sub-divided amongst the four *gafaelion* in a *tref*, the four *rhandiroedd* in a *gafael*, the four *tyddynnod* in a *rhandir* and the four *erwau* in a *tyddyn*.

[36] *Rec. Caern.*, p. 252.

[37] For examples see *S.D.*, p. 129, where the situation in *gafael Ieuaf ap Cynan* in Dincadfael is recorded: two-thirds of the *gafael*, held by co-heirs, pay 2½d. *twnc*; the remaining third, in the lord's hands by escheat, paid 1¼d. Ibid., pp. 279–80, the extent of Llanrwst, records five *gwelyau*, the eponyms of which were sons of a Rhufon; the *gwelyau* were clearly regarded as being of identical size for the purposes of the assessment of *twnc*. The full *twnc* assessment on one *gwely* was twelve pence and the unescheated portions of *gwelyau* paid corresponding proportions of twelve pence. It should be stressed that *gwelyau* are regarded in *S.D.* in this context as territorial units.

minus secundum quod plures illorum liberorum habuerint domos plures vel pauciores et eciam secundum quod ipsi liberi plures habuerint tenentes vel pauciores.[38]

But in some cases, *cylch* and *porthiant* are said to have been assessed according to the wealth in chattels of those liable to the render. The *pastus stalonis et garcionis* mentioned in the example from the customs of Rhufoniog above may be compared with the description of the same *cylch* in the customs of Cynmeirch:

> *Item omnes tenentes videlicet liberorum et Nativi seu ipsi liberi si tenentes non habuerint, solvent domino adinvicem per annum pro pastu Stalonis et garcionis vi s. viij d. ad festum Exaltacionis Sancte Crucis . . . Et colligitur consuetudo inter eos per porcionem catallorum quam unusquisque eorum optinuerit.*[39]

It is uncertain how far this represents pre-conquest practice, but it is probably significant in this context that the prince's *procuratio* described in the 1252 Bardsey concords was not levied on a fixed *per capita* basis, but varied according to the wealth of those from whom it was due. It is not clear on what basis their wealth was calculated: the possibility cannot be excluded that it was established in terms of both real and personal possessions. Those burdened with *procuratio* were divided into four classes according to their wealth, the members of each class paying at a rate different from that of other classes.[40] This contrasts with the method of assessment *per catalla* in the Denbigh lordship in 1334, where the commotal total for the *pastus* in question was pre-determined, and then apportioned amongst those liable to payment, on the basis of their wealth in chattels. It is, however, possible that this represents a fossilized form of assessment, and that the form mentioned in the Bardsey concords (which had apparently also become fossilized in the post-conquest period)[41] reflects

---

[38] Ibid., p. 148.
[39] Ibid., p. 47.
[40] *Rec. Caern.*, p. 252.
[41] See ibid., p. 221, for the petition of the abbot and convent of Bardsey against a charge of 68*s.* 6*d.* per year, which had unjustly been laid on them by Dafydd ap Gruffydd, when lord of Llŷn, *de putura sua.*

the original form of the *per catalla* levies of the Denbigh lordship in 1334. Certainly the cattle-tax of the 1270s which is discussed above is cognate in its basis with a form of assessment such as that seen in 1252, rather than with a levy *per catalla* where the ceiling of the tax was pre-fixed. The various forms of assessment which seem to have been developed by the princes, in particular a flexible levy based wholly or in part on moveable wealth, suggest attempts to exploit available resources as effectively as possible.

It would be interesting to know the identity of those who made the assessments, especially in cases where taxes reflected gradations of wealth amongst those subject to the due. In the laws the *gostegwr* (whose office, it has been suggested, had merged with that of the *rhingyll* by the later thirteenth century)[42] is given as the collector, or enforcer, of *twnc* payments.[43] It is not said, however, how the amount to be paid was established. The principal clue to the identity of the assessors is contained in the 1252 Bardsey concords. Here the rule is laid down that the four classes of *procuratio*-payers in the *abadaeth* (abbey lands) were to be established each year by the following means: the steward and the cellarer of the abbey (possibly reflecting the role of the *gostegwr-rhingyll*) were to elect each year four trustworthy men of the *abadaeth* who were to declare in which category each of their fellow-tenants should be placed.[44] It is by no means certain that this arrangement reflects those in force beyond the *abadaeth*, but the fact that it was made under the supervision of the secular lord of Cymydmaen suggests that this might be so. Another possible clue is furnished by the record of a Llŷn lay subsidy levied within a decade of the Edwardian conquest, wherein one of the inhabitants of Nefyn is described as *y gwestwr* (*yguestur*), which word, derived from *gwest*, or food-rent, may be rendered as 'the provisioner'.[45] It seems that the assessing and raising of taxation might involve the active participation of members of the local communities,

---

[42] See above, p. 45.
[43] *Ior.*, 90. 60.
[44] *Rec. Caern.*, p. 252.
[45] See T. Jones Pierce, 'A Lleyn Lay Subsidy Account', *B.B.C.S.*, V (1931) p. 145.

as was the case after the conquest in the lordship of Dyffryn Clwyd, where the community came to the church to divide the puture, or to appoint *divisores*.[46]

INCIDENTAL PAYMENTS

An important category of revenues, the value of which cannot be estimated with any precision, includes those incidental payments such as succession fees, trade tolls, and the profits of justice. Many of these forms of revenue were capable of extension in both scope and incidence, and were thus of great significance at a time when the princes needed to augment their income. The extent to which these incidental sources were being developed in the thirteenth century becomes clearer on detailed analysis of the various categories into which they fall.

One group of renders comprises payments due primarily as a result of some change in the status or condition of the individuals to whom they relate: such are the dues known as *ebediw*, *gobr estyn* and *amobr*. *Ebediw*, a due originally comparable to the Anglo-Saxon *heriot* in that it represented a render from a dead man's chattels to the ruler, was normally valued in the thirteenth century at ten shillings in the case of a freeman, and half a mark (6s. 8d.) or five shillings in the case of a bondman,[47] though certain classes seem to have paid less. T. P. Ellis argued[48] persuasively that *ebediw* was in origin a levy based on personal status rather than on tenure of land, but by the late-thirteenth century it was sufficiently closely associated with landholding for English officials to identify it as a form of relief.[49]

In the case of moveables, the legal texts make the ruler the heir to the goods of a man who dies childless, and so creates a

---

[46] *Ex. inf.* Professor R. R. Davies.
[47] The fact that these sums are the normal ones recorded in post-conquest extents makes it clear that they were considered as the amounts due to the independent princes. See *S.D. passim; Rec. Caern.*, 1–96 *passim*, and *Black Prince's Register, 1351–65*, III, p. 89.
[48] T. P. Ellis, *Welsh Tribal Law and Custom in the Middle Ages* (2 vols., Oxford, 1926), pp. 277 ff.
[49] The usual designation in post-conquest sources of a due which is clearly *ebediw* is *relevium*. The connection is made perfectly clear in cases such as that recorded in *S.D.*, p. 240: *Et iiii acr. dim. de eodem gavella sunt in manu domini pro dyffyk abbdeu quousque recti heredes satisfacere possint de releviis a retro existentibus.*

marwdy, or death-house.⁵⁰ This situation seems to have been complicated by the question of testamentary bequests. Thus, the Flintshire ministers' accounts for 1301–2 include a sum 'for the goods of Iorwerth Goch, deceased, which belong to the lord Prince by the custom of the country, because he died intestate'.⁵¹ It may be inferred from this that a childless man might bequeath his goods, but the corollary is that the children of a man who died intestate could not inherit his goods. Support for this reasoning is not wanting. The seventh item of the St. Asaph *gravamina* of 1276 against Llywelyn ap Gruffydd states of the prince that *testamenta non admittit aliquorum, nisi in egritudine condita, et ex qua egritudine decedat testatore: alioquin decedentium omnia bona tanquam sua propria occupat et distrahit ad libitum*.⁵² And the customs of commotes in the Denbigh lordship, recorded in 1334, make it clear that the goods of an unmarried man who died intestate went to the lord, whilst those of a married man were shared between the lord and the dead man's wife.⁵³

It is unlikely that the problem of intestacy affected the descent of land. Both legal sources and fourteenth-century extents reflect the rule that if a man died childless, he might be succeeded in his lands by his brother or some other relation within the third degree, upon the payment of *gobr estyn*, or investiture fee, which was assessed at the same value as the dead man's *ebediw*.⁵⁴ It seems possible that Llywelyn ap Gruffydd may have been attempting to extend the obligation to pay *gobr estyn* in some instances to the son or sons of a dead landholder. This inference may be drawn from post-conquest references to the plight of Iorwerth ap Philip.⁵⁵ Iorwerth's father, a freeman, had apparently been a substantial landholder in the Twrcelyn vill of Llechog, with some ten carucates of land. When Philip died, Iorwerth was a minor (i.e., under

---

⁵⁰ *Ior.*, 98. 19–21.
⁵¹ A. Jones (ed.), *Flintshire Ministers' Accounts, 1301–28* (1913), p. 12.
⁵² Haddan and Stubbs, *Councils*, 1, p. 513.
⁵³ *S.D.*, pp. 47, 152.
⁵⁴ In *S.D.*, this large payment is referred to simply as *relevium*, but its dual nature is brought out in *A.L.*, XIV. X. 15
⁵⁵ See E. A. Lewis, 'The Decay of Tribalism in North Wales', *Trans. Cymmr.*, 1901–2, p. 62, and *C. Inq. Misc.*, II, p. 528. For the partly illegible petition of Iorwerth Goch, see *Cal. Anc. Pet.*, pp. 275–6.

fourteen, it may be assumed), and Prince Llywelyn ap Gruffydd occupied the lands which Philip had held, until his son should pay £7 of relief and *gobr estyn*. Relief (*relevium*) here should almost certainly be understood as *ebediw*.

There are several points of interest about this episode, the most striking of which is the very large sum demanded by the prince, fourteen times the amount specified in the laws, and accepted by post-conquest administrators, as being due for *ebediw*. It is noteworthy that one of Iorwerth's petitions refers to his liability to pay relief and *gobr estyn* relating to his father and his other dead co-heirs. It is thus likely that Iorwerth ap Philip of Llechog (frequently denoted as Iorwerth Goch ap Philip) is the Iorwerth Goch of Con . . . , whose petition, preserved in an extremely defective manuscript, contains the following phrase in an otherwise illegible section: . . . *et ses cynk uncles moreront en le temps Lewelyn, jadis Prince de Gales, et* . . . It may be that Iorwerth Goch ap Philip was expected to pay relief and *gobr estyn* for lands belonging to his father and to five uncles: but even this would not explain why the payment due was set at £7. This extraordinary rate may be no more than a measure of Llywelyn's financial straits in the later years of his rule, but it may have a deeper significance. The Welsh laws contain no clear reference to a system of wardship: a freeman's son, even if he had not reached the age of majority (fourteen years), entered upon his father's privilege (*braint*) in the event of the latter's death.[56] However, in the customs relating to the escheat of land in the event of non-performance of services[57] there existed a theoretical basis for the development of wardship. As Iorwerth's minority is mentioned in the records relating to his case, it was clearly germane to his exclusion from his lands, and in one of his petitions he actually states that his wardship, as well as the lands of his father Philip, came into the hands of Llywelyn ap Gruffydd.[58] It is quite possible that this petition was framed in terms readily

[56] *Ior.*, 98. 8–9.
[57] It seems fairly clear that this was a pre-conquest custom. See, for example, the men listed in a Llŷn account of 1350–51 of whom it is recorded that *terras suas dimisserunt post guerram Madoci propter impotenciam eorundem et que captae fuerunt in manu Regis per consuetudinem patrie*. For this passage, see T. Jones Pierce, 'Lleyn Ministers' Accounts, 1350–51', *B.B.C.S.*, VI (1932), p. 258.
[58] *Cal. Anc. Corr.*, p. 478.

comprehensible to the English authorities, so that it may distort somewhat the situation existing under Llywelyn ap Gruffydd; but it seems likely that the prince had been moving towards a form of wardship. Quite clearly, a minor might be incapable, or deemed incapable, of performing certain obligations, particularly military ones. The large amount demanded from Iorwerth ap Philip by way of relief and *gobr estyn* may have been intended as a form of compensation to the prince for non-performance of obligations. In the event of non-payment, the land to which the minor had succeeded passed into the prince's hands.

Gobr estyn was also paid by a man who had gone through a formal ceremony of affiliation, and was 'legally admitted to land'.[59] It is particularly noteworthy in this context that the passage in *Llyfr Iorwerth* which describes the various forms taken by the ceremony of induction into a kindred has a reference to 'the man who represents the lord'.[60] There was probably a close connection between the appearance in the working of the kin system of a representative of the lord and the exaction of *gobr estyn* as a result of the ceremony concerned.

In view of the likelihood that Llywelyn ap Gruffydd, at least, was exacting *ebediw* and *gobr estyn* at rates higher than those prescribed in the laws and found in post-conquest accounts and surveys, it is difficult to form any estimate of the value of these dues to the princes. But it is significant that some twenty years after the conquest, when administration was once more settled after the turmoil of 1282-3 and 1294-5, reliefs and *gobrau estyn* in Anglesey, levied at regular rates, were reckoned to be worth £12 7s. 6d. annually:[61] this was a cash value higher, for example, than that of all the commuted renders and services in the commote of Dindaethwy in the pre-conquest period.

A further form of *gobr* was the *gobr merch* or *amobr*, due from both free and bond women at the same rate as *ebediw* in the case of their menfolk, according to the legal texts and post-

---

[59] *A.L.*, XIV. X. 15.
[60] *Ior.*, 103. 10.
[61] J. Griffiths, 'Early Accounts relating to North Wales *temp*. Edward I', *B.B.C.S.*, XVI (1956), p. 112.

conquest practice.⁶² *Amobr* was paid as a fine for fornication and as a render upon marriage. It was clearly a lucrative due: in the post-conquest period, and probably in the days of native rule, its collection within each commote required the attention of a specially designated officer, the *amobrager*. Some idea of the scale of this officer's activities is provided by the fact that the *amobrager's* office in the commotes of Rhos was surveyed as being worth £22 per annum in 1334.⁶³

Finally, a due was occasioned by a system almost akin to chevage, whereby a bondman purchased with an annual payment the right to live away from his bond vill. There are a few references which refer to the pre-conquest period. In the 1284 extent of Talybont there is recorded a payment of 3s. 4d. *de Heylin ap Roger villano de Talbont ut possit morari libere apud Towyn*. The sheriff's roll of 1308–9 for Merioneth records a fine of 12d. *de Ior' ap Hoydelo Croysak de quodam fine quondam facto cum L. principe ut non cogaretur morare in terris de Thlen sed quod posset morare pro voluntate sua in com' de Meryonith*. Again, in 1313, it was recorded that Anyann (Einion), sometime villein of Prince Llywelyn on his manor of Crogen, paid yearly a *gograid* of flour valued at 12d. for a licence to dwell elsewhere in the same commote at his will.⁶⁴ It is noteworthy that in two cases there is mention of a payment of 12d. or the equivalent: the larger payment made by Heilyn ap Roger may have been the result of his wish to settle in Towyn, one of the nascent boroughs of Gwynedd. It is quite impossible to say whether or not these payments reflect a common practice.

Another distinct category of renders from which the princes profited comprised a wide range of tolls on trade and other forms of economic activity. Among the oldest of these were ferry charges. It may have been to these that Gruffydd ap Cynan (*ob.* 1137) referred when he granted to his wife in his will *porthloedd Abermenei*.⁶⁵ There is a clear reference to ferry dues in Llywelyn ab Iorwerth's charter to Aberconwy abbey⁶⁶,

⁶² *Ior.*, 51. 25–34; *Rec. Caern.*, pp. 1–96 *passim*; *S.D.*, *passim*.
⁶³ *S.D.*, pp. 271–314.
⁶⁴ 'Extent of Merionethshire *temp.* Edward I', ed. M. C. J., *Arch. Camb.*, 3rd Ser., XIII (1867), p. 184; E. A. Lewis, art. cit., p. 58; *C. Inq. Misc.*, II, p. 43.
⁶⁵ A. Jones (ed.), *History of Gruffydd ap Cynan (1054–1137)* (Manchester, 1910), p. 156.
⁶⁶ For a discussion of this charter, see Appendix I, no. 1.

in which he granted to the monks freedom from tolls for the use of ferries and bridges throughout his lands. The ferries specified in the grant are those of Menai, Conwy, Abermaw and Dyfi. The first two of these were of particular importance in the internal communications of Gwynedd. The Menai ferries linked the uplands of Arfon and Arllechwedd, with their mainly pastoral economy, with the grain-producing area of Anglesey, whose principal trading centre, Llanfaes, was served by a ferry extended at £12 per year in 1284.[67] Along the straits was the ferry at Porthaethwy, surveyed at 53s. 4d. in 1284,[68] and apparently worked by a family closely associated with the princes' governance, the descendants of Mabon Glochydd.[69] It is noteworthy that the same family held lands in Creuddyn,[70] which may have served as the terminus of a ferry across the mouth of the Conwy: it may have been to such a ferry that Henry III referred in 1251 when he ordered the justice of Chester to allow the Friars Preacher of Bangor and their men freedom to carry goods *per aquam de Gannoc* (Degannwy).[71] This important communications route between upper and lower Gwynedd was reckoned in 1284 to yield £20 per year in tolls.[72] In a principality where the leading families, at least, were acquiring holdings scattered throughout several localities,[73] and in which trading activity was becoming increasingly important,[74] the princes' control of internal communications was of considerable and increasing importance in the thirteenth century.

The princes were also able to profit directly from the process of commerce by means of a wide range of market tolls, licences to trade and import duties, which have been so thoroughly illuminated by Professor Jones Pierce[75] that further analysis is scarcely necessary. The value of these levies was at least £30

---

[67] Seebohm, *Tribal System*, Appendix A, p. 3.
[68] Ibid., p. 5.
[69] See below, p. 120.
[70] *Rec. Caern.*, p. 1.
[71] *Close Rolls, 1247-51*, p. 401.
[72] See H. R. Davies, *The Conway and the Menai Ferries* (Cardiff), 1942), pp. 2-4, for a discussion of the princes' control of, and revenue from, the Conwy ferry.
[73] See below, pp.
[74] *Medieval Welsh Society*, pp. 103-26.
[75] Ibid., pp. 121-2.

per year from Gwynedd Uwch Conwy alone by 1284.[76] There are clear signs that the princes carefully regulated the life of the trading centres from which they profited: the fact that the boroughs tended to grow up at commotal centres[77] meant that their activities were easily kept under scrutiny. And the burgesses of Llanfaes after the conquest referred to *cartae principum*, which had clearly set out the rights and conditions under which they traded.[78]

The tolls derived from the processes of trade and production were, of course, liable to vary from year to year, but the princes also enjoyed profits from sources still more subject to fluctuation: wreck and treasure trove. The nature of the princes' exactions in these cases may be seen from the grants of privileges with respect to them, which were made to ecclesiastical centres. Llywelyn ab Iorwerth's charter to Aberconwy contains a very clear exposition of the princes' rights in cases of wreck:

> *concessi . . . ut uti et gauderi possint naufragio in omnibus terris suis et litoribus meliori modo quo in terris meis ego utor videlicet quecumque bona seu res per submersionem aut fractionem seu per aliud infortunium ad terras suas ad litora terrarum suarum coniuncta de mari evenerunt, ipsa bona totaliter et integre sint ipsorum Monachorum.*[79]

---

[76] Ibid., p. 123. This sum does not include fees derived from the regulation of another form of market activity, namely, transactions in land. Llinos B. Smith, 'The Gage and the Land Market in Late Medieval Wales', *Economic History Review*, 2nd Ser., XXIX (1976), pp. 537–50, argues cogently that in the post-conquest period the device of *prid* or Welsh mortgage was retained primarily in the lord's interest in order that fees for licences to *prid* might be exacted. It is possible that this represents pre-conquest practice, for *Llyfr Iorwerth* has a rule (*Ior.*, 88. 22) that no-one may sell land or *prid* it without the lord's consent. Llywelyn ab Iorwerth's charter to Cymer in 1209 contains the clause: *concessimus ut si quis de heredibus in omni terra que mee dicionis subiacet agrum vel stagnum ad tempus concesserit libertatum habeant suscipiendi eorumque fruetus tollendi.* See Keith Williams-Jones, 'Llywelyn's Charter to Cymer Abbey in 1209', *Jnl. Mer. Hist. Soc.*, III (1957), p. 56. It would seem from this that the lord or prince exercised control over alienation for a term and was in a position to license such transactions: in the Cymer charter he would seem to be waiving his licensing rights, which surely suggests that normally a fee for licensing was involved. In much the same way, it would appear from the Rhos Fyneich charter of 1230 (Appendix I, no. 13), by which Llywelyn recognized the purchase of kin-lands by Ednyfed Fychan in perpetuity, that the prince was in a position to license permanent alienation of lands.

[77] Examples are Llanfaes, Caernarfon, Pwllheli, Nefyn.

[78] The petition is printed in E. A. Lewis *The Medieval Boroughs of Snowdonia* (London, 1912), p. 295. Cf. *Cal. Anc. Pet.*, pp. 82–3.

[79] *Rec. Caern.*, p. 147.

The princes' practice with respect to wreck apparently varied during the course of the century. During the Bangor arbitration of 1261 between the bishop and the prince, it was recalled that Llywelyn ab Iorwerth had released wrecked goods if the owners had survived, or had not been involved in the wreck, and were thus able to demand their return.[80] This practice had, it seems, been abandoned by Llywelyn ap Gruffydd. So said the arbitrators in 1261, and Llywelyn ap Gruffydd's continued refusal to return shipwrecked goods to their owners is illustrated, some twenty years later, by the case of wreck which helped to poison relations between him and Edward I by 1282. The prince refused to return the goods of Robert of Leicester, claiming to retain them by right of wreck.[81] It is significant that Robert demanded the return of his goods not by virtue of the fact that he, as the owner, was alive and capable of claiming them, but on the plea that they had not been subject to wreck.

If Llywelyn ab Iorwerth had shown scruples about withholding shipwrecked goods from their owners, in another respect he had extended his claims, by seizing goods cast up on church lands, an example followed by his successors.[82] These claims also continued another of Llywelyn ab Iorwerth's apparent departures from previous practice, that is claiming treasure found on church lands:[83] here was an extension of the prince's right to treasure trove.

The value to the prince of such sources of revenue as wreck and treasure trove cannot of course be calculated: they represent occasional and unpredictable additions to the princes' revenue. But when a prince was able to profit from wreck or treasure trove there was every chance that the amounts involved would be considerable. The goods of Robert of Leicester, mentioned above, seem to have been worth £20 or £30.[84]

[80] Haddan and Stubbs, *Councils*, 1, pp. 489-90.
[81] *Cal. Anc. Corr.*, p. 89.
[82] Haddan and Stubbs, *Councils*, 1, loc. cit.
[83] Ibid.
[84] *Cal. Anc. Corr.*, p. 78. The goods are said to have been worth thirty (marks or pounds?): thirty shillings is an unlikely sum, as the justice of Chester distrained Llywelyn's goods to the value of £5 in retaliation, and then asked the king how he might levy further distraint, the implication being that the distraint of five pounds' worth of goods was not enough to bring Llywelyn to restore the merchant's goods.

THE PROFITS OF JUSTICE

In the case of many of the wide range of incidental dues discussed above, there was obviously a temptation for those subject to them to conceal from the princes' officials the fact that renders were owed; but if concealment was discovered, the prince stood to gain even more by way of retributory fines or distraint. Indeed, the profits of justice constitute perhaps the most remunerative of all the incidental revenues, and must be examined in some detail.

Much of the revenue from the profits of justice, dispensed either by the prince in person or in his name by his officials, accrued from fines imposed upon offenders which will be discussed below; but clearly of no little account were the sums which might be offered by parties to disputes, particularly disputes over land, as inducements to the prince or his bailiffs to hear their plaints or to grant them recourse to some specific form of procedure. The evidence for this practice is scanty, but nevertheless provides some idea of the amount of money which might be offered.

In a plea before the Hopton commission in 1278,[85] it was alleged that Madog ap Gruffydd had offered Llywelyn ap Gruffydd three hundred marks to enquire in his court regarding Madog's right to the land of Cydewain, and to do him full justice therein. This case of course concerned extensive claims to lordship in an area beyond Gwynedd, and the sum offered was very high. Probably more typical of payments made with respect to causes arising within Gwynedd was that mentioned by Tegwared ap John, one of the Welsh judges of Rhuddlan, when he gave evidence in 1281 before Edward I's commission enquiring into the operation of Welsh law.[86] Tegwared recalled a plea before Llywelyn ap Gruffydd and his judges, in which the sum of £6 was given to the prince in order that the case might be decided by inquisition. It is impossible to say how frequently, and in what proportion of cases, payments of this sort were made,[87] but it is at least fairly clear that the

---

[85] *Welsh Assize Roll*, p. 254.
[86] *C. Chanc. R., Various*, p. 200.
[87] Both Tegwared ap John and Einion ap Nest, another of the Rhuddlan judges, stated in general terms that the lord could grant a certain form of procedure for money or as of grace (ibid.).

prince regularly received a fee when he decided claims to land, for the legal texts mention the ruler's *gobyr am terfynu tir rhwng deu ymryson*.[88]

A somewhat sinister development of the idea of the sale of justice is seen in the agreement of the abbot and convent of Aberconwy to pay Llywelyn ap Gruffydd £40 *pro benivolentia (sic) prefati principis de quibusdam casibus et articulis nobis per eundem impositis optinenda*.[89] Here the abbot seems to be buying off the threat of attack by the prince.

Probably the most lucrative of the profits of judicial activity, however, were the fines exacted from wrongdoers. The lawbooks establish a gradation of penalties for a wide range of offences, the most frequently mentioned being the *camlwrw*, and the *dirwy* exacted for more serious offences: these were worth three kine or fifteen shillings, and twelve kine or £3, respectively.[90] A formula which appears frequently in the legal texts says that the *dirwy* applied to fighting, violence and theft (excluding theft in hand). This group of offences, conveniently and perhaps suspiciously grouped as a triad, may represent an original core of acts punished by *dirwy*, so that one may conclude, with Professor Jones Pierce, that 'other scattered references to offences subject to the same penalty— such as rape, failure of the compurgators in certain civil actions, bribery to commit, or acts accessory to, certain crimes, were new offences created at a somewhat later date'.[92]

Yet whatever the developments in the lawyers' statements regarding the scales of punishment, the generally rigid definitions in the legal texts of the penalties attaching to various offences clearly do not provide a proper reflection of the state of affairs in the thirteenth century. Evidence as to the actual nature of the penalties exacted at this period is presented by the examples cited before the assembly called in 1274 by the bishop and chapter of St. Asaph to determine the rights of the see in various cases in which offences had been committed by

---

[88] For a reference to this fee for settling the bounds of land between two claimants, see *A.L.*, XIV, X, 14.
[89] *Littere Wallie*, p. 25.
[90] *Ior.*, 104. 28–29.
[91] See for example *Bleg.*, 42. 29–30, and *Ior.*, 104. 30.
[92] *Medieval Welsh Society*, p. 305.

episcopal tenants.[93] A glimpse of the realities which must have often dictated the exaction of fines is to be had in the case of Gwilym ap Cadwgan of Llangernyw, who was taken in possession of a stolen cow at some time in the period 1240–5, and brought before Tudur ab Ednyfed, *rhaglaw* of Denbigh. Punishment had perforce to be limited by the culprit's capacity to pay: he had only two oxen, one of which went to the prince and the other to the bishop.[94]

Where the cases quoted in 1274 mention the sums of cash exacted as fines, they indicate the existence of a far wider range of penalties than that suggested by the legal texts. Between 1225 and 1233, a certain Elias (Elise?) who was found with a stolen sheep in his house was taken before the *rhaglaw* of Dinorben and fined twenty-five shillings.[95] Round about the years 1240–5, Madog Fugail, who was taken in possession of a stolen chest, was fined £4,[96] whilst Iorwerth ap Madog Foelgoch and Tegwared, the deacon's son, were fined £4 each, having been found in possession of two stolen oxen.[97] During Henry III's lordship in the Perfeddwlad (1247–54), one Rhicert Goch was fined £5 for unspecified theft;[98] Einion Fychan, who was captured with two ells of stolen woolcloth, was fined thirty shillings, and the same man was fined £3 for sheep-stealing.[99] A Rhicert 'Goec' (*Goch*?) suffered fines of £5 10s. for an unspecified theft, and £6 for rape.[100] In the period 1266–8, when the see of St. Asaph was vacant, a fine of twenty-five shillings was levied on Pyll ap Cynfrig for being in possession of a stolen cow.[101] Finally, it was recalled that in the years 1268–74 a fine of 2 £10s. had been exacted from an

---

[93] For discussion of the Latin and Welsh versions of the record, see below p. 119.
[94] NLW Peniarth MS. no. 231, p. 119.
[95] Ibid., p. 118. The date can be fixed approximately because it is recorded that the bishop at the time was Abraham (1225–32).
[96] Ibid., p. 120. The case was heard before the *rhaglaw* of Dinorben, and the prince at the time was David ap Llywelyn, who held Dinorben and its *cantref* of Rhos for most of the period 1240–45; after 1245 he was driven back across the Conwy by the forces of Henry III.
[97] Ibid.
[98] Ibid., pp. 123–4.
[99] Ibid., p. 124.
[100] Ibid., pp. 124–5.
[101] Ibid., p. 121.

RENDERS AND DUES 85

unnamed woman for sheepstealing[102] and a fine of £1 was levied on Goronwy ap Seisyll for an unspecified theft.[103]
There are few signs in the above list of the *dirwy* and *camlwrw* of the legal texts.[104] Moreover, there is little indication of a pattern of set penalties: the amount of fines may well have depended upon the nature of each individual offence, and on the discretion of the prince or his bailiff, rather than upon a broad categorization of offences. The lack of precise definition of the offences concerned in the record of 1274 makes it impossible to pick out any clear developments regarding the size of fines imposed at various periods during the century. But that the sort of fines mentioned in 1274 were of great importance in terms of the princes' total cash revenue becomes apparent when it is remembered, for example, that the annual *twnc* payments from the whole *cantref* of Rhos (i.e., the area governed by the *rhaglaw* of Dinorben) were no more than about £7 15s.[105]

It is also fairly clear, again in contrast to the picture supplied by some of the lawbooks, that a sentence of death, at least in cases of serious theft in hand, might be commuted for a cash payment.[106] The most important evidence on this point is once again provided by the record of the 1274 St. Asaph assembly. The general statement of rights previously enjoyed by the bishop and chapter of St. Asaph, which begins the record, declares that:

> *ballivi dominii seculariis (sic) et ministri in hominem episcopi et capituli diffamatum super furto manum non inicerent nisi prius vocatis iconomo ecclesie et suis conministris communi assensu habito talem caperent et si furtum esset evidens eum incarceratum ad aliquem locum carceralem dominii secularis ducerent ubi postea si talis a morte redimeretur medietas precii episcopo et capitulo erat assignanda.*[107]

---
[102] Ibid., p. 123.
[103] Ibid.
[104] See also the fine of £9 levied on the men of Llangernyw for an offence involving encroachment on lands, possibly in defiance of the prince's prohibition, ibid., p. 122, and the clearly 'political' fine of £100 imposed on Rhys ap Gruffydd ab Ednyfed in 1281 by Llywelyn ap Gruffydd for showing contempt and disobedience to the latter whilst at the court of Aberffraw: *Littere Wallie*, p. 31. Neither of these fines corresponds to penalties set out in the lawbooks.
[105] *S.D.*, pp. 268, 314.
[106] Compare especially *Bleg.*, 115. 6–8: *Tri dyn ny dyly brenhin eu gwerthu: lleidyr gwedy bamner y'r groc; a chynnllwynwr; a bradwr arglwyd.*
[107] NLW Peniarth MS. no. 231, p. 47.

This statement can, it is alleged in the record, be supported by many examples. Most of the cases cited contain no reference to redemption from execution, but the first piece of evidence provided by a canon of St. Asaph, Ieuaf ap Cadwgan, seems to come close to contradicting the general summary. Ieuaf said that in the time of his father, grandfather and great-grandfather,

> *consuevit mulcta hominis episcopi et capituli pro furto dum tale non esset furtum quod exinde iudicium mortis sequeretur equaliter dividi inter ecclesiam et dominium seculare. Si vero talis iudicaretur ad mortem et postea iuxta patrie consuetudinem a suspendio se redimeret tunc quia precium sanguinis est (sic) nihil episcopo reservabatur* . . .[108]

The record is manifestly corrupt in parts,[109] and it may be that one at least of the two statements quoted above has been significantly distorted during copying. If this is not the case, however, they seem to establish two categories of theft which might be followed by execution.[110] In the present context it is important to note that even the death penalty for serious cases of theft in hand might be averted by the payment of soul price.[111] This payment must have been a substantial one,

---

[108] Ibid. Unfortunately these early sections of the record are missing from the Welsh version, which would probably have elucidated the problem. The evidence of Ieuaf ap Cadwgan is supported by the case of men fined for stealing sheep from Princess Joan, the wife of Llywelyn ab Iorwerth, the unspecified fine being shared between the prince and the bishop, *a henne en enw cosp ac nyt en herwyd gwerth eneit, canys hunnu a berthynai ar er arglwydiaeth vyt ehun en digyfran ar escop mal e dywetpwyt uchot:* the sum paid, that is, was by way of punishment not 'soul-price', for the latter pertains to the secular lordship alone and is not to be shared with the bishop, as was explained previously; ibid., p. 118. See also the clause in the list of *articuli* drawn up by the bishop and chapter of St. Asaph, probably in the period 1274–6 (see note 116 below), which states that the bishop and chapter used to receive half of all fines up to £7 (the worth of the saleable thief in the lawbooks) levied on their men for theft: Haddan and Stubbs, *Councils*, 1, p. 491.

[109] See, for example, the comment that at some time in the past the bishops of St. Asaph *ei (sc. seculari dominio) concesserunt mulcte pro furto mediocri;* NLW Peniarth MS. no. 231, p. 46. The suggested emendation in Haddan and Stubbs, *Councils*, 1, is *mulctas* for *mulcte*, but the passage makes better sense if it is assumed that some such word as *medietatem* should stand with *mulcte*.

[110] It is perhaps significant that only in the second statement, that of Ieuaf ap Cadwgan, is there mention of *iudicium mortis*. This may be merely fortuitous, but it is possible that it reflects a statement in the legal texts regarding the saleable thief: if such a thief does not pay the price of £7 set upon him, and yet has the means to do so, he is to be executed. See, for the rule, *A.L.*, XIV, XII, 17. In such a case the initial sentence would involve payment rather than execution, but it was backed up by the threat of execution. By contrast, serious cases of theft in hand were clearly followed at once by *iudicium mortis*.

[111] NLW Peniarth MS. no. 231, p. 118.

probably of more than £7,[112] and thus beyond the means of many thieves,[113] though when levied it obviously provided a valuable augmentation of the prince's resources.

In the treatment accorded it in most of the legal texts, homicide, like serious theft in hand, stands outside the mass of offences punished by *dirwy* or *camlwrw*. Homicide was once the cause of feud, waged by the kin of the dead man upon the slayer and his kin, though the latter might buy off the feud by the payment of reparation to the victim's kin, the reparation, like the feud itself, being known as *galanas*. But that is not to say that cases of homicide might not by the thirteenth century involve considerable profit to the prince. Lords had long taken an enforcing third, the *traean cymell*, of the *galanas* payment.[114] In addition, Jones Pierce charts the rise of definitions of homicide which distinguish between simple killing and more serious forms, committed with intent, these latter being punished by a two-fold *dirwy*, *galanas* and penance, or possibly by the execution of the killer and the confiscation of his property by the prince.[115]

Key evidence for the situation in the thirteenth century is a clause which forms part of a list of articles closely related to the 1276 *gravamina* of the bishop and chapter of St. Asaph against Llywelyn ap Gruffydd.[116] The clause runs: *de homicidio in territorio Episcopi perpetrato res homicide remanebunt domino Episcopo propter homicidium in territorio suo perpetratum, emenda vero homicidii domino principi*. The use of the term *emenda* is interesting: it is used elsewhere in the list of articles to signify a fine due to the

---

[112] See note 108 above.
[113] The *gravamina* of 1276 contain a reference to the problem of punishment of men named as accomplices by thieves about to be hanged: Haddan and Stubbs, *Councils*, 1, p. 513, and compare ibid., p. 492.
[114] *Medieval Welsh Society*, p. 302.
[115] Ibid., p. 305.
[116] See Haddan and Stubbs, *Councils*, 1, pp. 491-3 for the *articuli*, and pp. 513-14 for the *gravamina*. The subject matter of the first ten clauses of the *articuli* corresponds exactly, and in the same order, to that of clauses nine to fourteen of the *gravamina*. The numerical discrepancy is accounted for by the fact that clauses nine to fourteen of the *gravamina* each consist of three sub-clauses. The twelfth and thirteenth clauses of the *articuli* likewise correspond to the fifteenth and sixteenth of the *gravamina*. In addition, all of the specific examples cited in the *articuli* relate to evidence given at the 1274 St. Asaph assembly. It thus seems clear that the *articuli* were drawn up after the evidence was gathered in 1274 and before 1277, when the lands of St. Asaph diocese passed out of the control of Llewelyn ap Gruffydd.

prince.[117] Its use in the present context thus illustrates a further stage in the development of the concept of homicide as an offence against the prince.

It is evident that marcher lords in the later medieval period continued to receive a proportion of *galanas* corresponding to the *traean cymell*.[118] Two passages from *Llyfr Colan*, probably a late-thirteenth-century lawbook from Gwynedd, reveal however that further developments had taken place there before the Edwardian conquest. Both passages refer to a similar problem, but give different rulings. In what seems to represent the earlier development, a new payment to the lord by the slayer, consisting of six 'corpse cows', is found alongside the *traean cymell* and the lord's established right of plunder.[119] In the other passage, a further step is indicated by the omission of any mention of *traean cymell*, an omission balanced by the doubling of the number of 'corpse cows' due to the ruler.[120] These passages may relate to the development of punishments for homicide with intent, traced by Jones Pierce, but they may also illuminate the use of *emenda*, or fine to the lord, in the clause of the *articuli* quoted above. The significance of this development lies in the fact that the prince's role in, and profit from, a case of homicide, was apparently ceasing to be regarded in terms of *galanas;* homicide had now a distinct aspect as a special concern of the lord. The prince and the victim's kin were thus virtually established as rivals, both with the object of exacting reparation for the act of homicide. The groundwork had thereby been laid in Gwynedd for a further decisive alteration of the role and expectation of victims' kin, and a corresponding development in those of the prince.

---

[117] Cf. the seventh clause: *Septimus est, de violenta virginum defloracione in territorio Episcopi cuius emende medietatem debet Episcopus cum suis canonicis recipere;* Haddan and Stubbs, *Councils*, 1, p. 492.

[118] See R. R. Davies, 'The Survival of the Bloodfeud in Medieval Wales' *History*, LIV (1969), p. 346.

[119] *Col.*, 322: *O derwyt bot bonedyc cannhwynawl en ur y vab uchelur ac ena e llat, e argluyd ef a dyly y gan y neb a'y lladrud vi byu keleyn ac argluyd a dely trayan kemell a kymyn ac a allo y anreythyau o'r pryt buygylyt.* For the antiquity of the provision regarding plunder see Latin Redaction A in *L.T.W.L.*, p. 140.

[120] *Col.*, 294. It must be admitted that the passages in this and the previous note are somewhat ambiguous; in the first passage the lord to whom the 'corpse cows' are owed may be the *mab uchelwr*.

It is perhaps well to keep in mind one final point about the profits to be derived from doing justice: it was not only the defendant in a case who faced the prospect of being fined. It is apparent from the legal texts that plaintiffs too faced fines if they were adjudged to have made false claims, or if they did not stand by the proper procedure.[121] It is possible that, stimulated by the fiscal needs of the princes, Welsh law was developing characteristics similar to those very clearly visible in England, whereby it became financially hazardous to appear in court in almost any capacity.[122]

MILITARY OBLIGATION

Labour services owed by both free and bondmen to the prince have already been mentioned, but by far the most important personal service due to the prince was military.[123] The lawbooks state that freemen were to serve within the country, that is, as a defensive force against outside attack, whenever the ruler wished. But they were also obliged to serve in the host in campaigns outside the country for six weeks per year.[124] References in record sources suggest that the picture presented by the lawbooks in this case broadly reflects thirteenth-century practice. Thus, in 1260 Henry III wrote to Hugh Bigod that he had been informed that Llywelyn ap Gruffydd had come with his army and siege-train so attack Builth, *praemuniendo suos quod cum victualibus ad quadraginta dies muniti venirent ibidem, exinde progressuri de Breckinok et Netherwent versus partes Marchie nostre ad devastacionem partium eorundem . . .*[125] The forty days here mentioned clearly correspond to the six weeks' service of the legal texts, and seem to begin with the arrival of the men at a point of assembly, the siege-camp outside Builth. If this

---

[121] *A.L.*, XIV, XI, 3. It is worth noting that the fourteenth book of 'anomalous' laws printed by Owen is a very interesting text: it seems to contain a more than usually chaotic mixture of archaic and 'revised' law, but can often be used with great effect to supplement the so-called Venedotian texts.

[122] Compare A. L. Poole, *Obligations of Society in the XII and XIII Centuries* (Oxford, 1946), pp. 77–91.

[123] See *A.L.*, XI, II, 2, which comments that the chief service from land is the lord king's hosting: *Penaf gwassanaeth dir yw llyd yr arglwyd urenhin.*

[124] *Iot.*, 92. 7–10: *Ny dele e brenhyn y'u wlat un lluyd ohoney ehun* (MS. E has *Ny dele e brenhyn duyn lluyd or wlat allan*) *namen un weyth pob bluyden, ac ny dele bot en hunnu namen pytheunos a mys. En e wlat ehun ryd vyd ydau pan venho.*

[125] *Close Rolls, 1259–61*, p. 268.

was so, then the actual period during which the men were absent from their localities may have been longer than forty days, depending on the areas from which they were levied. Again, in the extent of Merioneth compiled shortly after the Edwardian conquest, the section relating to Ardudwy states that *liberi tenentes, et villani de dominico Regis ibunt in exercitu cum Domino Rege per sex septimanas sumptibus suis*.[126] The significance of the reference to the service of bondmen will be discussed later; it is sufficient at present to note the six-week period of service with the ruler, at the cost of the men involved.

In the extents of the fourteenth century, the co-heirs of several *gwelyau* subject to immunity from most of the renders and services normally owed to the ruler, as a result of the grants of thirteenth-century princes, are said to be obliged to go with their lord in his war for forty days at their own cost, and thereafter at his cost.[127] It is clear from what has been said that the forty-day service at the individual's own cost simply reflects the normal duty of the freemen in the pre-conquest period.

It is sometimes assumed that the granting of tenurial immunities to leading freemen, a subject which will be discussed in greater detail below, represents the price which the princes paid to secure extended military service (i.e., service beyond the forty-day limit).[128] This assumption should be questioned, partly because it assumes 'policy' where there may have been none, and partly because it may involve a serious misapprehension of the manner in which extended military service was obtained. In no case in which the terms of the original grant are known, or in which some of the details are recorded, is there a reference to the prince providing for extended service. One grant, to Ednyfed Fychan, gives tenurial privileges without any mention of military service, whilst another, to Einion ap Maredudd, gives a list of immunities,

[126] 'Extent of Merionethshire *temp*. Edward I', p. 190.
[127] See, for example, *S.D.*, p. 205 (a *gafael* of Wyrion Eden in Llysaled); *Rec. Caern.*, pp. 73 (Trecastell, held by a branch of Wyrion Eden), 77 (half of Penmynydd and Erddreiniog, held by Wyrion Eden), 78 (four carucates of land in Ystrad-geirch). For Wyrion Eden, see below pp. 102–6.
[128] See, for example, F. M. Powicke, *The Thirteenth Century*, p. 387, and C. W. Lewis, 'The Treaty of Woodstock 1247; its background and significance', *W.H.R.*, II (1964), p. 63.

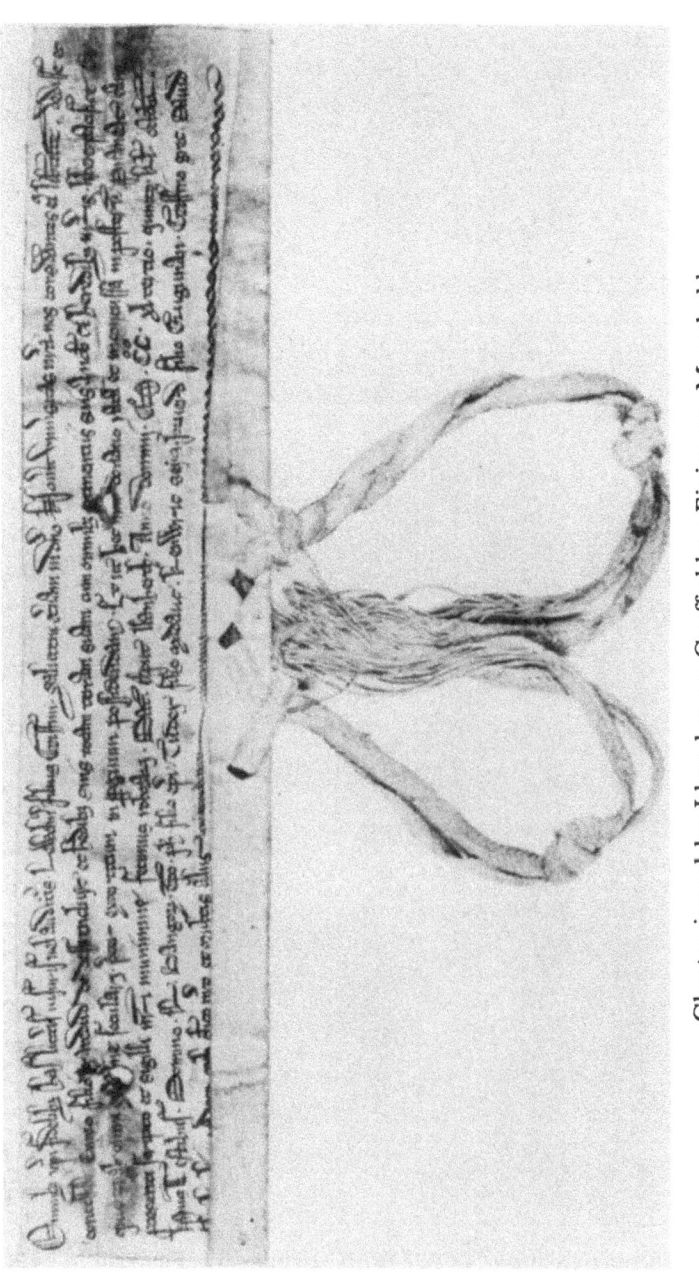

Charter issued by Llywelyn ap Gruffydd to Einion ap Maredudd.
Dated: 27 September 1243, Llannerch, Dyffryn Clwyd.

Reproduced by kind permission of the National Library of Wales.

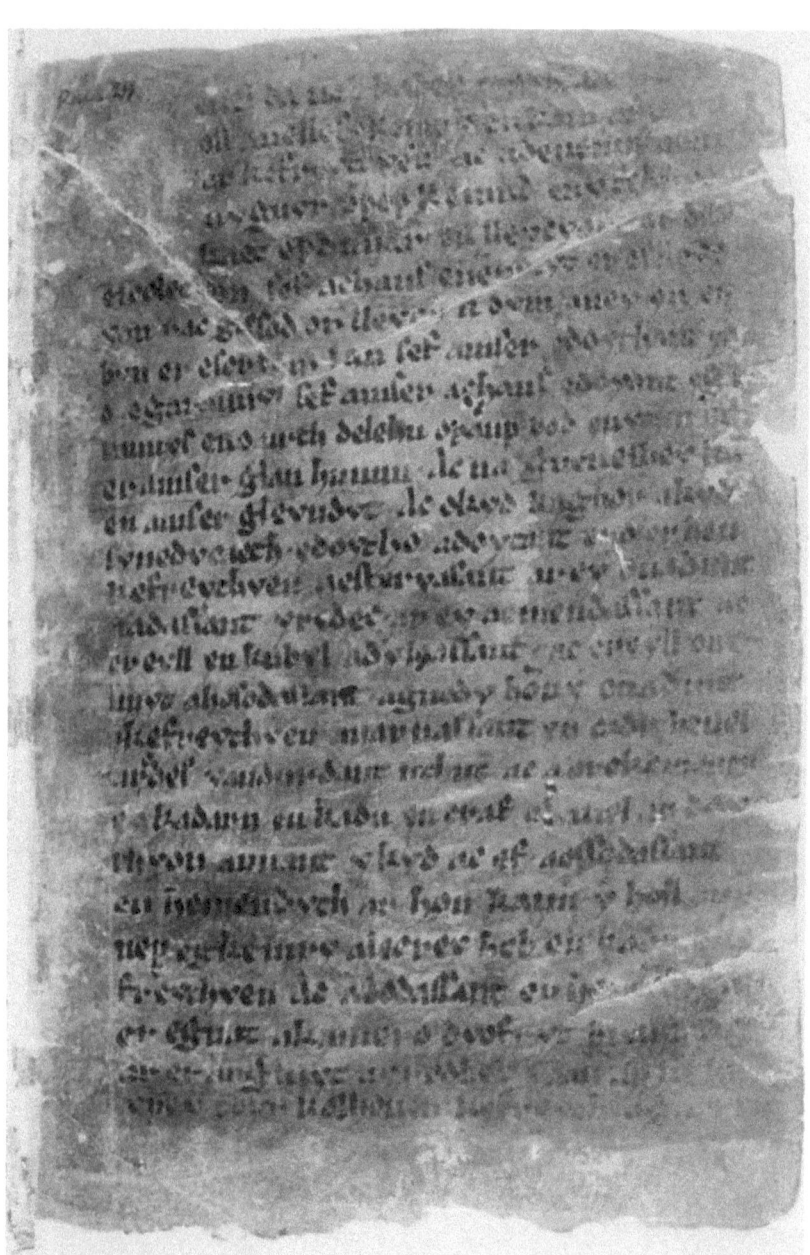

The opening section of *Llyfr Iorwerth* contained in Peniarth MS 29.

Reproduced by kind permission of the National Library of Wales.

but excepts from them the obligation of military service (*preter exercitum*).[129]

The important point is that the fourteenth-century sources in which the extended military service of otherwise privileged tenants is mentioned contrast the first forty days, when service was at the tenant's cost, with subsequent service at the lord's cost. Now, this distinction may not reflect directly the terms of the original grants: it may refer to fourteenth-century conditions, in which levies were generally paid from the start of their service.[130] In other words, where the terms of an original grant permitted it, the English authorities may have retained, in the case of some groups whose tenure was otherwise marked by fiscal immunities, the ancient obligation to serve for forty days at the subject's cost, possibly as a means of reducing the fiscal loss to the administration caused by the immunities enjoyed by the privileged groups. Some references to military service in the fourteenth-century extents state that privileged tenants serve with the prince in the army at the prince's own cost, with no mention of the forty-day period of service.[131] This omission probably reflects the difference between a grant of immunities *preter exercitum* and a grant which, by its silence, included military service within the list of obligations from which the beneficiaries were spared. Both sorts of grant presumably left open the question of military service bought by the prince. There is nothing to suggest that the purchase of voluntary extended service was not the usual method by which the thirteenth-century princes raised forces for long campaigns. In the majority of cases, the wage-bargaining might begin after forty days' service; in others (where individuals benefited from a grant of privileges which included immunity from military obligations), it would precede the start of service.

The lawbooks are not entirely consistent as to the age at which freemen became liable to perform military service. It is implied in *Llyfr Iorwerth* that fourteen was the age at which

---

[129] See Appendix I, nos. 13, 21.
[130] See H. J. Hewitt, *The Organisation of War under Edward III* (Manchester, 1966) ch. 1 *passim*.
[131] See, for example, *Rec. Caern.*, pp. 1 (Penrhyn, held by Wyrion Eden), 11 (Cwmllannerch, in the hands of tenants from several different kindreds), 33 (Crugeny, where four bovates were privileged as the result of a grant by Llywelyn ap Gruffydd).

obligation began,[132] but a later text states clearly that military service was demanded when a man reached twenty-one.[133] The difficulty is resolved, however, by a clause in the agreement between Llywelyn ap Gruffydd and the bishop of Bangor in 1261 which provided that men from episcopal lands should not be liable to military service before the 'legitimate age' of fourteen.[134] The clause makes it clear that Llywelyn had been attempting to impose military service on persons of less than fourteen years of age, and it is unlikely that the attempt had been confined to episcopal tenants alone. The reason for this may have been that the prince wished to swell the numbers of his armed forces. But the military value of such young recruits may be doubted,[135] and a list of *articuli* drawn up by the bishop and chapter of St. Asaph in the course of disputes with Llywelyn ap Gruffydd in the 1270s provides another possible motive for attempts to exact military service from those under fourteen. Some of the *articuli* relate to the consequences of non-performance of military service: neglect of the duty to join in a hosting was clearly punished by a fine,[136] whilst there are also references to the possibility of compounding in advance for non-performance. Any increase in the numbers of those liable to military service might thus be intended as much to increase revenue as to provide extra troops.

There remains the question of the military obligations of the bondmen. The lawbooks state that each bond *tref* was to supply, at the time of the hosting, one pack-horse, together with one man with an axe to make camps for the army.[137] These were to be provided at the cost of the ruler. Limited confirmation of these statements is afforded by an entry in the

[132] *Ior.*, 98. 12-14. The reference is, however, only to the process of becoming a lord's man; liability to military service is certainly not mentioned explicitly.

[133] *A.L.*, VIII, XI, 36, clearly contrasting the age at which one became a lord's man (fourteen) with the age of liability to military service.

[134] Haddan and Stubbs, *Councils*, 1, p. 490: *Quod homines Episcopi inhabiles ad arma (compelluntur) nobis videtur, quod de prius pretaxatis ante legitimam aetatem, sc. XIIII annorum non debet exigi expedicio, neque expedicionis redemptio.*

[135] Note that they are described in the clauses cited in the previous note as *inhabiles ad arma.*

[136] Haddan and Stubbs, *Councils*, 1, p. 493, where the twelfth clause has: *de expedicione: si contingat homines Episcopi ad expedicionem vocati remanere contra prohibitionem domini, et propter dictam negligentiam multari, medietatem illius mulcte debet Episcopus cum suis Canonicis recipere. Si autem homines Episcopi volunt concordari de suis rebus cum ministris Principis de sua expedicione, de tali redemptione nihil recipiet Capitulum.*

[137] *Ior.*, 43. 11-13: *E brenhyn a dele o pob byleyntref den a march a bueall e wneythur lluest e'r brenhyn, ac vynteu a deleant bot ar e cost ef.*

ministers' accounts for Llŷn in 1350–1, which reproduced sections of an extent made in the area shortly after the Edwardian conquest. Under the vill of Tref Madrun,[138] there is noted a payment from the bondmen of eight pence per year *pro cariagio I equi ad exercitum*. If this passage does relate to the pack-horse mentioned in the lawbooks, then the bond community, at least by the conquest, would seem in this case to have taken over from the prince the cost of supplying the horse. Whether such service might already be commuted in the pre-conquest period, as in the case of freemen, can only be conjectured. Again, the lawbooks' restriction to freemen of the general liability to personal service is reinforced by the restriction, in the Denbighland survey's statement of common customs in Rhufoniog, of the obligation to follow the lord in war to the *liberi de commoto*.[139] It has, however, been seen that in a statement of the customs of Ardudwy drawn up soon after the Edwardian conquest, the villeins of the royal demesne were liable to the same six-week-service period as the freemen.[140] And in the extent of the lands of the bishop of Bangor, drawn up in 1306, all of the tenants of many bond vills are said to be obliged to go with the lord in his war.[141] It would seem that at some time in the pre-conquest period the villeins of some, but by no means all, parts of Gwynedd had become liable for military service of the same kind as that performed by freemen.[142]

[138] T. Jones Pierce, 'Lleyn Ministers' Accounts, 1350–51', *B.B.C.S.*, VI (1932), pp. 259–60.
[139] *S.D.*, p. 145.
[140] See note 126 above.
[141] *Rec. Caern.*, pp. 97–110 *passim*.
[142] T. P. Ellis, *The First Extent of Bromfield and Yale, A.D. 1315* (Cymmrodorion Record Series, XI, 1924), p. 29, state that from the time of Gruffydd ap Cynan, military service was expected from many of the unfree as well as the free, and gave as evidence for this the fact that 'the greatest sufferers from escheat for having fought for prince Llywelyn, for having, in the euphemistic phrase of the Extents, "died against the peace", were the unfree'. If this argument were sound it would be possible to detect areas in which bondmen were liable to military service according to post-conquest records of deaths against the peace. But the phraseology of the extents does not betray anything of the institutional background (if there were any) of the bondmen's involvement in fighting. Ellis gave no explanation of his statement that bondmen's military service dated from the time of Gruffydd ap Cynan. It may rest on the reference to the latter's *bileinllu* found in A. Jones (ed.), *The History of Gruffydd ap Cynan (1054–1137)* (Manchester, 1913), p. 126: *a gossot (sc. Gruffydd) eu anheddeu ae fileinllu ar gwragedd ar meibion yn dyrysswch mynyddedd Eryri yn y lle ni ddioddefasant un perygl*. But here *bileinllu* probably means no more than 'all the bondmen', and is certainly included amongst the non-combatants sent into the mountains out of danger.

CONCLUSION

Patchy though the evidence is, it is quite clear that in the years before the Edwardian conquest the inhabitants of Gwynedd had been introduced to pressures of governance which were, potentially at least, as burdensome as those which confronted them after 1283. Writing of Llywelyn ap Gruffydd, Sir Maurice Powicke noted: 'How he contrived to raise the annual payments which, until the death of Henry III, were made to the English exchequer, has puzzled Welsh historians, as well it might . . .'[1]

Although it is not possible to solve that problem in precise quantitative terms, the range of fiscal resources set out above, and the capacity of many of them for extension in times of crisis, makes Llywelyn's achievement less puzzling. It should also be remembered that there were times when the prince was able to tap resources normally out of his reach: the vacancy of a see offered the prospect of plunder from episcopal lands which passed into the custody of the prince; the outbreak of war brought the chance to plunder neighbouring territories, to offer protection—at a price—to the wealthy and vulnerable ecclesiastical centres, and to raise ransoms from the more prominent prisoners taken.[2]

Even when it did not involve extortion, the intensive exploitation of resources had clearly involved rapid and unsettling change, as the demands of the prince eroded or overturned long-established customs. In many respects the English royal administration of the post-conquest period, with its constant reference to the extents and statutes of the 1280s, may have represented a return to stability in which, once more, custom triumphed.

---

[1] F. M. Powicke, *King Henry III and the Lord Edward*, p. 638.
[2] For 'protection' of religious houses see the account of the Margam annalist *sub.* 1231 with reference to Llywelyn ap Iorwerth: *de domo de Margan extorsit lx marcas argenti: Annales Monastici*, ed. H. R. Luard (Rolls Series, I, 1864), p. 39; for the Tewkesbury annalist's account of further extortion from Leominster priory on the same foray, see ibid., p. 80. For ransoms, see *C. Pat. R., 1247–58*, p. 663; *C. Lib. R., 1251–60*, pp. 436, 460.

Part 3
The Personnel of Administration
VII
RECRUITMENT AND REWARDS

A study of the men who received office from the princes serves to illuminate another aspect of governance. Office-holding was attractive: it brought prestige and, as will be seen, rewards of many sorts, from fees incidental to the exercise of official functions to lands and privileges granted by the prince in return for good service. Consequently, the granting of office might be used not only to secure the performance of the official duties discussed in chapter II, but also to attract loyalty and to strengthen certain individuals or families at the expense of others. The prince's ability to give and withhold office constituted, in short, an important means of political control.

THE REWARDS OF PRINCELY SERVICE

As well as giving a description of the responsibilities of the officers of the royal court, the laws of court also give an account of the perquisites attached to each office. It is probable that these descriptions, as with much of the material found in *Cyfreithiau Llys*, bear only occasional relevance to thirteenth-century conditions. Many elements must have been of considerable antiquity by that period, such as the right of the *distain* to a share of the skins of cattle slaughtered in the kitchen,[1] or the porter's right to a handful of each gift, such as berries, eggs or herrings, brought into the court.[2] Money perquisites sometimes have a more modern ring: thus, the *distain* is to have 24*d*. from every *swyddwr* when the latter is given office by the king, and 10*d*. from every pound given to the ruler *am tyr a dayar*.[3] Again, the holder of the office of

---
[1] *Ior.*, 8. 9-11.
[2] Ibid., 35. 4.
[3] Ibid., 8. 7-9, 14-15.

pengwastrawd, which may have survived, perhaps in the form of a sinecure, into the fourteenth century, is to have 4*d*. from anyone given a horse by the king,[4] while at a lower level the porter, whose office also survived into the post-conquest period, could claim 4*d*. from every prisoner on whom he closed the gate and 4*d*. from every *amobr* taken from the women of the *maerdref*.[5]

References in record sources to perquisites in cash or kind enjoyed by officers such as the *distain* are lacking, but record sources of both the thirteenth and fourteenth centuries provide some indication of the dues appurtenant to the officers of the commote. Mid-fourteenth-century records refer to the entitlement of *rhaglawiaid* to a proportion (twenty per cent or more) of the fines levied in the commote court, a proportion of reliefs levied in the commote, and to food and stabling for a horse and groom for one night per year from each bond tenant.[6] Similarly, *rhingylliaid* and woodwards are seen taking a proportion of fines,[7] and this is reinforced by evidence from the 1270s which shows the *rhingylliaid* of the Perfeddwlad taking certain items from the goods of malefactors subjected to distraint.[8]

Such considerations as the dues in cash or kind mentioned above undoubtedly acted as inducements to men to seek service under the prince, but in many cases they were not the main attraction involved. In the territorially-settled society of Gwynedd in the thirteenth century, it was land which constituted the most durable form, and the most reliable source, of wealth, in spite of the potential damage that could be caused by partible inheritance customs relating to land. In the accumulation of wealth and prestige, the amount of land which a man held, and the terms on which he held it, were of primary importance, and entry into the prince's service as one of his officials offered inviting prospects in both respects.

In the first place, it seems fairly clear that prominent servants of the prince might be rewarded with grants of land.

[4] Ibid., 11. 5–6.
[5] Ibid., 35. 6–7, 12–13.
[6] *Rec. Caern.*, pp. 141–2, 156–7.
[7] Ibid.
[8] NLW Peniarth MS. no. 231, pp. 48, 117.

Though recorded examples are few,[9] traditions of such grants survived, and the acquisition by leading ministers of lands well removed from the heartlands of their families is almost always to be attributed to grants made by the princes. Perhaps the clearest case is that of Ednyfed Fychan and his sons, who, though sprung from the stock of Marchudd in Rhos, held extensive lands elsewhere, notably in Anglesey.[10]

Secondly, *Llyfr Iorwerth* contains the information that the ruler's officers were allowed the considerable concession of holding their lands free from the various renders normally owed by freemen.[11] But it is clear that to a few eminent servants, an even greater favour was shown: in the fourteenth-century extents and surveys, all the heirs of some holdings, whether *gwelyau*, *gafaelion*, or vills, are described as holding their lands free from most renders and services. Though there are several possible explanations for the existence of such privileged conditions of tenure,[12] it is evident that they frequently arose from grants of hereditary tenurial immunities made by thirteenth-century princes to their servants. The descendants of Cynfrig ab Iorwerth, who included Ednyfed Fychan and formed for most of the period under discussion the core of ministerial groups surrounding the princes, held extensive lands both in Gwynedd Uwch Conwy and in the Perfeddwlad, quit of almost all the usual obligations, apparently as the result of a grant by Llywelyn ab Iorwerth.[13] But this family, which is discussed in greater detail below, was not the

---

[9] See Appendix I, nos. 13 (for a confirmation by Llywelyn ab Iorwerth of the purchase of land by Ednyfed Fychan) and 27 (for an exchange of lands between Llywelyn ap Gruffydd and Heilyn ap Tudur, which contains a reference to a grant by the prince to Heilyn's father). See also R. Fenton, *Tours in Wales (1804–1813)*, (Cambrian Archaeological Association 1917), p. 311, for a reference to a (lost) charter recording a grant of land in Creuddyn to Ednyfed Fychan by Llywelyn ab Iorwerth.
[10] See below, pp. 130–1.
[11] The phrase *ef a dely e tyr en ryd* occurs regularly at the outset of the treatment of each of the court officials from the *offeiriad teulu* to the *pencerdd*: see *Ior.*, 7–25, 27–37, 39–40.
[12] Some such grants would appear to have been made to lesser members of the princely house: see below, pp. 140–1. Other immunities had been conceded to ecclesiastical bodies, whether monastic houses, the bishops and chapters of Bangor and St. Asaph, or ancient churches on the *clas* model, which were frequently by the later thirteenth century in the hands of secular canons, *abbates* or portionaries: for an example, see *S.D.*, pp. 187–90.
[13] Ibid., pp. 228, 303.

only one to be thus honoured: other men whose service to the princes earned them and their descendants similar rewards were Einion ap Gwalchmai, Maredudd ab Iorwerth, Tudur ap Madog and Iorwerth ap Gwrgunon.

Einion ap Gwalchmai was one of Llywelyn ab Iorwerth's leading ministers in the period 1216–23.[14] The rarity of his patronymic makes it reasonably certain that he was the eponym of the privileged *gwelyau Einion ap Gwalchmai* and *Wyrion Einion ap Gwalchmai* in Cafflogion and in Trefddisteiniaid, Malltraeth, respectively.[15] It is noteworthy, however, that *gwely Einion ap Gwalchmai* in Lledwyganllys, Malltraeth, was recorded in the 1352 extent as being subject to normal renders and services,[16] whilst though *gwely Einion ap Gwalchmai* in Dindaethwy was recorded as enjoying considerable immunities, these were stated to have arisen from the fact that the lands concerned had been granted by way of exchange for the original site of the *gwely*, which formed part of the area on which Beaumaris had been built.[17] This indicates that grants of hereditary tenurial privileges might be made in respect of certain of the grantee's lands only: they may in some cases have applied only to lands, newly granted by the prince, beyond the patrimony of the recipient.

There can be little doubt that the eponym of *gwely Maredudd ab Iorwerth* in Ysgeifiog, recorded in 1352 as being subject to privileged tenure by the grant of Llywelyn ab Iorwerth,[18] was the Maredudd ab Iorwerth who appears as a servant of both Llywelyn ab Iorwerth and, it seems, his grandson Owain ap Gruffydd.[19] Detailed discussions of the genealogical connections of Maredudd ab Iorwerth, given below, will indicate that the holding in Ysgeifiog was not the only land granted to him and his heirs on privileged terms.

Another eminent member of the ministerial group in the thirteenth century who seems to have received grants of

---

[14] See Appendix II, *sub* Einion ap Gwalchmai.
[15] *Rec. Caern.*, pp. 31, 46.
[16] Ibid., p. 44.
[17] Ibid., p. 76. The original site of the *gwely* may have been, of course, subject to privileged tenure.
[18] Ibid., p. 78.
[19] See below, pp. 110–12, and for a summary of Maredudd's appearances as a minister of the princes, see Appendix II, *sub* Maredudd ab Iorwerth.

hereditary tenurial privileges was Tudur ap Madog, though it is possible that he was not the first of his family to benefit from such grants.[20] Tudur ap Madog appears in record sources as a servant of both David ap Llywelyn and of Llywelyn ap Gruffydd,[21] and is almost certainly the man whose descendants enjoyed rights of immunity from services and renders in the two *gwelyau Tudur ap Madog* and the *gwelyau Wyrion Iarddur* and *Wyrion ap Cynddelw* (sic) in Dindaethwy.[22] The co-heirs of these lands in 1352 can be shown, by comparison with the genealogies, to have been descended from Iarddur ap Cynddelw, who is traditionally supposed to have been living in the principate of Llywelyn ab Iorwerth.[23] Iarddur's son, Madog, witnessed Llywelyn ab Iorwerth's charter to Aberconwy abbey, which was granted at the close of the twelfth century,[24] and Madog in turn had a son, Tudur, who would thus seem to have flourished at the same period as the Tudur ap Madog of thirteenth-century records. Moreover, the genealogies give Tudur ap Madog ab Iarddur a son called Gruffydd, and an inquisition of 1289 revealed that Gruffydd ap Tudur and his brother had greater rights in lands in Pennant Gwernogof, by hereditary right after the death of their father, Tudur ap Madog, than did the prior of Beddgelert by reason of a grant of David ap Llywelyn, then prince of Wales.[25] This indicates that the Tudur ap Madog of the line of Iarddur enjoyed princely favour in the period when the Tudur ap Madog of mid-century records is known to have been in the princes' service.

Yet Tudur cannot be conclusively identified as the sole grantee of the tenurial privileges enjoyed by his descendants. Iarddur ap Cynddelw apparently enjoyed the favour of Llywelyn ab Iorwerth, who was traditionally supposed to have granted him lands in Arllechwedd Uchaf, though the precise nature of this grant, as well as the circumstances which

---

[20] See below, p. 100.
[21] See Appendix II, *sub* Tudur ap Madog.
[22] *Rec. Caern.*, pp. 73, 77.
[23] See Dwnn, *Heraldic Visitations*, II, pp. 264-5, 340, and P. C. Bartrum, 'Pedigrees of the Welsh Tribal Patriarchs', *N.L.W.J.*, XIII, pp. 128-9.
[24] For a discussion of this charter, see Appendix I, no. 1.
[25] *C. Inq. Misc., 1216-1307*, p. 416.

occasioned it, are unknown.[26] There was in 1352 a *gafael Iarddur* recorded in Arllechwedd Uchaf,[27] which was held by descendants of Iarddur ap Cynddelw but not, however, on privileged terms. Of Iarddur's two sons, Iorwerth was reputed in later centuries to have been deprived of his lands by Llywelyn ab Iorwerth for his failure to perform military service:[28] but no such stain dishonoured Iarddur's other son, Madog. His appearance as a witness to Llywelyn's Aberconwy charter has been noted. He may have been Llywelyn's minister, and he may have received some grant of hereditary privileged tenure. Indeed, *gwely Wyrion Iarddur* and *gwely Wyrion ap Cynddelw* were in 1352 recorded as being subject to somewhat different privileges from those relating to the *gwelyau Tudur ap Madog*.[29] This may indicate that the grants were made in respect of these lands at different times. It remains probable, of course, that Tudur ap Madog was the grantee of privileges enjoyed by his descendants in at least some of their lands.

Finally, Iorwerth ap Gwrgunon, who served Llywelyn ap Gruffydd in the period c. 1243-63,[30] may be identified as the founder of a holding, *gwely Iorwerth ap Gurgen* in Twrcelyn,[31] which was recorded in 1352 as being subject to considerable immunities.

It is noteworthy that holdings associated with men who were reputed to have been prominent officials of Owain Gwynedd in the mid-twelfth century are recorded in 1352 as

---

[26] Glyn Roberts discusses the alleged grant of land in Arllechwedd Uchaf to Iarddur by Llywelyn ab Iorwerth in *Aspects of Welsh History*, p. 206, and his article 'Griffiths of Penrhyn' in *D.W.B.*, p. 1123. It is also necessary to refer to Sir John Wynn's *Survey of Penmaenmawr*, ed. J. O. Halliwell (1859) where it is stated that 'Jarddur was owner of all the landes in that commotte . . . savinge Aber and Wieg, which did not belong to the Prince . . .' The sense here may not be that Iarddur held the whole commote, but instead all the former demesne lands of the prince except those specified. See Francis Jones, 'The Heraldry of Gwynedd', *Trans. Caerns. Hist. Soc.*, XXIV (1963), p. 56, for the tradition that Iarddur was 'sometime Forester of Snowdon'.
[27] *Rec. Caern.*, p. 14.
[28] *Survey of Penmaenmawr, ut supra.*
[29] The holders of *gwely Wyrion Iarddur* and *gwely Wyrion ap Cynddelw* (sic) paid relief, *gobr* and *amobr*, whereas immunity from these was apparently enjoyed by the holders of *gwelyau Tudur ap Madog*.
[30] See Appendix II, *sub* Iorwerth ap Gwrgunon.
[31] *Rec. Caern.*, p. 68.

being subject to normal renders and services.³² And of considerable significance is the fact that *gwelyau* apparently founded by Gwyn ab Ednywain, *distain* to Llywelyn ab Iorwerth in the early years of the thirteenth century, also appears as unprivileged in 1352.³³ It thus seems highly probable that the early or middle years of the principate of Llywelyn ab Iorwerth saw the origin of grants of hereditary tenurial privileges as a means of rewarding prominent ministers. Whether it is quite apt to refer to the creation of a ministerial aristocracy, as does Glyn Roberts,³⁴ is somewhat doubtful. Terms such as *nobiles* or *magnates*, as employed in late-thirteenth-century documents, were clearly not confined in their application to men who enjoyed tenurial privileges granted by a prince as a reward for official service.³⁵ These terms seem to have been used loosely to indicate powerful or wealthy men. Princes' servants, it is true, were by the nature of their employment powerful, and by virtue of the rewards attaching to office they were well placed to become wealthy; yet the attributes of wealth and power were certainly not exclusive to them. Again, it is apparent that the tenurial privileges granted to prominent servants set them apart from other freemen: there were ways in which privileged tenure might arise, other than as a reward for service, but it seems that the ways in which tenurial privileges had originated were well remembered even in the fourteenth century.³⁶ Here an important point emerges: one

---

³² For the tradition that Llywarch ap Bran and Hwfa ap Cynddelw were officials of the court of Owain Gwynedd, see T. Pennant, *Tours of Wales*, ed. John Rhys (Caernarvon, 1883) III, pp. 428–30. For *gwelyau* named after the sons of Llywarch, see *Rec. Caern.*, p. 56, and for those named after the sons of Hwfa, see ibid., p. 51. The one of the latter subject to tenurial privileges is *gwely Matusalem ap Hwfa*: significantly Matusalem's grandson, Iorwerth ap Maredudd, was probably connected with the court of Llywelyn ap Gruffydd, and is the only one of Hwfa's descendants to appear in this context: *Littere Wallie*, p. 185. His own descendants were noted partisans of the English kings: J. B. Smith, 'Welsh Dominicans and the Crisis of 1277', *B.B.C.S.*, XXII (1968), pp. 354–6.
³³ *Rec. Caern.*, pp. 39–40.
³⁴ *Aspects of Welsh History*, p. 181.
³⁵ See, for example, the terminology used by the surveyors of Talybont in 1284, when they note payments *de quodlibet terram tenente exceptis magnatibus*, . . . ('Extent of Merionethshire *temp.* Edward I', p. 185.) This seems to reflect the statement in the 1334 Denbighland survey regarding the discharge of obligations by the tenants of landholders rather than by landholders themselves; for which see *S.D.*, p. 149.
³⁶ Thus, in the extents of the mid-fourteenth century the source of a claim to immunity from renders is frequently stated.

may perhaps talk of the immunists discussed here as an aristocracy whose origin was ministerial, but the enhanced status derived from tenurial privileges was not, when these were made hereditary, dependent upon continued service in subsequent generations, after the grant. Whether or not grants of hereditary tenurial privileges did create a tradition of service within descent groups will be examined in the discussion of leading ministers and their families which follows. It is worth remembering at the outset that what began as privileges to be striven for soon became rights to be protected in the most effective way possible. When success attended the policies of the princes, such protection was normally achieved by the continuing service of the grantee or his descendants. But in times of adversity a transfer of loyalties might serve the same purpose more effectively: there can be little doubt that this was amongst the considerations which induced many members of the official group, and their descendants, in Gwynedd to desert the cause of Llywelyn ap Gruffydd in the period of his decline, and thereafter to serve the conqueror as they or their forebears had served the Welsh princes. Before the analysis can be carried further forward, it will be necessary to establish the identity of as many of the princes' ministers as possible.

DESCENDANTS OF CYNFRIG AB IORWERTH

Undoubtedly the greatest ministerial family of the thirteenth century was that whose representatives in the fourteenth century were known as Wyrion Eden, the grandsons, or descendants of Ednyfed.[37] Ednyfed was Ednyfed Fychan, the great minister of Llywelyn ab Iorwerth and David ap Llywelyn.[38] The designation is slightly misleading, for, in fact, it includes all of the descendants of Ednyfed Fychan's father, Cynfrig ab Iorwerth, who is stated by the Denbighland survey of 1334 to have been the original grantee of the hereditary

---

[37] For a discussion concentrating on the Anglesey 'Tudur' branch of the family, see *Aspects of Welsh History*, pp. 179-214.

[38] For his career, see Appendix II, *sub* Ednyfed Fychan. In this and subsequent cases the evidence supporting points of biographical detail discussed in the text will not be cited in full in footnotes, but will be given in the relevant entry in Appendix II. In cases where points made relate to persons not covered by entries in Appendix II, footnote citations are of course given.

tenurial privileges enjoyed by Wyrion Eden.³⁹ As Glyn Roberts has pointed out, this may imply that Cynfrig preceded his son in Llywelyn ab Iorwerth's service.⁴⁰ But the account as preserved in the Denbigh survey may be confused, and even if accurate, it would still be easy to imagine how the term Wyrion Eden arose, for Ednyfed was by far the most famous of Cynfrig's sons. He was not, however, the only one to be a prince's official, for of the three other sons with whom Cynfrig is credited in the genealogies, two, Gorowny and Heilyn, can also be identified as prominent servants of Llywelyn ab Iorwerth and David ap Llywelyn.⁴¹

That the Goronwy ap Cynfrig who appears in the ranks of the servants of Llywelyn ab Iorwerth and of his son, David, was Ednyfed's brother is proved by two pieces of evidence. First, the Patent Roll of 1232, recording the names of a group of Llywelyn ab Iorwerth's envoys, contains a direct reference to Goronwy as Ednyfed's brother. Secondly, it appears that in 1241 Goronwy ap Cynfrig was handed over to Henry III by David ap Llywelyn as a hostage for the prince's good behaviour. He was still in English hands in 1247 when, however, he was apparently re-instated in his lands in the Perfeddwlad. The lands in question were specified, and amongst them are several which were recorded in 1334 as settlements of Wyrion Eden.⁴² It seems that in 1245 Goronwy had become a collaborator with the English government in its attempt to curb the rising power of David ap Llywelyn. He never reappears in the service of a prince of Gwynedd, and it is possible that his defection was too blatant to permit this. It is a possibility, but no more, that the Cynfrig ap Goronwy who was bailiff of Rhuddlan in the 1270s was a son of Goronwy ap Cynfrig.⁴³

In the case of Heilyn ap Cynfrig, who appears in the service of the princes in the years 1222–41, there is not the same

---

³⁹ *S.D.*, p. 303.
⁴⁰ *Aspects of Welsh History*, p. 182.
⁴¹ For these men, see Appendix II, *sub* Goronwy ap Cynfrig, Heilyn ap Cynfrig.
⁴² Amongst Goronwy's lands mentioned were Brynffanugl (*S.D.*, p. 261); Twynnan (ibid., p. 297); Bodlennyn (ibid., p. 251); Maesgwyn (ibid.) and ? Toronyth (ibid., p. 265).
⁴³ See Appendix II, *sub* Cynfrig ap Goronwy. Several of the coheirs of *gwely Cynfrig ab Iorwerth* in Brynffanugl in 1334 (*S.D.*, p. 261) were grandsons of a Cynfrig who must have flourished at about the time when this Cynfrig ap Goronwy was active.

weight of evidence as exists for Goronwy to prove that he was the brother of Ednyfed Fychan, but this is highly probable on the basis of his chronological location. It is, moreover, quite certain that the Goronwy ap Heilyn who appears as the servant of both Llywelyn ap Gruffydd and Edward I in turn in the years 1277–81 was the grandson of Cynfrig ab Iorwerth.[44] It is known that he was one of the magnates who led the Welsh rising of 1282–3, and that in 1283 he was *distain* to Dafydd ap Gruffydd, so that it is of great significance that the Denbigh survey of 1334 contains references in its description of the lands of Wyrion Eden to the escheated holdings of Goronwy ap Heilyn Sais ap Cynfrig, who died against the peace.[45] It would seem from the designation *Sais* (the Englishman) applied to Heilyn that he had strong English connections.

It remains true that the branch of Cynfrig ab Iorwerth's descendants which has the most spectacular history of prominence in princely service is that of Ednyfed Fychan himself. It has been seen that Ednyfed was *distain* to Llywelyn ab Iorwerth and David ap Llywelyn, and that he was followed in that office by two at least, and probably three, of his sons, Gruffydd, Goronwy and Tudur.[46] Amongst Ednyfed's other sons, Cynfrig and Rhys appear as servants of Llywelyn ap Gruffydd, and amongst his grandsons, Rhys ap Gruffydd was a prominent official of the same prince; Heilyn ap Tudur and Tudur ap Goronwy appear to have received Llywelyn ap Gruffydd's favour in his later years, and may therefore have been his servants.[47]

The history of Ednyfed's family in the thirteenth century is not, however, one of unmixed loyalty to the princes of

[44] See Appendix II, *sub* Goronwy ap Heilyn.
[45] *S.D.*, pp. 239 (Goronwy ap Heilyn Sais), 295 (Goronwy ap Heilyn Sais), 297 (Goronwy ap Heilyn ap Cynfrig).
[46] See above, pp. 17–18, and Appendix II, *sub* Goronwy ab Ednyfed, Gruffydd ab Ednyfed and Tudur ab Ednyfed.
[47] See Appendix II, *sub* Cynfrig ab Ednyfed, Rhys ab Ednyfed and Rhys ap Gruffydd. For Llywelyn's grant of lands in Dinllaen to Heilyn ap Tudur, see *Rec. Caern.*, p. 211, and for his grant of lands in Aber to Tudur ap Goronwy, ibid., p. 217, and *Cal. Anc. Corr.*, p. 108. On the other hand, the grant in Dinllaen was by way of an exchange. In the 1240s and 1250s, Heilyn had been a hostage in England for his father's good behaviour, but in 1263 he was released by royal mandate: this is surprising, because Tudur had long since returned to the service of Llywelyn ap Gruffydd and the English government was about to launch an attack on the prince. The only explanation is that Henry was convinced of Heilyn's pro-English sympathies.

Gwynedd. Gruffydd ab Ednyfed is traditionally reputed to have been forced to flee to Ireland in the time of Llywelyn ab Iorwerth as a result of a slander concerning the prince's wife, Joan.[48] It is perfectly consistent with this story that Gruffydd ab Ednyfed appears as prominent in the service of Llywelyn ap Gruffydd, whose father, David's half-brother, was so sternly treated by Llywelyn ab Iorwerth.[49]

It was the later years of the century, however, which saw the greatest strain between Ednyfed's descendants and their prince. In 1269 Rhys ab Ednyfed had to provide sureties for his future good behaviour towards Llywelyn, though the background to this episode is unknown. Further stress is visible in the crisis of 1276-7, when the Dominican friar, Llywelyn ap Gruffydd, himself a grandson of Ednyfed Fychan, acted as the intermediary between Edward I and his own brother Rhys, Prince Llywelyn's former minister, together with his kinsmen, Gruffydd ab Iorwerth and Hywel ap Goronwy, in their plot to defect to the king.[50]

Mr. J. B. Smith has very plausibly argued that Hywel ap Goronwy was another of Ednyfed Fychan's grandsons.[51] The causes of their planned, but ultimately abortive, defection are uncertain: it may simply have been that Rhys had decided that the prince was doomed to defeat, and therefore sought to secure his interests by a timely submission to Edward I. Indeed, the Treaty of Conwy included a clause ordering Llywelyn to free Rhys ap Gruffydd and restore him 'to the status which he held when he first treated with the lord king about coming to his peace'. Thereafter, Rhys passed into the service of Edward, and in 1281 incurred Llywelyn's anger and a fine of £100 on account of some act of disobedience and contempt shown to the prince whilst Rhys was with him at Aberffraw. The brother of Rhys, Hywel ap Gruffydd, was one of Edward I's bailiffs in the Perfeddwlad after 1277 and, in the company of the invading English forces, was killed at the battle of the Menai in 1282.[52]

---

[48] Dwnn, *Heraldic Visitations*, II, p. 101.
[49] See below, pp. 152-3.
[50] J. B. Smith, 'Welsh Dominicans and the Crisis of 1277', *B.B.C.S.*, XXII (1968), pp. 356-7.
[51] Ibid., pp. 355-6.
[52] *C. Chanc. R., Various*, pp. 164, 169, 171, 173, and J. G. Edwards, 'Sir Gruffydd Llwyd', *E.H.R.*, XXX (1915), p. 601.

It is clear that the ministerial tradition amongst Wyrion Eden did not die with their alienation from Llywelyn ap Gruffydd in his final years. The family passed from the service of the native princes to that of English rulers,[53] except for a brief period in 1294-5, when several of Ednyfed's descendants appear in the witness-list of a charter granted by Madog ap Llywelyn, the rebel prince, to one Bleddyn Fychan. One of the witnesses, Tudur ap Goronwy ab Ednyfed, is designated as Madog's steward. Neither Tudur nor his kinsmen amongst the witnesses seem to have suffered unduly for their part in Madog's revolt.[54]

THE FAMILY OF EINION FYCHAN

Einion Fychan[55] was a leading minister of three princes, Llywelyn ab Iorwerth, David ap Llywelyn and Llywelyn ap Gruffydd, whilst his son, Dafydd ab Einion Fychan,[56] was a very prominent servant of the last-named prince. The genealogical background of these important men is, however, extremely mysterious, and before any real progress can be made in its elucidation it is necessary to fix as far as possible the locality with which they can be most closely associated. There are several grounds for supposing that they were primarily connected with Anglesey.

By 1246 Einion Fychan, Goronwy ap Cynfrig and Tudur ab Ednyfed were amongst those men of Gwynedd who had come into the hands of Henry III as a result of his conflicts with David ap Llywelyn. In that year, Henry made arrangements for the release of Einion and Tudur, and probably of Goronwy also. In May 1247 John de Grey, justice of Chester, was ordered by the king to restore Goronwy and Tudur to their

---

[53] As well as the entries *sub* Rhys ap Gruffydd and Goronwy ap Heilyn in Appendix II, and the references cited in notes 37 and 52 above, see the entries in *D.W.B.*, *sub* Ednyfed Fychan, Sir Gruffydd Llwyd and Rhys ap Gruffydd (d. 1356).

[54] See *Aspects of Welsh History*, pp. 186-7. For the charter of Madog ap Llywelyn, see *Royal Commission on Ancient Monuments in Wales and Monmouthshire, Merioneth Inventory*, 1921, p. 40n. With Tudur ap Goronwy were Goronwy Fychan, his brother, and Gruffydd ap Rhys, almost certainly his second cousin.

[55] See Appendix II, *sub* Einion Fychan.

[56] Ibid., *sub* Dafydd ab Einion. His identity is established by a reference to him as Dafydd ab Einion Fychan in 1274.

lands in the Perfeddwlad.⁵⁷ No such order survives regarding Einion Fychan. Though hardly conclusive in itself, this raises the suspicion that Einion's lands lay in Gwynedd Uwch Conwy, and this suspicion is strengthened by his appearance in 1247 among the witnesses to a confirmation by Owain ap Gruffydd of a grant of Llywelyn ap Gruffydd to Ynys Lannog priory.

The situation becomes clearer in the case of Dafydd ab Einion Fychan. In the first place, careful note should be taken of a letter written by Edward I to the bishop of Bangor in January 1278, regarding complaints made to him by a Dafydd ab Einion,

> *quod quidam de partibus illis, asserentes quedam blada, que idem David a Willielmo Burnell et hominibus suis emit in Anglesey vestre diocesis dum fuerunt ibidem in servicio nostro sua esse quandam crucem super blada predicta . . . apponi fecerunt, occasione cuius crucis predictus David aliquam administracionem de bladis illis habere non potest.*

The identity of this Dafydd ab Einion is not certain, but it would appear from Edward's concern in the matter that he was a man of some consequence, so that it is at least possible that he was the son of Einion Fychan. It is known that Llywelyn ap Gruffydd and his court visited Edward I in London at Christmas 1277,⁵⁸ and as Dafydd ab Einion Fychan was one of Llywelyn's leading ministers at this period it is probable that he was present in the prince's entourage; this might provide the background to his apparently direct complaint to the king. And it is clear that the complainant had interests in Anglesey.

Secondly, English records of the 1290s refer to a Dafydd Fychan ap Dafydd ab Einion who held his father's land in Dindaethwy, Anglesey, for a fine of £5 per year.⁵⁹ On first

---

⁵⁷ *Close Rolls, 1242–47*, p. 510. That the Einion ab Owain also mentioned here was not Einion Fychan is proved by *C. Lib. R., 1245–51*, p. 76, where both men are referred to in totally different circumstances.

⁵⁸ Lloyd, *Hist. Wales*, II, p. 760.

⁵⁹ See *C. Close R., Various*, p. 325; John Griffiths, 'Two early ministers' accounts for North Wales', *B.B.C.S.*, IX (1939), p. 68 (which fixes the commote as Dindaethwy); idem, 'Early accounts relating to North Wales *temp.* Edward I', *B.B.C.S.*, XIV (1952), pp. 241, 303, 309. In *C. Pat. R., 1343–45*, p. 232, Dafydd Fychan ap Dafydd ab Einion is given as one of the men of Anglesey who did homage and fealty to Prince Edward in 1301.

examination, there is nothing, apart from the fact that the chronology is not obviously improbable, to indicate that Dafydd Fychan was a grandson of Einion Fychan, servant of the princes. Fortunately, however, other evidence can be brought to bear upon the problem. After the death of Tudur ab Ednyfed in 1278, the name of Llywelyn ap Gruffydd's *distain* is nowhere given in the record sources. But in 1281 Dafydd ab Einion appears at the head of the witness-list in a document issued by Llywelyn: this was the position usually accorded to the *distain*, who was normally preceded only by princelings or ecclesiastical dignitaries. Further, there is a reference in *Brut y Tywysogyon* to Llywelyn's *distain* in this period: in 1282 he was sent by the prince to take homages in Brycheiniog.[60] He is not named, and nothing is said of his fate. Amongst the ministers' accounts of the fourteenth century, however, is a reference to an Anglesey man, Dafydd ab Einion Fychan,[61] who died *contra pacem* in south Wales. If Dafydd ab Einion was indeed the prince's *distain*, who was sent in 1282 to organize resistance to Edward I in the south, where he met his death, and if Dafydd Fychan was his son, then this would explain why the latter held his father's lands conditionally on the payment of a fine. In the pattern here constructed, there is, of course, a clear enough connection of Dafydd ab Einion with Anglesey and, more particularly, with Dindaethwy.

The evidence of some of the record sources having been examined, it can now be compared with the information supplied by the genealogies. These supply two men called Einion Fychan who were members of prominent families in Gwynedd, and who must have flourished at about the time of the Einion Fychan of the records. The first of these men is Einion Fychan ab Einion Ddu ap Cynfrig, a nephew of Ednyfed Fychan.[62] He is indeed credited with a son called Dafydd, a fact which is, however, not as conclusive as it appears. This branch of the family of Cynfrig ab Iorwerth is seen in record sources only in the 1334 Denbigh survey, where

---

[60] *B.T., Pen. 20,* p. 228.
[61] E. A. Lewis, 'The Decay of Tribalism in North Wales' *Trans. Cymmr.*, 1902-3, p. 38.
[62] Dwnn, *Heraldic Visitations*, II, p. 278.

it is called *progenies David ap Eynon ap Ken' ap Ior'*, holding land in Dinorben Fychan.[63] The appearance of this line here, holding by hereditary privileged tenure, hardly accords with the reconstruction suggested above of the local background and eventual fate of Dafydd ab Einion Fychan. If Dafydd died *contra pacem*, as is suggested, then one would expect lands specifically associated with him to escheat, as was the case elsewhere in the Denbigh lordship with men who had died in similar circumstances.

The genealogies do, however, provide another Einion Fychan, the son of Einion ap Gwalchmai, himself the servant of Llywelyn ab Iorwerth and an eminent poet.[64] No genealogy has come to light which credits him with a son named Dafydd, but this need not be greatly significant. More important is the fact that Einion ap Gwalchmai was an Anglesey man, whose father and grandfather, Gwalchmai and Meilir, both gave their names to Anglesey *trefi*. One of the co-heirs of *gwely Einion ap Gwalchmai* in Dindaethwy in 1352 was Dafydd ap Gruffydd ap Dafydd Fychan.[65] There is no objection on chronological grounds to the suggestion that this was the grandson of Dafydd Fychan ap Dafydd ab Einion of Dindaethwy who flourished in the 1290s, and the great-grandson of the Dafydd ab Einion Fychan who, it has been suggested, died *contra pacem* in 1282-3 after a career of nearly thirty years in princely service. Again, it is noteworthy that in 1352 one of the holders of *gwely Einion ap Gwalchmai* in Trefddisteiniaid in Aberffraw was Llywelyn ap Dafydd Gethin.[66] This is clearly the son of Dafydd Gethin ap Dafydd Fychan of Aberffraw who petitioned the king early in the fourteenth century regarding land held by his father in Trefor Fychan in Dindaethwy, which formed part of the site of Beaumaris.[67] This places a Dafydd Fychan of Dindaethwy, who must have flourished in the late-thirteenth century, as a

[63] *S.D.*, p. 228.
[64] Dwnn, op. cit., II, pp. 261-2. For Einion ap Gwalchmai, see Appendix II, *sub nomine*.
[65] *Rec. Caern.*, p. 76. Dafydd ap Gruffydd ap Dafydd Fychan, described as one of the co-heirs of *gwely Einion ap Gwalchmai*, is given as one of the holders of *gwely Iorwerth Fychan & Einion Mon*, and is differentiated from the other holders of that *gwely* in that he pays no relief, *gobr* or *amobr*.
[66] *Rec. Caern.*, p. 46.
[67] *Cal. Anc. Pet.*, p. 444.

descendant of Einion ap Gwalchmai. Dafydd Gethin's petition records the fact that Dafydd Fychan had served Edward I in the second war in Scotland, and it may be as a result of such service that Dafydd Fychan and his descendants escaped from the necessity of paying the annual £5 fine recorded in the early 1290s.

It is true that the identification of Einion Fychan as a son of Einion ap Gwalchmai rests entirely on coincidental evidence. But the cumulative force of the large number of coincidences involved, all of which fit together quite easily, is impressive. If the identification is accepted as a probable one, then it reveals the family with the longest continuous history of prominence in the princes' service which has come to light, for Gwalchmai had almost certainly been household poet to Owain Gwynedd, and Meilir had served his predecessor, Gruffydd ap Cynan.[68] This family, moreover, furnishes one of the few prominent ministers of Gwynedd who died fighting for his prince in the final crisis of Llywelyn's rule.

DESCENDANTS OF LLYWARCH AP BRAN

A branch of the progeny of Llywarch ap Bran provides another example of a family with a strong ministerial tradition. Llywarch himself was reputed to have been steward to Owain Gwynedd; his grandson Maredudd ab Iorwerth is known to have been a prominent minister of Llywelyn ab Iorwerth and, probably, of Owain ap Gruffydd,[69] and it seems likely that at least one of Maredudd's sons was a servant of the princes also.

Information on the descendants of Maredudd ab Iorwerth may be obtained from the genealogies and from the names of *gwelyau* and their tenants recorded in the 1352 extents of Anglesey and Caernarvonshire. In the present context, it is the latter which provide the most valuable source. It is first necessary to examine *gwelyau* which can definitely be associated with Maredudd ab Iorwerth: such are *gwely Maredudd ab Iorwerth* in Ysgeifiog,[70] probably *gwely Maredudd ab Iorwerth* in Llanfigel, recorded as being held *de sancto Machuto*,[71] and

[68] Lloyd, *Hist. Wales*, II, pp. 531–2.
[69] See above, p. 98 and Appendix II, *sub* Maredudd ab Iorwerth.
[70] *Rec. Caern.*, p. 78.
[71] Ibid., p. 62.

certainly *gwely Iorwerth ap Llywarch* in Trelywarch,[72] the eponym of which was Maredudd's father. The recorded holders of these *gwelyau* in 1352 were as follows: Ieuan Wyddel and Tudur ap Hywel ap Tudur, in Ysgeifiog; Iorwerth Fychan ab Iorwerth ap Tudur and Iorwerth ap Hywel ap Tudur in Trelywarch; Maredudd ap Cad[wgan?] and Iorwerth Fychan in Llanfigel. Assuming that the last-named is identical with the Iorwerth Fychan ab Iorwerth ap Tudur holding in Trelywarch, there are thus four known descendants of Maredudd ab Iorwerth, together with a possible fifth descendant in Iorwerth ap Hywel ap Tudur. Three of this group are descendants of a Tudur. Reckoning a generation at about thirty years, the man, or men, named Tudur in the family of Maredudd ap Iorwerth would have flourished about 1290. As Maredudd flourished in the second quarter of the thirteenth century, a genealogy of Tudur ap X ap Maredudd ab Iorwerth may be suggested. Now, Iorwerth ap Hywel and Iorwerth Fychan, the named holders of *gwely Iorwerth ap Llywarch* in Trelywarch, are also the only recorded holders of *gwely Tudur ap Gruffydd* in Clegyrog.[73] And Iorwerth Fychan, together with Tudur ap Hywel, one of the holders of *gwely Maredudd ab Iorwerth* in Ysgeifiog, are named as co-heirs of *gwely Gruffydd ap Maredudd* in Llanfair Prysgoel.[74] The genealogy suggested above can thus be completed with some confidence as Tudur ap Gruffydd ap Maredudd ab Iorwerth.[75]

Such a genealogy illuminates a reference to political events in the mid-thirteenth century which is contained in an inquisition of about 1284.[76] The inquisition concerned a Gruffydd ap Maredudd, and it was found that he was not seised on the day he died of any land, for he held of 'Sir Owain' against Llywelyn, sometime prince, on the day when he was taken,[77] and the same Gruffydd was outlawed from Wales and died in England. But when he took his way to England he was seised

[72] Ibid., p. 56.
[73] Ibid., p. 61.
[74] Ibid., p. 19.
[75] Only enough evidence is here adduced to make the necessary identifications: these conclusions can be buttressed by consideration of the names and tenants of other *gwelyau*. See D. Stephenson, 'The Governance of Gwynedd under the thirteenth-century Princes' (Oxford D.Phil. thesis, 1977), p. 149.
[76] *C. Inq. P. M.*, II, p. 327.
[77] This clearly refers to the events of 1255.

of a fourth part of the town of Klegyraut (Clegyrog), which he had of the gift of David son of Llywelyn, then prince of Wales, and a small township called Bodwrdyn, and the township of Thlysleu (Llysllew) which he had of the gift of Owen, sometime prince. These he enjoyed in addition to his part of the inheritance of his father, which Tudur and Maredudd, his sons, now held.

Two facts connect the persons mentioned here with the family which has been discussed above. First, the inquisition provides a line running as Tudur ap Gruffydd ap Maredudd, which is identical with the pedigree established for the descendants of Maredudd ab Iorwerth ap Llywarch. Secondly, it will be observed that Clegyrog, one of the areas in which Gruffydd ap Maredudd is said to have been granted lands, was the site of *gwely Tudur ap Gruffydd* in 1352.[78] The conclusion is obvious, namely, that the Gruffydd ap Maredudd discussed in the inquisition was the son of Maredudd ab Iorwerth ap Llywarch. Maredudd himself was, significantly in view of his son's loyalties, not amongst the witnesses to any of Llywelyn ap Gruffydd's charters issued in 1247, but was a witness to Owain ap Gruffydd's confirmation of one of his brother's grants.

Gruffydd almost certainly followed his father in the prince's service; this assumption most satisfactorily explains his large rewards at the hands of David and Owain. It was a progress on the model of other official families, and which was cut short by Gruffydd's loyalty to Owain in 1255, but resumed, in the person of Gruffydd's son, Tudur, under Edward I.[79]

DESCENDANTS OF IARDDUR AP CYNDDELW

It has already been seen that both Iarddur ap Cynddelw and his son, Madog, may have been servants of Llywelyn ab Iorwerth, and that Madog ab Iarddur's son, Tudur, was certainly the minister of Llywelyn ap Gruffydd.[80] By the period of Tudur's prominence, the family had benefited substantially from grants of land and privileges by the princes.

---

[78] See note 73 above.

[79] It may be added that in the 1290s royal pensions were paid to Tudur ap Gruffydd and his brother Maredudd, of Anglesey. These were clearly the persons referred to in the inquisition: J. Griffiths, 'Early accounts relating to North Wales temp. Edward I', *B.B.C.S.*, XIV (1952), p. 306.

[80] See pp. 99–100 above.

RECRUITMENT AND REWARDS 113

But Tudur is last seen in 1258, and none of his sons appears in the entourage of Llywelyn ap Gruffydd. In view of the fact that there survive documents of the two decades following 1258, which apparently indicate quite fully the composition of the ministerial group surrounding Llywelyn ap Gruffydd,[81] it may be that the family of Tudur ap Madog was out of favour with the prince. But, perhaps significantly, ministerial activity in the family revived with two of Tudur's sons after the Edwardian conquest. Tudur is known to have had a son called Gruffydd,[82] and post-conquest records have many references to a man or men of this name who held official posts. A Gruffydd ap Tudur was Edward I's constable of Dolwyddelan castle for some years after 1284,[83] and a man of the same name was *rhaglaw* of Tegeingl around the turn of the century,[84] and in a rather different context a Gruffydd ap Tudur was in the entourage of Madog ap Llywelyn during his revolt of 1294–5.[85] There is some reason to suppose that the last-mentioned Gruffydd is identical with the constable of Dolwyddelan and, possibly, with the *rhaglaw* of Tegeingl.[86] It also seems likely that these references relate to the son of Tudur ap Madog. Again, the Tudur Fychan who in 1284 was granted the township of Nantmawr for life,[87] and in 1290 was granted £20 by Edward I,[88] in both cases for his good service, was almost certainly a son of Tudur ap Madog; in 1305 he is stated as holding in Penhwnllys[89] in Anglesey, a vill held in 1352 by the co-heirs of *gwely Tudur ap Madog*.[90] The appearance of these men in the royal service so soon after the conquest suggests that they had long been favourable to Edward I. Gruffydd and Tudur Fychan may indeed have resided in the

---

[81] See, for example, *Littere Wallie*, pp. 77, 85, 99.
[82] Dwnn, op. cit., II, pp. 262–3.
[83] *Littere Wallie*, p. 186; *C. Chanc. R., Various*, pp. 324–5.
[84] R. Stewart-Brown (ed.), *Cheshire in the Pipe Rolls*, Appendix, *passim*.
[85] *Royal Commission on Ancient Monuments in Wales and Monmouthshire, Merioneth Inventory*, p. 40n.
[86] It is noteworthy that one of the other witnesses to the charter, Daykin Grach, had been keeper of the vaccaries of Dolwyddelan. This suggests that Dolwyddelan may have been a centre of the revolt: see J. Griffiths, art. cit., p. 312.
[87] *C. Chanc. R., Various*, p. 288.
[88] Ibid., p. 326.
[89] *Rec. Caern.*, pp. 219–20.
[90] Ibid., p. 73.

Perfeddwlad rather than in Gwynedd Uwch Conwy, at least after 1277, for men of these names are recorded as witnesses from Dyffryn Clwyd in the 1281 inquiry into the operation of the law of Hywel Dda; the family had certainly acquired land in this area by the late 1280s.[91]

THE FAMILY OF IORWERTH AP GWRGUNON

Iorwerth ap Gwrgunon (or Grugunon) was one of Llywelyn ap Gruffydd's prominent servants from the early 1240s, when Llywelyn was an exile in the Perfeddwlad, until the early 1260s.[92] The pedigrees mention a Iorwerth ap Gwrgunon ap Cyfnerth ap Rhufon,[93] and a tradition[94] associated with the family places Rhufon in the period of Owain Gwynedd (d. 1170) and associates him with the Conwy valley where, as will be seen, his descendants in the fourteenth century held extensive lands. Such a genealogy would accord well with the identification of the Iorwerth ap Gwrgunon of record sources as a descendant of Rhufon. According to a tradition recorded by Pennant[95] on the authority of Gruffydd Hiraethog, other members of the same line also served the princes. Pennant states that 'Rhufon's grandchild (and Madoc Goch ap Jorwerth ap Gwrgynon ap Cyfnerth, his son) were stewards to Llywelyn ap Jorwerth, Prince of Wales'. This story is clearly somewhat garbled: Madog Goch ab Iorwerth could not possibly have been a steward to Llywelyn ab Iorwerth. He may, however, be the Madog ab Iorwerth who appears in the entourage of Llywelyn ap Gruffydd in 1281. It is also possible that he was the Madog Goch who was Llywelyn's bailiff of Penllyn in 1282.[96] It may be assumed that Iorwerth ap Gwrgunon, the minister of Llywelyn ap Gruffydd, was the eponym of the privileged *gwely Iorwerth ap Gwrgen'* in Bodhunod, Twrcelyn.[97] One of the named co-heirs of that *gwely* in 1352 was Ieuan ap Hywel, who was also one of the co-heirs of *gwely*

---

[91] *C. Chanc. R., Various*, pp. 199–200.
[92] See Appendix II, *sub* Iorwerth ap Gwrgunon.
[93] Dwnn, *Heraldic Visitations*, II, p. 115.
[94] T. Pennant, *Tours in Wales*, ed. John Rhys (3 volumes, Caernarvon, 1883) III, p. 436.
[95] Ibid.
[96] See Appendix II, *sub* Madog Goch ab Iorwerth.
[97] *Rec. Caern.*, p. 68.

Cyfnerth ap Rhufon in Gwydir, Nantconwy.[98] In the survey of this last *gwely*, there is a reference to the special privileges enjoyed by the heirs of Gwrgunon ap Cyfnerth ap Rhufon. This may lend some support to Pennant's apparent claim that Gwrgunon was steward to Llywelyn ab Iorwerth, though there is no record evidence for this; Pennant may simply have written grandchild in error for great-grandchild. Iorwerth is the only son known to have been born to Gwrgunon, so that a grant of hereditary privileges to Iorwerth would in effect benefit all the heirs of Gwrgunon.

DESCENDANTS OF RHODRI AB OWAIN GWYNEDD

Rhodri ab Owain Gwynedd was one of the more prominent contenders in the struggle for supremacy in Gwynedd in the last quarter of the twelfth century from which Llywelyn ab Iorwerth emerged victorious.[99] A study of Rhodri's descendants reveals an apparent attempt by Llywelyn ab Iorwerth and his successors to integrate, within the ranks of their ministers, representatives of other branches of the princely house. As will be argued in a later chapter,[100] this almost certainly represents one of several such attempts.

Central to a discussion of the progeny of Rhodri ab Owain is the *History of the Gwydir Family*, written by Sir John Wynn (1553–1627).[101] Sir John's treatment of medieval Welsh history contains at least one patent fabrication,[102] as well as some obvious inaccuracies, as when he attempts to deal with wider matters than the fortunes of his family.[103] Again, much of what he wrote cannot be confirmed by reference to earlier extant sources, so that the usefulness of his work as a source for the study of events in the thirteenth century is *prima facie* doubtful. Yet, closer examination suggests that it may be used with some confidence, at least where specific questions of family history are concerned.

[98] Ibid., p. 11.
[99] Lloyd, *Hist. Wales*, II, pp. 587–90.
[100] See below, ch. VIII.
[101] Sir John Wynn, *The History of the Gwydir Family*, ed. John Ballinger (Cardiff, 1927).
[102] This is the fictitious account of Edward I's massacre of the bards, ibid., p. 24. See Ballinger's discussion in his Introduction, ibid., pp. xvii–xviii.
[103] Thus, the year of the death of Gruffydd ap Cynan is given as 1253 (ibid., p. 9) instead of 1200.

The prime purpose of the early sections of Wynn's narrative was to provide the lineage of his family as far back as Owain Gwynedd, through Thomas ap Rhodri ab Owain. The inclusion of information about Rhodri's other sons does not further this aim, so that there would seem to be no obvious reason for Wynn to falsify such information. He attributes to Rhodri three sons, Gruffydd, Thomas and Einion. For the existence of the last-named, a Welsh chronicle copied by Thomas Wiliems is Wynn's authority.[104] This chronicle, which seems to be lost, was clearly not one of the known versions of *Brut y Tywysogyon*, for the information which Wynn claims to have derived from it differs from the account of events given in these texts.[105] Nevertheless, the chronicle, whatever its nature and antiquity, can be shown to have been accurate enough for its authority to carry some weight.[106] And in the early years of the thirteenth century there appears in the witness-list to a charter of Llywelyn ab Iorwerth an Einion ap Rhodri, who attests after Llywelyn's *distain*, Gwyn ab Ednywain.[107]

The existence of Gruffydd ap Rhodri is well supported by record evidence. Included in Wynn's narrative is King John's grant in 1212 of three *cantrefi* in the Perfeddwlad to Owain ap Dafydd and Gruffydd ap Rhodri,[108] the grandsons of Owain Gwynedd, a concession made by John as a means of putting added pressure on Llywelyn ab Iorwerth during his attempt to crush the power of the prince. Two years later Gruffydd ap Rhodri is recorded as a captain of Welsh troops in the king's service.[109] Wynn knew nothing of Gruffydd's later career, but record evidence reveals a Gruffydd ap Rhodri as prominent in Llywelyn's service in the 1220s and 1230s.[110] The same man

---

[104] Ibid., p. 6.
[105] Wynn gives the chronicle copied by Wiliems as the source of his erroneous statement that 'in end llywelyn [sc. ab Iorwerth] killed his uncle david and all his posterityie at Conwey'. This does not appear in *Brut y Tywysogyon*.
[106] For example, in the case referred to in the previous note, though Wiliems's chronicle was wrong about the death of David and his son Owain, a battle was fought at the mouth of the Conwy in 1194, when Llywelyn and his allies inflicted a crucial defeat on David.
[107] See Keith Williams-Jones, 'Llywelyn's charter to Cymer abbey in 1209', *Jnl. Mer. Hist. Soc.*, III (1957), p. 57.
[108] Sir John Wynn, op. cit., p. 5.
[109] *Rot. Claus.*, I, p. 210.
[110] See Appendix II, *sub* Gruffydd ap Rhodri.

was one of the guarantors found by David ap Llywelyn for his observance of the terms of the Treaty of Gloucester in 1240. This man may well be identical with the English partisan of 1212 and 1214. The change of allegiance which such an identification involves may quite possibly have taken place in the twelve years before the later date and the first appearance of Gruffydd ap Rhodri in ministerial circles. It must be admitted that the evidence is only coincidental for identifying as grandsons of Owain Gwynedd the Gruffydd and Einion ap Rhodri who appear in the entourage of Llywelyn ab Iorwerth. But Rhodri was a very rare name at this period, its only identifiable bearers being members of the princely house, and to find otherwise unidentified men of these names in the correct chronological setting creates a strong possibility that they represent members of the progeny of Owain Gwynedd, at least one, and possibly both, of whom had entered the service of Llywelyn ab Iorwerth.

Thomas ap Rhodri, from whom Wynn traced his family's descent, does not appear in thirteenth-century records, but evidence for his existence is provided by genealogical texts earlier in date than Wynn's history.[111] Nothing is known of his career, nor is anything certainly established regarding that of his son, Caradog, though the latter may be Llywelyn's envoy of that name (no patronymic being given) who is noted in 1222 and 1237.[112]

Caradog had at least two sons, Gruffydd and Einion, who can have been little more than youths during the later years of the rule of Llywelyn ab Iorwerth. They are not seen amongst the ministerial group, comprising most of Llywelyn's prominent servants, which remained loyal to David ap Llywelyn in the troubled period that followed his accession, and Wynn records a tradition that the brothers were hostile to that prince, their hostility provoking a long struggle as a result of which they were forced to flee David's territories and seek safety at the court of Llywelyn ap Gruffydd in the Perfeddwlad.[113] That the story may contain a considerable element of truth is

---

[111] See, for example, Dwnn, *Heraldic Visitations*, II, pp. 6, 9.
[112] See Appendix II, *sub* Caradog.
[113] Sir John Wynn, op. cit., pp. 10–11.

suggested by a charter of Llywelyn ap Gruffydd to Ralph Mortimer (*ob.* 1246) which is undated but presumably was drawn up in the early 1240s;[114] in its witness-list is found the name of Einion ap Caradog. The appearance of Einion in these circumstances would certainly seem to indicate his disaffection with Prince David. Of the career of Gruffydd ap Caradog, nothing is known except that he was granted hereditary tenurial privileges with respect to lands at Bryncelyn[115] by Llywelyn ap Gruffydd, who may also have granted him the lands about Denbigh recorded in 1334 as having been held by his descendants.[116] For his part, Einion became one of Llywelyn ap Gruffydd's greatest ministers. He was one of the parties to the Scotto-Welsh agreement of 1258, and for almost twenty years after that date is regularly found acting in a ministerial capacity. Einion had two sons, Tudur and one whose name is unknown. There is no record of their acting as ministers to Llywelyn ap Gruffydd, but apparently both died in the service of Edward I.[117]

The extent to which Einion was integrated into the ranks of the ministerial groups surrounding Llywelyn ap Gruffydd remains unclear. They were certainly his regular companions; he equally certainly performed functions similar to theirs; and he married into the greatest of the ministerial families, for his wife was a daughter of Gruffydd ab Ednyfed Fychan.[118] In the post-conquest period, petitions by the heirs of Tudur ab Einion ap Caradog make it clear that Einion held extensive lands in Penychen, Eifionydd, where by tradition he held a *llys*, and Penyberth and Pennarfynydd in Llŷn.[119] Yet possession of these lands did not mark Einion out as obviously more amply endowed than many of his fellows in the prince's service. It is, however, uncertain whether Einion's lands were

---

[114] See Appendix I, no. 20, and Appendix IV.
[115] T. Jones Pierce, 'Lleyn Ministers' Accounts, 1350–51', *B.B.C.S.*, VI (1933), p. 266.
[116] *S.D.*, pp. 27–8, and compare ibid., pp. 278, 285.
[117] *Cal. Anc. Pet.*, pp. 339, 454.
[118] Ibid., p. 454, where Einion's daughters claim that their mother was the sister of Friar Llywelyn of Bangor. J. B. Smith, 'Welsh Dominicans and the Crisis of 1277', *B.B.C.S.*, XXII (1968), p. 354, demonstrates the probability that Friar Llywelyn was the son of Gruffydd ab Ednyfed Fychan.
[119] Sir John Wynn, op. cit., p. 7; *Cal. Anc. Pet.*, p. 339. See also Colin Gresham, *Eifionydd: A study in Landownership from the Medieval Period to the Present Day* (Cardiff, 1973), pp. 345–6.

RECRUITMENT AND REWARDS 119

wholly or in part a residue of territories once held by Rhodri ab Owain; the extent to which Einion benefited from the grants of territory and tenurial immunities which applied to other leading servants of the thirteenth-century princes is unknown. It will, therefore, be necessary to omit his case from a detailed analysis of the operation of the system of grants in reward for service.[120]

LOCAL OFFICIALS: EVIDENCE FROM THE PERFEDDWLAD

Only rarely is it possible to discover the names of the princes' officials of *cantref* and commote, whilst it is even more unusual to be able to identify a sequence of local officials in a given area. However, a remarkably full sequence of holders of the office of *rhaglaw* in the *cantref* of Rhos, together with less comprehensive information regarding the *rhaglawiaid* of Tegeingl, may be established, mainly from evidence cited before an assembly called by the bishop of St. Asaph in 1274 to establish the rights of the see in legal cases involving the distraints of goods of episcopal tenants.[121] The evidence brought forward to establish precedents in 1274 was dated by reference to the name of the contemporary prince and bishop, together with that of the prince's *rhaglaw* in the *cantref* in which each case was heard. The approximate date of the appearance of each *rhaglaw* may thus be fixed by comparing the known dates of the principate and episcopate of the men with whom he is linked in the references. The information thus gathered, together with that obtained from other sources, is set out below in Table 1.

Several of the *rhaglawiaid* of Dinorben may be identified with some confidence. Heilyn Sais, who held office at some

---

[120] For this analysis, see below, pp. 124-35.
[121] The proceedings of the 1274 assembly are to be found in a Latin text in NLW Peniarth MS. no. 231, pp. 45-52, and in a Welsh text ibid., pp. 116-25. The Welsh text lacks the whole of the introduction, describing the circumstances in which the inquiry was held: it begins abruptly in the middle of one of the cases being cited. On the other hand, the Welsh text contains in its later sections several cases not given in the Latin text. The question of which text represents, or is closest to, the original is difficult to resolve. The fact that each text has in some respects advantages over the other suggests that neither provides an accurate reflection of the original: the Welsh text has much fuller versions of the recurrent formulae, whereas in some cases in which the statements of the two texts clash, the Latin version would seem to be the more reliable: see the notes to Table 1 below.

time between 1225 and 1232, and Goronwy ap Heilyn, *rhaglaw* under Edward I in the period 1279–81, may be fairly clearly identified as son and grandson respectively of Cynfrig ab Iorwerth, and thus members of probably the most prominent descent group in the Perfeddwlad. Again, Rhys ab Ednyfed, *rhaglaw* at some time in the years 1268–74, was almost certainly the son of Ednyfed Fychan ap Cynfrig, as was Tudur ab Ednyfed, *rhaglaw* of Denbigh or Dinorben at some time between 1240 and 1245 and again between 1266 and 1268. Further, two of the four or five known *rhaglawiaid* of Rhuddlan (Tegeingl) were Cynfrig ap Goronwy, possibly a grandson of Cynfrig ab Iorwerth, and Hywel ap Gruffydd, grandson of Ednyfed Fychan. The local influence of the progeny of Cynfrig ab Iorwerth in the Perfeddwlad is thus apparent even from this limited number of examples.[122]

Amongst the *rhaglawiaid* of Dinorben there appear to be two representatives of another prominent Rhos family. Madog ab Iorwerth Goch is recorded as *rhaglaw* between 1240–5, 1266–8 and again between 1268 and 1276. He appears in the pedigrees as the great-grandson of Mabon Glochydd, whilst Bleddyn ap Madog, *rhaglaw* at some stage in the period 1240–5, may be the eponym of one of three *gwelyau* in Mochdref in Rhos, which are connected with descendants of Mabon. Bleddyn ap Madog seems to have been the grandson of Mabon, and thus the uncle of Madog ab Iorwerth Goch. The family of Mabon Glochydd thus seems to have been closely involved in the administration of Dinorben under the thirteenth-century princes. It may well be that this ministerial activity goes some way towards explaining the fact that the holdings of the descendants of Mabon Glochydd appear in the records of the fourteenth century as subject to an irregular pattern of immunities.[123]

---

[122] For a discussion of the progeny of Cynfrig ab Iorwerth, see above pp. 102–6. The known careers of all of the *rhaglawiaid* discussed here are set out in Appendix II *sub nominis*.

[123] For pedigrees relating to Mabon, see P. C. Bartrum, *Welsh Genealogies A.D. 300–1400* (8 vols., Cardiff, 1974), *sub nomine*. It is uncertain how far the pedigrees are complete or accurate: as will be seen, the fourteenth-century extents refer to a Dafydd ap Mabon, whose existence cannot be proved from the pedigrees. Descendants of Mabon Glochydd are found holding in *gwelyau* named after Iorwerth ap Madog, Bleddyn ap Madog and Gwion ap Madog, in Mochdref (Rhos) and Gloddaeth (Creuddyn). In the former vill the co-heirs of each *gwely*

Thus, both of these descent groups—that of Mabon Glochydd and that of Cynfrig ab Iorwerth—had an interest in the office of *rhaglaw* of Dinorben. This may point to an element of actual or potential conflict between them. The descendants of Mabon Glochydd seem to have enjoyed superiority in the period before the temporary English conquest of the area around mid-century. It is, however, extremely difficult to work out a satisfactory chronology of succession to office in Llywelyn ap Gruffydd's principate. The problem is caused by the fact that one of the two texts, Latin and Welsh, which record the proceedings of the 1274 assembly is corrupt, and quite possibly both are, so that it is difficult to establish whether Tudur ab Ednyfed was *rhaglaw* of Denbigh or of Dinorben, and whether some of the officials given only in the Welsh text are given their correct names and assigned to the correct administrative area. Again, it is a matter of guesswork whether Rhys ab Ednyfed's apparent spell as *rhaglaw* of Dinorben should be placed before or after the disgrace which he seems to have suffered in 1269, when he had to find sureties for his good behaviour towards the prince.[124] The evidence will, however, support some tentative conclusions. Madog ab Iorwerth Goch seems to have been a consistent and stalwart servant of Llywelyn ap Gruffydd: in particular, he did not pass into the service of Edward I after the war of 1277, but is known to have remained in the service of the prince.[125] In contrast, the descendants of Cynfrig ab Iorwerth seem more

were said to claim immunity from *amobr*, a claim which had been denied by the lords of the commote: *S.D.*, pp. 306–7. The tenants of the Gloddaeth *gwelyau* were said in 1352 to owe rent of half a mark, suit of court and service with the prince: *Rec. Caern.*, p. 1. Mabon's progeny also held in *gwely Wyrion Mabon* at Carnan in Menai, ibid., p. 81; *gwely Dafydd ap Mabon* in Porthaethwy, and Cerrigtegfan in Dindaethwy: ibid., pp. 77–8. One member of the progeny, Gruffydd ap Madog Gloddaeth, held in Nantfychan, Twrcelyn, in 1352: ibid., p. 69. The tenants of the Carnan *gwely* owed only suit to the hundred court and a rent of six pence a year; those of the Cerrigtegfan *gwely* owed suit of court and a rent of 6s. 1d. per year, and of the Porthaethwy *gwely* suit of court only, though their bondmen owed *cylch*. At Nantfychan, Gruffydd ap Madog Gloddaeth owed suit of court only. A further possible explanation of at least some of the immunities is the fact that the tenants of the Porthaethwy *gwely Dafydd ap Mabon*, who included men of the line of Madog ap Mabon, appear in 1352 as the custodians of the Porthaethwy ferry: indeed, the location of several of the holdings of this progeny suggest a connection with, or control of, ferries. Such activity may even provide the explanation for Mabon's curious epithet.

[124] See Appendix II, *sub* Rhys ab Ednyfed and Tudur ab Ednyfed.
[125] See Appendix II, *sub* Madog ab Iorwerth Goch.

flexible and their loyalty more suspect: the *rhaglaw* of Dinorben after 1277 was Goronwy ap Heilyn, a former servant of Llywelyn; and of Ednyfed's sons, the disgrace of Rhys has already been mentioned, whilst Tudur, who may have been *rhaglaw* at Dinorben, had for long in the 1250s and early '60s been an English prisoner. Indeed, two sources of potential conflict may have been related, namely, rivalry for office and the problem of loyalty to the prince in an area relatively susceptible to English attack.

Of the other *rhaglawiaid* mentioned in 1274, Goronwy ap Seisyll, who held office in Rhos at some period between 1225 and 1232, also appears in the entourage of Llywelyn ab Iorwerth in the early 1220s and in that of David ap Llywelyn in 1240.[126] A more interesting case is that of Gruffydd Gryg,[127] *rhaglaw* of either Denbigh or Rhuddlan (probably the latter) while Henry III controlled the area around mid-century, and who was made *magister satellitum* of Dyffryn Clwyd and Tegeingl in 1251 by the king. Gruffydd Gryg first appears in record sources as a member of the entourage of Llywelyn ap Gruffydd in the Perfeddwlad in 1243, but clearly did not follow his master when Llywelyn attempted to establish himself in Gwynedd Uwch Conwy. It may not be entirely fanciful to identify Gruffydd Gryg as the brother of Einion ap Caradog, discussed above:[128] Gruffydd ap Caradog is reputed to have joined Llywelyn ap Gruffydd in the Perfeddwlad in the early 1240s and at some stage he obtained lands in Ysgeibion in Ceinmeirch. Llywelyn ap Gruffydd is perhaps unlikely to have exercised sufficient power in the Perfeddwlad before 1245 to have been able to make such a grant, and after his seizure of power in Gwynedd Uwch Conwy it seems as though Gruffydd ap Caradog may have returned to his native area of Llŷn-Eifionydd. Perhaps the most likely grantor of lands to Gruffydd in Ceinmeirch was Henry III, especially if he was one of the king's local officials in the area of the Perfeddwlad.

Again, Cynfrig ap Goronwy appears as the *rhaglaw* in Rhuddlan of Henry III, Llywelyn ap Gruffydd and Edward I

---

[126] Ibid., *sub* Goronwy ap Seisyll.
[127] Ibid., *sub* Gruffydd Gryg.
[128] See above, pp. 117–19.

successively.[129] He seems to have been an official whose services were so valuable, and his loyalties so flexible, that he was insulated from the effects of changes in political supremacy. In a different category was Madog ap Maredudd ap Dafydd, *rhaglaw* of Dinorben under Henry III. He is almost certainly to be identified as the Madog ap Maredudd who appears as *magister satellitum* in Rhos after the English conquest of the area in 1277.[130] He never appears in the service of Llywelyn ap Gruffydd.

These last three cases, together with that of the descendants of Cynfrig ab Iorwerth, indicate the sort of support, amongst Welshmen capable of assuming official responsibilities, on which English kings might rely when they attempted to annex areas of Gwynedd. On the one hand were men whose attachment to office seems to have proved stronger than their loyalty to the prince, and on the other men consistently disaffected towards the prince of Gwynedd, as seems so have been the case with Madog ap Maredudd ap Dafydd.

It may finally be observed that in the very few cases in which the identity of local officials in other areas is known, the officials of Llywelyn ap Gruffydd seem to be drawn from descent groups which had probably already benefited from grants of hereditary tenurial privileges: this seems to follow a pattern seen in Rhos and Tegeingl, where the earlier *rhaglawiaid* frequently cannot be fitted into the genealogies of privileged families, whereas the *rhaglawiaid* of Llywelyn ap Gruffydd can be so located. Thus, the Dafydd ab Einion who was *rhaglaw* of Eiryoes in the Perfeddwlad in the early 1270s may be the descendant of Einion Ddu, brother of Ednyfed Fychan, who held lands near Dinorben.[131] Secondly, the *rhaglaw* of Arllechwedd Uchaf in the later years of Llywelyn ap Gruffydd and under Edward I was one Hywel ap Cyn': the patronymic is uncertain, possible forms being Cynfrig or Cynddelw.[132] It is known, however, that Hywel held lands in

---

[129] See Appendix II, *sub* Cynfrig ap Goronwy.
[130] *Registrum epistolarum Johannis Peckham*, II, p. 450.
[131] See *S.D.*, p. 228, which may give a truncated version of the genealogy: cf. Bartrum, op. cit.
[132] For Hywel ap Cyn', see Appendix II *sub nomine*. From *Cal. Anc. Pet.*, p. 397 and *C. Chanc. Warr.*, I, p. 323, it would appear that the patronymic is to be read as Cynfrig. In *C. Pat. R.*, *1343–45*, p. 231, it is recorded that amongst those who did homage to Prince Edward at Conwy in 1301 was a Hywel ap Cynfrig.

Bodfeio,[133] and it would not seem unreasonable to place him amongst the descendants of Iarddur ap Cynddelw, who held *gafael Iarddur* in Bodfeio.[134] Lastly, in 1305 Goronwy Grach petitioned Prince Edward,[135] claiming that he and his ancestors had held the office of *rhingyll* in the commote of Menai. From other sources it appears that Goronwy Grach held in Tregarnedd, a vill held by the descendants of Gruffydd ab Ednyfed Fychan.[136] Goronwy should thus probably be identified as a grandson of Gruffydd.

It may be that as the century progressed there developed a tendency for those families, which derived their privileged status from the rewards given in return for official service, to fill the more important and prestigious offices of commote or *cantref*. To this extent, the princes may have been successful in creating a tradition of service by their grants of land and tenurial privilege.

SOME CHARACTERISTICS OF THE MINISTERIAL ÉLITE

The term 'ministerial élite' will be used in the present context to denote men who were prominent in the princes' service and who had benefited from grants of hereditary tenurial privileges and, generally, of lands. It would be unwise to claim that the attributes and patterns of behaviour here ascribed to the élite necessarily characterize only that group: it is highly likely and in some cases evident, that men beyond the ministerial élite manifested characteristics similar to some of those set out below; but it does seem probable that the particular circumstances of members of the ministerial élite heightened those characteristics in their case.

---

[133] *Cal. Anc. Pet.*, p. 397.
[134] *Rec. Caern.*, p. 14. For the descent of a Hywel ap Cynfrig from Iarddur, see Bartrum, op. cit., and Dwnn, op. cit., II, p. 200.
[135] Ibid., p. 219.
[136] N. M. Fryde (ed.), *List of Welsh Entries in the Memoranda Rolls* (Cardiff, 1974), p. 17. It is interesting to note that Goronwy, in the course of a complaint that he is being charged too much rent for the demesne of Rhosfair, which he holds on lease with two other men, names one of them as Hywel ap Cynfrig: this looks like a reference to the *rhaglaw* of Arllechwedd Uchaf, for whom see above, notes 132–4. The episode suggests one of the means by which the ministerial élite was bound to the new régime after 1283. For the possession of Tregarnedd by descendants of Gruffydd ab Ednyfed, see *Rec. Caern.*, p. 169, and *Aspects of Welsh History*, pp. 183, 274; cf. *C. Chanc. R., Various*, p. 285.

Members of the families of Cynfrig ab Iorwerth, Iarddur ap Cynddelw, Gwalchmai ap Meilir, Llywarch ap Bran, Iorwerth ap Gwrgunon and Rhodri ab Owain Gwynedd account for almost all of the known prominent ministers of the princes' *curia* in the thirteenth century. It seems probable that the ministerial élite was numerically small, and that the addition of new members to its ranks was very restricted, for of those lines which are known to have enjoyed hereditary tenurial privileges as a result of service to a prince, none seems to have emerged later than the middle of the century. Thus, the first grants of hereditary tenurial immunity in the case of each family seem to have been made as follows: in the case of the family of Cynfrig ab Iorwerth, the first grant was made either to Cynfrig or to Ednyfed Fychan (*fl. c.* 1215–46); in the case of the line of Gwalchmai, the first grant seems to have been made to Einion ap Gwalchmai (*fl. c.* 1216–23); with the line of Iarddur ap Cynddelw the initial grant was possibly to Madog ab Iarddur or to Tudur ap Madog (*fl. c.* 1243–58); with the line of Llywarch ap Bran the first grant was made to Maredudd ab Iorwerth (*fl. c.* 1237–47); finally, in the case of the family of Iorwerth ap Gwrgunon, the initial grant was made either to Gwrgunon ap Cyfnerth or to Iorwerth ap Gwrgunon (*fl. c.* 1243–63).[137] For this phenomenon there may be sound economic reasons. There was clearly a limit to the number of descent groups which could be thus honoured by grants of hereditary tenurial privileges, as the renders from which immunity was granted constituted a vital part of the princes' revenues.[138] Yet once the practice was established, men entering the upper levels of the princes' service would presumably expect to share in it, or to receive some equivalent benefits. But as the century wore on, the princes' resources were alternately cut back by English conquests or stretched to meet the costs of military and diplomatic success.[139] These observations may account for the apparent lack of movement

---

[137] For discussion of these grants, see above, pp. 97–115.
[138] The extent of the privileges granted of course varied from one case to another. But the most general form of privilege enjoyed by the above-mentioned beneficiaries was immunity from all fiscal renders, and in some cases from military and other services. In the case of most holdings of Wyrion Eden', military service continued to be demanded: see above, pp 90–1.
[139] See above, pp xxx–xxxi.

into the ranks of the privileged families with a ministerial tradition, and raise the suspicion that the princes found it increasingly difficult to satisfy the aspirations of their more ambitious subjects.

Again, in view of the fact that hereditary privileges granted in respect of certain lands were shared by all of the grantee's co-heirs in those lands, whether they followed him in princely service or not, those who did so follow him might well have felt that some extra rewards were due to them in order to distinguish them from their non-ministerial co-heirs, and there is some indication that some such additional grants were made.[140] But the attempts of members of ministerial families to accumulate lands subject to hereditary privileged tenure could achieve only incomplete success as a result of the obvious limiting factors described above. A failure of the established reward system may help to account for the breaks, often coinciding with the later years of Llywelyn ap Gruffydd's principate, in the tradition of service of many ministerial lines. It is perhaps significant that in such cases the tradition of service generally revived in the immediate post-conquest period, when other sources of rewards became available.[141]

The extent to which ministerial lines were alienated from Llywelyn ap Gruffydd in his later years is difficult to gauge, but was apparently considerable. In some instances, a fall from favour of members of a ministerial line can only be guessed at, as in the case of the sons of Tudur ap Madog, and possibly, of those of Einion ap Caradog.[142] In others, there is firm evidence of alienation from the prince. The expulsion of Gruffydd ap Maredudd of the line of Llywarch ap Bran, after the internal strife of 1255, provides one example,[143] whilst the fluctuating relations with the princes of the members of the line of Cynfrig ab Iorwerth have been set out above.[144] Events were to show that such men could be ignored or rejected by a prince only at

---

[140] See, for example, the grants made by Llywelyn ap Gruffydd to Tudur ap Goronwy of the line of Ednyfed Fychan, and Hywel ap Cynfrig probably of the line of Iarddur, from the lands of his vill of Aber, cited in *Rec. Caern.*, p. 217.
[141] The most common of these alternative sources was the granting of an annual pension or the farming out of a bailiwick. For a list of such grants to favoured Welshmen in 1278, see *C. Chanc. R., Various*, pp. 175–6.
[142] See above, pp 113, 118.
[143] See above, pp 111–12.
[144] See above, pp 102–6.

his peril, for members of each of the lines which had fallen from ministerial status under Llywelyn ap Gruffydd can be identified as, or assumed to have been, English partisans in the period of the final decline of the prince, and many of them were prominent in post-conquest administration.

Writing of the reactions to the Edwardian conquest in Wales, and by implication in Gwynedd in particular, A. H. Dodd commented[145] as follows: 'That the *uchelwyr* hastened to come to terms with the conqueror—a point emphasized by Glyn Roberts—is not surprising. The only alternative was to see the whole administration turned over to aliens . . .' There is clearly a substantial core of truth in Professor Dodd's analysis, but it perhaps ignores the fact that a fairly large and important group of *uchelwyr*, including many of the ministerial élite, had come to terms with the English well before the final conquest. In some cases there may well have been a strong element of opportunism in their actions, a determination not to be caught on the wrong side; during and after 1277 the balance of power in Wales had fairly decisively tipped against the prince. Yet signs of stress in the relations between Llywelyn ap Gruffydd and members of the ministerial lines are visible before 1277, and in different circumstances from those of 1277-82. It can perhaps never be firmly established whether the English successes against Llywelyn ap Gruffydd after 1276 were the cause of, or the excuse for, the many known defections from the side of the prince, but it would surely be unrealistic to assume that loyalties which snapped so frequently and decisively in 1277 were entirely firm before then.

It would, of course, be unwise to attempt to quantify the importance of the various factors which resulted in the Edwardian conquest of Gwynedd, but clearly of no little significance was the fact that a large proportion of the ministerial élite was in league with Edward. The desertion of members of distinguished families must have weakened Llywelyn's prestige within Gwynedd, whilst Edward, with a body of native officials or members of ministerial lines at his disposal with which to replace those loyal to Llywelyn, could

---

[145] A. H. Dodd, 'Nationalism in Wales: A Historical Assessment', *Trans. Cymmr.*, 1970, p. 39.

more readily think in terms of permanent conquest rather than of punitive expeditions or a stronger assertion of overlordship. Whether the creation of the ministerial élite contributed to the rise of overmighty subjects is unclear, but it may be suspected that Llywelyn ap Gruffydd finally paid the penalty for the fact that a governing class had been created, notably by Llywelyn ab Iorwerth, and many of its members had subsequently, for whatever reasons, been excluded from government, whilst admission to its ranks had perforce been restricted.

It is noteworthy that during the thirteenth century the territorial basis of most of the component families of the ministerial élite became diffused within Gwynedd. The descendants of Cynfrig ab Iorwerth, whose homeland was in Rhos in the Perfeddwlad, were granted lands in Anglesey and other areas of Gwynedd Uwch Conwy, as well as lands in the eastern Perfeddwlad and beyond Gwynedd altogether. Iorwerth ap Gwrgunon, whose family lands were in the Conwy valley, received land in Anglesey; the family of Iarddur ap Cynddelw spread from Arllechwedd Uchaf to Anglesey, and perhaps to the Perfeddwlad; descendants of Gwalchmai moved over much of Anglesey and were given land in Llŷn, and a somewhat similar progress, within Anglesey and southwards to the mainland, was followed by the line of Llywarch ap Bran.[146] Such a process may have strengthened the principality in some respects: it may have produced ministers whose attitudes and preoccupations were less marked by localism than those of their predecessors; it almost certainly widened the geographical distribution within Gwynedd of prominent men and descent groups closely associated with one branch of the princely house, though the effects of this would of course be reversed by the alienation of such families from a prince. This process of territorial diffusion of ministerial lines had some interesting limitations, which will be analysed below in greater detail.

A final feature of the ministerial élite which deserves mention is the closeness of the links of its members with England. Such links might be formed in many ways. For example, a number of the princes' more prominent servants were fairly frequently

---

[146] This process is examined in detail below.

involved in diplomatic missions to England.¹⁴⁷ Records relating to contacts with the royal court and royal servants furnish the bulk of the evidence of diplomatic activity, but it is probable that the princes' ministers were also involved in many less systematically recorded contacts with the lords of the March. Again, the hostage system, used by the English government at times of ascendancy over the princes in order to secure their good behaviour, took many men who were, or who were to be, prominent officials into honourable captivity in England. Such men were sometimes joined in captivity by ministers taken by the English at times of open conflict.¹⁴⁸ These categories included men such as Einion Fychan, Goronwy ap Cynfrig, Tudur ab Ednyfed and Goronwy ap Heilyn. Further, as has been noted, members of ministerial lines who had fallen from favour in Gwynedd often found a refuge in England.

It is possible to suggest one important effect of the process outlined here. Contacts with England and the English are likely to have lessened the cultural differences between members of the ministerial élite of Gwynedd and their English counterparts: many of the princes' leading servants were, in short, becoming Anglicized: whilst the court poets were still picturing the English as the natural foe of the Welsh, members of the ministerial élite and their families were receiving lands and pensions from English kings, were sometimes serving the latter, and were marrying into the ranks of the English magnates.¹⁴⁹ Such a process of assimilation may have had as its consequence a decline in the significance of political frontiers towards England and her marcher satellites, and, correspondingly, a decline in the determination to maintain those frontiers by the class of Welshmen most affected.

---

¹⁴⁷ See, for example, Appendix II, *sub* Ednyfed Fychan, Einion Fychan, Dafydd ab Einion, Einion ap Caradog.
¹⁴⁸ For hostages, see ibid., *sub* Einion Fychan, Gorowny ap Cynfrig and Goronwy ap Heilyn. The most prominent of the princes' servants to be captured and detained was Tudur ab Ednyfed.
¹⁴⁹ For examples of men who received substantial gifts of land, money or other valuables from the English kings, see ibid., *sub* Ednyfed Fychan, Tudur ab Ednyfed, Goronwy ap Heilyn. For an example of marriage into the ranks of a prominent marcher family, see ibid., *sub* Rhys ap Gruffydd; such marriages merely followed the example set by the members of the princely house itself.

THE DISTRIBUTION OF LAND-GRANTS TO THE MINISTERIAL ÉLITE

It has already been suggested that the princes' practice of allocating parcels of land in widely diffused areas of Gwynedd to prominent ministers and their descendants may have helped to establish a degree of territorial cohesion within Gwynedd. Closer analysis of the known and probable allocations seems, however, to reveal a concentration of the territorial interests of leading families with ministerial traditions in a nucleal area of Gwynedd, comprising broadly those territories which were to constitute the post-conquest counties of Anglesey and Caernarvon. These lands were nucleal in the sense that they were those least susceptible to removal from the control of the lords of Aberffraw, and in the related sense that they formed the geo-military power-base of the princes of Gwynedd.[150]

Two broad distributional tendencies emerge. First, families whose previous settlements were outside the nucleal area were generally allocated lands within it. The principal descent group in this category is the progeny of Cynfrig ab Iorwerth, of the line of Edrud ap Marchudd. The patrimonial lands of Cynfrig ab Iorwerth lay in Rhos in the Perfeddwlad.[151] Members of his progeny were granted lands in Penrhyn in Creuddyn, Aber and Cororion in Arllechwedd Uchaf, Dinsylwy Rys, Trecastell, Erddreiniog and Penmynydd in Dindaethwy, Gwredog and Trysglwyn in Twrcelyn, Bodorfach in Llifon, Dindryfwl in Malltraeth and Tregarnedd in Menai.[152] Some lands in the Perfeddwlad (i.e., outside the 'nucleal area') acquired by Ednyfed Fychan, Cynfrig's son, were gained by purchase rather than by allocation.[153] It is not known how he acquired *gafael Ednyfed Fychan* in Llysaled in Rhufoniog Uwch Aled.[154] Tudur ab Ednyfed may have held lands in Tegeingl and Dyffryn Clwyd, which possibly stand as exceptions to the process described here; land which he held in Maenan, in Rhos, however, was granted to him by Henry III while the

---

[150] See above, pp. xiii–xv, and for a much fuller discussion, G. R. J. Jones, 'The Military Geography of Gwynedd in the Thirteenth Century', esp. p. 104.
[151] *S.D.*, pp. 261, 265, 295, 297, 303.
[152] *Rec. Caern.*, pp. 1, 12–13, 48, 53, 68–9, 72–3, 77, 169, 217.
[153] See Appendix I, no. 13.
[154] *S.D.*, p. 205.

latter controlled the Perfeddwlad.[155] Again, it appears that Tudur ab Ednyfed Fychan was granted land in Penllyn by Llywelyn ap Gruffydd; it is, however, significant that in 1281 Tudur's son, Heilyn, exchanged the lands in Penllyn for territory in Llŷn.[156]

Another minister whose patrimony lay partly outside and partly on the very edge of the nucleal lands, and who was allocated land inside these was Iorwerth ap Gwrgunon, a descendant of Cyfnerth ap Rhufon, whose patrimonial lands lay in the Conwy valley.[157] Iorwerth himself seems to have been granted land in Twrcelyn.[158]

It is difficult to establish where the patrimony of Mabon Glochydd, seemingly the founder of another ministerial line, was located: *gwelyau* apparently founded by his son, Dafydd, are found in Dindaethwy, and by his son, Madog, in Creuddyn and adjacent land in Rhos.[159] It is possible that no significant movement between extra-nucleal and nucleal land took place. As the line of Mabon is called in the genealogical sources one of the 'short lineages',[160] it is possible that both the Anglesey and the mainland territories represent original allocations to Mabon, possibly coinciding with his assumption of some sort of responsibility for the keeping of ferries.

In contrast with this first group, ministers whose patrimonial lands lay within the nucleal area were generally allocated supplementary lands in other localities within that area, but not beyond it. There are three principal descent groups affected by this pattern of allocation, the first being that of Einion ap Gwalchmai, whose patrimonial lands probably lay in Mall-

---

[155] For the Maenan grant, see *Welsh Assize Roll*, p. 261. That Tudur ab Ednyfed held Nant in Tegeingl and Llangynhafal in Dyffryn Clwyd is assumed by Glyn Roberts, *Aspects of Welsh History*, p. 253, but it seems that in the case of the latter vill at least he may have been mistaken: *Ruthin Court Rolls temp. Edward I*, ed. R. A. Roberts, Cymmrodorion Record Series, II (London, 1893), p. 44 (citing the record of a court of 1299: cf. p. 45), makes it clear that Llangynhafal was held by Gruffydd ap Tudur and Tudur his brother, who are certainly to be identified as sons of Tudur ap Madog ab Iarddur. In view of the fact that Gruffydd ap Tudur was particularly closely associated with Tegeingl (cf. *C. Pat. R., 1343-45*, p. 229), it may be that he was also the holder of Nant.
[156] *Rec. Caern.*, p. 211.
[157] See above, p. 104.
[158] *Rec. Caern.*, p. 68.
[159] See note 125 above.
[160] See P. C. Bartrum, 'Pedigrees of the Welsh Tribal Patriarchs', *N.L.W.J.*, XIII, p. 125.

traeth. Einion is not associated with Trewalchmai in that commote, where there are found instead three *gwelyau* associated with others of Gwalchmai's sons, but a *gwely Einion ap Gwalchmai*, significantly unprivileged, is found in nearby Lledwygan Llys.[161] If this represents Einion's share of the patrimony, he and his descendants seem to have received additional territories in Malltraeth, in Bodffordd and Trefddisteiniaid and, more significantly, in Bodwrog in Llifon, Trefor Fychan in Dindaethwy and Marchros in Cafflogion.[162]

The line of Iarddur ap Cynddelw seems to have been established in Arllechwedd Uchaf by the late-twelfth century.[163] Members of this line apparently received grants of land in Penhwnllys, Twrgarw, Trefraint, and Crymlyn in Dindaethwy, and on the mainland, it seems, at Pennant Gwernogof, the location of which is uncertain but was almost certainly in the nucleal area.[164] By the late-thirteenth century, Iarddur's great-grandson Gruffydd ap Tudur, is found holding land in Dyffryn Clwyd.[165] It is not, however, certain when this land was granted: it may be a post-conquest grant, for Gruffydd was a prominent figure in post-conquest administration, or it may represent a grant of the period before 1245, when Llywelyn ap Gruffydd seems to have held sway over part at least of Dyffryn Clwyd, and when Gruffydd's father, Tudur ap Madog, was in his entourage: thus the pattern of allocation is not necessarily broken in this case.

Third in this category is Maredudd ab Iorwerth, the grandson of Llywarch ap Bran. His patrimony was itself scattered, lying in Trelywarch in Talybolion, Porthaml in Menai, and Botandreg in Is Gwyrfai,[166] which indicates that the dispersal of settlements established by servants of the rulers of Gwynedd was not an innovation of the thirteenth

---

[161] *Rec. Caern.*, p. 44. One group of tenants, the descendants of Llywelyn ab Ednyfed, were not required to pay relief or *amobr*, an immunity which dated from the pre-conquest period.
[162] Ibid., pp. 31, 44, 55, 76. *Cal. Anc. Pet.*, p. 444. Cf. the discussion above, pp.
[163] See above, pp 99–100.
[164] For Pennant Gwernogof, see *C. Inq. Misc., 1216–1307*, p. 416, recording a grant made by David ap Llywelyn. As Tudur's sons contested the lands with the prior of Beddgelert, it may be presumed to have been near that place. For the other lands, see *Rec. Caern.*, pp. 73–7.
[165] See note 155 above.
[166] *Rec. Caern.*, pp. 19, 56, 81.

century. Maredudd ab Iorwerth received other grants of land in the commotes of Menai and Is Gwyrfai, at Ysgeifiog and Llanfair Prysgoel respectively,[167] while his son Gruffydd received grants of land in Bodwrdin in Malltraeth, Llysllew in Menai and Clegyrog in Talybolion.[168]

Finally, it is worth noting the case of the ministerial branch of the progeny of Thomas ap Rhodri ab Owain Gwynedd. The patrimony of his grandsons, Einion and Gruffydd ap Caradog, seems to have been in the Llŷn-Eifionydd region,[169] and there is evidence that they received further grants in that area.[170] Gruffydd at least also received lands in the Perfeddwlad, but these may well have been granted by Llywelyn ap Gruffydd in the period before 1245, when Einion certainly, and Gruffydd probably, formed part of his entourage. If Gruffydd remained in the Perfeddwlad after 1245, as has been tentatively suggested above, the grants may possibly have been made by Henry III.[171]

It is, of course, possible to place undue emphasis upon the pattern here described: it is of necessity impressionistic. Of the ministerial families or individuals who received grants in areas other than those in which their patrimonial lands lay, some may not have been considered for want of evidence. New settlements, even those subject to privileged tenure, may not always have been acquired by a prince's grant, but by some other means, such as purchase. The regularity of the pattern may be exaggerated by inadequacies of the evidence for some, but certainly not all, of the extra-nuclear areas.[172] There were, finally, periods in the thirteenth century when the extra-

---

[167] Ibid., pp. 19, 78.
[168] Ibid., p. 61, for Clegyrog. For the grants of all three, see *C. Inq. P. M.*, II, p. 327.
[169] See above, pp 118–19.
[170] See T. Jones Pierce, 'Lleyn Ministers' Accounts, 1350–51', *B.B.C.S.*, VI (1933), p. 266.
[171] See above, p 122.
[172] The earliest extent of Merionethshire containing details of the settlement pattern dates from 1422 and is printed in *Rec. Caern.*, pp. 261–92; by this time many of the signs which denote or suggest allocation of land by the native princes, such as remarks of jurors or unusual tenurial conditions, may have been obscured. The 1324 extent of Dyffryn Clwyd, translated and summarized in R. I. Jack, 'Records of Denbighshire Lordships, II. The Lordship of Dyffryn Clwyd in 1324', *Trans. Denb. Hist. Soc.*, XVII (1968), pp. 7–53, is not as full as might be wished in its treatment of the pattern of tenure, and there is no early extent of Tegeingl. The 1334 extent of Denbigh lordship (*S.D.*) is, however, very detailed.

134 RECRUITMENT AND REWARDS

TABLE 1. *RHAGLAWIAID* IN THE PERFEDDWLAD

(a) Dinorben

Rhaglaw	Date	Source
Maredudd ap Iorwerth	c. 1200–c. 1224	NLW Peniarth MS., no. 231, pp. 47, 116
Heilyn Sais	? 1225–? 1232	Ibid., pp. 48–9, 116–17
Cynfrig Wenkwys	? 1225–? 1232	Ibid., pp. 49, 117
Goronwy ap Seisyll	? 1225–? 1232	Ibid., pp. 49, 118
Bleddyn ap Madog	? 1240–? 1245	Ibid., pp. 50, 119
Madog ab Iorwerth Goch	? 1240–? 1245	Ibid., pp. 51, 119
Madog ap Maredudd ap Dafydd	? 1247–? 1254	Ibid., p. 124
Madog ab Iorwerth Goch	? 1266–? 1268	Ibid., pp. 52, 121–2
Madog ab Iorwerth Goch	? 1268–? 1276	Ibid., p. 123
Rhys ab Ednyfed	? 1268–? 1276	Ibid., p. 123
Goronwy ap Heilyn	? 1279– 1281	See Appendix 2, *sub* Goronwy ap Heilyn

(b) Dinorben or Denbigh

Rhaglaw	Date	Source
Tudur ab Ednyfed	? 1240–? 1245	Ibid., pp. 50, 119[a]
Tudur ab Ednyfed	? 1266–? 1268	Ibid., pp. 52, 121[a]

(c) Rhuddlan

Rhaglaw	Date	Source
Tegwared ab Ithel	? 1225–? 1232	Ibid., pp. 49, 118[b]
Maredudd ab Ieuaf *or* Madog ab Iorwerth	? 1225–? 1232	Ibid., pp. 50, 119[b]
? Gruffydd Gryg	? 1247–? 1254	Ibid., p. 124[c]
Cynfrig ap Goronwy	? 1247–? 1254	Ibid., p. 124
Cynfrig ap Goronwy	? 1256–? 1266	Ibid., pp. 51, 120
Hywel ap Gruffydd	1277	See Appendix 2, *sub* Hywel ap Gruffydd
Cynfrig ap Goronwy	? 1279– 1281	Ibid., *sub* Cynfrig ap Goronwy

NOTES TO TABLE 1

(a) The Latin text has Tudur as *rhaglaw* of Dinorben, the Welsh has *rhaglaw* of Denbigh. The cases concerned involve people from Llangernyw, which was within the area controlled from Dinorben, though there is no evidence that the offences took place in Llangernyw itself and it is perhaps significant that Llangernyw lies close to the border between Rhos and Rhufoniog.

(b) The Welsh version has Madog ap Iorwerth.

(c) Gruffydd's area of authority is not given in the text: but the fact that he was master-serjeant of Dyffryn Clwyd and Tegeingl in 1252 (see Appendix 2 *sub* Gruffydd Gryg), suggests that he may have been *rhaglaw* in one of those areas. Tegeingl is the more likely, as Dyffryn Clwyd was in the diocese of Bangor and thus less likely to be mentioned in a St. Asaph enquiry.

nucleal areas were withdrawn from the control of the lords of Aberffraw (one of the factors, indeed, which renders them 'extra-nucleal'), though these periods were broken by others in which the princes, having recovered those territories, were free to make grants of land within them.

In spite of the need to treat with caution the pattern of allocation of lands, and though there were certainly exceptions to it, the degree of regularity involved remains impressive. It seems to represent an effort, conscious or unconscious, to maximize the landed interests of men or families important in the princes' service, within the nucleal area of Gwynedd. Such a development, which cannot have taken place without at least the acquiescence of the princes, suggests accommodation to segmentary tendencies rather than an attempt to erase them.

Part 4
Problems of Political Control

Thus far, the emphasis has been placed upon the internal workings of the princes' governance; but it must be remembered that the princes and their officials did not represent the only source of power and authority within Gwynedd. There were, for example, recurrent attempts made by the kings of England to stamp their authority upon Gwynedd not only by securing the homage and fealty of the princes but also by taking homage, hostages, and oaths from the princes' leading subjects to perform specific obligations within Gwynedd for the benefit of the kings. Moreover, the princes had to share power and authority within Gwynedd with other individuals and groups over whom they sometimes exercised only partial control. It is the object of the following chapters to investigate the princes' relations with three such groups: other representatives of the princely house; the great ecclesiastics, the bishops and abbots of Gwynedd; and various forms of kin groups.

VIII

THE PRINCES AND THE LORDS OF THE PRINCELY HOUSE

The custom by which the territories of a ruler were partitioned on his death amongst his sons is well known to have been one of the principal factors in the instability which characterized Welsh political life in the centuries before the Edwardian conquest. It was a custom well grounded in the Welsh law of partible inheritance which, moreover, did not even distinguish between the rights of legitimate and illegitimate offspring.[1] Indeed, the distinction between legitimacy and illegitimacy drawn by, say, the church or by English lawyers had little meaning in the context of Welsh law and custom.

It is true that a ruler might designate one of his sons or other near kin as his principal heir, who was generally known in the thirteenth-century lawbooks as the *edling*. The legal texts state that the *edling* is to be the most privileged of the ruler's kin, the one who will rule after him.[2] But they lay down no principle according to which the *edling* is to be chosen, nor do the different texts agree on the limits of the kin relationship to the ruler within which a man is eligible for the position.[3] Even more important, *Llyfr Iorwerth* apparently betrays some uncertainty as to how many men might enjoy the dignity of an *edling* at any one time: after determining the *aelodau* of a king as his sons, nephews and cousins, the lawbook continues: 'some say that every one of these is an *edling;* others say that only he to whom the king gives hope and expectation is an *edling*.'[4]

---

[1] This was certainly the situation in the thirteenth century, for one of the grievances of the bishop and chapter of St. Asaph against Llywelyn ap Gruffydd in 1276 was that *hereditatem illegitime natis indistincte concedit*, though they added that this was no more than was customary: Haddan and Stubbs, *Councils*, p. 514.
[2] *Ior.*, 4. 1–2; *Bleg.*, 4. 17–18; 5. 15.
[3] According to *Ior.*, 4. 3–4, he is to be a son or nephew of the king; *Bleg.*, 4. 20–21, has a son or brother; *Llyfr Cyfnerth* (*W.M.L.*, 3) has a brother, son or nephew.
[4] *Ior.*, 4. 14–17.

This imprecision may reflect no more than a dispute over the precise meaning of *edling* amongst the thirteenth-century jurists; there still existed an apparently older word, *gwrthrych*, sometimes treated as synonymous with *edling*, but which may have had a more precise application.[5]

The fact remains, however, that even the designation of a single *edling* could not prevent the fragmentation of a ruler's territories, in order to provide for any other sons whom he might have. There are indications that a distinction was made in Welsh law between the descent of the kingdom and that of the kingship, or at least that the provisions of the law were such that they might permit such a distinction to arise. Within each of the three areas into which Wales was traditionally divided, that is Gwynedd in the north, Powys in the east and Deheubarth in the south, the lawbooks recognized a chief seat. In the case of Gwynedd, the chief seat was the court of Aberffraw in Anglesey, and whoever held Aberffraw was in theory overlord, if not direct ruler, of the whole of Gwynedd.[6] In fact the practical implications of overlordship might be virtually non-existent. Certainly the 'ground-plan' of governance did not assume the existence of a single directing force in Gwynedd, for the commote or *cantref*, itself a principality in miniature, with its own court and demesne land, its own integral organization for raising taxation and suppressing disorder, was the unit of division most frequently and naturally employed in any partition.[7] The wider principality was thus only an aggregation of smaller ones, and the lord of Aberffraw was often merely a *primus inter pares*. The lack of definition in the situation made it almost inevitable that internecine wars for 'ambition of governement', in Sir John Wynn's phrase,[8] should

---

[5] *Gwrthrych* is sometimes found with agent suffix-*iad*. *Gwrthrych* and *Gwrthrychiad* were certainly obsolescent at this period (cf. T. M. Charles-Edwards, 'The heir-apparent in Irish and Welsh law', *Celtica*, IX, pp. 185–86), but may have retained their significance amongst the jurists.

[6] See *L.T.W.L.*, pp. 207, 317 for the principal seats of Aberffraw and Dinefwr, and see Llywelyn ab Iorwerth's reference to Dinefwr in 1221: *ad quod tanquam ad caput Suthwalliae olim pertinebant dignitates totius Suthwalliae; Royal and other Historical Letters . . . Henry III*, I, pp. 176–7.

[7] See ch. IV, note 1 for the commote and the *cantref*, which also served as a unit of administration. J. G. Edwards, *The Normans and the Welsh March* (British Academy Raleigh Lecture, Oxford, 1957), has much to say on the commote as the basic unit of governance.

[8] *Gwydir Family*, p. 7.

be chronic. It is true, however, that the legal texts contain a provision by which a ruler's kin might be territorially settled without the damaging effects of a general partition of territory.

According to the picture (certainly over-simplified in thirteenth-century terms) drawn by the legal texts, Welsh society consisted of three types of men: kings, freemen and bondmen.[9] The privileges of the king's near kin, his *aelodau*, were to be reckoned in terms of those of the king until, say the lawbooks, they took land.[10] It is clear that this phrase may refer to more than a general partition of the kingdom, for the rule is elaborated as follows: a member of the king's near kin taking land should thenceforth be privileged according to the privilege associated with that land, unless it were bondland, in which case the privilege of the land itself would increase until it became free.[11] A process thus seems to have existed for the reduction of members of the ruling house to the status of freemen,[12] and it would not be surprising to find that such men were settled on privileged terms in order to distinguish them from freemen of less exalted birth and so induce them to accept the change in status. There is a little evidence of the application of such a process in Gwynedd.

In the Anglesey vill of Bodlew there were in 1352 three *gwelyau* whose eponyms were Philip ab Owain, Llywelyn ab Owain and Madog ab Owain.[13] The first two of these enjoyed immunity from almost all the renders and services associated with ordinary free tenure, and the third was subject to only a small annual rent. It may therefore be significant that Philip, Llywelyn and Madog are found in genealogical sources as three of the sons attributed to Owain Gwynedd.[14] And the heir of *gwely Philip ab Owain* in 1352 was Hywel ap Llywelyn,

---

[9] *L.T.W.L.*, p. 207; implied in *Ior.*, 42. 4–8, 11–19.
[10] *Ior.*, 4. 13–14, 24–8.
[11] Ibid., 4. 25–7.
[12] It should be noted that *Llyfr Iorwerth* makes the process applicable to the *edling* as well as other *aelodau* of the king. If one of these was settled at a commotal *llys*, then presumably his privilege became kingly. See however *A.L.*, XIV, X, 19, which glosses the term *gwahalaeth* as follows: *sef yw hwnnw mab arglwydd ny bo nac edling na phenteulu; o chymer dir gan arglwydd yr caethet y tir a gaffo ni bydd llei y ebediw na chweugeint: a llyna y gwr a freinia y tir.* The passage clearly rules the *edling* out of the process of taking land, but it is interesting that it makes that process a possible, but not a necessary, eventuality.
[13] *Rec. Caern.*, pp. 52–3.
[14] P. C. Bartrum (ed.), *Early Welsh Genealogical Tracts* (Cardiff, 1966), p. 97

OF THE PRINCELY HOUSE 141

who also held on privileged terms in Lledwigan Llan,[15] and who was almost certainly a direct descendant of Cynan ab Owain Gwynedd. It will be argued[16] that Hywel's father was settled in Lledwigan Llan by Llywelyn ap Gruffydd and it may be that he was similarly settled in *gwely Philip ab Owain*. Again, in the Eifionydd vill of Pennant, there was recorded in 1352 a *gwely Wyrion Cynan*,[17] which was also characterized by immunities from renders and services. Sir John Wynn recorded a tradition[18] that the Cynan in question was Cynan ab Owain Gwynedd. But even if this were so, no clue survives as to the conditions under which the *gwely* was established.

The *gwelyau* discussed above constitute cases in which one may possibly see the emergence of examples of tenurial immunities from the process of settlement of rulers' kin. It is clear, however, that the rule relating to such settlement does not envisage that privileges would normally be created for the benefit of rulers' kin settled on free land. If special tenurial conditions were not created, then the detection of such holdings in the extents is made extremely difficult: we are forced back on guesswork. For example, the founder of *gwely Einion ap Rhodri* in Gelleiniog in Anglesey (a vill which in 1352 still contained demesne of the prince and had once contained more)[19] may have been a son of Rhodri ab Owain Gwynedd.[20]

Fascinating though the conjectures are, it is impossible to say how far the thirteenth-century princes wished, or were able, to avail themselves of this peaceful method of eliminating dynastic rivals. It may have removed from the scene some of the descendants of Owain Gwynedd, but enough of them remained to produce the long series of dynastic conflicts which brought Llywelyn ab Iorwerth to power.

When Llywelyn set about establishing a foot-hold in Gwynedd in 1188, he was faced with one uncle, Dafydd ab Owain, holding the Perfeddwlad, another, Rhodri ab Owain,

---

[15] *Rec. Caern.*, p. 45.
[16] See below, pp. 143–7.
[17] *Rec. Caern.*, p. 39.
[18] Wynn, *Gwydir Family*, p. 7.
[19] *Rec. Caern.*, p. 52. See ibid., for one carucate remaining in demesne in 1352; Rhys W. Hays, *The History of the Abbey of Aberconway*, pp. 17–18, for Gruffydd ap Cynan's grant of lands in Gelleiniog to the abbey.
[20] Wynn, *Gwydir Family*, p. 6.

holding Anglesey, Nantconwy, Arllechwedd, Arfon and Llŷn, and two cousins, Gruffydd and Maredudd ap Cynan ab Owain, holding Eifionydd, Ardudwy and Meirionydd.[21] Profiting from his skill in diplomacy and warfare, and from the fortuitous death of some of his rivals, Llywelyn had made himself the direct ruler of most of Gwynedd by the start of the thirteenth century. His descendants were to dominate Gwynedd until the Edwardian conquest. It is proposed to examine two aspects of their domination: first, how far and by what means they were able to preserve their hold on Gwynedd in the face of the claims of other branches of the princely house, and secondly, how far they succeeded in developing a theory and practice of succession in the principality more conducive to political stability.

By the early years of the century, Rhodri ab Owain was dead, though as has been seen, he left sons;[22] Dafydd ab Owain, an old man, was an exile in England, but he too had a son, Owain.[23] Gruffydd ap Cynan had died in 1200, and in 1202 his son, Hywel, had driven Maredudd ap Cynan from his land of Meirionydd and then submitted to Llywelyn ab Iorwerth.[24] Hywel died in 1216, still a young man;[25] whether or not he had sons is unknown. Maredudd ap Cynan, who died in 1212, did have sons, Llywelyn Fawr and Llywelyn Fychan, and it is the problems presented by this line which will be examined first.

There is no sign that the sons of Maredudd ap Cynan were imprisoned or exiled during Llywelyn ab Iorwerth's principate. That they were not permitted to rule in Meirionydd is indicated by the fact that at some date before 1221 Llywelyn ab Iorwerth had clearly entrusted to his son, Gruffydd, the task of ruling Meirionydd and Ardudwy.[26] Thereafter, Llywelyn seems to have retained these areas in his own hands, and it may have been in the period 1221-40 that he secured his hold on

---

[21] See above, p. xvii.
[22] See above, pp. 116-17.
[23] Lloyd, *Hist. Wales*, II, p. 590.
[24] *BT*, *R.B.H.*, p. 184. Hywel may have ruled in Meirionydd as well as in part of his father's lands until his death. In 1215, however, he was accompanied on an expedition under Llywelyn ab Iorwerth by Llywelyn ap Maredudd ap Cynan, who may have ruled in part of Maredudd's former territory: ibid., p. 207. See also note below.
[25] Lloyd, op. cit., II, p. 647, note 180.
[26] See p. 152 below.

Meirionydd by the building of Castell y Bere.[27] But in 1241 Meirionydd was restored to Llywelyn Fawr and Llywelyn Fychan by the power of Henry III,[28] and some years later Llywelyn Fawr promised the king that *si forte contigerit quod in aliquo quod absit contra dominum regem racionabiliter fuero convictus, concedo pro me et heredibus meis domino regi et heredibus suis totam terram meam quod cedat ei et heredibus suis in dominicum* . . .[29] Meirionydd was clearly held immediately of the king by Llywelyn, who refers to his status as that of one of the king's Welsh barons: for a time, then, Meirionydd had been taken from the control of the prince of Aberffraw. Llywelyn Fawr's son, Maredudd, seems to have succeeded him as lord of Meirionydd and was in turn succeeded by his son, Llywelyn.[30] It was not until 1256 that Llywelyn ap Gruffydd succeeded in driving the lord of Meirionydd and some of his family into exile in England.[31] Llywelyn ap Maredudd received an English pension for some years after 1256, and died in somewhat mysterious circumstances in 1263.[32] It has been well established that the ejected lord of Meirionydd had a son, Madog, who was the leader of the Welsh revolt in north Wales in 1294–5 and who was imprisoned in the Tower of London after his capture.[33] It is also clear that Madog ap Llywelyn held the vill of Lledwigan Llan in Anglesey before his revolt.[34]

The little that has been certainly established about Madog's earlier career reveals that Llywelyn ap Gruffydd's action in 1256 had not solved the problem of the claim to Meirionydd of the line of Maredudd ap Cynan. For in 1277, during the first of Edward I's Welsh campaigns, Madog ap Llywelyn is recorded as receiving payments from the king,[35] and in the

---

[27] E. D. Evans, 'Castell y Bere', *Jnl. Mer. Hist. Soc.*, III (1957), p. 35.
[28] *BT, R.B.H.*, p. 236. By 1245, Llywelyn Fawr and Llywelyn Fychan had joined forces with David ap Llywelyn: see *Close Rolls, 1242–47*, p. 347.
[29] *Littere Wallie*, p. 14.
[30] Lloyd, *Hist. Wales*, II, pp. 709, note 92, and 718. Maredudd succeeded in 1251: see *Close Rolls, 1247–51*, p. 555.
[31] *BT, R.B.H.*, p. 246. Compare p. 144 below.
[32] For the pension, see *C. Lib. R., 1251–60*, pp. 436, 472, 506, and ibid., *1260–67*, pp. 4, 50, 72, 102. Llywelyn's death is noticed in *Annales Cambriae*, p. 100.
[33] See J. G. Edwards, 'Madog ap Llywelyn, the Welsh leader in 1294–95' *B.B.C.S.*, XIII (1950), pp. 207–10.
[34] E. A. Lewis, 'The Decay of Tribalism in North Wales' *Trans. Cymmr.*, 1902–3, p. 36.
[35] J. G. Edwards, art. cit.

following year Madog, appearing before the king's justices, claimed against Llywelyn ap Gruffydd the whole land of Meirionydd.[36] There is no record that judgement was given, just as there is none that Meirionydd was ever restored to Madog. It may be that his claims were used simply as a threat by Edward to ensure Llywelyn ap Gruffydd's good behaviour.

It is generally assumed that between 1256 and the Edwardian conquest, Madog ap Llywelyn was in exile in England.[37] But a different story was told in the course of an inquisition in the Meirionydd commote of Ystumanner in 1308.[38] It was recalled that a former lord, Llywelyn Fawr ap Maredudd ap Cynan, had four sons, Madog, David, Llywelyn and Maredudd, who ought to have succeeded him. But immediately after his death, Llywelyn ap Gruffydd, then prince of Wales, ejected the sons and seized the commote into his own hand, assigning to Madog and David certain small lands in Anglesey, but nothing to Llywelyn and Maredudd. This account is interesting in that it reveals that the jurors assumed that the lordship of Meirionydd was partible between the four sons, Madog, David, Llywelyn and Maredudd. However, their version of events in the mid-thirteenth century is clearly wrong at some points: Llywelyn Fawr ap Maredudd last appears in 1246;[39] the Llywelyn ap Maredudd driven from Meirionydd in 1256 was almost certainly his grandson. The pedigree of the line of Meirionydd thus seems to have been shortened by the omission of two generations. But in other respects the 1308 account seems quite trustworthy. Most significantly, its ascription of a brother called David to Madog ap Llywelyn finds confirmation in a grant made by Edward II in 1312 to Madog's son, Maredudd.[40]

Maredudd ap Madog was granted the Anglesey vill of Llanllibio, which had belonged to David ap Llywelyn and was in the king's hands by his death and the imprisonment of

---

[36] *Welsh Assize Roll*, pp. 238–9.
[37] See, for example, John Griffiths, 'The Revolt of Madog ap Llywelyn in 1294–95', *Trans. Caerns. Hist. Soc.*, 1955, p. 14.
[38] *C. Inq. Misc., 1307–49*, p. 14.
[39] R. F. Walker, 'The Anglo-Welsh Wars, 1216–1267' (unpublished University of Oxford D.Phil. thesis, 1954), p. 546, note 314, re-dating the submission of Llywelyn Fawr to Henry III printed in *Littere Wallie*, p. 14.
[40] *C. Fine R., 1307–19*, p. 135; *C. Pat. R., 1307–13*, pp. 461–2.

Madog ap Llywelyn, to whom it should descend by hereditary right. In all probability, then, David and Madog ap Llywelyn were brothers. This is of great interest in view of grants made by Edward I in 1284 to Gruffydd ab Iorwerth and his *nepos*, David ap Llywelyn, and to Elise ab Iorwerth and his *nepos*, Madog ap Llywelyn, by which they were allowed to hold all their lands in Wales by barony, as their ancestors had done.[41] The brothers Gruffydd and Elise ab Iorwerth are easily identified as descendants of Owain Brogyntyn of the ruling house of Powys. They were lords of Edeirnion.[42] But the names of their *nepotes* David and Madog ap Llywelyn are not to be found in any of the other records or pedigrees relating to this line. The only contemporary figures of these names whose ancestry might justify their being granted tenure by barony would seem to be the representatives of the line of Meirionydd. Indeed, as has been seen, Llywelyn Fawr ap Maredudd had promised fealty to Henry III in 1246 on condition that the king should maintain him and his heirs according to the uses and customs of Welsh barons.[43]

There was apparently no question of the restoration of Meirionydd to David and Madog ap Llywelyn in 1284; shortly before Edward's grant Meirionydd had been made into shire ground by the statute of Rhuddlan.[44] The only other lands ever recorded as being held by David and Madog are the two Anglesey vills of Llanllibio and Lledwigan Llan. By the time of the making of the 1352 extent, Llanllibio had passed out of the family, but Lledwigan Llan seems to have been held by Madog ap Llywelyn's son, Hywel, doubtless as a tenant at will or for life in view of his father's revolt.[45] And in 1352 Lledwigan Llan was held by one of the most comprehensive privileged tenures in Anglesey: Hywel owed no renders, no suit to the hundred court but only to one county court per year and, with his villeins, to the two great tourns of the prince.

[41] *C. Chanc. R., Various*, p. 286.
[42] See the genealogical table in Lloyd, *Hist. Wales*, II, p. 769.
[43] *Littere Wallie*, p. 14. See note 39 above.
[44] The draft version of the grants to Gruffydd and Elise and their *nepotes* seems to have been prepared in May 1284: see A. D. Carr, 'Some Edeyrnion and Dinmael Documents', *B.B.C.S.*, XXI (1965), p. 246. The Statute of Rhuddlan was issued over a month earlier: *Statutes of the Realm*, I, p. 55.
[45] *Rec. Caern.*, p. 45. See also Glyn Roberts, 'Biographical Notes: Madog ap Llywelyn', *B.B.C.S.*, XVII (1956), pp. 41-2.

In the scope of these immunities, at least, Hywel's tenure of Lledwigan Llan was comparable to Welsh barony.[46]

It is important to note that the immunities which Hywel enjoyed are not said in the extent to have resulted from the grant of an English ruler, though several other cases of privileged tenure are noted as having arisen in this way.[47] Again, Edward I's concession of tenure by barony was couched in terms of a confirmation of a pre-existing right with respect to lands already held rather than in those of an original creation. These considerations raise the interesting question of when Madog and David received their Anglesey lands. If the theory of the brothers' exile in England between 1256 and the Edwardian conquest is accepted, the lands can hardly have been given by Llywelyn ap Gruffydd, as was stated in the 1308 Ystumanner inquisition. The exile theory is, however, difficult to prove. There is a record of payments made in 1260 by Henry III to Llywelyn ap Maredudd, the expelled lord of Meirionydd, for himself, his wife, and his children.[48] But it may be that some, but not all, of Llywelyn ap Maredudd's children accompanied him into exile. Three brothers were attributed to Madog in 1308, and only he and David were said to have been provided for by Llywelyn ap Gruffydd. Secondly, as has been seen, Madog received payments from Edward I in 1277. But that was the year of Edward's first great assault on the prince of Wales, in the course of which many Welshmen came in to the king from Llywelyn ap Gruffydd's lands. Some of them were Anglesey men,[49] amongst whom may have been Madog ap Llywelyn. Finally, though it is by no means a conclusive point, it should be noted that no trace has come to light of an Edwardian grant of land in Anglesey to David and Madog ap Llywelyn. So, the strong

---

[46] That is not to say, of course, that Hywel's tenure *was* Welsh barony. The grants of barony to Madog and David ap Llywelyn in 1284 expressly allowed them free gallows, view of frankpledge, jurisdiction over all pleas pertaining to court baron and free hunting in their lands and woods. For other references to Welsh barony, see *C. Inq. P.M.*, VI, pp. 42 and 150.

[47] For immunities granted as compensation for post-conquest exchanges of territory with Edward I, see *Rec. Caern.*, p. 74.

[48] *C. Lib. R., 1251–60*, p. 506.

[49] For the case of Iorwerth Foel, see *Rot. Parl.*, I, p. 5, and for that of Gruffydd ab Iorwerth, *Cal. Anc. Corr.*, p. 74; see also J. B. Smith, 'Welsh Dominicans and the Crisis of 1277', *B.B.C.S.*, XXII (1968), pp. 353–7.

possibility at least must be admitted that the brothers had indeed been settled in Lledwigan Llan and Llanllibio by Llywelyn ap Gruffydd. By such a settlement the prince of Gwynedd may have hoped to keep potential rivals for the loyalty of part of his principality under surveillance, away from their natural followers in Meirionydd, whilst at the same time enabling them to live in reasonably dignified circumstances. His plan may well have succeeded in the case of David ap Llywelyn, but it is clear that Madog remained conscious of his rights to more than a vill in Anglesey.

Yet attempts by Llywelyn ab Iorwerth and his successors to integrate representatives of other branches of the princely house into the ranks of the privileged freemen were worth making, for if such princelings were allowed or forced to find refuge in England or in the lands of marcher lords unsympathetic to the prince, the consequences for the latter might prove embarrassing. In this context, Sir John Wynn's statement is noteworthy that Dafydd ab Owain Gwynedd, finally sent into exile in England by Llywelyn ab Iorwerth by the late 1190s,[50] 'often assayed by the power of the king of England to recover the principality against Prince Llywelyn his nephew'.[51] And there is recorded the grant of 1212 whereby King John conceded to Owain, Dafydd ab Owain's son, and to Gruffydd ap Rhodri, another of Owain Gwynedd's grandsons, three of the four *cantrefi* of the Perfeddwlad.[52] In addition, Owain and Gruffydd were to have Arfon, Arllechwedd and Llŷn, if they could win them from Llywelyn ab Iorwerth. The grant was made by John as a means of putting added pressure on Llywelyn as he attempted to curb the growing power of the prince. It is a good example of the threat to political stability in Gwynedd if the king of England were able to champion the interests of exiled or dissident members of the princely house. For John was not claiming for Owain and Gruffydd any more than was arguably their due in terms of Welsh custom. Owain and Gruffydd, however, received little substantial aid from John: the king's military offensive against Llywelyn ab Iorwerth had

---

[50] Lloyd, *Hist. Wales*, II, p. 590.
[51] *Gwydir Family*, p. 5.
[52] *Rotuli Chartarum*, I, p. 188; cf. *Gwydir Family*, loc. cit.

already petered out before he made his grant to them,[53] and events elsewhere soon distracted his attention from Wales. The grant of 1212 represents the last recorded intervention in the affairs of Gwynedd by the line of Dafydd ab Owain. Owain ap Dafydd had already been granted lands in England by John,[54] and may have preferred to live peacefully on his English manors than to fight for his inheritance in Gwynedd.

The rise in Gwynedd in the thirteenth century of a group of 'ministerial' families, enjoying hereditary privileges which distinguished their members from the bulk of freemen, provided the princes with a means of inducing members of other branches of their house to forego claims to rule over commotes or *cantrefi* in Gwynedd. There is indeed evidence that attempts were made to integrate such princelings within the ministerial group. Such a process, if successful, might lead to a restructuring of the ambitions of the families concerned. Assimilation seems to have gone furthest in the case of the descendants of Rhodri ab Owain Gwynedd who have been discussed elsewhere:[55] one of them was Gruffydd ap Rhodri, the beneficiary, in theory at least, of John's grant of 1212, and who was by the later 1220s sufficiently reconciled to Llywelyn's supremacy to serve among his officials. A further example is provided by a study of the descendants of Cadwaladr ap Gruffydd, the brother of Owain Gwynedd, and in this case the limitations inherent in the process are more clearly apparent. It is first necessary to establish the genealogical connections.

For several years after 1246, Owain and Llywelyn ap Gruffydd were faced with a certain Maredudd ap Rhicert, who asserted, with the support of Henry III, a hereditary right to the *cantref* of Llŷn.[56] A letter written by Owain and Llywelyn to King Henry in 1249–50 reveals that Maredudd

---

[53] Lloyd, *Hist. Wales*, II, p. 639.
[54] Ibid., p. 616, note 26.
[55] See pp. 115–19 above.
[56] *C. Pat. R., 1232–47*, p. 496. For Maredudd's pension from Henry III, see *C. Lib. R., 1245–51*, and ibid., *1251–60*, *passim*. Though Maredudd was granted the pension on the grounds that he was disinherited on the king's account, the following note makes it clear that he still had lands in Llŷn in 1249–50. The references to Maredudd's being disinherited probably indicate that he did not hold all of the lands to which he laid claim.

refused to give any renders or services to the brothers.⁵⁷ In short, his claim was to something like princely status in Llŷn. There is no immediately apparent source for such a claim. But there are references to a Rhicert who was prominent in Llŷn some years earlier, and who may prove to have been Maredudd's father. An inquisition of 1323 heard that Rhicert ap Cadwaladr, *rhaglaw* of Dinllaen, one of the commotes of Llŷn, had once been paid a sum of money from the lands of Haughmond abbey, in Nefyn.⁵⁸ It is clear from the account given in the course of the inquisition that Rhicert had been *rhaglaw* at some time during the first third of the thirteenth century,⁵⁹ a point broadly confirmed by the appearance of Rhicert ap Cadwaladr in the witness lists of two of Llywelyn ab Iorwerth's charters: the first, relating to the Penllyn lands of Basingwerk abbey, was issued before 1230, and the second, relating to the lands in Llŷn of Haughmond, apparently was issued shortly after 1230. The appearance of Rhicert amongst the witnesses to the latter charter confirms his identification as an official in Dinllaen.⁶⁰ Again, in 1281, Llywelyn ap Gruffydd granted to Heilyn ap Tudur some lands in Dinllaen which had belonged to a Rhicert ap Cadwaladr.⁶¹

It is noteworthy that the original grant of land in Nefyn to Haughmond abbey had been made by Cadwaladr ap Gruffydd ap Cynan,⁶² brother of Owain Gwynedd, who is indeed credited in the genealogies with a son called Rhicert.⁶³ Just as there is no chronological difficulty in the way of an identification of Maredudd ap Rhicert as the son of Rhicert ap Cadwaladr, *rhaglaw* of Dinllaen, so there is none in the way of identifying the latter as the son of Cadwaladr ap Gruffydd ap Cynan. A

---

⁵⁷ *Royal and other historical letters . . . Henry III*, II, pp. 65–66 and *Cal. Anc. Corr.*, p. 33, where it is shown that the letter was written in the period October 1249 to June 1250.
⁵⁸ *C. Inq. Misc., 1307–49*, p. 166.
⁵⁹ The payment had been made to Rhicert ap Cadwaladr in the time of Llywelyn ab Iorwerth. But by 1232 (eight years before Llywelyn's death), Rhicert had been succeeded as *rhaglaw* by Philip ap Gilbert.
⁶⁰ See Appendix II *sub* Rhicert ap Cadwaladr.
⁶¹ *Rec. Caern.*, p. 211. For the location of Nant Gwrtheyrn, see Melville Richards, *Welsh Administrative and Territorial Units* (Cardiff, 1969), p. 163.
⁶² Edward Owen (ed.), *A Catalogue of the Manuscripts relating to Wales in the British Museum* (London, 1900–22), II, p. 451.
⁶³ P. C. Bartrum, 'Achau Brenhinoedd a Thywysogion Cymru', *B.B.C.S.*, XIX (1961), p. 208.

line of descent running Maredudd ap Rhicert ap Cadwaladr ap Gruffydd ap Cynan, of course, explains Maredudd's claim to princely status, and if his father had been entrusted with the government of at least part of Llŷn, and if his grandfather had had sufficient interests in the area to endow Haughmond with lands there, an explanation is provided of why Llŷn was the region in which he asserted his rights.

It is interesting that Rhicert ap Cadwaladr seems to have been *rhaglaw* over part of the land in which his father had exercised lordship. It is tempting to think that in such a case the grant of the office of *rhaglaw* was little more than a recognition, in terms of a formal position within the prince's government, of a *de facto* supremacy in a commote or *cantref* exercised by a scion of the ruling house. Yet it seems clear that Llywelyn ab Iorwerth had no intention of allowing the office of *rhaglaw* to become vested in the stock of such princelings. For though Maredudd ap Rhicert seems to have been a member of the entourage of David ap Llywelyn in 1229,[64] he clearly did not succeed his father as *rhaglaw* of Dinllaen, or if he did, he failed to retain his hold on the office: by 1232 the *rhaglaw* was apparently one Philip ap Gilbert,[65] of whom nothing more is known.

During the principate of David ap Llywelyn, Maredudd ap Rhicert apparently continued to act in a ministerial capacity, for he appears as one of a group of envoys sent by David to Henry III in 1245. But he certainly took advantage of the weakness of Owain and Llywelyn ap Gruffydd in the years after 1246 to attempt a restoration of the eminence of his line. The circumstances of his death are not certain: as a royal partisan, who claimed to have lost lands in the king's service, Maredudd received a pension from Henry III in the years 1247–57.[66] There is no mention of him after the latter date. It may be that the cessation of the pension represents an economy on Henry's part, but it is ominous that in 1257 Llywelyn ap Gruffydd was well launched on the career of conquest which was to make him the dominant figure in Wales; royal power

[64] See Appendix II *sub* Maredudd ap Rhicert.
[65] See notes 58–9 above.
[66] See note 64 above.

in Wales was at a low ebb, and royal partisans were vulnerable. Maredudd ap Rhicert may have met a violent end.[67]

In general, however, a salient feature of the treatment accorded by Llywelyn ab Iorwerth and his successors to members of other lines of the princely house is an absence of the mutilation and killing which characterized Welsh political life before the thirteenth century,[68] and which indeed continued to characterize it in some areas beyond Gwynedd.[69] If this reflects an attitude deliberately adopted by the princes, then it may not be entirely fanciful to see as at least one factor in it the influence of the monastic and religious orders which became firmly established in Gwynedd in the thirteenth century.

In contrast to the eremitical style of the ancient Celtic monasticism, the new orders, especially the Cistercians at Cymer and Aberconwy, were closely bound up with the political life of the principality.[70] Their members, even their houses and granges, occupied a central place in many aspects of the princes' governance. Though purely a matter for speculation, it is possible that the relatively lenient treatment accorded by the princes to the members of the line of Meirionydd may not be unconnected with the fact that both Cymer and Aberconwy owed their early endowments to the sons of

---

[67] It is possible, however, that Maredudd escaped and that he may have held lands beyond Gwynedd itself, though whether he held these simultaneously with his Llŷn lands or came into possession of them many years later, after 1277, is a matter for pure speculation. Cadwaladr ap Gruffydd had been associated with Ceredigion in the mid-twelfth century, and Maredudd may have made good a claim to lands south of the Dyfi. West Wales ministers' accounts for the closing years of the thirteenth century refer to the land of Mareduc ap Richard let to farm, and in 1304–5 refer to the part-payment of a fine of £200 from Maredudd Fychan, son of Maredudd ap Rhicert (Ricard): if the fine was for lands, they were clearly extensive ones. See Myvanwy Rhys, *Ministers' Accounts for West Wales, 1277–1307* (Cymmrodorion Record Series, XIII, 1936) pp. 68–9, 384–6.
[68] For twelfth-century attempts, made within a framework provided by Welsh law, to resolve potential conflicts, see above pp. 140–1.
[69] *BT*, *R.B.H.*, *passim*. Cf. the influence of 'wise men' in preventing recourse to violence at critical points in the history of Gwynedd in the thirteenth century, as in the case of Llywelyn ab Iorwerth's confrontation with his son Gruffydd in 1221 (ibid., p. 220) and in that of the arrival in Gwynedd of Owain ap Gruffydd in 1246 (ibid., p. 240).
[70] See pp. 33–4 above.

Cynan ab Owain Gwynedd.[71] A measure of reluctance to indulge to the full in the traditional brutalities toward real or potential rivals for power is also apparent in the internal politics of the line of Iorwerth ab Owain Gwynedd: imprisonment rather than slaying or mutilation was the weapon usually adopted when more peaceful stratagems failed or proved unattractive.[72]

Llywelyn ab Iorwerth expended much energy and employed much diplomatic skill in the latter half of his principate in attempting to ensure that clear overlordship within the principality that he had built up should be enjoyed after his death by his legitimate son, David, at the expense of the older but 'illegitimate' Gruffydd. The radicalism and consistency of Llywelyn's attitude to the succession can, however, be overstated. It is frequently assumed that Llywelyn's policy was one of total disinheritance of Gruffydd. Yet clearly this was not the case at all times, for Llywelyn seems to have made several attempts to provide Gruffydd with a share of his lands. Gruffydd had been settled in Meirionydd and Ardudwy before 1221, for in that year Llywelyn was forced to eject him from that area as a result of his harsh rule.[73] Gruffydd was restored to favour by 1223, when he is recorded in *Brut y Tywysogyon* as leading forces for his father in Ystrad Tywi;[74] and he was quite clearly given lands once more, this time beyond Gwynedd, for there survives a charter issued by him to Strata Marcella abbey,[75] by which he made extensive grants and confirmations in Powys Wenwynwyn. In 1228 Gruffydd was imprisoned by his father for six years, but on his release in 1234 he was granted half of Llŷn and later received most of

---

[71] Gruffydd ap Cynan ab Owain was an early benefactor of Aberconwy: a charter of his granting Gelleiniog to the abbey is the earliest recorded donation to that house: see H. Ellis (ed.), *The Register and Chronicle of the Abbey of Aberconway*, Camden Miscellany I (London, Camden Society, 1843) pp. 7–8. In the 1209 charter of Llywelyn ab Iorwerth to Cymer, for which see Keith Williams-Jones, 'Llywelyn's Charter to Cymer, 1209', *Jnl. Mer. Hist. Soc.*, III (1957), pp. 54, 57, Gruffydd ap Cynan, Maredudd ap Cynan and Hywel ap Gruffydd are all named as previous benefactors.

[72] The exception to this general rule is the alleged involvement of Dafydd ap Gruffydd in the plot to kill Llywelyn ap Gruffydd in 1274, for which see *Littere Wallie*, pp. 136–8.

[73] *BT, R.B.H.*, p. 220.

[74] Ibid., p. 224.

[75] E. D. Jones, N. G. Davies, B. F. Roberts, 'Five Strata Marcella Charters', *N.L.W.J.*, V (1947), pp. 53–4.

Powys Wenwynwyn and the remainder of Llŷn.[76] It is interesting that Llywelyn should repeatedly attempt to settle Gruffydd in territories which had been either held by the line of Cynan ab Owain (i.e., Llŷn, Ardudwy, Meirionydd), representatives of which were still alive and might attempt to re-establish themselves, or had been seized from Gwenwynwyn of Powys, whose sons might also assert their rights to lordship. The available evidence, then, suggests that Llywelyn ab Iorwerth intended to make some fairly substantial territorial provision for Gruffydd, albeit in potentially 'difficult' areas; Gruffydd was to be a lord, but not a prince.

It is, of course, true that the enunciation of the principle that a legitimate rather than an illegitimate son should always be a ruler's principal heir represents a possible modification of Welsh custom which, as depicted in the legal texts, knew no rule according to which an *edling* was to be chosen from the ruler's *aelodau*. Yet the principle of the primacy of legitimate over illegitimate sons was, so far as is known, only put forward by Llywelyn on two occasions, both in the early 1220s: once in a letter to Pope Honorius III in 1222, and once on an earlier occasion when the prince apparently issued a proclamation against the enjoyment by illegitimate sons of equal rights of inheritance with legitimate sons.[77] The proclamation was said to have been issued with the consent of King Henry, and by the authority of Pandulf the legate and the archbishop of Canterbury. Llywelyn may well have reasoned that the men with whom he was dealing on these occasions, the pope, the legate, the archbishop and the councillors of Henry III, might be more likely to lend support to a plan to establish David as the principal heir if that plan were expressed not in terms of Welsh custom (which, possibly, it might have been), but in terms of custom and law which were bound to be acceptable to them: that is, in terms of canon law and feudal custom. It remains uncertain on what grounds, if any, Llywelyn justified

---

[76] In 1238, David ejected Gruffydd from his lands in Powys, leaving him in possession of Llŷn: *BT*, *R.B.H.*, p. 234.
[77] The gist of Llywelyn's letter to Honorius can be guessed from the papal reply, in *Cal. Papal Letters*, I, p. 87, which also supplies the evidence for Llywelyn's earlier proclamation, which was quite possibly issued in May 1220, as suggested by F. M. Powicke, *King Henry III and the Lord Edward*, p. 630, note 1.

to his fellow Welshmen his choice of David as his principal heir.[78]

David's complete dispossession and imprisonment of his brother after Llywelyn ab Iorwerth's death in 1240,[79] however necessary it may have been in order to establish his control of Gwynedd proper, certainly played into the hands of Henry III. For the king was able to use David's manifest break with Welsh customary law as one of the means of rallying Welsh support against the prince of Gwynedd. For a consideration of six hundred marks, promised by Gruffydd's wife, Senena, and backed by a formidable array of marchers and Welsh lords acting as pledges, Henry undertook, *inter alia*, to allow Gruffydd *iudicium curie sue secundum legem Walensem ei et heredibus suis . . . super porcione que eum contingit de hereditate que fuit predicti Lewelini patris sui et quam predictus David ipsi Griffino deforciat*.[80] It is significant that it was not, for Henry, a question of replacing David by Gruffydd; his policy depended on adhering to the idea of partibility. Thus, Gruffydd, if his claim so a share of the *hereditas* should succeed, was to keep a firm peace with David *super porcione que eidem David remanebit de hereditate predicta*.[81] In the event, Gruffydd simply passed out of David's prison into Henry's. The king presumably found him of more use in captivity, where he could be held as a threat to David, than at liberty in Gwynedd.[82]

David's power in the early 1240s seems to have been curbed further by the appearance in Dyffryn Clwyd of one of Gruffydd's four sons, Llywelyn, who almost certainly acted as a magnet for dissident elements in David's territory. It seems highly probable that Llywelyn acted, at least during the period 1241–3, with the connivance of Henry III and the active support of Ralph Mortimer.[83] There are signs that Henry's

---

[78] It is uncertain whether the 1220 proclamation was intended to influence opinion inside or outside Wales.
[79] For a detailed reconstruction of the sequence of events after Llywelyn's death, see G. A. Williams, 'The Succession to Gwynedd, 1238–47' *B.B.C.S.*, XX (1964), pp. 393–413.
[80] *Littere Wallie*, p. 52.
[81] Ibid.
[82] There were persistent reports from witnesses before the Edwardian laws commission of 1281 that some kind of plea between David and Gruffydd actually took place before Henry III: *C. Chanc. R., Various*, pp. 193, 195, 198, 203.
[83] For detailed analysis, see Appendix IV.

policy towards David had begun to falter even before the death of Gruffydd in 1244. He had delayed long over the issue of Gruffydd's inheritance in Gwynedd; his continued detention of the latter must have drained much of the dynamic from his exploitation of the idea of partible inheritance. It is clear that many of the Welsh lords began to realize that Henry himself was proving a significant threat to Welsh custom. The death of Gruffydd whilst attempting to escape from the Tower of London enabled David to present his opposition so Henry III in a new light, and to rally the Welsh lords to his side.[84]

Amongst those who went over to David's side was Llywelyn ap Gruffydd; he was the only one of his father's four sons in Gwynedd at the time of David's death in 1246. Llywelyn was not able to derive much profit from this situation, however, for his brothers were in the hands of Henry III, who thus possessed the means for a return to the policy of divide and rule. Owain, Llywelyn's elder brother, had been maintained at Chester by the king since the death of Gruffydd ap Llywelyn, clearly as a means of drawing support away from Prince David.[85] It is noteworthy that in November 1244 Owain promised fealty to Henry III on pain of losing the two *cantrefi* which had been committed to him, and all the other lands which were his by hereditary right.[86] Even though Henry's patronage of Owain was not immediately useful, it probably enabled the latter to gather the nucleus of supporters and to make the contacts within Gwynedd which almost certainly underlay his entry into the principality on David's death and his subsequent partition of most of Gwynedd above Conwy with Llywelyn.[87]

The counsel of wise men which, according to *Brut y Tywysogyon*, persuaded the brothers to divide Gwynedd,[88] confirmed once more the vitality of the principle of partible inheritance as applied to the lands of the principality. A third

---

[84] See G. A. Williams, art cit., p. 409. It is perhaps significant that the Welsh chronicles refer to David's anger at the death of his half-brother: *BT, R.B.H.*, p. 238; *Cronica de Wallie*, p. 13. For the Welsh chiefs who rallied behind David, see *Close Rolls, 1242-47*, p. 347. For the appearance in 1245 of Tudur ap Madog, one of Llywelyn ap Gruffydd's followers, as an envoy of David, see *C. Pat. R., 1232-47*, p. 461.
[85] *C. Pat. R., 1232-47*, p. 446.
[86] *Littere Wallie*, p. 16.
[87] *BT, R.B.H.*, p. 240.
[88] For the territorial division, see below pp. 156-8.

brother, Rhodri, had clearly been released into Gwynedd[89] by King Henry in 1248, though it is uncertain whether or not he received a share of the inheritance, and the fourth brother, Dafydd, was in Gwynedd by 1252, when he appears as lord of Cymydmaen in the Llŷn peninsula.[90] Little progress has hitherto been made in establishing the allocation of lands on which the brothers agreed. A study of the pattern of grants of lands and privileges made by them may help to resolve the problem.

Sir John Lloyd pointed out[91] that Llywelyn ap Gruffydd's grant to Ynys Lannog priory in 1247 may be taken as evidence that Llywelyn held Dindaethwy, the commote in which lay the lands granted. It is thus interesting that a man prominent in Llywelyn's entourage in the years before and after 1246, Iorwerth ap Gwrgunon, was the eponym of a privileged *gwely* recorded in 1352 in the commote of Twrcelyn,[92] adjacent to Dindaethwy. If, as seems quite possible, Llywelyn granted these lands to Iorwerth soon after he was established as lord of part of Gwynedd Uwch Conwy, then it follows that he held Twrcelyn as well as Dindaethwy.

In the case of Owain, an inquisition taken shortly after the Edwardian conquest revealed that he had made grants to Gruffydd ap Maredudd of the line of Llywarch ap Bran in Bodwrdin and Llysllew.[93] Bodwrdin lay in Malltraeth commote and Llysllew in Menai: Owain thus probably held these two south-western commotes of Anglesey. His hold on Menai is confirmed by a record of a grant made by him to the priory of Beddgelert of land in Tre'r beirdd in that commote.[94] In view of the location in Malltraeth of the *llys* of Aberffraw, it is reasonable to suppose that Owain held the whole of Aberffraw *cantref*, the other constituent commote of which, Llifon, seems to have contained no *llys*, and so to have been dependent on *llys Aberffraw* as its administrative centre. There is no clear

---

[89] *Littere Wallie*, p. 19.
[90] *Rec. Caern.*, p. 252.
[91] Lloyd, *Hist. Wales*, II, p. 707, note 76. See also Appendix I, no. 22.
[92] *Rec. Caern.*, p. 68.
[93] *C. Inq. P.M., Ed. I*, II, p. 327.
[94] See Appendix I, no. 35, and reference cited. C. A. Gresham, *Eifionydd*, Cardiff, 1973, p. 63, assumes that the grant, by *dominus Owain*, was made by Owain Gwynedd. This is most unlikely.

indication as to which of the brothers held the northern commote of Talybolion, but for the remainder of Anglesey an east-west pattern of partition emerges, with Llywelyn holding the eastern and Owain the western commotes.

There are clear signs that the east-west division was reproduced on the mainland, though as far as the extent of territory held was concerned, the division seems to have been far from equitable. Once more Sir John Lloyd supplied an initial clue when he observed that Llywelyn's grant in 1247 to Basingwerk abbey of lands in Penllyn indicates that this *cantref* formed part of his share of Gwynedd.[95] The grant to Basingwerk was dated at Bangor,[96] which would appear to place Llywelyn in control of Arfon. This is confirmed by a grant made by Llywelyn to Beddgelert priory, mentioned in a list, drawn up after the Edwardian conquest, of grants to the house, the texts of which have not survived.[97] The grants are undated as they appear in the list, but may well have been arranged in chronological order: the grant of Llywelyn ap Gruffydd in question is placed before one made by Owain, almost certainly Llywelyn's brother, which must have been made by 1255. The fact that Owain's grant was of land in Menai and not in the vicinity of the priory itself suggests that he did not control the latter area. Llywelyn is recorded as having granted to Beddgelert the land of the sons of Ithel of Pennardd, and an exchange of lands in 1269 between the prior of Beddgelert and the prince[98] refers to the land of the sons of Ithel ap Dafydd in Pennardd in Arfon: this must be the Pennardd located near Clynnog Fawr, so that Llywelyn apparently held Arfon above and below Gwyrfai. Again, in a grant similarly placed in the list before Owain's gift, Llywelyn is recorded as giving to Beddgelert land in Trefan and Llecheiddior in Eifionydd, which indicates that he also held the commote to the south of Arfon.

For Llŷn the situation is a complex one. It is noteworthy that Dafydd ap Gruffydd appears in 1252 as lord of Cymydmaen, the commote at the tip of the peninsula. According

---

[95] Lloyd, *Hist. Wales*, II, loc. cit.
[96] Appendix I, no. 23.
[97] Appendix I, nos. 32-9.
[98] Ibid., no. 33.

to the *Cronica de Wallia*, Dafydd was *dux familie* to Owain,[99] and so it is quite probable that he was provided with Cymydmaen from lands originally held by Owain. In view of the fact that the lands to the east of Llŷn seem to have been held by Llywelyn, it would be natural to assume that the whole of the *cantref* had been consigned to Owain. However, in a letter to Henry III written about 1249[100] Owain and Llywelyn together complained of Maredudd ap Rhicert, a magnate associated particularly with Llŷn, *qui de magnis terris quas tenet de nobis non respondet nobis in aliquo*. It is uncertain, then, whether both Owain and Llywelyn held in Llŷn, or whether Maredudd's lands extended beyond Llŷn into territory which was certainly in the lordship of Llywelyn. It may perhaps be assumed that Llywelyn took the lands to the east of his territories of Arfon and Eifionydd, namely, the *cantref* of Arllechwedd and the commote of Ardudwy: any other allocation would have produced a strangely discrete distribution of territory.[101]

In the first few years after 1246, Owain and Llywelyn seem to have avoided facing the problem of which of them should be accorded primacy. Owain's name precedes that of Llywelyn in the documents issued by them, and his position might have been the more prestigious: he seems to have held Aberffraw, and it may be significant that the priory of Ynys Lannog

---

[99] *Rec. Caern.*, p. 252; *Cronica de Wallie*, p. 14.
[100] *Royal letters* . . . *Henry III*, II, pp. 64–6.
[101] The division of Gwynedd Uwch Conwy north of Meirionydd suggested here would explain many things. It makes readily understandable the resentment felt by Owain towards Llywelyn. Though initially possessed of a large (and perhaps the larger) part of the highly productive areas of Llŷn and Anglesey, Owain seems to have been obliged to relinquish some of his lands to make provision for Dafydd: no corresponding grant by Llywelyn is known and, in view of Dafydd's adherence to Owain in 1255, it is unlikely that one was made. Again, Llywelyn's possession of the upland areas, whilst not a source of great revenue for him, gave him the prestige of extensive territories and, with all, or most, of the stone castles in the joint lordship, a great strategic superiority. An acceptable context is also provided for the battle of Bryn Derwin in 1255, at which Llywelyn defeated and captured Owain and Dafydd. Bryn Derwin is to be located mid-way along the border between Arfon and Eifionydd: that is, within Llywelyn's territories. That this was the case is suggested by the chroniclers' accounts: *Cronica de Wallia*, p. 14, states that Owain and Dafydd attacked Llywelyn, and were for a time successful in disinheriting him, a statement which may be construed to mean that Llywelyn lost territories in his brothers' initial onslaught. *Brut y Tywysogyon*, too, has Llywelyn awaiting his brothers' attack on Bryn Derwin, thus seeming to place him on the defensive. It may well be that Owain and Dafydd succeeded in wresting from Llywelyn his lowland territories, but were defeated when Llywelyn gave battle on ground of his own choosing on the edge of his mountain stronghold.

thought it well to obtain his confirmation of a charter granted by Llywelyn ap Gruffydd.[102] On the other hand, the styles used by the brothers give no indication of any difference of status between them: thus, in 1251 they refer to themselves as *Owenus et Lewelinus filii Griffini quondam principis, heredes Norwallie*.[103] The king had, it seems, successfully confused during these years the issue of the succession to the principate with that of the inheritance of the lands comprised within the principality of Gwynedd.

After 1252, however, the need to provide a suitable lordship for Dafydd precipitated the problem of leadership.[104] Henry III seems to have attempted to stabilize the situation and to preserve the power vacuum in Gwynedd by calling the brothers before his justices to settle their disputes,[105] but in 1255 Llywelyn defeated and imprisoned Owain and Dafydd.[106] That Llywelyn realized how far his victory had negated royal policy in Gwynedd is seen from his subsequent efforts to placate the king.[107]

No broad principles of succession to the principate emerged from the establishment of supremacy in Gwynedd by Llywelyn: there is no sign that he claimed to rule by designation, election or the grace of God. Nor did Llywelyn succeed in turning to his own advantage the confusion regarding what distinction, if any, was to be made between succession to the principate and inheritance of the patrimony of the princely house; it is indeed somewhat misleading to refer to an attack by him on the custom of partible inheritance, as applied to the principality lands, for by many of his actions Llywelyn confirmed rather than refuted the validity of that concept. Thus, in 1272 he induced his brother, Rhodri, to quitclaim to him all his rights in Wales in return for a promised payment of one thousand

---

[102] See Appendix I, no. 24.
[103] *Littere Wallie*, p. 160.
[104] Llywelyn's agreement with Gruffydd ap Madog of Bromfield in 1250, for which see *Littere Wallie*, p. 148, may reveal early signs of a rift between the brothers, and certainly betokens an independent attitude on Llywelyn's part.
[105] *Close Rolls, 1253–54*, pp. 109–10: letters of January 1254 to Llywelyn, Dafydd and Owain, which make it fairly clear that the cause of friction was the poor relationship between Llywelyn and Dafydd.
[106] *BT, R.B.H.*, p. 246; cf. *Cronica de Wallia*, p. 14.
[107] *Close Rolls, 1256–59*, p. 104: reference to gifts offered to the king by Llywelyn in the matter of his brothers.

marks.¹⁰⁸ The terms of the agreement are revealing, for Rhodri quitclaimed *totum ius, hereditatem et clamium quod habemus et habere debemus in terris et possessionibus apud Norwalliam vel alibi per totum principatum Wallie*. The phrase leaves little doubt that the quitclaim merely made an exception to the accepted rule of partibility. It is generally assumed that Rhodri had been long in Llywelyn's prison before the making of this agreement, but there are signs that this was not the case. A short chronicle of thirteenth-century affairs in Wales,¹⁰⁹ possibly drawn up by one of Peckham's clerks, says of Llywelyn that *Rotherum quartum fratrem suum quem obsidem posuerat liberare postmodum non curavit*. Now, it certainly seems that Rhodri had been released by Henry III in 1248,¹¹⁰ when his future good conduct was guaranteed by Owain and Llywelyn. But the Cheshire accounts for the years 1250–54 contain payments for the whole of that period to a custodian and three hostages, one of whom was Rhodri ap Gruffydd.¹¹¹ It thus looks as though at some stage Llywelyn handed Rhodri back to the king. This may explain why Rhodri is not mentioned in the chronicles or the records in the context of the 1255 crisis. The possibility also arises that the initiative in the 1272 agreement came from Rhodri, perhaps at the instigation of the royal government. In 1277, with only fifty of the promised thousand marks having been paid, Rhodri claimed before the king's justices his share of Gwynedd, a claim which he only abandoned when Llywelyn agreed to carry out the provisions of the 1272 agreement.¹¹² Again, only a year after his imprisonment of Owain and Dafydd in 1255, Llywelyn released the latter and made over to him large areas of Gwynedd.¹¹³ The view has been advanced that the cause of Dafydd's defection to the English in 1263 was that he had not been given a share of the Perfeddwlad (specifically Rhufoniog and Dyffryn Clwyd) and of Gwynedd Uwch Conwy;¹¹⁴ but there exists a charter granted by Dafydd

---

¹⁰⁸ *Littere Wallie*, p. 85.
¹⁰⁹ J. W. Willis-Bund, 'Archbishop Peckham', *Trans. Cymmr.*, 1900–1, p. 83.
¹¹⁰ *Close Rolls, 1247–51*, p. 45.
¹¹¹ *Cheshire in the Pipe Rolls*, p. 98.
¹¹² *Welsh Assize Roll*, pp. 238–9; *C. Close R., 1272–79*, pp. 506–7. Rhodri had served Edward I in the war of 1277: *Welsh Assize Roll*, p. 50, note 2.
¹¹³ *Annales Cestrienses*, ed. R. C. Christie (Lancs. and Cheshire Rec. Soc., London, 1887), p. 72.
¹¹⁴ Ralph Maud, 'David, the last Prince of Wales', *Trans. Cymmr.*, 1968, pp. 47–8.

in 1260 which reveals that he was lord of at least Dyffryn Clwyd and part of the Llŷn peninsula.[115] It is thus instructive that the Chester annalist believed that Dafydd defected from Llywelyn because he wished to liberate his brother, Owain.[116] According to the *Cronica de Wallia*, Dafydd had served Owain as his *dux familie*,[117] presumably, that is, as his *penteulu*, and it may indeed be that there was a bond of affection between the two brothers.[118] If Dafydd had succeeded in liberating Owain, a further division of Gwynedd would almost certainly have resulted.

Nor did the English kings fail to exploit the opportunities offered to them to limit Llywelyn ap Gruffydd's power by the persistence of the idea of the partibility of Gwynedd. Even the Treaty of Montgomery in 1267, which Henry III negotiated from a position of some weakness, contained traces of the principle of partition in operation: Dafydd ap Gruffydd was to be permitted by Llywelyn to regain the lands which he had held before he went over to the king in 1263. And that Henry III intended that Dafydd should receive his lands not as the gift of Llywelyn but as his share of the *hereditas* is indicated by the subsequent provision of the treaty: if Dafydd should not be content with the lands which he had held before 1263, his portion should be increased according to the judgement of five named Welsh magnates, *quibus si David noluerit esse contentus, quod voluerit petet, de quo secundum leges et consuetudines Wallie iusticia sibi fiat, uno vel duobus presentibus quos domino regi transmittere placuerit ad videndum que et qualis iusticie sibi fiet*.[119] There can be little doubt that the *leges et consuetudines* which Henry and his advisers had in mind embraced the custom of partible inheritance.

A decade later, in the Treaty of Conwy, negotiated under wholly different circumstances from that of Montgomery, the rights of Llywelyn's brothers in his now severely truncated

---

[115] J. C. Davies, 'A Grant by David ap Gruffydd', *N.L.W.J.*, III (1943), pp. 29–32.
[116] *Annales Cestrienses, ut supra*, p. 82.
[117] *Cronica de Wallia*, p. 14.
[118] It is entirely consistent with the picture built up here that in 1277 Edward I stated that Dafydd had petitioned him as earnestly on Owain's behalf as on his own: *Littere Wallie*, p. 103.
[119] Ibid., p. 3. The subsequent settlement is recorded in NLW Peniarth MS no. 231, pp. 67–9.

principality were underlined anew. Edward I accepted Llywelyn's hold on Gwynedd Uwch Conwy for the prince's lifetime, but it was explicitly stated that the land thus held included territory due to his brother Dafydd by hereditary right.[120] Owain was to be allowed to claim his portion of the inheritance by legal process,[121] and was apparently settled by Llywelyn in Llŷn: it would appear that Owain did not live to enjoy his renewed lordship for very long.[122] Finally, the Conwy treaty stipulated that the claims of Rhodri were to be met.[123]

It is clear that throughout the thirteenth century right up to the eve of the final conquest of Gwynedd, the kings of England were able to use the idea of partible inheritance as a means of dividing Gwynedd against itself, for they were able to intervene in the affairs of the principality in support of a practice believed to be reasonable and just by a large number of Welshmen.[124] The inability of the princes to define the pattern of inheritance within the princely house in a way at once acceptable in terms of Welsh custom and compatible with the development of a strong unitary principate in Gwynedd thus imposed a recurrent limiting factor upon their achievements.

It should not be overlooked, however, that with regard to many aspects of their relations with lesser members of their house, the achievements of the princes were considerable; their extent is suggested by some interesting developments in political terminology during the thirteenth century. The distinction between the impartible *regnum*, or principate, and the partible patrimony is an important one, and is made in

---

[120] *Littere Wallie*, p. 120.
[121] Ibid., p. 119: *Item dictus Lewelinus Owenum fratrem suum liberabit sub hac forma quod aliqui ex parte domini regis venient et ipso liberato dabunt ei opcionem aut quod componat cum fratre suo predicto et in formam certam pacis gratis consenciat et postmodum supplicet domino regi quod illam pacem approbet et confirmet, aut quod ponat se in custodia domini regis donec secundum leges et consuetudines Wallie in loco ubi transgressus est de eo fuerit iudicatum et si sic liberatus fuerit repetat hereditatem suam si sibi viderit expedire et coram rege firmabitur via quam eligere voluerit de predictis.* Owain seems to have followed the first of the alternative procedures offered to him.
[122] *BT, R.B.H.*, pp. 266–8. But see the grant by Llywelyn ap Gruffydd to Heilyn ap Tudur of lands in Dinllaen in 1281, given in *Rec. Caern.*, p. 211. Either the settlement had not yet been made or Owain was already dead.
[123] *Littere Wallie*, p. 121.
[124] *Welsh Assize Roll*, p. 247: a vigorous statement of the need for an equitable partition of lands amongst a ruler's sons, made by Owain and Gruffydd, sons of Gruffydd Maelor II.

many of the legal texts.[125] Nevertheless, the practice of partitioning the patrimony was not, as has been seen, without implications for the concept of *regnum:* hence the notion that all lords of commotes or *cantrefi* wielded kingly power.[126] Dr. Richter has suggested [127] that an important step towards the creation of a unitary polity in Wales had been taken in the late-twelfth century with the emergence of the title of *princeps*, of which, he claims, there was recognised to be but one bearer in each of the principalities of Gwynedd, Powys and Deheubarth. But that seems to over-simplify the situation. In a letter apparently written by a group of Welsh rulers before 1202,[128] we find one prince of Gwynedd—Llywelyn ab Iorwerth—two of Powys and four of Deheubarth. This letter was quite probably drafted by Giraldus Cambrensis, who may have obscured the true nature of the designation *princeps*, but in his Cymer charter of 1209 Llywelyn ab Iorwerth refers to his fellow princes of a few years previously,[129] and in his late-twelfth-century Aberconwy charter the same ruler styles himself *princeps totius Norwallie*,[130] a title which, while embodying an assertion of overlordship in Gwynedd, does suggest that it might be possible to be prince of something less than the whole of north Wales.

The situation with regard to the various concepts of *principatus* in the late-twelfth and early-thirteenth centuries was probably somewhat confused. It did, however, become clearer

---

[125] A brief but extremely telling discussion of this point is to be found in J. B. Smith, 'Owain Gwynedd', *Trans. Caerns. Hist. Soc.*, 1971, p. 13. As Mr. Smith points out, the legal rules relating to succession in the royal house are couched in terms which assume that the kingship was indivisible. Yet the fact of frequent partitions of the kingdom or principality is undeniable, and as has been seen (note 6 above), the legal texts imply, and certainly do not preclude, the partibility of the kingdom. It has also been seen (p. 138 above), that *Llyfr Iorwerth*, with its uncertainty over how many men should be allowed the status of an *edling*, may betray confusion in the minds of the jurists over the question of the partibility of the kingship itself.
[126] See note 7 above.
[127] Michael Richter, 'The Political and Institutional Background to National Consciousness in Medieval Wales', in T. W. Moody (ed.), *Nationality and the Pursuit of National Independence* (Belfast, 1978), pp. 37–55.
[128] Haddan and Stubbs, *Councils*, p. 431; *Giraldi Cambrensis Opera*, III, pp. 244–6: cf. Lloyd, *Hist. Wales*, p. 627 n. 73.
[129] Keith Williams-Jones, 'Llywelyn's Charter to Cymer Abbey in 1209', *Jnl. Mer. Hist. Soc.*, III (1957), p. 54.
[130] *Rec. Caern.*, p. 147. For discussion of the date of this charter, see Appendix I, no. 1.

as the thirteenth century progressed, as the title of *princeps* became restricted in its use at any one time to a single man in Gwynedd, and, indeed, in Wales. Other members of the ruling house in Gwynedd, and of the old royal lines of Powys and Deheubarth confined themselves to the use of *dominus*, a development which quite clearly reflects the political successes of the Llywelyns. This process would explain the increasing use in thirteenth-century legal texts of the term *arglwydd* (lord) which replaces *brenin* (king) in many contexts. Professor Dafydd Jenkins attributes this process of replacement largely to the growth in thirteenth-century Gwynedd of franchisal jurisdiction exercised by privileged laymen such as Wyrion Eden.[131] This may be so, but there is no evidence that Wyrion Eden and the like exercised wider jurisdictional rights than those normally enjoyed by freemen who held tenanted lands. The claims to more extensive jurisdictional rights in the mid-fourteenth-century *Quo Warranto* proceedings were all put forward by descendants of old ruling houses, holding by Welsh barony.[132] It would seem reasonable to assume that the compilers of the legal texts were becoming more aware during the thirteenth century of a distinction between one type of ruler, the prince, who might still be referred to conservatively as *brenin*,[133] and the other type of ruler, a lesser member of the ruling house within Gwynedd or a representative of one of the former kingly lines beyond Gwynedd, whom it was now unrealistic to denote as a king, and who appears instead in the texts as *arglwydd*.

Whatever had been the case in the twelfth century, there is evidence that in the thirteenth relations between princes and lords were being worked out with rigour. The retention of their lordship by the *domini* was, it seems, dependent on their carrying out obligations formally entered into, namely, the performance of homage, and the maintenance of fealty to the prince. As the century progressed, increasing numbers of documents survive to record the establishment of precise obligations owed by lords.

---

[131] Dafydd Jenkins, 'Kings, Lords and Princes: the Nomenclature of Authority in Thirteenth-Century Wales', *B.B.C.S.*, XXVI (1976), pp. 451–62, esp. pp. 460–1.
[132] See the *Quo Warranto* proceedings in *Rec. Caern.*, referred to by Dafydd Jenkins, loc. cit.
[133] Or even as *mechdeyrn*, for which see *L.T.W.L.*, p. 207.

to the prince.[134] These obligations were clearly a matter for negotiation, and thus varied with political circumstances, but amongst them are found agreements to render money to the prince, to give up hostages, and to take part, under specific circumstances, in military expeditions. It is hard to resist the conclusion that a qualitative change, in the direction of a clearer definition of obligations, was being worked in the relations between the princes and the lords of Gwynedd and, indeed, of the lands beyond Gwynedd.

---

[134] See *Littere Wallie*, pp. 45, 104–5, 111–13; NLW Peniarth MS. no. 231, pp. 67–9.

IX
PRINCES, BISHOPS AND ABBOTS

It is the aim of the present chapter to examine the extent to which the princes were able to enlist the goodwill and co-operation of the leading ecclesiastics within Gwynedd in the governance of the principality. The acquiescence of these men in princely policy was of great importance: many leading ecclesiastics had considerable territorial influence by virtue of the estates of their see or abbey,[1] and might in addition be members of prominent families.[2] Again, in the event of conflict between the prince of Gwynedd and the king of England, the latter was generally able to rely on the support of the archbishop of Canterbury,[3] under whose metropolitan sway lay the bishoprics of Gwynedd. Such support normally involved attempts to secure the censure of the prince by the leading

---

[1] See, for example, the extents of the lands of the see of Bangor in 1306 in *Rec. Caern.*, pp. 93–115 (for the date, see below, Appendix VI), and of the lands of the see of St. Asaph in the fourteenth century in NLW SA/MB/22, ff. 19r–21r. The lands of the abbey of Aberconwy about the beginning of the thirteenth century are described in Llywelyn ab Iorwerth's charter, discussed in Colin Gresham, 'The Aberconwy Charter', *Arch. Camb.*, XCIV (1939), pp. 123–62, and R. W. Hays, *The History of the Abbey of Aberconway*, pp. 9–19. The Cymer abbey lands are detailed in Keith Williams-Jones, 'Llywelyn's Charter to Cymer Abbey in 1209', *Jnl. Mer. Hist. Soc.*, III (1957), pp. 45–78.

[2] It is unfortunate that more is not known of the genealogical connections of leading ecclesiastics in Gwynedd. But Bishop Hywel II of St. Asaph (1240–7) may have been a son of Ednyfed Fychan, whilst Anian II of St. Asaph was a distant kinsman of Llywelyn ap Gruffydd himself: see O. E. Jones, 'Llyfr Coch Asaph: A Textual and Historical Study' (unpublished University of Wales M.A. thesis, 1968), II, pp. 178–9.

[3] The point was well made in the letter sent by the Welsh princes in support of Giraldus's plans to secure metropolitan status for St. David's: *Ad haec etiam, quoties Anglici in terram nostram et nos insurgunt, statim Archiepiscopi Cantuarienses totam terram nostram sub interdicto concludunt; et nos qui pro patria nostra solum et libertate tuenda pugnamus, nominatim, et gentem nostram in genere, sententia excommunicationis involvunt: et id ipsum Episcopis nostris, quos ipsi ad libitum suum nobis, ut diximus, creant, et qui eis in hoc libenter obediunt, faciendum iniungunt. Unde accidit, ut quoties in bellicis conflictibus pro patria tuenda cum gente excommunicati cadunt.* The letter is given in *Giraldi Cambrensis Opera*, ed. J. S. Brewer *et al.* (Rolls Series, London, 1861–91), III, pp. 244–6. For practical examples of excommunication of the princes of Gwynedd which plainly served English royal policy, see Haddan and Stubbs, *Councils*, pp. 462–3, for the excommunication of Llywelyn ab Iorwerth in 1231; ibid., pp. 472–3, for the excommunication of David ap Llywelyn in 1244; ibid., pp. 487–8, for the order of Boniface of Canterbury to the incumbents of Welsh sees to excommunicate Llywelyn ap Gruffydd in 1260.

clerics within his territory, a censure which might undermine the loyalty to the prince of those of his subjects whose allegiance was conditional on their confidence in his prospects of success. It was thus useful for the lord of Aberffraw to have at hand prominent clerics who might be relied upon to quiet the misgiving of the hesitant by proclaiming the justice of the prince's cause. Nor, it seems, was Llywelyn ab Iorwerth averse to using the weapon of interdict, pronounced by a compliant bishop, against recalcitrant subjects or vassals: thus, he had the lands of Madog ap Gruffydd Maelor laid under interdict when the latter planned a marriage of which Llywelyn did not approve.[4] It is hard to resist the assumption that Llywelyn ab Iorwerth's example was followed by his successors.

It was not, however, simply a question of establishing the rightness of the prince's actions and the iniquity of those of his opponents in the eyes of his subjects in Gwynedd or elsewhere in Wales. In view of the pope's position as a potential political protector, and of the influence enjoyed by the papacy in England, particularly during the reign of Henry III, it was advisable for the prince of Gwynedd to ensure that his activities were well regarded at the papal court. In this, the obvious intermediaries and advocates were the bishops and abbots of Gwynedd, who might, of course, be joined on occasion by their colleagues of Powys and Deheubarth.

Finally, good relations between the princes and leading ecclesiastics were made the more vital to the former because the bishops and abbots controlled scarce resources, such as stone buildings suitable for the storing of documents, and skilled subordinates, drafters of documents, learned men suitable to employ as diplomatic envoys, all of whom were of great value to the princes for the efficient conduct of their affairs.

These, then, were some of the principal factors which drove the princes to seek good relations with the leading dignitaries of the church in Gwynedd. The relationship was by no means one-sided, however: powerful forces impelled the clerics to seek the favour of the princes. Such favour might, for example, be translated into grants of land and privileges. Just as significant

---

[4] *Cal. Anc. Corr.*, p. 3: the episode is dated 1215–17.

was the fact that the lord of Aberffraw was the most obvious source of protection and, indeed, of oppression for most of the clerical centres of Gwynedd,[5] while their status as great landholders gave these last a vested interest in aiding the prince to maintain peace and stability within his dominions.

In contrast, it should be noted that there were forces making for conflict in the relations between princes and leading clerics. In the first place, clerical obedience to the metropolitan authority of Canterbury, or to the orders of the pope, might involve clashes with the prince. Secondly, the leading clerics in areas most subject to English or marcher pressure might be led by considerations of political prudence to withhold their full support from the prince. Lastly, in times when a prince's fiscal and other resources were hard pressed, he was likely to resent, and possibly ignore, the ecclesiastics' territorial and other privileges, which limited his ability to exploit to the full the resources of Gwynedd.

Perhaps the most prominent of the ecclesiastics of Gwynedd were the bishops of Bangor and St. Asaph, whose sees covered the whole of Gwynedd and extended far beyond it to the south and the east.[6] A broad developmental survey of the relationship between the princes and these bishops, such as will be attempted below, may well prove somewhat misleading, because the evidence is unevenly distributed, being far fuller for the principates of David ap Llywelyn and Llywelyn ap Gruffydd than for that of Llywelyn ab Iorwerth and the joint rule of Llywelyn and Owain ap Gruffydd. The last case is hardly surprising: for the whole of the joint rule, St. Asaph diocese stood outside the area subject to the brothers, while Bishop Richard of Bangor seems to have been in almost uninterrupted exile from his diocese. There is, however, every reason to accept Lloyd's general statement with regard to the situation under Llywelyn ab Iorwerth that 'the ecclesiastical air was untroubled'.[7] The bishops of Bangor, Robert (1197–

---

[5] There were exceptions to this rule, of course, in particular the clerical centres sited near the borders with royal and marcher territory: see below, pp. 182–3.
[6] See William Rees, *Historical Atlas of Wales* (London, 1967), plate 33.
[7] *Hist. Wales*, II, p. 689.

1212), Cadwgan (1215–36) and Richard (1237–67), and those of St. Asaph, Reiner (d. 1224), Abraham (1225–32) and the two Hywels (1235–40 and 1240–47),[8] seem not to have clashed with Llywelyn so decisively as to make a conflict worth recording or recalling in their, or following, generations, while several of them seem to have been active in promoting the prince's plans. For his part, Llywelyn almost certainly contrived to influence the succession to the bishoprics within his territories,[9] presumably striving to secure the adoption of men well disposed towards him. The good relations between Llywelyn and the bishops apparently survived encroachments by the former upon episcopal rights.[10] The acquiescence of the bishops of Bangor and St. Asaph in the actions and policies of Llywelyn ab Iorwerth can be inferred from such incidents as that of 1231, when Henry III called the bishops of the province of Canterbury to a conference to discuss the excommunication of Llywelyn: the bishops of St. David's and Llandaff were summoned, but those of Bangor and St. Asaph were not.[11]

The internal calm which characterized the principate of Llywelyn ab Iorwerth was not, however, maintained under his successors. For most of his principate David ap Llywelyn had to contend with the active opposition of Richard of Bangor—largely, it seems, because of David's breach of faith in seizing his half-brother Gruffydd at a parley held under Bishop Richard's protection in 1241.[12] Richard's opposition was maintained outside the lands controlled by David, though

---

[8] Ibid., and *BT, Pen. 20, Tr.*, p. 104 and notes. For the two Hywels, see Haddan and Stubbs, *Councils*, pp. 465–6.
[9] As pointed out by Lloyd, *Hist. Wales*, II, p. 688, it appears from the account of Giraldus (*Giraldi Cambrensis Opera*, IV, pp. 161–7) that Llywelyn influenced the election of Cadwgan to Bangor in 1215. It is a reasonable assumption that the prince's influence was behind the elevation of Hywel ab Ednyfed to St. Asaph in 1240.
[10] One of the clauses in the April 1261 Bangor arbitration (for which see further pp. 171–2 below) contains the phrase, regarding Llywelyn ap Gruffydd: *Quod res proiectas in terram Ecclesie occupat similiter et thesauros inventos in terra Ecclesie; non recolimus alium talia recepisse praeter solum principem Lewelinum et suos successores.* Haddan and Stubbs, *Councils*, p. 490.
[11] Ibid., pp. 462–3.
[12] For a reconstruction of events, see G. A. Williams, 'The Succession to Gwynedd, 1238–47', *B.B.C.S.*, XX (1964), pp. 393–413; the absence of Richard of Bangor from David's entourage at Gloucester in May 1240, when Hywel of St. Asaph was present, may well indicate that Richard was already at odds with David. See *Littere Wallie*, pp. 5–6. It is a little odd that Richard seems to have been used as an envoy by him in the summer of 1241: see ibid., p. 153.

he certainly appeared in territory nominally within the latter's dominions, where he may have added dignity to the apparent attempts of the young Llywelyn ap Gruffydd to usurp his uncle's position.[13] The attitude of Hywel of St. Asaph is uncertain after the initial months of David's rule, when he seems to have lent his support to the prince.[14] When hostilities broke out between David and Henry III in 1241, Hywel seems not to have been regarded by the English government as a partisan of the prince:[15] the vulnerable position of his see probably inclined him to circumspection, a quality which would prove useful after the Treaty of Gwern Eigron (1241) had consigned part of the see, Tegeingl, to English occupation, and essential after 1245, when the whole of the see was over-run by English forces. It is possible that Hywel engaged in the diplomatic negotiations of Llywelyn and Owain ap Gruffydd with Henry III at Woodstock in 1247, as he died a little later in the same year at nearby Oxford.[16]

Even after the death of David and the succession of Owain and Llywelyn in 1246, Richard of Bangor maintained his exile from Gwynedd Uwch Conwy for some years, though he is known to have paid a visit to Dafydd ap Gruffydd's lordship of Cymydmaen in 1252.[17] The reasons for the continued exile are unclear: it is possible that Richard had been alienated from Llywelyn ap Gruffydd when the latter reached an accommodation with Prince David about 1245. Alternatively, the bishop may simply have been waiting to see how the unstable political situation created in 1246–7 would resolve itself. After Llywelyn had established himself as master of Gwynedd above and below Conwy in 1255–6, and beaten off Henry III's attempt to humble him in the autumn of 1257, the desirability of coming to terms with the prince would have become obvious to Bishop Richard. At the same time Llywelyn, if he was to

[13] See Appendix IV.
[14] *Littere Wallie*, pp. 5–6, 10. He seems to have acted as David's agent in concluding peace with Henry III in August 1241: see *C. Pat. R., 1232–47*, p. 257.
[15] Shortly after the treaty of Gwern Eigron in September 1241, Henry III granted Bishop Hywel protection without term for himself, his clerks and other men: ibid., p. 258. Hywel seems to have fled to royal territory in the war which broke out in 1244, for in April 1246 the king issued a safe conduct to the bishops of Bangor and St. Asaph and their men, who were returning to Wales: ibid., p. 478.
[16] *BT, R.B.H.*, p. 240.
[17] *Rec. Caern.*, p. 252.

establish the respectability of his rule in Gwynedd, could hardly afford to allow one of the leading clerics of the principality to remain in exile.

Richard was, it seems, still in England in January 1258, but he had returned to Gwynedd by 1259[18] and, in this and the following years, was several times employed by Llywelyn as an envoy—though always, significantly, accompanied by trusted servants of the prince.[19] These missions were the practical outcome of the recognition by both prince and bishop that an *entente* was to their mutual advantage. The basis of this *entente* seems to have been the settlement of territorial and other disputes between them in 1261. It was inevitable that after Richard's long exile the respective rights of bishop and prince in several areas should have become blurred and subject to dispute. The territorial agreement of August 1261 is unremarkable as far as its scope is concerned:[20] it seems to represent an attempt to tie up loose ends left after the more important concordat of April on princely and episcopal rights,[21] which was itself preceded by another agreement, the contents of which are largely unknown and which was drawn up at Llandrillo.[22] The date of the Llandrillo agreement is not known, but it is not unreasonable to guess that it was made soon after Richard's return from exile, in an attempt to settle the most pressing points at issue.

The agreements, of which texts have survived, resulted from arbitrations by persons acceptable to both parties. Llywelyn seems to have been anxious to arrange, from a position of strength, an equitable settlement. It is difficult to establish whether prince or bishop gained more from the April agreement, for no set of *gravamina* drawn up in advance by either

---

[18] *C. Pat. R., 1258–66*, p. 57.
[19] See above, p. 32.
[20] *Littere Wallie*, pp. 97–8. The dispute over boundaries in Talyllyn was judged in favour of Llywelyn. The agreement did not settle the dispute over the bounds between Llanwnda and Bodellog, but provided the machinery for settlement: the outcome is unknown.
[21] Haddan and Stubbs, *Councils*, pp. 489–91.
[22] Ibid., p. 490, where a question of sacrilege is dealt with thus: *respondemus ut continetur in litteris de Llan-Terillo;* and ibid., p. 491, where the arbitration is concluded with the phrases: *Partes vero supradictae ad ista inviolabiliter servanda teneantur; et ad ea servanda subobligatae sub eadem pena sint, que in litteris inter ipsas confectis apud Llanderillo fuerint obligatae.*

side survives.²³ The topics covered in the agreement were wide-ranging: the doing of justice on clerks of the diocese; the powers of the prince over the bishop's lay vassals; problems of sanctuary; the punishment of sacrilege; and the arrest of excommunicate persons by the prince. In at least one case, a clause relating to rights of wreck, the arbitrators considered that Llywelyn should give ground, but were evidently not anxious to press the point.²⁴ In other cases, however, their decision was clearly favourable to the bishop,²⁵ and it may be assumed that the agreement marked something of a diminution of the freedom of action which Llywelyn must have enjoyed *vis-à-vis* the see of Bangor during Richard's absence.

It is convenient to note at this point that in 1260 Llywelyn had agreed to an arbitration in a dispute between himself and the bishop of St. Asaph over rights in the vill of Henllan.²⁶ Anian I of St. Asaph had succeeded to the bishopric in 1249, following a two-year vacancy of the see. In 1256 the lands of Gwynedd Is Conwy in the northern part of the diocese were overrun by Llywelyn ap Gruffydd, who strengthened his hold on them by his campaigns during the next four years. Anian, like Richard of Bangor, doubtless saw the advantages of a settlement with a prince who so obviously held the political initiative. Taken as a whole, the Henllan arbitration, the agreement at Llandrillo, and the two agreements with Richard of Bangor in 1261 suggest that in these years Llywelyn was attempting a general settlement of disputes with the bishops, undoubtedly as a means of consolidating his authority within Gwynedd, and inducing the bishops to co-operate with him.

In the case of Richard of Bangor, the concord thus established did not last for very long: by 1265 conflict had arisen between

---

²³ In the collection of extracts from the Red Book of Asaph in which the record of the 1261 arbitration is preserved, NLW Peniarth MS. no. 231, the arbitration is followed by a list of thirteen *articuli*, which purport to set out the ways in which the prince had oppressed the church. The *articuli* follow the arbitration without an obvious break, and are so printed in Haddan and Stubbs, *Councils*, pp. 491–92, as though they formed, in some way, part of that settlement. But an examination of the content and lay-out of the *articuli* reveals that they were composed in, or after, 1274, and that they relate to St. Asaph diocese: see above, ch. VI, note 116.
²⁴ See the clause cited in note 10, above.
²⁵ See, for example, the clauses relating to offences of clergy, the exaction of military service and the commandeering of horses by the prince and his officers, and the obligation of the prince to arrest persons under sentence of excommunication.
²⁶ NLW SA/MB/22, f. 21v.

PRINCES, BISHOPS AND ABBOTS 173

Llywelyn and the bishop, who had placed an interdict on the prince's chapel.[27] The reasons for the conflict are unclear, but it seems that tenurial rights were at issue.[28] It may be that Llywelyn's re-entry into hostilities with the marcher lords in 1263, which clearly involved him in considerable expense, led him to encroach upon episcopal rights in an attempt to utilize all available resources; on the other hand, it may simply be that by 1265 Llywelyn was confident of securing formal recognition from the English government of his supremacy in Wales, and felt able to abandon his former politic restraint towards the bishop. Two years later, Richard died, after requesting permission to resign his see in terms which suggest that he was isolated and friendless in his diocese.[29] The prince's relations with Anian I of St. Asaph after 1260 have largely to be inferred, but there is no record of any major clash between them before Anian's death in 1266.

Thus, at a time when his plans to establish his supremacy in Wales were bearing impressive fruit, Llywelyn was offered the chance to secure in both dioceses of Gwynedd prelates who would prove compliant. The situation was the more auspicious because the chapter of Bangor was dominated by men favourably inclined to Llywelyn and frequently employed by him on diplomatic and other tasks,[30] while he had conciliated the chapter of St. Asaph with a loan of £20 in 1266,[31] and by allowing the *custos* appointed, presumably by Llywelyn himself after Anian's death, to issue a charter of liberties and a confirmation of charters to the canons in 1266-7.[32] By November 1267 Richard had been replaced at Bangor by another Anian, while at St. Asaph the Dominican, Anian II,

---

[27] *Close Rolls, 1264-68*, p. 117.
[28] The mandate of the English government to Richard, cited in the previous note, ordering him to lift the interdict, contains the accusation that the bishop had acted *pro causis non ad forum ecclesiasticum immo ad curiam laicalem mere pertinentibus, ut de laicalis feodis* . . . No doubt the bishop saw the matter differently. The episode is a good indication that Llywelyn took ecclesiastical censure within his territories seriously—otherwise, he could not have made efforts to persuade the English government to put pressure on the bishop.
[29] Haddan and Stubbs, *Councils*, pp. 496-7.
[30] See above, pp. 35-7.
[31] *Littere Wallie*, pp. 39-40.
[32] See, for the grant of liberties, Haddan and Stubbs, *Councils*, pp. 495-6.

had succeeded to the bishopric late in 1268.[33] But if Llywelyn had expected these men to be tractable, he was greatly deceived; the remaining years of his principate saw the development of conflict between the prince and the bishops on a scale unparalleled at any earlier time in the century.

For some years there is no sign of overt conflict: both bishops appear occasionally in circumstances which suggest that they were co-operating with Llywelyn.[34] Some problems with Anian II of St. Asaph had clearly arisen as early as 1269, when Llywelyn granted to the bishop a charter confirming in general terms diocesan liberties, and setting up machinery to establish by inquisition episcopal and princely rights in disputed cases. If tension had been mounting, the 1269 charter may have dispelled it for a time, although a reference to the excommunication in 1270 of violators of the privileges of St. Asaph may relate to a further clash between prince and bishop.[35] Anian of Bangor began to show signs of opposition to the prince by December 1274 when, with his colleague of St. Asaph, he protested to Llywelyn against his treatment of his brother, Dafydd.[36] Thereafter, the bishop of Bangor's opposition seems to have been muted, but when he fled to the English in 1277 he revealed the depth of hostility between himself and the prince: he had, so he claimed, lost sixty of his kinsmen in the war, a loss at which Llywelyn was rejoicing.[37] The episode is a good illustration of the point that the mere attainment of high ecclesiastical office did not mean that a man had severed the bonds of kinship.

The rift with Anian of St. Asaph, which had opened up by late 1274, was more apparent and more harmful to Llywelyn's

---

[33] For a study of some aspects of the career of Anian II see T. Jones Pierce, 'Einion ap Ynyr (Anian II), bishop of St. Asaph', *Flintshire Hist. Soc. Publications,* XVII (1957), pp. 16–33. There is interesting evidence quoted in Lloyd, *Hist. Wales,* II, p. 745, note 149, that a John was consecrated to St. Asaph in November 1267 but died soon afterwards: this would imply that Llywelyn made little attempt to exploit the vacancy of the see for his own profit, as alleged later by Anian: see Haddan and Stubbs, *Councils,* p. 512.

[34] Lloyd, op. cit., II, p. 745; *Cal. Anc. Corr.,* p. 10; *Littere Wallie,* p. 58.

[35] Haddan and Stubbs, *Councils,* pp. 497–8 and note a. See p. 184 below, and note 80.

[36] *Littere Wallie,* pp. 179–80: this reply of Llywelyn's makes it clear that his treatment of Dafydd and Gruffydd was not the only matter complained of in the bishops' letters.

[37] *Cal. Anc. Corr.,* p. 112.

cause before 1277 than that with the bishop of Bangor. The basis of the conflict seems to have been Llywelyn's alleged usurpation of many of the bishop's financial rights over episcopal tenants, especially the right to a share of the fines, or in some cases all of the fines, of delinquent *homines episcopi*; though Anian seems progressively to have broadened his attack on the prince. The bishop of St. Asaph's campaign was certainly under way by October 1274, when he called a diocesan assembly to establish the validity of his claims to various financial rights alleged to have been usurped by Llywelyn.[38] In December, Anian joined with his namesake of Bangor in sending warning letters to Llywelyn on the subject of the prince's attempts to bring to heel his brother Dafydd, who was suspected of treachery. A major reason for the sending of the letters was the fact that the settlement between Llywelyn and Dafydd, reached in 1269, had established that any subsequent dispute should be settled by the arbitration of the bishops of Bangor and St. Asaph.[39] Llywelyn may have considered that a papal confirmation of the settlement, which had been obtained by him in August 1274,[40] enabled him to proceed against Dafydd on his own terms: it is certainly significant of the decline in relations between Llywelyn and the two Anians since 1269 that the prince was not prepared to let the case of Dafydd go before the bishops, but instead called his brother before his council.[41]

It was presumably late in 1274 or early in 1275 that Anian succeeded in bringing to his aid the pope himself, for a letter to Gregory X defending Llywelyn, and sent under the names of several of the Cisterican abbots of Wales in March 1275,[42]

[38] NLW Peniarth MS. no. 231, pp. 45-52 (Latin) and pp. 116-25 (Welsh).
[39] Ibid., pp. 67-9. The relevant passage, on p. 68, is: *Si autem transgressiones alique offense seu rancores in posterum inter nos mutuo emerserint, prefati episcopi adiectis sibi probis viris ex communi assensu nostro electis non suspectis alicui partium dictas transgressiones offensas et rancores inter nos et dictum David corrigi facient et sopiri*.
[40] Haddan and Stubbs, *Councils*, pp. 501-2. It is interesting that Gregory X's confirmation of the 1269 agreement, and of a settlement by the bishops of certain obscurities which it contained (a settlement provided for in the agreement), contains no obvious reference to the clause set out in the previous note.
[41] *Littere Wallie*, p. 137. The bishops may have been members of the council: see above, p. 9.
[42] Haddan and Stubbs, *Councils*, p. 498. The date given by the editors is March 7, 1274. This is a rendering of: *anno Domini M°CC°LXX°IIII° septimo die Martii*. As the Cistercians dated their year from the end of March, it is clear that the letter was issued in the year 1275, by modern reckoning.

refers to a complaint made by Anian II to Gregory and the latter's subsequent condemnation of Llywelyn.[43] As might be expected, the archbishop of Canterbury was also brought into the reckoning by Anian: in May 1275 Llywelyn wrote to the archbishop, himself a Dominican like Anian, to defend himself against the bishop of St. Asaph's accusations.[44] Nor was the clash between prince and bishop confined to claim and counter-claim: Anian seems to have worked against the prince by informing King Edward of Llywelyn's activities within Wales during the period of diplomatic and military manoeuvring which preceded the war of 1277.[45]

In December 1276, just a month after Edward had formally declared war on Llywelyn, Anian unleashed his final and most comprehensive attack on the prince: a long list of *gravamina* in which the prince's alleged offences against the bishop, the clergy, tenants and rights of the see of St. Asaph during the past decade were minutely detailed.[46] It seems likely that the 1276 *gravamina* were not intended primarily for consideration by Llywelyn. In the charter of liberties which the prince issued to the bishop and chapter, probably early in 1277 when under severe political pressure, Llywelyn was clearly not responding primarily to the *gravamina* but apparently was acting in answer to one of the papal directives to him to restore Anian to his rights.[47] The impression is strong that both bishop and prince

---

[43] It is possible that the *articuli* referred to in note 23 above formed the basis of the bishop's appeal. There is, indeed, some correspondence in terms of subject matter and phraseology between the *articuli* and the charter of liberties to St. Asaph issued by Llywelyn in 1276–77; the last document clearly reflects a papal mandate based on Anian's appeals.

[44] Haddan and Stubbs, *Councils*, pp. 503–5.

[45] See *Cal. Anc. Corr.*, p. 105, for a report by Anian II to Edward I on a cornage exacted by Llywelyn; for the date, see F. M. Powicke, *King Henry III and the Lord Edward*, p. 638.

[46] Haddan and Stubbs, *Councils*, pp. 511–16.

[47] Ibid., pp. 519–21. After an initial clause conceding cases relating to wills, marriage, tithe, usury and sacrilege to the church, the other clauses are headed: *Volumus insuper salubribus Apostolice sedis monitis parere pariter et mandatis, que circa reformacionem status Assavensis Ecclesie meminimus recepisse dudum, in articulis infrascriptis.* Some of the phrases used in the charter of liberties seem to reflect the reply of the Cistercian abbots in March 1275 (see note 42 above) to a papal mandate to Llywelyn, which reply fairly incorporates many of the words of the original mandate. In particular, in a reference to exactions by the prince from churches and monasteries, both the charter and the abbots' letter contain the words *personis . . . degentibus contradicentibus et invitis*. This phraseological recurrence has added significance, of course, as a further indication that the Cistercians were involved in the drafting of the prince's documents.

were acting out the final moves in their conflict largely for their diplomatic value. Llywelyn was trying not only to influence Welsh opinion but also to mollify the pope, whose assistance he was seeking about this time in his efforts to secure the release of his wife, Eleanor, from King Edward's custody.[48] Anian may have been anticipating a royal victory in the impending clash between Llywelyn and Edward, and may have been using the *gravamina* as a statement of the rights of his see which were, or had been, the subject of dispute. If this was the spirit in which the *gravamina* were issued, they cannot be taken as an accurate reflection of the extent of Llywelyn's encroachment on episcopal rights in 1276. The prince's charter of liberties to St. Asaph failed to mollify Anian, who took himself and his household into English custody in February 1277.[49] Thereafter, with the English victory and occupation of the Perfeddwlad and the restoration of Powys to Gruffydd ap Gwenwynwyn, the diocese of St. Asaph passed out of the control of the prince of Gwynedd.

Having thus established the chronological framework of the clash between Llywelyn and Anian II of St. Asaph in 1274–7, some of the more striking characteristics of the conflict can be discussed in some detail. The episode illuminates many aspects of Llywelyn's governance. Accepting that Anian II was an unusually combative bishop, it does seem that his opposition to Llywelyn must have been sparked off by the threat at least of increased princely pressure on the rights of his see. The period after 1268 was certainly one of intense pressure upon Llywelyn's fiscal resources: the building of Dolforwyn castle in 1273–4[50] represented a new charge on revenue, whilst up to 1272 at least the prince had been paying out large sums, totalling some 15,000 marks, in discharge of the obligation to pay 25,000 marks, and an additional 5,000 marks for the homage of Maredudd ap Rhys, in accordance with the Treaty of Montgomery in 1267. Llywelyn had also entered, in 1272, into an obligation to pay his brother Rhodri 1,000 marks.[51] The evidence taken before the diocesan assembly of 1274,

[48] See J. B. Smith, 'Offra Principis Wallie Domino Regi', *B.B.C.S.*, XXI (1966), p. 365.
[49] *C. Pat. R., 1272–81*, p. 196.
[50] *Littere Wallie*, p. 23.
[51] Ibid., p. li, and for the 1272 agreement with Rhodri, p. 85.

selective though it might be, suggests that Llywelyn's encroachments upon the bishop's right to profits of justice were of recent origin, for cases were then cited in which the bishop's rights had been exercised without impediment from the time of Llywelyn's predecessors, from that of his own principate, and as recently as the episcopate of Anian II himself.[52] It should be stressed, however, that it was quite obviously in Anian's interests to make Llywelyn's alleged encroachments appear both recent and clearly at variance with previously accepted practice.[53]

In a sense, however, both the prince's motives and the veracity of the bishop's claims are of secondary importance: the fact is that the conflict with Anian II gave the prince's political opponents another field in which they could claim that he was subverting Welsh social and political traditions.[54] The bishop, whether wittingly or not, took his place alongside such men as the exiled Dafydd ap Gruffydd and the disinherited members of the house of Meirionydd,[55] as well as all those who were alarmed by the heavy, and probably growing, burden of Llywelyn's government—in short, all those with a vested interest in claiming that the régime of Llywelyn ap Gruffydd was running contrary to the best traditions of the Welsh past.

[52] NLW Peniarth MS. no. 231, p. 123, contains cases from Anian II's episcopate.
[53] It should, nevertheless, be pointed out that O. E. Jones's comment ('Llyfr Coch Asaph: A Textual and Historical Study' (unpublished University of Wales M.A. thesis, 1968) II, pp. 106-7) that 'Anian's claims on the issue of vassals of the church and prince caught fighting each other suggest some inconsistency on the part of the bishop' should be questioned. Jones argues that 'on the one hand, Anian claimed to have half the fines of his vassals convicted of fighting against the prince's men on the prince's territory; that is, the claim was made on the rule that it was not the venue of the cause of action which determined jurisdiction, but the homage which the defendant owed. On the other hand, the bishop maintained that the prince was to receive nothing when the fighting occurred on church land; jurisdiction was also territorial.' But there is, in fact, no inconsistency in the bishop's claims, at least none which would benefit him: if fighting takes place on the prince's land, the bishop claims half of the fine of his own man, but allows that the prince should take the whole fine of *his* man. See Haddan and Stubbs, *Councils*, pp. 492, 513. It would seem that homage was regarded by Anian as the determining factor in the question of who should receive the fines of offenders, but that he conceded to the prince the right to half of the fine of an episcopal tenant convicted of fighting on the prince's territory.
[54] The title of the *articuli* of 1274-6 (in Haddan and Stubbs, *Councils*, pp. 491-92) is significant: *Hii sunt articuli de quibus dominium seculare presumit Ecclesiam fatigare contra instituciones Wallorum principum*. The confirmation of the liberties of St. Asaph by Edward I in November 1275 (*C. Pat. R., 1272-81*, p. 112) was no doubt intended to stand in sharp contrast to the oppression of Llywelyn.
[55] See above, pp. 144-7.

PRINCES, BISHOPS AND ABBOTS 179

A second striking feature of the clash between prince and bishop is the very considerable publicity which Anian was able to give to his cause. Even within Gwynedd, Anian was able to call the attention of many to his claims by the tactic of holding diocesan assemblies and enquiries, to which were summoned both clergy and laymen.[56] And from such meetings resulted appeals to Canterbury and to Rome.[57] Anian of St. Asaph seems to have enjoyed a remarkable freedom of action under Llywelyn, the explanation of which may well lie in geographical factors and, perhaps, in a failure on the prince's part to follow in St. Asaph a course which appears to have proved successful in Bangor. This was the isolation of the bishop in his see, achieved by surrounding him with men who were associated with the prince's government and aspirations. There is clear evidence that canons of Bangor were associated with Llywelyn from an early stage of his principate.[58] In such an environment, with his isolation underlined by the location of his cathedral in the heart of Gwynedd, the bishop of Bangor was particularly vulnerable to any political pressures which might be exerted by the prince. Thus in 1277, after escaping from Gwynedd following his excommunication of Llywelyn, Anian of Bangor wrote to Edward I that he had been the prince's confessor and unable to stir a foot except under the prince's power.[59] In the diocese of St. Asaph, the situation was manifestly different: the position of the see, contiguous to, and embracing, marcher territory, made the isolation of the bishop difficult: any act of repression directed against him was far more likely to become known beyond Gwynedd and thereby supply propaganda to those anxious to undermine Llywelyn's moral standing. The difficulty of conducting a repressive campaign against the bishop was compounded by Llywelyn ap Gruffydd's apparent failure to gain the support of the chapter of St. Asaph, in contrast to his achievement in Bangor:

---

[56] According to the preambles to the records of their proceedings, the diocesan assembly of October 1274 was attended by *clericis ac laicis fidedignis*, and the assembly which preceded the issue of the *gravamina* of December 1276 was held *evocatis ad hoc specialiter clero et populo*. But these are, admittedly, hardly objective descriptions.
[57] See notes 43 and 47 above, and Haddan and Stubbs, *Councils*, pp. 503–5, 516.
[58] See pp. 35–7 above.
[59] *Cal. Anc. Corr.*, p. 66.

Anian II seems to have enjoyed the active co-operation of many of his canons and diocesan clergy in his clash with Llywelyn.[60] The war of 1277 produced a political situation in which the see of Bangor occupied a position rather similar to that of St. Asaph before the outbreak of hostilities. It is, therefore, interesting to note that relations between Llywelyn and Anian of Bangor altered radically after that date, in a manner favourable to the bishop. Llywelyn apparently began to lose his control over the Bangor chapter,[61] whilst the imminence of the power of Edward I was felt throughout Gwynedd Uwch Conwy, and the bishop was amongst those who benefited.[62]

During 1278 Edward I more than once ordered Llywelyn to treat the bishop of Bangor justly, and a letter from Peckham[63] to Llywelyn in the following year charges the prince with financial oppressions against the clergy and episcopal tenants. The conflict between Llywelyn and the bishop of Bangor lasted until 1280 when, according to Archbishop Peckham, a settlement was imminent.[64] The *rapprochement* did not, however, prevent Anian from taking refuge in English-held territory on the outbreak of hostilities in 1282.[65] There is no evidence that Anian of Bangor's attitude to Llywelyn in the years 1278–82 reached the level of active hostility and subversion which

---

[60] There is an impressive number of witnesses, including canons of St. Asaph, in favour of Anian's case at the diocesan assembly of October 1274. See especially NLW Peniarth MS. no. 231, p. 51, for the comment *hoc dicunt Bledynt goch & maior pars capituli*.

[61] In 1280, Llywelyn was involved in a dispute with the archdeacon of Bangor: Haddan and Stubbs, *Councils*, p. 527. And after the war of 1277 the archdeacon of Anglesey appears as a royal agent concerned with the administration of the lands of the dead Madog Fychan of Bromfield: *C. Chanc. R., Various*, p. 183. The loss of control was not, of course, complete, but it is notable that, in addition to the archdeacons of Anglesey and Bangor and the dean of Bangor, Gregory, canon of Bangor, also received a payment from the king's agents in 1284, of £3 10s. *pro dampnis in ultima guerra michi illatis: Littere Wallie*, p. 66. It is not certain who was responsible for the damages, but the relatively large sum paid to Gregory perhaps suggests that he was a royal partisan.

[62] See Haddan and Stubbs, *Councils*, pp. 524–5, for an instance in which Anian of Bangor acted as Edward's agent in settling a case which had arisen as a result of the occupation of Anglesey by royal forces.

[63] Ibid., p. 525; *Registrum . . . Peckham*, I, p. 77.

[64] It is usually assumed that a settlement had been reached, but this interpretation receives no support from the text: *De composicione autem inter vos et dominum Episcopum Bangorensem amicabiliter deducenda gaudemus plurimum, Altissimum deprecantes ut dignetur illi tractatui vestro Sui spiritum consilii destinare*.

[65] He was with Edward by July 1282: *Littere Wallie*, pp. 165–6.

characterized the conduct of the bishop of St. Asaph towards the prince in the years 1274–7. But it is surely not without significance that in the last crisis of his rule the most substantial ecclesiastic in Llywelyn's principate was virtually a royal representative.

From the close of the principate of Llywelyn ab Iorwerth, then, the support of the bishops of Bangor and St. Asaph for the rulers of Gwynedd was at best uncertain and frequently non-existent. One can surely not accept the conclusion of Sir Maurice Powicke that 'on the whole . . . Richard and Anian of Bangor, Anian I and Anian II were accommodating (*sc.* to the princes)', nor, without very considerable qualifications, the same writer's assertion that these bishops were 'loyal Welshmen'.[66]

It was, indeed, the fact that the political support of the bishops could not be taken for granted that made more valuable to the princes the friendship of another group of clerics sufficiently prestigious within Gwynedd and influential beyond it to provide an adequate ecclesiastical prop to their régime, namely the Cistercians. There were, of course, others to whom the princes might turn: Franciscans were established at Llanfaes by Llywelyn ab Iorwerth,[67] and their warden was used as an envoy by Llywelyn ap Gruffydd.[68] The Dominicans, too, were installed at Bangor and Rhuddlan by the mid-thirteenth century,[69] but were not, it seems, much patronized by the princes, and were significant mainly in their opposition to Llywelyn ap Gruffydd.[70] Anian II of St. Asaph was himself a Dominican, and the Dominicans have been shown by Mr. Beverley Smith to have been closely involved with dissident elements in Gwynedd in 1277.[71]

The Cistercian houses within Gwynedd which were of greatest importance to the princes were those of Cymer and Aberconwy, both largely, though not originally, endowed by

---

[66] F. M. Powicke, *The Thirteenth Century* (2nd ed.), pp. 390–1.
[67] *BT, R.B.H.*, p. 234.
[68] See Appendix III *sub* William of Llanfaes.
[69] See *Aspects of Welsh History*, pp. 217–18.
[70] Ibid., pp. 217–23, for a brief survey of relations between the prince and the Black Friars.
[71] J. B. Smith, 'Welsh Dominicans and the Crisis of 1277', *B.B.C.S.*, XXII (1968), pp. 353–7.

Llywelyn ab Iorwerth.[72] The very considerable lands and privileges granted to Cymer and Aberconwy bought for Llywelyn's successors the support of these houses. It was a support worth having: it has already been seen that the two abbeys were closely associated with the princes' governance, especially under Llywelyn ap Gruffydd.[73] David ap Llywelyn, too, was able to take advantage of Cistercian help for, when he was apparently without the co-operation of either the bishop of Bangor or the bishop of St. Asaph, it was the abbots of Aberconwy and Cymer whom he employed as his intermediaries and agents in an audacious and only narrowly unsuccessful attempt to invoke papal aid against Henry III in 1244.[74] In 1274, Llywelyn ap Gruffydd employed the abbot and prior of Cymer to try to persuade the fugitive Gruffydd ap Gwenwynwyn to return to the principality.[75] Again, when, in the course of his clash with Llywelyn ap Gruffydd, Anian II of St. Asaph appealed to Pope Gregory X, it was a group of Cistercian abbots, including those of Aberconwy and Cymer, which wrote to Gregory in Llywelyn's defence, describing him as *tutor strenuus ac praecipuus ordinis nostri, singulorumque ordinum et ecclesiasticarum in Wallia personarum*.[76]

Amongst the Cistercian abbots who did not come to Llywelyn's aid in 1275 was the head of the house at Basingwerk. Basingwerk, like the other two Cistercian houses of Gwynedd, had received substantial endowments from the princes,[77] though not, it seems, on quite the same scale: unlike Aberconwy and Cymer, it seems never to have played a significant part in the princes' governance. Indeed, monks of Basingwerk were conspicuous mainly for their part in opposing the princes of Gwynedd: in 1241 and 1276-77, the house was apparently aligned with those hostile to David ap Llywelyn and Llywelyn

---

[72] In both cases, earlier endowments had been made by members of the house of Meirionydd: see ch. VIII, note 59. For early co-operation between Llywelyn ab Iorwerth and Aberconwy, see R. W. Hays, op. cit., pp. 26-31.
[73] See pp. 33-4 above.
[74] Lloyd, *Hist. Wales*, II, p. 702.
[75] *Littere Wallie*, p. 138.
[76] Haddan and Stubbs, *Councils*, p. 499.
[77] See Appendix I, nos. 4, 19, 23.

ap Gruffydd respectively.[78] This exception to the rule of co-operation between the princes and the Cistercians in Gwynedd is interesting. As Basingwerk was situated close to the north-eastern edge of the princes' dominions even at their furthest extent, and in an area particularly susceptible to English incursions, it may have seemed inexpedient to the monks to identify themselves with the princes' governance. It is, perhaps, significant in this context that in the years after the war of 1277, when the abbey of Aberconwy occupied a position on the border of Llywelyn's territory, rather as Basingwerk had done before 1277, there is a hint of a breakdown in the pattern of good relations between Llywelyn and Aberconwy itself: for some unspecified reason, the abbey had incurred the prince's ill-will which it was forced to buy off with a payment of £40.[79]

On the basis of the available evidence, then, it seems that the achievements of Llywelyn ab Iorwerth in attracting widespread and, apparently, remarkably consistent support from the prominent ecclesiastics of Gwynedd was never matched by the later princes, except, perhaps, by Llywelyn ap Gruffydd in the years around 1260. The story after 1240 is one of uneasy and frequently hostile relations between the princes and many of the leading ecclesiastics, especially in areas in which military

---

[78] In August 1241, the abbot of Basingwerk was commissioned by Henry III to bring Hywel of St. Asaph and Master David, clerk of David ap Llywelyn, to speak with the king's council, whilst Brother Gregory of Basingwerk was given power by the king to conduct the bishop of Bangor's harness to Rhuddlan: *C. Pat. R., 1232-47*, pp. 257-8. In January 1276, Edward I gave the abbot and convent of Basingwerk protection for two years, but in December of that year Llywelyn's oppression of the abbey was included in the *gravamina* of St. Asaph: *C. Pat. R., 1272-81*, p. 129; Haddan and Stubbs, *Councils*, p. 515. Disputes with the same abbey were still causing trouble for Llywelyn in 1278: ibid., p. 525.

[79] See *Littere Wallie*, p. 25, for the record of the agreement of the abbot and convent of Aberconwy to pay Llywelyn forty marks *pro benivolentia (sic) prefati domini principis de quibusdam casibus et articulis nobis per eundem impositis optinenda, quandoque ab eodem fuerimus requisiti, predictis articulis et rancoribus nobis remissis et omnino cassatis*. R. W. Hays, *The History of the Abbey of Aberconway, 1186-1537* (Cardiff, 1963) p. 56, minimizes the significance of this document: he assumes that the abbot was buying exemption from earlier payments imposed by Llywelyn, 'perhaps for war expenses': it is, however, certain that something far more serious was involved. The references to *articuli* suggest that an attack on the abbey's privileges may have been involved, whilst the mention of Llywelyn's rancour is ominous.

confrontation between the princes and their political opponents was likely. It may be that disproportionate attention has been paid to the period of apparently severe conflict between the prince and the bishop of St. Asaph in the years 1274–7, particularly as there is evidence that in previous years the princely and episcopal administrations had worked closely and generally harmoniously together. Moreover, it is clear that in some cases, at least, the prince was prepared to lend support to the bishop to maintain the latter's rights: after setting up the process of inquests in 1269 to determine episcopal liberties, Llywelyn seems to have acquiesced in the punishment for encroachment of several of his local officials in the Perfeddwlad.[80]

It should not be assumed that clashes between princes and bishops were simply the result of wilful oppression by the former. The bishops were great immunists, who benefited from a share at least of a very wide range of judicial profits accruing from penalties levied on malefactors amongst their tenants, or on those who committed misdeeds on episcopal lands. The bishops also benefited from a range of dues such as *amobr*, *ebediw* and *gobr estyn* and food renders, which derived from their lordship over men or land. In view of the very wide scope of the lordship claimed by the bishop, and of the extent of the episcopal lands throughout which that lordship was exercised, it is hardly to be wondered that disputes over infractions of their rights should arise. It is quite possible that many of the alleged instances of encroachment on episcopal rights were no more than isolated, exceptional cases, to which the bishop reacted sharply. Again, the rights of the bishops seem to have been founded in the main on unwritten custom[81]

---

[80] The series of sureties found for payment to the bishop by men identifiable as local officials of the prince, given in NLW Peniarth MS. no. 231, pp. 79–80, almost certainly relates to this period, though the text of the dating clause is corrupt.

[81] *Ior.*, 83. 13, does contain the information that from episcopal land the king is owed hosting and (fines for) theft: but this and similar passages in the legal texts are concerned primarily with establishing the minimum rights of the king *vis-à-vis* the bishop, and not with defining those of the bishop as against the king. In the struggles of the bishops against Llywelyn ap Gruffydd, they never cite the text of charters issued to them or their predecessors by the princes, nor, except for a vague reference to *instituciones Wallorum principum* in Anian II of St. Asaph's *articuli* (Haddan and Stubbs, *Councils*, p. 491), are such grants even suggested.

PRINCES, BISHOPS AND ABBOTS

rather than on the charters of the princes or other documentary acknowledgements, in contrast to the rights and privileges of other ecclesiastical institutions, such as the houses of the Cistercians or Hospitallers. Some, at least, of the *gravamina* and *articuli* set forth by the bishops may represent issues where the cause for complaint was slight or even non-existent, but in which the bishop was trying to force a written acknowledgement of his rights. Moreover, for some of his protestations of 1276, Anian II of St. Asaph does not claim the sanction of custom, and by implication rejects it in some cases;[82] in such instances, he may thus have been taking the offensive against the prince.

Complex though they were, the crises of the 1270s were of clear significance in that they tested the stability and effectiveness of the régime which had been built up in Gwynedd and beyond by the princes, and they served to reveal some of its weaknesses. There seems every possibility that many of the factors which operated to produce strained relations between princes and ecclesiastics, such as the fiscal pressures of the former, the oppression of local officials over whom the prince might have little effective control, or the need, acute in frontier areas, to avoid identification with a prince whose political control might not be permanent, might not affect churchmen alone. When due allowance has been made for imbalances in, and the limitations of, the evidence, it may be that the relations of the princes with the bishops, abbots and other leading ecclesiastics of Gwynedd can be used as a rough index of the degree of political stability attained within the principality by the rulers of Aberffraw.

---

[82] See, in particular, the eighteenth clause of the *gravamina* of St. Asaph in 1276: ibid., p. 514.

X
THE STATE AND KINSHIP GROUPS

The term 'state' is something of a neologism when used in the context of the thirteenth century in so far as it carries connotations not borne by the Latin word *status* from which it is derived and which is frequently found in thirteenth-century sources.[1] It seems quite reasonable, however, to use the term as a tool of analysis, and it is here employed to denote a structure of subordination, established within defined territorial limits, and involving a coercive organisation differentiated from other forms of socio-political organisation as the executive agency of a central source of authority. In the present context this source of authority is ultimately the prince, though for practical purposes it may be represented in some areas by a lord of the princely house. It should also be stressed that the forms and extent of kinship-groups were variable, differing according to circumstances. Thus, when an individual established his kin relationships for the purpose of a claim to land through kin and descent, or for the payment of *galanas* (composition of feud), or when a lord sought and held the near kin of an offender in order to force the latter to stand to justice, the kin groups concerned were each different, though probably overlapping.[2] In the last case, the kin involved were not part of a formally constituted hostage-group, but were selected *ad hoc* by the lord's agents. Underlying all of these various forms of kinship-group, however, is the strength of kinship ties and their importance as a means of social control.

One of the most important problems to be considered is the extent to which state organisation was susceptible to influence

---

[1] See, for example, René Fedou, *L'État au Moyen Age* (Paris, 1971) p. 5.
[2] For the four-generation agnatic kindred on which claims to land were frequently based, see *Ior.*, 85. 1–4; the payment of *galanas* by those within seven degrees of kinship to the offender (i.e., by descendants of his great-great-great-great-grandfather) is illustrated in *Ior.*, 106. 17–19. For subsequent modifications of this system, by which *galanas* was collected within four degrees of kinship see R. R. Davies, 'The Survival of the Bloodfeud in Medieval Wales', *History*, LIV (1969), p. 345. For the seizure by the lord of 'hostages' from amongst an offender's kin, see notes 22 and 23 below.

or even obstruction by kin groups. At a simple level this involves the degree to which certain kin groups were able to control or influence the succession to offices through which the princes sought to impose their will upon Gwynedd. The lawbooks contain passages in the midst of tracts which clearly relate to pre-thirteenth-century conditions and which make it clear that some, at least, of the offices within the framework of governance employed by Welsh kings had lain in the control of kindred groups. Thus the office of *maer* might be in some sense hereditary,[3] and the *pencenedl* or chief of kindred seems to have exercised absolute control over appointments to certain, unspecified, offices.[4] At the same time, other passages in the legal texts, probably archaic by the thirteenth century, make it clear that the need to differentiate state from kin organisation was appreciated at a relatively early stage, for it is stated that no-one may hold the offices of *maer*, whose duty lay in enforcing the ruler's rights, and *pencedl* simultaneously.[5]

Record evidence from the thirteenth and fourteenth centuries enables us to test assumptions derived from the legal texts. At the highest level, it has already been seen that the office of *distain* was held by descendants of Cynfrig ab Iorwerth from about 1215 until 1278 and again in 1282–3,[6] while in the period 1278–82 the office may have been held by Dafydd ab Einion Fychan, himself a member of a family with a long tradition of service to princes of Gwynedd.[7] Again, members of a small number of descent groups appear with significant frequency in ministerial roles, both in the age of the Llywelyns and in the early post-conquest period.[8] The limited evidence suggests, however, that many, and probably most, offices of importance were not held as of right by a single descent group, though the eminence of such a group at court or in a locality may well have given its members a strong claim to selection by the prince. It may in fact be somewhat misleading to refer to

---

[3] This may be the significance of references in the legal texts to the purchase by a man of the office of *maer que sua sit iure*. See, for example, *L.T.W.L.*, p. 120.
[4] Ibid., p. 139: *Quecumque officialis dignitas fuerit in potestate illius qui cephas est gentis sue, eius erit.*
[5] Ibid., p. 120.
[6] See above, pp. 17–18.
[7] See above, pp. 106–10.
[8] See above, pp. 124–9.

succession to offices of importance in the context of the central *curia*. It has been noted that the majority of ministers of the itinerant court are not accorded titles in the records.[9] The absence of precise designations probably indicates the unspecialized nature of their work and, further, suggests that they were not regarded as dignitaries, but as functionaries. When the concept of office as function rather than *dignitas* has been established (and it need not, of course, be established in the manner suggested here) there arises the problem of aptitude for office, which militates strongly against the tenure of a specific post by a given descent group as of right.

At the local level, there are signs that some offices were vested in a particular lineage. Thus, in 1305 Goronwy Grach, probably a descendant of Ednyfed Fychan, referred to the fact that *ipse et Antecessores sui tempore Regis et Prin[cipum]*? *tenuerunt officium Ringildi commoti de Meney*, and quitclaimed for himself and his heirs to Prince Edward any claim to the office.[10] This does not, however, represent a universal pattern. The remarkably full evidence which exists for the study of the succession to the office of *rhaglaw* of Dinorben in the Perfeddwlad suggests that two descent groups, the progeny of Cynfrig ab Iorwerth and of Mabon Glochydd had an 'interest', though by no means an exclusive one, in the office: one may, perhaps, postulate an element of competition between the two descent groups.[11] Such competition might prove useful to the prince as a means of extracting an office from the grip of a single descent group and making it more responsive to his will.

The situation with regard to the influence upon the distribution of office exerted by certain kindred groups was thus a complex one: what needs to be stressed here is that one is dealing only with certain descent groups, not with the problem of kindred *tout court* in this context.

In a more general sense, state and kinship organisation may be seen as being in some measure potentially in opposition in terms of political functions. For example, while the kinship group is responsible, either in law or in fact, for achieving a settlement in the case of offences committed by or against its

[9] See above, pp. 24–5.
[10] *Rec. Caern.*, p. 219.
[11] See above, pp. 119–24.

members, it prevents the state both from limiting disorder on its own terms and from reaping material rewards, in the form of confiscations or fines, from peace-keeping or peace-restoring activity. In this context the main lines of development by the Edwardian conquest have been suggested by Professor Jones Pierce, who has pointed to a process of encroachment by the state upon the former functions of the kindred.[12] Thus, the old system of *galanas*, kin-vengeance and kin-compensation for slaying, had declined by the thirteenth century under the forces of the unwillingness of the offenders' kin to bear responsibility for the misdeeds of others, and of the prince's replacement of composition payments to the kin by fines paid to the prince himself, a development facilitated and perhaps necessitated by the ineffectiveness of the kinship-groups as a pursuing agency. It is doubtless true that it was never a simple matter of the replacement of one agency by another. The laws themselves provide evidence of intermediate developments by which the lord and the kin co-operated in the exaction of *galanas;* such was the *traean cymell*, which can be traced in the March in the later middle ages.[13] Doubtless, too, the concept of kin-vengeance persisted throughout the thirteenth century in Gwynedd, but its expression was no longer necessarily the core of the retributive system.[14] Jones Pierce explains the continued emphasis placed upon the *galanas*-sharing kin in the legal texts of the thirteenth century and later as the result of the fact that 'a knowledge of the structure of parantellic kindred or *cenedl* was still of supreme importance for the efficient operation of *rhaith* or compurgation (operative in many forms of personal actions), a procedure which normally demanded oath-helpers . . . drawn from paternal and maternal kindred in the

---

[12] *Medieval Welsh Society*, pp. 20–6; 296–308.
[13] See generally R. R. Davies, 'The Survival of the Bloodfeud in Medieval Wales', *History*, LIV (1969), pp. 338–57.
[14] Ibid., p. 343, note 25. The examples given by Professor Davies illustrate the survival of the concept of kin-vengeance in late-thirteenth-century Gwynedd, but do not indicate how far it was systematized. In situations where both the state and kinship groups may be seen to have shared interests, it is easy to assume encroachment by the state on the sphere of action of the kin, and equally tempting to assume that the process of displacement involved confrontation. In practice, the emergence of a state interest alongside that of kinship groups may have served to facilitate, rather than to obstruct, the operations of the latter: the development of the lord's *traean cymell* in the levying of *galanas*-payments represents a case in point. Nevertheless, shared interests, however developed, may easily provide occasions for conflict.

proportion of two to one.'[15] Forms of legal process, then, continued frequently to be based on principles and procedures founded in kinship organisation, though again Jones Pierce has commented on the frequent isolation of the individual from his kinsmen in the legal process.[16]

One of the crucial points of contact between state and kindred lay in the matter of the control of the allocation and descent of land. If such control lay in the hands of the prince he might hope both to check the influence in a locality of powerful kindreds or individuals and to reward those whose services he valued. It seems clear that in the case of actions for real property the most effective claim to occupation of land might by the mid-thirteenth century be that based upon proof of investiture by the lord,[17] that is, a claim based upon the authority of the state or some agency reproducing the activity of the state, rather than upon standing within a kindred. Nor was the control of a kindred group over the territory which it occupied an absolute control: a patrimony, say the legal texts, might be forfeited to the ruler for failure to render to him those obligations which attached to the land. In the same way, as a result of the principle, underlying much of the discussion of real property law in the legal texts, that kin-lands were held not by absolute right of ownership but conditionally upon trust for subsequent generations of the kin, alienation in perpetuity of kin-lands was not in theory permissible. This principle is, however, significantly qualified in the legal texts by the information that the sale or *prid* of land was allowed only with the permission of the lord,[18] and evidence from the earlier thirteenth century survives to show Llywelyn ab Iorwerth supervising the permanent alienation of kin-lands in the Perfeddwlad.[19] Professor Jones Pierce argued that the restriction of alienation was upheld by the conservatism of kindred groups, but Dr. Llinos Smith's analysis establishes the strong suspicion that prohibition was maintained by the princes in order that they might benefit from fees charged in return

---

[15] *Medieval Welsh Society*, p. 259.
[16] Ibid., p. 24.
[17] Dafyd Jenkins, 'A Lawyer looks at Welsh Land Law', *Trans. Cymmr.*, 1967, pp. 220–48.
[18] See above, chapter 6, note 76.
[19] See ibid.

for the giving of permission to alienate.[20]

In many cases, including some of those discussed above, it is misleading to see the kin-state relationship in terms of confrontation, for there were several respects in which the state might exploit in its own interests the strength of kinship ties or organisation. Thus, in a few cases, such as that of *amobr*, the kinship tie was utilized by the state to ensure payment of dues.[21] In a somewhat different fashion, the state exploited kin relationships in order to bring offenders to justice: a passage from a collection of documents included in the Record of Caernarvon and alleged to have been found *in recordis Northwallie*[22] runs thus:

> *Item lex Wallensica hec est et habetur de recordo quod si aliquis Wallensis pro aliquo delicto aut forisfacto fugam fecerit et ad largum in patria se tenuit et legi parere noluit parentes cognati et alligati propinquiores sui arestari debent per Justiciarium et eius Officiarios et in Castris detineri quousque talis malefactor per ipsos et suos captus fuerit vel legi paruerit.*

From another source we learn that this was a statement of contemporary practice made by a Welsh judge shortly after the Edwardian conquest,[23] and it may therefore be safely taken as a guide to pre-conquest circumstances.

It has already been seen that at an earlier stage of Welsh political development the *pencenedl* seems sometimes to have been able to exercise control over certain of the offices through which the ruler sought to enforce his will. To judge by the evidence of some of the legal texts, the office of *pencenedl* declined in importance during the thirteenth century,[24] though record evidence reveals that it persisted in Gwynedd and neighbouring territories into the fourteenth century. There are two references to holders of the office in Powys in the 1270s, and early in the fourteenth century Llywelyn ap Gruffydd ab Iorwerth described himself as *pencenedl* of the line of Hwfa ap

---

[20] See ibid.
[21] See, for example, the common customs of Rhufoniog Is Aled, in *S.D.*, p. 151: *Et si non habeat unde solvere (sc. amobr) propinquiores parentes eius solvent pro ea.*
[22] *Rec. Caern.*, p. 131.
[23] *Cal. Anc. Corr.*, p. 234.
[24] Latin Redaction B of the laws has as its list of three causes for which a man may lose his patrimony the following: *regis proditionem, penkenedyl mactationem, et kynllwyn*, but adds a fourth: *si quis cesserit iure hereditario quia non onera et servitia hereditarie imposita sustineret. L.T.W.L.*, p. 231. In the thirteenth-century legal text from Gwynedd, *Llyfr Colan*, the clause relating to the *pencenedl* has been dropped from the list, and its place taken by the clause which appears as the fourth cause in Redaction B. See *Col.* and Dafydd Jenkins, art. cit., pp. 231–2.

Cynddelw.[25] No further information is given in the case of one of the Powys references,[26] but in the other the office is referred to not in terms of its relation to a kindred group but in territorial terms: Gruffydd ap Meurig was *pencenedl* of Cegidfa, a large administrative township in Swydd Llannerch Hudol.[27] And it is interesting that, in the case of Llywelyn ap Gruffydd ab Iorwerth, Hwfa ap Cynddelw was traditionally identified as a hereditary dignitary in the court of Owain Gwynedd,[28] and that Llywelyn's grandfather was possibly a member of the entourage of Llywelyn the Last, while his father was a partisan of Edward I and his brothers, like himself, were prominent servants of Edward II.[29] This territorialization of the office of *pencenedl* in Powys and its association with a prominent ministerial family in Anglesey may suggest that the office only persisted when it could be accommodated within the framework of state activity. In this context it is perhaps significant that *Llyfr Iorwerth* contains references to situations in which the *pencenedl* features, but provides for the case in which there is no *pencenedl*: instead there appears the man 'who is in place of the lord'.[30]

It is hard to extract from the veiled hints of the legal texts and the rare references in record sources a glimpse of the realities of thirteenth-century kinship organization, but it does at least seem clear that as a formal institution the kinship group was offering little resistance to the activity of the state, but that where the kinship group persisted as a central element in the insularity of the local communities (and that must have been the situation throughout most areas of Gwynedd, despite the increasingly wide geographical distribution of the landed interests of families connected with the princes' administration), it represented an association which the princes might sometimes exploit but which they could never ignore.

[25] *Cal. Anc. Pet.*, p. 84.
[26] *C. Chanc. R., Various*, p. 179, has a reference to a Gervase, who was *pencenedl* in the witness-list to a charter of 1277 of Gruffydd ap Gwenwynwyn.
[27] *Littere Wallie*, p. 132, has a reference to Gruffydd ap Meurig, *pencenedl* of Cegidfa, amongst the witnesses to a 1271 grant by Gruffydd ap Gwenwynwyn.
[28] See T. Pennant, *Tours in Wales*, ed. J. Rhys (Caernarfon, 1883), III, p. 428; 'His [*sc.* Hwfa ap Cynddelw's] office, by inheritance was to bear the Prince's coronet, and to put it upon his head when the Bishop of Bangor annointed him (as Nicholas, Bishop of Bangor, affirmeth)'.
[29] J. B. Smith, 'Welsh Dominicans and the Crisis of 1277', *B.B.C.S.*, XXII (1968), p. 355.
[30] *Ior.*, 103. 10.

Part 5
Assessment

Since the mid-twelfth century, the princes of Gwynedd had been anxious not merely to impress their superior status upon their fellow-rulers in Wales, but to gain recognition of this supremacy from a wider community of rulers. Their marriages[1] into the English royal house and the Anglo-Norman aristocracy are a symptom of this desire, as are such matters as their adoption of personal styles intelligible to political society beyond Wales, and their attempts to set the political and constitutional problems of their principality into a wider European context.[2]

The attempt to win an acknowledged place in the framework of European polities required careful management: the princes had to ensure that they were well represented by men able to match the diplomatic skills of the servants of other rulers, and capable of impressing upon the latter the elevated status of their master. The wider political perspectives of the rulers of Gwynedd were the corollary of the attainment of political supremacy within Wales, which in turn required the creation of an effective power-base in Gwynedd itself. In consequence, the princes required the services of men capable of controlling the more complex and extensive forms of governmental activity which were being introduced in Gwynedd: with administration still almost wholly non-departmentalized,[3] these servants of the princes had to be versatile men, knowledgeable in many matters of government. The princes' control over Gwynedd and then

---

[1] See A. J. Roderick, 'Marriage and Politics in Wales, 1066–1282', *W.H.R.* IV (1968–69), pp. 1–20.

[2] On the question of princely styles, see the use of forms derived from English rather than Welsh, namely, *princeps North-wallie, princeps Wallie*. This was not, of course, always the practice adopted by the princes: Llywelyn ab Iorwerth styled himself *princeps Aberffraw et dominus Snowdonie* in the years 1230–40, and Llywelyn ap Gruffydd combined his title of *princeps Wallie* with that of *dominus Snowdonie* in the period 1258–82: such fluctuations may well be a valuable pointer to the changing focus of a ruler's policy. On attempts to present constitutional problems in a broader context see *Cal. Anc. Corr.*, pp. 24, 86; *Welsh Assize Roll*, p. 266.

[3] See ch. II–IV above.

over a wider Welsh principality rested in the first instance largely upon extensive military activity requiring major deployment of men and materials of war; moreover, whatever was achieved by force of arms had to be secured by means which also involved massive expenditure, such as the building of castles like Castell y Bere, Ewloe or Dolforwyn, or the payments, running into many thousands of pounds, by which Llywelyn ap Gruffydd bought from Henry III recognition of the greatness which he had attained in 1267.

Fighting men, skilled administrators and diplomatic representatives, and large quantities of cash were resources in high demand by the thirteenth-century princes. The problems which they encountered in developing these resources were more complex than those of opposition provoked by increasing pressures of governance (though this they undoubtedly met). A deeper problem lay in the fact that their attempts to develop any one category of resources tended to limit their capacity to exploit others. An obvious example of this is provided by the need to recruit clerical servants: grants of lands and immunities helped to secure the specialized services and the influential support of important clerical centres in Gwynedd,[4] but the grants reduced the revenue resources at the princes' disposal. A second illustration is to be found in the princes' attempts to maximize their resources by eliminating the control exercised by other members of the princely house over large areas of Gwynedd.[5] But the methods of elimination were costly: representatives of minor branches of the princely house might be forcibly resettled (though apparently generally on privileged terms) in areas where they had no traditional support; those nearer in blood to the prince might suffer imprisonment or exile, a fate which might be shared by the princes' more distant kin. In any of these cases, however, the dispossessed princeling remained a potential rival for general or local power, and might continue to enjoy the support, covert or overt, of his erstwhile retainers and friends. Some attempts were made to induce princelings to reconcile themselves to the loss of their status as petty chiefs: it required a promise of

[4] This is not to say that the grants were necessarily made with a view to securing such support.
[5] See ch. VIII above.

1,000 marks from Llywelyn ap Gruffydd to persuade his brother, Rhodri, to relinquish his rights in the principality. In the case of men more distantly related to the prince, it was sometimes possible to integrate them within the emerging ministerial élite, but this reduced the availability of places within that élite for men of non-princely descent: as service brought rewards which cut into the princes' resources, it became necessary to restrict the size of the ministerial group.

The practice of granting hereditary tenurial privileges to leading ministers[6] was potentially damaging for the princes, for it tended to produce a growing complex of lands, particularly within the nucleal area of Anglesey, Llŷn, Arfon, and Arllechwedd, which the princes were unable to exploit as they did the lands of unprivileged freemen.

In other, and more paradoxical, ways, the development of certain categories of scarce resources had the effect of weakening the capacity of the rulers to use Gwynedd as the powerbase of a principality which would endure in the face of almost certain opposition from English kings and Anglo-Norman marcher lords. The development of the ministerial élite is important in this respect. The members of this group, by virtue of the work which they did, became, in Professor Glyn Roberts's words, 'sophisticated men of the world, frequently in touch with the king's court, whether as envoys or hostages ... very much at home in baronial circles. The princes of Gwynedd were not their sole source of royal patronage, and their wide travels enabled them to mix on intimate terms with their traditional enemies.'[7] Indeed, they not infrequently turned to those traditional enemies for shelter and support if they incurred the ill-will of the prince of Gwynedd. For the servants of the princes, conflict with the English king or the marcher lords was no longer a stark clash of alien cultures: not for them the resolution of men who knew that their way of life would be at an end if their princes were defeated and their land conquered. For in reality—and it is hard to imagine that they did not grasp this—their usefulness to a conqueror was such that they stood a good chance of retaining their power and prestige under a new dispensation. Moreover, in the later

[6] See ch. VII above for this and subsequent points.
[7] *Aspects of Welsh History*, p. 301.

years of the rule of Llywelyn ap Gruffydd, when the prince was attempting apparently to restrict the scale of his grants to leading ministers, and increasingly threatened to encroach upon the privileges already granted to servants or favourites by himself or his predecessors, annexation by the English king might well have been seen as offering the possibility of more ample rewards in the future and a more secure guarantee of the inviolability of privileges already held.

A study of the governance of the thirteenth-century princes not only reveals the methods by which they created a powerbase from which to extend their sway in Wales, but also serves to expose some of the less obvious factors which contributed to their ultimate failure. It is ironic that had the princes been less vigorous and less successful in their development of the nascent state in Gwynedd, Edward I might have been content, and indeed constrained, to exercise no more than a feudal overlordship over a people whom his ancestor, Henry II, described as 'desperate men . . . [who] could not be tamed'.[8] For it cannot be gainsaid that governance in a quantitative sense was increasing in the thirteenth century. Given the paucity of evidence, its uneven distribution which makes an evolutionary view difficult, and the fact that it frequently emanates from partisan sources, it remains clear that the presence of the prince was felt more strongly in Gwynedd during the later principate of Llywelyn ap Gruffydd than at the outset of the century. If the princes shared many aspects of the control of men and land in Gwynedd with lords of the princely house, great ecclesiastical institutions and kindred groups, it nevertheless seems true that the princes' share in that control was generally increasing through the century. And in the areas subject to their direct control, more was being demanded by way of renders and services, and new dues and obligations were being introduced which the framework of governance was well developed to exact, and more cash as opposed to produce was being demanded.[9] Meanwhile, all

---

[8] See Michael Richter, *Giraldus Cambrensis. The growth of the Welsh Nation* (Aberystwyth, 1972), p. 80.
[9] See ch. VI above.

over Gwynedd were being built stone castles[10] for the lords of Aberffraw: Ewloe, Degannwy, Dolwyddelan, Dolbadarn, Cricieth, Carn Dochan and Castell y Bere, all of which were built or strengthened during the first three-quarters of the century, served to remind the local communities they dominated of the might of the princes.

The castles were not the only additions to the landscape that denoted the extension of princely authority. The century saw the appearance in increasing numbers of trading boroughs which depended on, and were controlled by, the princes.[11] The pattern of land-distribution, too, was being modified throughout the period, most notably by the grants of land to great ecclesiastical houses and to favoured servants of the princes, whilst it is clear that the princes were allowing the purchase of kin-lands by favoured individuals.[12] This was merely one way in which the princes were encouraging the disintegration of traditional social structures, another being the manner in which distinctions between bond and free status were blurred as the obligations proper to each began to overlap under pressure of the princes' requirements.[13]

Thus were governance and the acceptance of governance firmly implanted in Gwynedd. The area which had been longest and most defiantly resistant to English domination had not been untouched by the pressures of governance of a nascent state which in its vigour and extent rivalled anything which the English might import. By the reign of Edward I the permanent conquest of Gwynedd was a viable, if expensive, proposition.

---

[10] For a convenient short survey of the stone castles, see Lord Harlech, *North Wales* (Volume V of *Illustrated regional guides to Ancient Monuments in the ownership or guardianship of the Ministry of Works*) (London, H.M.S.O., 1948), esp. pp. 19–20.
[11] It is perhaps worthwhile to point out that the development of boroughs in Gwynedd did not begin in the thirteenth century: a late-twelfth-century charter of Maredudd ap Cynan granting land in Nefyn to Haughmond abbey has amongst its witnesses *Roberto et Stephano burgensibus de Nevin*. See the Haughmond Cartulary, Shrewsbury Public Library MS. I, f. 149r.
[12] See p. 80 above.
[13] See pp. 66, 92–3 above.

APPENDIX I

A CHECK-LIST OF CHARTERS ISSUED BY THE THIRTEENTH-CENTURY RULERS OF GWYNEDD

The following list is confined to the formal documents issued in the name of the princes and recording their grants and confirmations of territories or privileges, or both. In some cases, textual problems which bear upon questions of authenticity are discussed, but no attempt is made to edit the texts, or to provide a full textual commentary upon them. Where printed texts of a high standard exist, only these are cited; references to texts preserved in the rolls of the English royal government are normally given *via* the texts or calendars published by the P.R.O.; in other cases, manuscript references are given, sometimes accompanied by citations of readily available translations.

1(a). *Lewelinus gervasii filius tocius norwallie princeps*, to Aberconwy abbey.
   Dated: 6th ides January 1198, in the tenth year of my principate, i.e., 8 January 1199.
   Grants and confirms extensive lands in Gwynedd, and privileges.
   Texts in Dugdale, *Monasticon*, V, pp. 272–74; *Rec. Caern.*, pp. 146–48.* The topographical sections are printed, and the charter discussed, in C. A. Gresham, 'The Aberconwy Charter', *Arch. Camb.*, 1939, pp. 123–62. Further discussion is in R. W. Hays, *The History of the Abbey of Aberconway, 1186–1537* (Cardiff, 1963), pp. 6–23.

1(b). Same to the same. Same date.
   Grants further privileges.
   Text: *Rec. Caern.*, p. 148.

These two charters are, perhaps, the most puzzling of any issued by the princes. It has hitherto been assumed that the dating of the charters at least cannot be correct, on the grounds that Llywelyn was not in a position to make, as he does in 1 (a), extensive territorial grants in Gwynedd Uwch Conwy because this area was controlled in 1199 by Gruffydd ap Cynan ab Owain and his brother Maredudd. But the ascription to Gruffydd of pre-eminence in Gwynedd Uwch Conwy until his death in 1200, most forcefully argued by Lloyd, *Hist. Wales*, II, pp. 588–89, 612–13, rests on very insecure foundations, and principally on the eulogies of the poets who describe Gruffydd as *rwyf kemeis* and *rwy dygannwy*. See Lloyd, op. cit., II, p. 589, note 74, for these phrases from Prydydd y Moch.

There seems no good reason why the validity of the dating clauses in the charters now under discussion should be thus lightly rejected. They present no obvious internal inconsistencies: the use of the style Llywelyn son of Iorwerth, prince of all North Wales, is at once assertive, as though stating a novel position, and its inclusion of Llywelyn's patronymic means that it is almost certainly to be dated before the end of the first decade of the thirteenth century; the normal style after the first decade of the century was simply Llywelyn, prince of North Wales.

Again, the placing of January 1199 in the tenth year of Llywelyn's principate is reasonable, if one assumes that he reckoned his principate from the date when he first began to assert his rights to a share of Gwynedd, and that, according to Giraldus, was in 1188: see *Giraldi Cambrensis Opera*, ed. J. S. Brewer *et al.*, VI, p. 134. The use of the first person singular denotes this as a very early charter.

*See also *C. Chart. R., 1327–41*, p. 268.

APPENDIX I

A full re-assessment of the validity of the dating of these charters would involve an extensive and detailed re-evaluation of the political development of Gwynedd in the 1190s, a project beyond the scope of the present work. It must suffice here to make the following points:
   (a) Many of the territorial grants in Gwynedd Uwch Conwy may be confirmed in 1(a) by Llywelyn acting as political overlord rather than as the direct ruler of the territories.
   (b) Such a position of overlord is unlikely to have been exercised by Llywelyn as long as we assume, with Lloyd, that in 1199 he was in direct control only of territory east of the Conwy. But the references of Prydydd y Moch to Gruffydd's being in possession of Degannwy and Cemais may refer to the political control which he undoubtedly exercised in those areas in the early 1190s. (See Giraldus's account in *Opera*, VI, pp. 126-7, of the expulsion of Rhodri ab Owain from Anglesey by Gruffydd and Maredudd ap Cynan, an action which almost certainly implies their control of the mainland opposite the island.) In the war of 1194, when Llywelyn and the sons of Cynan joined forces against Dafydd ab Owain, it is well known that there was a major battle at the mouth of the Conwy, where Dafydd was defeated. But the poets who laud Llywelyn's part in this go on to describe as part of this campaign, or another which followed hard upon it, a crossing of the Menai at Porthaethwy and a battle which Llywelyn won in the heart of Anglesey at Coedanau. The role of Rhodri ab Owain in these events is not clear: some sources make him a member of the coalition which defeated Dafydd, while others set him on the losing side (see Lloyd, op. cit., II, p. 588, notes 72, 73). It may be that Rhodri was initially amongst the victorious allies but subsequently fell victim to a drive by Llywelyn to establish himself above the Conwy, a drive which took him into Arfon and then Anglesey. It is, perhaps, significant that Rhodri, though possibly the founder of Aberconwy abbey (see R. W. Hays, op. cit., p. 6), was not buried there, but at Caer Gybi, a site which suggests that his death took place in Anglesey when Aberconwy was in territory controlled by an opponent. The above reading of the situation would confine the area controlled by the sons of Cynan to Llŷn, Dunoding and Meirionydd. It is interesting that *Brut y Tywysogyon* makes no mention of any drive into Gwynedd Uwch Conwy by Llywelyn ab Iorwerth after Gruffydd's death in 1200. Finally, it is noteworthy that Giraldus (*Opera*, VI, p. 134) states in the second (1197) edition of his *Itinerarium Cambriae* that Llywelyn held *Venedotia fere tota*, from which he had driven out both Dafydd *and* Rhodri, a phrase which would have been wholly inappropriate had Llywelyn held only the Perfeddwlad.

The political situation in the period 1194-1200 set out above would clearly enable Llywelyn to regard himself as the dominant force in Gwynedd, and to issue a charter to Aberconwy confirming previous grants and probably adding new ones. Charter 1(b) still presents something of a problem. It may represent a rather later document, issued for convenience with the same dating-clause and witness-list, but probably representing an afterthought, a group of clauses not thought out when the first charter was drafted, possibly in advance of its being formally conferred upon the abbey.

   2. Llywelyn, *Norwalle princeps*, to Strata Marcella abbey.
      Dated: 7th before the Kalends of December (?1208), Dinorben.
      Grants lands and privileges.
      Text: E. D. Jones, N. G. Davies, B. F. Roberts, 'Five Strata Marcella Charters', *N.L.W.J.*, V (1947), p. 52.

APPENDIX I

The use of the first person singular throughout marks this charter out as one issued early in Llywelyn's principate. In 1208 Llywelyn overran the territory of Gwenwynwyn in which lay Strata Marcella: see *B.T.*, *R.B.H.* p. 188.

3. *Lewelinus Gervasii filius Norwallie princeps* to Cymer abbey.
Dated: 1209.
Grants and confirms lands and privileges.
Text: the basis of all serious study of this charter should be the edition and analysis in Keith Williams-Jones, 'Llywelyn's Charter to Cymer Abbey in 1209', *Jnl. Mer. Hist. Soc.*, III (1957), pp. 45–78.

4. Llywelyn, *princeps Northwallie*, to Basingwerk abbey.
No date.
Grants lands and privileges.
Text: Dugdale, *Monasticon*, V, p. 263; cf. *C. Chart, R., 1257–1300*, p. 291.
The use of the first person singular throughout suggests that the charter is very early, but this is hardly conclusive as it may reflect drafting by grantees: David ap Llywelyn's charter of 1240 (see below, no. 19) also employs the first person singular. But it would seem that Llywelyn ab Iorwerth needed little prompting to offer his protection and favour to Cistercian abbeys (see nos. 1, 2, 3 above), of which Basingwerk was one, so that an early date is to be expected. In addition, the witness-list contains none of the names of Llywelyn's servants who appear with some regularity from about 1215 onwards: it does not even contain the name of Master Ystrwyth or Gwyn ab Ednywain, and so may be very early.

5. Llywelyn, *princeps Norwallie*, to Haughmond abbey.
No date.
Grants lands and privileges in Ellesmere.
Text: Shrewsbury Public Library, MS. 1, f. 128v; Eyton, *Shropshire*, X, p. 251 (English).
The combination in the text of first person singular and plural, and the presence in the witness-list of Gwyn ab Ednywain, suggests that this grant falls between 1205, when Llywelyn acquired Ellesmere, and 1210, when he was for a time deprived of it.

6. Llywelyn *princeps Norwallie*, to Haughmond abbey.
No date.
Confirms grants of lands in Ellesmere.
Text: Shrewsbury Public Library, MS. 1, f. 209v; Eyton, op. cit., X, p. 250.
The confirmation of a grant made by Owain ap Dafydd perhaps suggests that the date of this charter may be close to that of no. 5 above, i.e., in the period of Llywelyn's first occupation of Ellesmere.

7. Llywelyn *princeps Norwallie*, to Haughmond abbey.
No date.
Grants lands in Ellesmere with the consent of Geoffrey de Vere and Robert fitz Aher.
Text: Shrewsbury Public Library, MS. 1, f. 152; Eyton, op. cit., X, p. 250.
Possibly about the same date as nos. 5 and 6 above.

8. Llywelyn *princeps Norwallie*, to Morgan Gam.
No date.
Grants lands for service of one knight's fee.
Text: G. T. Clark, *Cartae . . . Glamorgan*, (Cardiff, 1910) III, p. 1083.
It has been assumed in the past (see Keith Williams-Jones, art. cit., p. 51,

APPENDIX I

note 40) that this charter belongs to 1231. But by that date Llywelyn had abandoned the style 'prince of North Wales'. It seems clear from the witnesses, who include Madog ap Gruffydd Maelor, Maredudd ap Rhotpert, Ednyfed (Ethenwit), Einion ap Gwalchmai (who otherwise does not appear after about 1223), Madog ap Rhirid, Maelgwn ap Rhys Gryg (a mistake, presumably, for Maelgwn ap Rhys—*ob.* 1230, Lloyd, op. cit., II, p. 674—and Rhys Gryg) and Rhys ap Gruffydd, that the charter was issued during Llywelyn's southern expedition of 1215, or possibly during the Aberdyfi assembly of 1216. See *BT, R.B.H.*, p. 206.

9. Llywelyn *princeps Northwallie*, to Ynys Lannog priory.
   Dated: 15 October 1221, Caernarfon.
   Grants lands and privileges.
   Text: Dugdale, *Monasticon*, IV, pp. 581–82 (witness-list incomplete); cf. *C. Chart. R., 1257–1300*, p. 459.

10. Llywelyn *princeps de Aberfrau et dominus Snaudonie*, to the Hospital of St. John, Dolgynwal.
    Dated: *apud Ruthin in octabis Sancti Martini anno regni Henrici Junioris Regis Anglie X^{mo}* (18 November 1225).
    Grants lands and privileges.
    Text: Eyton, *Shropshire*, X, p. 247; cf. *C. Pat. R., 1313–17*, p. 576.
    A most puzzling document. The designation of Henry III as *junior* is unusual and may relate to his minority. But if the date is, indeed, 1225, this is an unusually early use by Llywelyn of the style 'prince of Aberffraw, lord of Snowdon', which does not appear elsewhere until 1230. It is tempting to suppose that X^{mo} in the dating clause should read *XX^{mo}*, though by that date Henry III was no longer *junior*. On internal grounds the charter appears sound enough, and the witness-list is compatible with a date of 1225 (but also with one after 1230).

11. Gruffydd, *filius Lewelini principis Norwallie*, to Strata Marcella.
    Dated: 1226.
    Grants and confirms lands.
    Text: E. D. Jones, N. G. Davies, B. F. Roberts, 'Five Strata Marcella Charters', *N.L.W.J.*, V (1947), pp. 53–54.

12. David *filius domini L. principis*, to Ynys Lannog.
    Dated: 22 February 1229.
    Confirms territory and privileges.
    Text: Dugdale, *Monasticon*, IV, p. 582 (witness-list incomplete); *C. Chart. R., 1257–1300*, p. 459.

13. Llywelyn *princeps Aberfraw dominus Snowdon*, to Ednyfed Fychan.
    Dated: May 1230.
    Acknowledges and permits purchase of land by Ednyfed.
    Text: J. G. Evans, *Report*, II, p. 859.

14. Llywelyn *princeps de Aberfrau dominus Snowdini*, to Haughmond.
    No date: ? 1230–32.
    Confirms liberties in Nefyn.
    Text: Shrewsbury Public Library, MS. 1, f. 149*v*.
    The presence of Rhicert ap Cadwaladr (for whom see Appendix II *sub nomine*) in the witness-list suggests that the charter should be dated between 1230 (suggested by Llywelyn's style) and 1232 (when Rhicert apparently ceased to be *rhaglaw* of Dinllaen).

APPENDIX I 203

15. Llywelyn, *princeps de Aberfrau dominus Snawdonie*, to Ralph Mortimer.
    No date: *c.* 1230–40.
    Quitclaims lands in Norton and Knighton.
    Text: B.L., Harleian MS. 1240, f. 68*v*; Eyton. op. cit., XI, p. 348.
    This should be dated 1230–40 in view of the title adopted by Llywelyn.

16. Llywelyn *princeps de Aberfrau et dominus Snaudonie*, to Ynys Lannog.
    Dated: 10 April 1237, Rhosfair.
    Grants lands and privileges.
    Text: Dugdale *Monasticon*, IV, p. 582 (witness-list incomplete); cf. *C. Chart. R.*, *1257–1300*, p. 460.

17. David *filius domini Lewelini*, to Ynys Lannog.
    Dated: 21 February 1238.
    Confirms lands and privileges.
    Text: Dugdale, *Monasticon*, IV, p. 582.

18. David *filius domini Lewelini principis de Aberfrau domini Snaudonie*, to Haughmond.
    No date: ? 1238–40.
    Confirms lands in Trefeglwys.
    Text: Shrewsbury Public Library, MS. 1, f. 215.
    The presence of Richard, bishop of Bangor, as a witness indicates that the charter is later than 1237. It was possibly issued in 1238, when David ejected his brother Gruffydd from Powys.

19. David *filius Lewelini princeps Northwallie*, to Basingwerk.
    Dated: 25 July 1240, Coleshill.
    Confirms lands and privileges.
    Text: Dugdale, *Monasticon*, V, p. 263.

20. Llywelyn *filius Griffini filii Leulini quondam principis Norwallie* to Ralph Mortimer.
    No date: probably *c.* 1241.
    Quitclaims rights to Maelienydd and Gwerthrynion.
    Texts: J. B. Smith, 'The Middle March in the Thirteenth Century', *B.B.C.S.*, XXIV (1970), pp. 88–9, 92.

21. Llywelyn ap Gruffydd to Einion ap Maredudd.
    Dated: 27 September 1243, Llannerch, Dyffryn Clwyd.
    Confirms lands and privileges.
    Text: J. Conway Davies, 'A grant of Llywelyn ap Gruffydd', *N.L.W.J.*, III, (1943), p. 158.

22. Llywelyn ap Gruffydd to Ynys Lannog.
    Dated: 6 January 1247, Llanfaes.
    Confirms lands and privileges.
    Texts: Dugdale, *Monasticon*, IV, p. 582 (witness-list incomplete); cf. *C. Chart. R.*, *1257–1300*, p. 460.

23. Llywelyn ap Gruffydd to Basingwerk.
    Dated: 8 April 1247, Bangor.
    Confirms lands and privileges.
    Text: *C. Chart. R., 1257–1300*, p. 291.

24. Owain ap Gruffydd to Ynys Lannog.
    Dated: 17 September 1247, Bagenig (Bancenyn).
    Confirms lands and privileges.
    Text: Dugdale, *Monasticon*, IV, p. 582 (witness-list incomplete); cf. *C. Chart. R.*, *1257–1300*, p. 460.

25. *Dominus David filius Grufini* to Madog ab Einion ap Maredudd.
Dated: *Anno MCCxlxix, xi Kallendas februarii:* apparently to be read as 22 January 1260.
Confirms lands and privileges.
Text: J. Conway Davies, 'A Grant by David ap Gruffydd', *N.L.W.J.*, III (1943), p. 29.

26. Llywelyn, *filius Gruffini princeps Wallie dominus Snawdonie*, to the bishop and chapter of St. Asaph.
No date: see above, pp. 176–7 for the suggestion that the date of the charter is late 1276/early 1277.
Confirms diocesan liberties.
Text: Haddan and Stubbs, *Councils*, pp. 519-21.

27. Llywelyn ap Gruffydd, *princeps Wallie dominus Snaudonie*, to Heilyn ap Tudur ab Ednyfed.
Dated: 7 August 1281.
Confirms an exchange of lands between them.
Text: *Rec. Caern.*, p. 211 (defective).

28. Llywelyn, *filius Griffini, princeps Wallie et dominus Snowdon*, to Roger Mortimer.
Dated: 9 October 1281, Radnor.
Quitclaims lands in Gwerthrynion.
Text: J. B. Smith, art. cit., p. 90.

29. David *filius Griffini princeps Wallie dominus Snowdonie*, to Rhys Fychan.
Dated: 2 May 1283, Llanberis.
Text: *Littere Wallie*, pp. 74–5.

CHARTERS OF WHICH THE TEXTS HAVE NOT SURVIVED

A. **To Aberconwy Abbey**
30. Grant by Llywelyn ap Gruffydd of first voidance of the chapels of Cemais and Caernarfon.
Source: *C. Chart. R., 1327–41*, p. 269. See R. W. Hays, op. cit., pp. 116–17

B. **To Basingwerk Abbey**
31. Grant by Llywelyn ab Iorwerth, prince of North Wales.
Source: the existence of this grant is revealed by comparison of nos. 4 and 19 above; cf. *C. Chart. R., 1327–41*, p. 100.

C. **To Beddgelert Priory**
32. Charter of *Llywelyn Magnus*, granting land in Pennant.
33. Charter of Llywelyn ap Gruffydd, granting land in Pennardd.
34. Charter of Llywelyn ap Gruffydd, granting land in Cefnyfynydd and Llecheiddior.
35. Charter of *Dominus Owain*, granting land in Trefyfeirdd (Tre'r beirdd).
36. Charter of Llywelyn ap Gruffydd, confirming land in Beddgelert.
37–39. Three charters of *Dominus Dafydd*, granting land in Pennant.
Source: *Rec. Caern.*, p. 166.

D. **To Strata Marcella**
40. Grant by David *filius Lewelini principis Aberfrau*.
Source: *C. Chart. R., 1300–26*, p. 441.

APPENDIX II
A BIOGRAPHICAL GAZETTEER OF LAYMEN IN THE SERVICE OF THE THIRTEENTH-CENTURY PRINCES

Only persons who can be identified with reasonable certainty as being in the service of one or more of the princes are included in the following gazetteer. It must be emphasized that it does not include the name of every man appearing in the witness-lists of the princes' charters, since it is quite possible that men other than princes' servants appear in such lists. The recurrence of a name in two or more witness-lists has, however, been tentatively accepted as an indication of ministerial status. In most cases, the criteria for inclusion in the gazetteer are self-evident; where this is not so, explanation is provided in the notes.

In the case of officials of Llywelyn ap Gruffydd who passed into the service of the English king or marcher lords after the Edwardian conquest, references to the post-conquest phase of their service are not exhaustive in most cases, but are intended merely to prove continued ministerial activity.

Types of reference excluded from the gazetteer are those which relate to events covered by other citations used in the same biographical entry and which add nothing to the information there provided. Also excluded are those which illustrate a minister's genealogical background, rather than his career: these have been discussed, in most cases, in the main text above. Charters are designated by the numbers given to them in Appendix I.

Bleddyn ap Llywelyn
1274:
  renders account as castellan of Dolforwyn. *Littere Wallie*, p. 23.
1305:
  petitions Prince Edward that the justice of north Wales is demanding two shillings per year from him for two acres of land in Aber which Prince Llywelyn gave him to hold free of renders. *Rec. Caern.*, p. 217.

Bleddyn ap Madog
?1240–5:
  rhaglaw of Dinorben. NLW Peniarth MS. no. 231, pp. 50, 119.

Bleddyn ap Meurig
1223:
  one of a group of arbitrators appointed by Llywelyn ab Iorwerth to determine the limits of the lands held by certain of the south Welsh chiefs. *Patent Rolls, 1216–25*, p. 413.
1226:
  witnesses charter 11.
1244:
  amongst a group of Welshmen whom Henry III ordered to be brought to Chester. *C. Lib. R., 1240–45*, pp. 252–3.

Caradog (ap Thomas?)
1221:
  acts as Llywelyn ab Iorwerth's envoy to Henry III. *Rot. Claus.*, I, p. 457.
1237:
  acts as Llywelyn ab Iorwerth's envoy to Henry III. *C. Lib. R., 1226–40*, p. 272.

APPENDIX II

Cynfrig Wenkwys
?1224–32:
rhaglaw of Dinorben. NLW Peniarth MS. no. 231, pp. 49, 117.

Cynfrig ab Ednyfed
1256:
one of a group of envoys sent by Llywelyn ap Gruffydd to treat with Henry III concerning Llywelyn's affairs. *C. Pat. R., 1247–58*, p. 471.
1263:
one of a group of arbitrators appointed in the agreement between Llywelyn ap Gruffydd and Gruffydd ap Gwenwynwyn to determine any future readjustments of territory between the two parties should Gruffydd lose lands in war. *Littere Wallie*, p. 78.
one of a large group witnessing the performance of homage by Gruffydd ap Gwenwynwyn to Llywelyn ap Gruffydd. Ibid., p. 77.
1268:
amongst the envoys of Llywelyn ap Gruffydd who handed over 4,000 marks to Henry III's receivers. Ibid., p. 143.
1274:
one of the arbitrators appointed to determine the *causa accusacionum* against Gruffydd ap Gwenwynwyn and his son Owain. Ibid., p. 109; amongst the witnesses to the record of the settlement. Ibid., p. 99.

Cynfrig ap Goronwy
?1249–54:
rhaglaw of Rhuddlan. NLW Peniarth MS. no. 231, p. 124.
?1254–66:
rhaglaw of Rhuddlan. Ibid., pp. 51, 120.
1269:
as bailiff of Rhuddlan, stood surety of forty shillings for Rhys ab Ednyfed's fidelity to the prince. *Littere Wallie*, p. 23.
1272:
amongst the witnesses to the quitclaim by Rhodri ap Gruffydd to Prince Llywelyn of all his lands in Wales. Ibid., p. 85.
1278:
one of a group of Welshmen 'for whom the king will provide'; granted a fee of six pounds per year. *C. Chanc. R., Various*, p. 176. For Cynfrig's subsequent career as royal bailiff of Rhuddlan, 1279–81, see *C. Close R., 1272–79*, p. 563; *Cal. Inq. Misc.*, I, p. 343; *C. Chanc. R., Various*, p. 189. For his complaints to Edward I in 1282, see *Registrum . . . Peckham*, II, p. 462.

Cynfrig ap Madog
1283:
keeper of Castell y Bere. *Littere Wallie*, p. 189.

Dafydd ab Einion (Probably not the man listed below)
c. 1270:
rhaglaw of Eiryoes. NLW Peniarth MS. no. 231, p. 79.

Dafydd ab Einion
1247:
possibly the David ab Evin who witnessed charter 24.
1256:
one of a group of envoys sent by Llywelyn ap Gruffydd to treat with Henry III concerning Llywelyn's affairs. *C. Pat. R., 1247–58*, p. 471.

APPENDIX II 207

1258:
amongst the parties to the Scotto-Welsh agreement. *Littere Wallie*, p. 185.
1259:
amongst those whom Llywelyn ap Gruffydd announced had sworn to a truce at Montgomery between himself and Henry III. *Littere Wallie*, p. 28.
1263:
one of a large group witnessing the performance of homage to Prince Llywelyn by Gruffydd ap Gwenwynwyn. Ibid., p. 77.
1267:
with Einion ap Caradog (*q.v.*) negotiated the Treaty of Montgomery; swore to uphold the treaty. *C. Pat. R., 1266–72*, p. 102 (for the safe conduct); *Littere Wallie*, p. 4.
1268:
one of the arbitrators chosen by Llywelyn ap Gruffydd to settle his dispute with Gilbert of Clare. Ibid., p. 102.
1272:
amongst the witnesses to Rhodri ap Gruffydd's quitclaim to Prince Llywelyn of all his lands in Wales. Ibid., p. 85.
1274:
one of the arbitrators appointed to give judgement in the *causa accusacionum* against Gruffydd ap Gwenwynwyn and his son Owain. *Littere Wallie*, p. 109; amongst the witnesses to this settlement. Ibid., p. 99.
1277:
together with Goronwy ap Heilyn (*q.v.*), swore *pro se et aliis de consilio . . . principis* to ensure that Llywelyn ap Gruffydd would surrender to Edward I hostages for his observance of the terms of the Treaty of Conwy. Ibid., p. 121.
1278:
probably the Dafydd ab Einion whom Edward I (in a letter to the bishop of Bangor) said had complained to him that he was being denied the use of his corn. Haddan and Stubbs, *Councils*, pp. 524–5.
1281:
headed the witness-list to an agreement between the abbot of Cymer and Prince Llywelyn. *Littere Wallie*, pp. 45–6.

Dafydd ap Gruffydd
1247:
appeared at the head of the witness-list of charter 22; he is followed by Tudur ap Madog and Iorwerth ap Gwrgunon (*q.v.*), all three apparently being styled 'stewards of the grantor'.

Ednyfed Fychan
1215:
amongst the witnesses to charter 8; name given simply as 'Ethenwit'.
1218:
heads the list of Llywelyn's men named in the Treaty of Worcester as obliged to withdraw from his homage and fealty should he break the agreement. *Rot. Claus.*, I, p. 397.
1222:
amongst the witnesses to Llywelyn ab Iorwerth's agreement with Ranulf of Chester for the marriage of the prince's daughter Helen to John the Scot. Owen, *Catalogue*, III, p. 526.
1223:
one of a group of arbitrators appointed by Llywelyn ab Iorwerth to determine the limits of the lands held by certain of the southern Welsh chiefs. *Patent Rolls, 1216–25*, p. 413.

APPENDIX II

1225:
witnessed charter 10: designated as 'steward'.
1229:
granted letters of protection for his lands in south Wales and elsewhere by Henry III. *Patent Rolls, 1225–32*, p. 271.
1230:
grantee of charter 13; designated as 'steward'.
?1230–40:
witnessed charter 14.
?1230–40:
witnessed charter 15; designated as 'steward'.
1231:
amongst the small group of Welshmen, mainly chiefs, who sealed the agreement by which the truce between Llywelyn ab Iorwerth and Henry III was extended for a year. *Patent Rolls, 1225–32*, p. 453.
1232 (May):
together with Einion Fychan and, later, Princess Joan, received a safe-conduct from Henry III for negotiations with the English government. *Patent Rolls, 1225–32*, pp. 471, 475–6.
1232 (November):
headed a group of envoys from Llywelyn who were given a safe-conduct to go to Shrewsbury to negotiate with Henry III's representatives; designated as 'steward'. *C. Pat. R., 1232–47*, pp. 3–4.
1233:
granted a safe-conduct by Henry III to go to Worcester to treat of peace between Henry and Llywelyn. Ibid., p. 17.
1234:
possibly acted with Prince Llywelyn to fix a day for judicial proceedings regarding disputed land in Llangollen. *C. Chart. R., 1257–1300*, p. 458.
1235 (June):
issued by Henry III with a safe-conduct for himself and those with him who were passing through England *en route* to the Holy Land. *C. Pat. R., 1232–47*, p. 100.
1235 (June):
Simon Pateshul, treasurer, is ordered by Henry III to find out where Ednyfed, steward of Prince Llywelyn, is staying in London *en route* to the Holy Land, and to give him a silver cup, worth five marks. *Close Rolls, 1234–37*, p. 101. Cancelled, *quia non habuit*.
1237:
Henry III requested that when Llywelyn sent his son to him, he should also send *dominum de Sancto Asapho et Edenevet fidelem ipsius principis*, with full power to agree peace terms. Ibid., pp. 526–7.
1238:
headed a list of ministers who Llywelyn announced had sworn, on his soul, to observe a one-year extension of the truce with Henry III. *C. Pat. R., 1233–47*, pp. 225, 237.
1240 (May):
one of three men from Gwynedd appointed in the Treaty of Gloucester to act as arbitrators in the settlement of disputes over land between David ap Llywelyn and *barones regis*. One of four men who swear to ensure David's observance of the treaty. *Littere Wallie*, pp. 5–6.
1240 (July):
witnessed charter 19.

APPENDIX II

?1240–4:
giving evidence before Edward I's inquiry into the use of the laws of Hywel Dda, Hywel 'de Sochlac' recalled that Ednyfed represented David ap Llywelyn in a plea between the latter and Gruffydd ap Llywelyn. *C. Chanc. R., Various*, p. 193.

1241:
together with Bishop Hywel of St. Asaph (probably his son), he swore to ensure that David ap Llywelyn observed the treaty of Gwern Eigron. *Littere Wallie*, p. 10.

1245:
headed a group of David ap Llywelyn's envoys who were given safe-conducts to parley with Henry III and his council at Degannwy. *C. Pat. R., 1232–47*, p. 461.

1246:
notice of Ednyfed's death in the Chester annals: he is styled *justiciarius Wallie*. Christie (ed.), *Annales Cestrienses*, p. 66.

Reference of uncertain date:
an inquisition of 1278 heard that Llywelyn and Owain, lords of Mechain, pleaded in a case regarding disputed lands in Mechain before Ednyfed Fychan, then justice of the prince. *C. Inq. Misc.*, I, p. 333.

Ednyfed
1270:
rhingyll of Dinorben. NLW Peniarth MS. no. 231, p. 79.

Einion
1270:
rhingyll of Denbigh. Ibid.

Einion ap Caradog
c. 1240:
by tradition, he is supposed to have taken Gruffydd ap Llywelyn's part against David ap Llywelyn, and to have been expelled by the latter from his lands. Wynn, *Gwydir Family*, p. 11.

c. 1241:
amongst the witnesses to charter 20.

1258:
one of the parties to the Scotto-Welsh alliance. *Littere Wallie*, p. 185

1261 (April):
one of a group of arbitrators between Llywelyn ap Gruffydd and the bishop of Bangor in a dispute over ecclesiastical rights and privileges; one of a further group of arbitrators elected to settle a possible case of violation of sanctuary. Haddan and Stubbs, *Councils*, pp. 489–90.

1261 (Aug.):
one of a group of arbitrators who settled a dispute over boundaries in Talyllyn between the prince and the bishop of Bangor; one of a group assigned to ensure that the jury chosen to pronounce in a similar case involving the boundary between Llanwnda and Bodellog was up to strength. *Littere Wallie*, pp. 97–8.

1263:
amongst a large group witnessing the agreement of Gruffydd ap Gwenwynwyn to do homage to Llywelyn ap Gruffydd. Ibid., p. 78.

1267:
with Dafydd ab Einion (*q.v.*) negotiated the Treaty of Montgomery. *C. Pat. R., 1266–72*, p. 102, for safe-conduct; *Littere Wallie*, p. 4, for the negotiations; ibid., for oaths taken to observe the treaty.

1272:
 amongst the witnesses to the quitclaim by Rhodri ap Gruffydd to Llywelyn ap Gruffydd of all his lands in Wales. Ibid., p. 85.
1274 (18 April):
 one of the arbitrators in the *causa accusacionum* against Gruffydd ap Gwenwynwyn and his son Owain. Ibid., p. 109.
 amongst the witnesses to the settlement drawn up. Ibid., p. 99.
1274 (22 April):
 headed the list of auditors of the account of the keeper of Dolforwyn. Ibid., p. 23.
1275:
 with Tudur ab Ednyfed (*q.v.*), mentioned by Llywelyn ap Gruffydd as a possible arbitrator in his dispute with the bishop of St. Asaph. Haddan and Stubbs, *Councils*, p. 505.
1277:
 headed a list of sureties for the release by Llywelyn ap Gruffydd of Dafydd Goch ab Iorwerth ap Dafydd. *Littere Wallie*, p. 44.

Einion ap Gwalchmai
1215:
 amongst the witnesses to charter 8.
1218:
 amongst a group of Llywelyn's men named in the Treaty of Worcester as obliged to withdraw from his homage and fealty should he break the agreement. *Rot. Claus.*, I, p. 397.
1221:
 headed the lay witnesses to charter 9.
1223:
 one of a group of arbitrators appointed by Llywelyn ab Iorwerth to determine the limits of the lands held by certain of the south Welsh chiefs. *Patent Rolls, 1216-25*, p. 413.
Reference of uncertain date:
 giving evidence before Edward I's 1281 enquiry into the operation of the law of Hywel Dda, Cynfrig Sais recalled that in a case between Llywelyn ab Iorwerth and Gwenwynwyn (of Powys) before the king's justices at Westminster, Einion ap Gwalchmai was associated with the justices and they judged together. The date is presumably 1208-10. *C. Chanc. R., Various*, p. 195.

Einion ap Llywarch
1271:
 headed a group of attorneys for Llywelyn ap Gruffydd who handed over £1,000 to Henry III's receivers. *Littere Wallie*, p. 140.
1283:
 a record of men from Rhos Uwch Dulas who gave bonds for keeping the peace includes Anyan fil' Lywer'. *B.B.C.S.*, XIII (1949), p. 143.

Einion Fychan
1221:
 amongst the witnesses to charter 9.
1225:
 amongst the witnesses to charter 10.
1232 (May):
 together with Ednyfed Fychan (*q.v.*) and, later, Princess Joan, he received a safe-conduct from Henry III for negotiations with the English. *Patent Rolls, 1225-32*, pp. 471, 475-6.

APPENDIX II

1232 (November):
amongst a group of envoys of Llywelyn ab Iorwerth given safe-conducts by Henry III for negotiations at Shrewsbury. *C. Pat. R., 1232–47*, pp. 3–4.

1232 (December):
Henry III ordered the release of the son of Einion Fychan, kept as a hostage in return for the delivery of the hostages for William de Braose. *C. Pat. R., 1232–47*, p. 6.

1235:
one of a group sent by Llywelyn ab Iorwerth to settle infractions of the truce with Henry III. *Close Rolls, 1234–37*, p. 179.

1237:
headed the witness-list to charter 16.

1238:
one of a group of ministers whom Llywelyn announced had sworn, on his soul, to observe a one-year extension of the truce with Henry III. *C. Pat. R., 1232–47*, pp. 225, 237.

1240 (May):
one of three men from Gwynedd appointed in the Treaty of Gloucester to act as arbitrators in the settlement of disputes over land between David ap Llywelyn and *barones regis*; and one of four men responsible for ensuring David's observance of the treaty. *Littere Wallie*, pp. 5–6.

1240 (July):
amongst the witnesses to charter 19.

1241 (March, April):
amongst a group of proctors acting for David ap Llywelyn in proceedings concerning claims against the prince by the marcher lords. *Littere Wallie*, p. 18; *Close Rolls, 1237–42*, p. 357.

1241–6:
detained as a hostage by Henry III. See note.

1246 (September):
granted twenty-five marks from the issues of Salop and Stafford to buy himself a horse, of the king's gift. *C. Lib. R., 1245–51*, p. 81.

1246 (September):
did homage to Henry III for all his lands in Wales. *Littere Wallie*, p. 49.

1246 (September):
granted all of his lands in Wales which he had on the day when David ap Llywelyn gave him to the king as a hostage for faithful service. *C. Chart. R., 1226–57*, p. 305.

1247:
amongst the witnesses to charter 24.

1258 (March):
one of the parties to the Scotto-Welsh agreement. *Littere Wallie*, p. 185.

1258 (August):
? one of the witnesses to the agreement whereby Hywel ap Rhys did homage to Llywelyn ap Gruffydd. *Ibid.*, p. 45.

1261 (April):
one of a group of arbitrators between Llywelyn and the bishop of Bangor in a dispute over ecclesiastical rights; one of a further group chosen to settle a possible case of violation of sanctuary. Haddan and Stubbs, *Councils*, pp. 489–90.

1261 (August):
one of a group of arbitrators who settled a dispute over boundaries in Talyllyn between Llywelyn and the bishop of Bangor: one of a group assigned to ensure that the jury chosen to pronounce in a similar case involving bounds between Llanwnda and Bodellog was at full strength. *Littere Wallie*, pp. 97–8.

APPENDIX II

NOTE

In December 1241 the king issued a mandate to the justice of Chester, John Lestrange, to deliver Einion Fychan and Goronwy ap Cynfrig (*q.v.*) from prison and to let them go where they wished, upon the delivery to him by David ap Llywelyn of over twenty named hostages: *C. Pat. R., 1232–47*, p. 267. Whether or not these last were delivered is unclear, but it seems fairly certain that Einion Fychan and Goronwy ap Cynfrig were not released. Lestrange's accounts do not provide conclusive evidence either way, but of some significance is a letter which he wrote to Henry III informing him that Einion Fychan and Goronwy ap Cynfrig, who were then in the king's prison at Chester, had offered to cause their wives and children to come to the king's territory to be loyal to the king, and to do all possible harm to his enemies and give him such security as he should think fit. J. G. Edwards suggested that the date of the letter 'might be as early as 1241': *Cal. Anc. Corr.*, pp. 22–3; but it is surely to be connected with the transfer in November 1245 of Goronwy ap Cynfrig to the king's house of La Mare in Chester, for his own use and that of any men whom he could attract to the king's service. Einion Fychan apparently retracted his offer to serve the king, or else it was refused, for in August 1246 he, along with Philip de Calxston, was still in the prison at Chester: *C. Lib. R., 1245–51*, p. 76.

Giles
1233:
Llywelyn's messenger to Henry III. *C. Lib. R., 1226–40*, p. 238.

Goronwy ap Cynfrig
1221:
amongst the witnesses to charter 9.
1225:
probably the Wrenno used as an envoy to Henry III. *Rot. Claus.*, II, p. 18 (a).
1230:
amongst the witnesses to charter 13.
1232:
one of a group of envoys sent by Llywelyn ab Iorwerth to negotiate with Henry III's representatives at Shrewsbury. *C. Pat. R., 1232–47*, p. 3.
1235:
one of a group of envoys sent by Llywelyn ab Iorwerth to settle infractions of the truce with Henry III. *Close Rolls, 1234–37*, p. 179.
1240:
amongst the witnesses to charter 19.
1241 (February–March):
amongst a group of proctors assigned by David ap Llywelyn to act for him in proceedings concerning claims against the prince by the marchers. *Littere Wallie*, p. 20.
1241–5:
detained as a hostage in Chester by Henry III. See note *sub* Einion Fychan.
1245:
granted the king's house of La Mare in Chester for the reception of himself and those whom he can attract to the king's service. *C. Pat. R., 1232–47*, p. 465.
1246 (April):
Hywel ap Cynfrig mentioned as a hostage for Goronwy ap Cynfrig. *C. Lib. R., 1245–51*, p. 38.
1246 (June):
granted ten pounds of the king's gift. Ibid., p. 57.

1246 (September):
   granted all his lands in Wales which he had on the day when David ap Llywelyn gave him to the king as a hostage for faithful service. *C. Chart. R., 1226–57*, p. 305.
1247:
   justice of Chester ordered to put Goronwy in seisin of his lands in the Perfeddwlad. *Close Rolls, 1242–47*, p. 510.

Goronwy ab Ednyfed

1222:
   possibly the Goronwy ab Ednyfed who was amongst the witnesses to Llywelyn ab Iorwerth's agreement with Ranulf of Chester. Owen, *Catalogue*, III, p. 526.
1258:
   one of the parties to the Scotto-Welsh agreement. *Littere Wallie*, p. 185.
1259:
   appeared amongst a group who Llywelyn ap Gruffydd announced had sworn to a truce at Montgomery between the prince and Henry III. Ibid., p. 28.
1261 (April):
   one of a group of arbitrators between Llywelyn ap Gruffydd and the bishop of Bangor in a dispute over ecclesiastical rights; one of a further group of arbitrators elected to settle a possible case of violation of sanctuary. Haddan and Stubbs, *Councils*, pp. 489–90.
1261 (August):
   one of a group of arbitrators who settled a dispute over boundaries in Talyllyn between Llywelyn and the bishop of Bangor; one of a group assigned to ensure that the jury chosen to pronounce on a similar case involving the boundary between Llanwnda and Bodellog was at full strength. *Littere Wallie*, pp. 97–8.
1262:
   led a Welsh attack on Gwent. *Cal. Anc. Corr.*, p. 52.
1263:
   one of a group of arbitrators appointed in the agreement between Llywelyn ap Gruffydd and Gruffydd ap Gwenwynwyn to determine any future readjustments of territory between them. *Littere Wallie*, p. 78.
1265:
   amongst those who attested letters patent of Llywelyn announcing the conclusion of peace terms with Henry III. *Royal Letters . . . Henry III*, II, p. 284.
1267:
   one of those who swore to observe the Treaty of Montgomery. *Littere Wallie*, p. 4.
1268:
   one of the arbitrators chosen by Llywelyn ap Gruffydd to settle his dispute with Gilbert of Clare. Ibid., p. 102.
1268:
   death of Goronwy recorded in *Brut y Tywysogyon. BT, Pen 20*, p. 218.

Goronwy ap Heilyn

1248:
   held as a hostage in England. *Close Rolls, 1247–51*, p. 45.
1277:
   with Tudur ab Ednyfed (q.v.), granted powers by Llywelyn ap Gruffydd to conclude peace with the English; with Dafydd ab Einion (q.v.), swore *pro se et aliis de consilio . . . principis* to ensure that Llywelyn ap Gruffydd surrendered to Edward I hostages for his observance of the treaty. *Littere Wallie*, pp. 118, 121.

1277–8:
: with the priors of Bangor and Rhuddlan, made four journeys to Snowdon and Anglesey on the king's service. R. Stewart-Brown (ed.), *Cheshire in the Pipe Rolls*, 1938, p. 124.

1278–81:
: claimed expenses for his journeys to Wales to negotiate with Llywelyn about his dispute with Gruffydd ap Gwenwynwyn. *Cal. Anc. Corr.*, p. 40.

1278 (January):
: sent by Llywelyn ap Gruffydd to treat with Eleanor de Montfort at Windsor Castle. *C. Chanc. R., Various*, p. 170.

1278:
: granted a fee of £6 per year by Edward I. Ibid., p. 176.

1278–81:
: served Edward I as bailiff of Rhos and as a member of several judicial commissions. *C. Chanc. R., Various*, pp. 168, 189, 198; *Welsh Assize Roll*, p. 261; *C. Inq. Misc.*, I, p. 343.

1282:
: presented a list of grievances against the English, including a complaint that he had been removed from his bailiwick. *Registrum . . . Peckham*, II, pp. 458–59.

1283 (May):
: amongst the witnesses to charter 24.

1283:
: died *contra pacem*. *S.D.*, p. 297.

Goronwy ap Seisyll

?1224–32:
: *rhaglaw* of Dinorben. NLW Peniarth MS. no. 231, pp. 49, 118.

1225:
: amongst the witnesses to charter 10.

1240:
: amongst the witnesses to charter 19.

Gruffydd Gryg

1243:
: amongst the witnesses to charter 21.

1250:
: granted by Henry III the town of 'Moston' of the king's demesne, to hold at pleasure until the king gave him other lands. *C. Pat. R., 1247–58*, p. 64.

1251:
: appointed by Henry III master-serjeant in Tegeingl and Dyffryn Clwyd. Ibid., p. 113.

?1249–54:
: *rhaglaw* of Henry III, somewhere in the Perfeddwlad—possibly Rhuddlan. NLW Peniarth MS. no. 231, p. 124.

Gruffydd ab Ednyfed

Pre-1240:
: traditionally held to have been forced to flee to Ireland during the principate of Llywelyn ab Iorwerth as a result of some slander concerning Princess Joan. Dwnn, *Heraldic Visitations*, II, p. 101, note 7.

1247:
: headed the witness-list to charter 23.

1256:
: headed a group of envoys sent by Llywelyn ap Gruffydd to treat with Henry III. *C. Pat. R., 1247–58*, p. 471.

?1247-56:
  alleged in a genealogical source to have been *distain* to the prince. *Cronica de Wallia*, p. 16.

Gruffydd ap Rhodri
1226:
  headed the lay witnesses to charter 11.
1230:
  followed David ap Llywelyn in the witness-list to charter 13.
?1230-2:
  headed the witness-list to charter 14.
1231:
  amongst a small group of Welshmen, mainly princelings, who sealed an agreement extending for one year the truce between Llywelyn and Henry III. *Patent Rolls, 1225-32*, p. 453.
?1230-40:
  amongst the witnesses to charter 15.
1233:
  granted safe-conduct by Henry III for a journey to Jerusalem on pilgrimage. *C. Pat. R., 1232-47*, p. 17.
1240:
  one of a small group of men from Gwynedd who agreed to ensure David ap Llywelyn's observance of the Treaty of Gloucester. *Littere Wallie*, p. 6.

Gwyn ab Ednywain
Pre-1200:
  probably headed the witness-list to a charter of Gruffydd ap Cynan to Aberconwy abbey. H. Ellis (ed.), *Register and Chronicle of Aberconway Abbey*, p. 8.
c. 1199:
  amongst the witnesses to charter 1.
c. 1205-10:
  witnessed charter 5.
?1208:
  amongst the witnesses to charter 2.
1209:
  headed the laymen in the witness-list to charter 3.
1209:
  with master Ystrwyth (*q.v.*), he acted as receiver of expenses paid to Llywelyn ab Iorwerth by King John. *Rot. Regn. Johan.*, p. 126.

Heilyn ap Cynfrig
1222:
  amongst the witnesses to Llywelyn's agreement with Ranulf of Chester. Owen, *Catalogue*, III, p. 526.
1223:
  probably the Heilyn who acted as envoy for Llywelyn to Henry III. *Patent Rolls, 1216-25*, p. 383.
?1224-32:
  rhaglaw of Dinorben. NLW Peniarth MS. no. 231, pp. 48-9, 116-17.
1237:
  amongst the witnesses to charter 16.
1240:
  amongst the witnesses to charter 19.

Heilyn ab Iddig
1222:
amongst the witnesses to Llywelyn's agreement with Ranulf of Chester. Owen, *Catalogue*, III, p. 526.
1225:
amongst the witnesses to charter 10.

Hywel ap Cynfrig
Bailiff of Arllechwedd Uchaf under both Llywelyn ap Gruffydd and Edward I. *Rec. Caern.*, p. 219.

Ieuaf ap Ll(ywelyn?)
1252:
ballivus of Neigwl under Dafydd ap Gruffydd. *Rec. Caern.*, p. 252.

Iorwerth ap Gwrgunon
1243:
amongst the witnesses to charter 21.
1247:
amongst the witnesses to charter 23.
1247:
amongst the witnesses to charter 22; one of those at the head of the list, designated as 'stewards of the grantor'.
1256:
one of a group of envoys sent by Llywelyn ap Gruffydd to treat with Henry III. *C. Pat. R., 1247-58*, p. 471.
1258:
amongst the parties to the Scotto-Welsh agreement. *Littere Wallie*, p. 185.
1261:
perhaps the Iorwerth appointed as an arbitrator to settle a possible case of violation of sanctuary between the prince and the bishop of Bangor. Haddan and Stubbs, *Councils*, p. 490.
1263:
one of the large group who witnessed the agreement by which Gruffydd ap Gwenwynwyn agreed to do homage to Llywelyn ap Gruffydd. *Littere Wallie*, p. 78.

Ithel ap Bleddyn
pre-1276:
keeper of Ewloe castle for Llywelyn ap Gruffydd. *Cal. Anc. Pet.*, p. 93; *27th Report of Deputy Keeper of the Public Records*, p. 101.
1279:
permitted by Edward I to remain in the service of Llywelyn ap Gruffydd, conditional on fealty to the king. *C. Close R., 1272-79*, p. 563.

Ithel ap Tegwared
c. 1270:
rhingyll of Denbigh. NLW Peniarth MS. no. 231, p. 180.

Madog Goch
1282:
constable of Penllyn, one of the leaders of the Welsh attack on Oswestry on Palm Sunday. *Welsh Assize Roll*, p. 352.

Madog ap Bleddyn ap Meurig
c. 1270:
woodward of Rhos. NLW Peniarth MS. no. 231, pp. 179-80.

APPENDIX II

Madog ab Iorwerth Goch
?1240–5, ?1266–76:
  rhaglaw of Dinorben. Ibid., pp. 51–2, 119, 121–3.
1279:
  permitted by Edward I to remain in the service of Llywelyn, conditional upon fealty to the king. *C. Close R., 1272–79*, p. 563.
1281:
  amongst the witnesses to Llywelyn ap Gruffydd's agreement with the abbot of Cymer. *Littere Wallie*, pp. 45–6.
1283:
  possibly the Madog ab Iorwerth of Rhos Uwch Dulas who gave his bond for keeping the peace. *B.B.C.S.*, XIII (1949), p. 143.

Madog ab Iorwerth?/Maredudd ab Ieuaf?
?1240–5:
  rhaglaw of Rhuddlan. NLW Peniarth MS. no. 231, pp. 50, 119.

Maredudd ab Iorwerth
1237:
  amongst the witnesses to charter 16.
1247:
  amongst the witnesses to charter 24.
  Probably not the Maredudd ab Iorwerth who was *rhaglaw* of Dinorben at some time in the first quarter of the century: NLW Peniarth MS. no. 231, p. 47.

Maredudd ap Rhicert
1229:
  headed the witness-list to charter 12.
1245:
  one of a group of envoys sent by David ap Llywelyn to treat with Henry III at Degannwy. *C. Pat. R., 1232–47*, p. 461.
1247–57:
  recipient of a pension from Henry III. *C. Lib. R., 1245–51, passim;* ibid., *1251–60, passim.*

Owain the chamberlain
1225:
  witnessed charter 10.

Philip ap Gilbert
c. 1232:
  rhaglaw of Dinllaen. *C. Inq. Misc.*, II, p. 166.

Rhirid ap Madog
Pre-1282:
  constable of Penllyn? *Registrum . . . Peckham*, II, p. 455.

Rhys ab Ednyfed
1241:
  amongst a group of hostages demanded by Henry III from David ap Llywelyn in exchange for Einion Fychan and Goronwy ap Cynfrig. *C. Pat. R., 1232–47*, p. 267.
1258:
  amongst the parties to the Scotto-Welsh agreement. *Littere Wallie*, p. 185.
c. 1268?:
  rhaglaw of Dinorben. NLW Peniarth MS. no. 231, p. 123.

1269:
   obliged to find sureties for his fealty to Llywelyn. *Littere Wallie*, pp. 23, 24, 29.

Rhys ap Gruffydd
1258:
   headed the witness-list to the record of a grant by Llywelyn ap Gruffydd to Hywel ap Rhys. *Littere Wallie*, p. 45.
1272:
   amongst the witnesses to the quitclaim by Rhodri ap Gruffydd to Llywelyn of all his lands in Wales. *Littere Wallie*, p. 85.
1274:
   amongst the witnesses to the settlement of the case between Llywelyn ap Gruffydd and Gruffydd ap Gwenwynwyn. *Littere Wallie*, p. 99.
1277 (January):
   the town of Morton was found by English forces to be in Rhys ap Gruffydd's hands: it was taken into the king's hands. *C. Inq. Misc.*, I, p. 327.
1277 (May):
   together with his brother Hywel, Rhys received safe-conduct from Edward I to come to his peace. *C. Pat. R., 1272-81*, p. 211.
1277 (July):
   Friar Llywelyn, his brother, attempted to secure favourable treatment for Rhys and others when they came to the king's allegiance. *B.B.C.S.*, XXII (1968), pp. 353-7.
1277 (November):
   a clause of the Treaty of Conwy required Llywelyn ap Gruffydd to restore Rhys ap Gruffydd to the position which he had when he first negotiated with the king about coming to his peace. *Littere Wallie*, p. 119.
1278:
   amongst those appointed by Edward I to hear and determine pleas in the marches and Wales. *C. Chanc. R., Various*, pp. 163, 168.
1279:
   Edward I ordered an inquiry into the rights in Caeo of Rhys and Hywel ap Gruffydd against Rhys ap Maredudd. *Ibid.*, p. 179.
1281:
   pledged £100 to Llywelyn ap Gruffydd on account of the disobedience and contempt which he showed to the prince at Aberffraw. *Littere Wallie*, p. 31.
c. 1283-84:
   councillor of Edward I; keeper of the county of Caernarvon. *E.H.R.*, XXX (1915), p. 601.

Rhicert ap Cadwaladr
c. 1210:
   headed the witness-list to charter 4.
pre-1232:
   rhaglaw of Dinllaen. *C. Inq. Misc.*, II, p. 166.
?1230-40:
   witnessed charter 14.

Tegwared ab Ithel
?1224-32:
   rhaglaw of Rhuddlan. NLW Peniarth MS. no. 231, pp. 49, 118.

Tudur ab Ednyfed
?1240-5:
   rhaglaw of Dinorben or Denbigh. *Ibid.*, pp. 50, 119.

APPENDIX II

1241:
headed a group of proctors acting for David ap Llywelyn in proceedings concerning claims against the prince by marcher lords; designated as *senescallus*. *Littere Wallie*, p. 18; *Close Rolls, 1237-42*, p. 357.

1245 (November):
Henry III orders Gruffydd ap Gwenwynwyn to deliver Tudur ab Ednyfed to John Lestrange, who is to send him to London. *C. Pat. R., 1232-47*, p. 466.

1245 (November):
Henry III ordered the sheriff of Oxford to find serjeants at arms to help escort Tudur ab Ednyfed, the king's prisoner of Wales, to London. *C. Lib. R., 1245-51*, p. 7.

1245 (November):
Henry III ordered the constable of the Tower of London to keep Tudur ab Ednyfed *in medio stado eiusdem Turris*. *Close Rolls, 1242-47*, p. 369.

1246 (August):
Henry III ordered the constable of the Tower to hand Tudur over to John Mansel, to take him where the king had ordered. Ibid., p. 457.

1246 (August):
Tudur gave up two sons as hostages, to be kept in the Tower, *extra prisonem*. Ibid.

1246 (September):
promised fealty to Henry III on his release from captivity. *Littere Wallie*, p. 51.

1246 (September):
Henry III ordered the justice of Chester to allow Tudur twenty-five marks from the issues of Cheshire to buy a horse of the king's gift. *C. Lib. R., 1245-51*, p. 79.

1246 (September):
did homage for all his lands in Wales, and swore fealty to Henry III. *Littere Wallie*, p. 50.

1246 (?September):
Madog Fychan of Bromfield stood surety of fifty marks for Tudur's fidelity to the king. Ibid., p. 30.

1247 (January):
Henry III granted Tudur his part of the lands which his father held on the day of his death, as well as the lands which he possessed of right when he was taken in the war, to be held by him and his heirs for as long as they are in the king's fealty and service. *C. Pat. R., 1232-47*, p. 496.

1247 (May):
Henry III ordered the justice of Chester to put Tudur and others in seisin of their lands in the Perfeddwlad. *Close Rolls, 1242-47*, p. 510.

1247 (November):
Henry III ordered the justice of Chester to allow Tudur ab Ednyfed to enjoy peaceful possession of his wife's inheritance *in terra nostra Wallie que est in ballive sua*. *Close Rolls, 1247-51*, p. 5.

1248 (July):
granted land to keep himself in the king's service, until the king shall provide something else. Ibid., p. 72.

1248 (July):
granted £10 *per annum* at the exchequer of Chester to keep him in the king's service, until the king provided for him otherwise. *C. Pat. R., 1247-58*, p. 23; cf. *C. Lib. R., 1245-51, passim*.

1251:
Henry III ordered the justice of Chester to allocate Tudur ten librates of land for life. *Close Rolls, 1247-51*, p. 518.

APPENDIX II

c. 1251–4:
Henry III grants Tudur the vill of Maenan. *Welsh Assize Roll*, p. 261.

1258:
Tudur ab Ednyfed and his brothers have fifteen marks from the king's wardrobe for their expenses. *C. Pat. R., 1258–66*, p. 45.

1259:
acted as an envoy from Henry III to Llywelyn in truce negotiations. *C. Lib. R., 1251–60*, p. 480.

1260:
acted as an envoy from Henry III to Llywelyn in truce negotiations. *C. Pat. R., 1258–66*, pp. 57, 65, 69.

1261:
one of a group of arbitrators who settled a dispute over boundaries in Talyllyn between Llywelyn ap Gruffydd and the bishop of Bangor. *Littere Wallie*, p. 97.

1263 (February):
his son Heilyn, formerly held hostage, was delivered to him by Henry III. *C. Pat. R., 1258–66*, p. 248.

1263 (December):
one of a large group who witnessed the performance of homage to Llywelyn ap Gruffydd of Gruffydd ap Gwenwynwyn; one of a group of arbitrators appointed to determine any future readjustments of territory between Llywelyn and Gruffydd. *Littere Wallie*, p. 78.

?1266–68:
rhaglaw of Dinorben or Denbigh. NLW Peniarth MS. no. 231, pp. 52, 121.

1267:
one of those appointed in the Treaty of Montgomery to decide what lands should be given to Dafydd ap Gruffydd if he should be dissatisfied with the lands provided for him in the treaty. *Littere Wallie*, p. 3; swore to uphold the treaty. Ibid., p. 4.

1268:
one of the arbitrators chosen by Llywelyn ap Gruffydd to settle his dispute with Gilbert of Clare. Ibid., p. 102.

1271:
a group of men standing surety for Meurig ap Gruffydd of Elfael stated that *procuravimus sigillum Tuderi filii Etnyved iusticiarii Wallie*. Ibid., p. 26.

1272:
headed the witness-list to Rhodri ap Gruffydd's quitclaim to Llywelyn ap Gruffydd of all his lands in Wales; designated as *senescallus Wallie*. Ibid., p. 85.

1274:
as *justiciarius domini principis*, headed the list of arbitrators in the *causa accusacionum* against Gruffydd ap Gwenwynwyn and his son Owain. Ibid., p. 109.
amongst witnesses to the settlement. Ibid., p. 99.

1275:
with Einion ap Caradog (*q.v.*), mentioned by Llywelyn ap Gruffydd as a possible arbitrator in his conflict with the bishop of St. Asaph. Haddan and Stubbs, *Councils*, p. 505.

1277 (November):
together with Goronwy ap Heilyn (*q.v.*), given special powers to conclude peace by Llywelyn ap Gruffydd; swore *in animam principis et in animam propriam* to ensure that Llywelyn surrendered to Edward I hostages for his observance of the Treaty of Conwy. *Littere Wallie*, p. 121.

1277 (November):
possibly the Tudur ab Ednyfed included with Ralph de Fremingham and Walter de Hopton in a commission of oyer and terminer regarding the persons who took the beasts of Alice, late the wife of William le Bellward at Oswestry. *C. Pat. R., 1272-81*, p. 283.

Tudur ap Madog
c. 1241:
amongst the witnesses to charter 20.
1243:
amongst the witnesses to charter 21.
1245:
one of a group of Welsh envoys sent by David ap Llywelyn to negotiate with Henry III at Degannwy. *C. Pat. R., 1232-47*, p. 461.
1245-46:
granted lands in Pennant Gwernogof by David ap Llywelyn. *C. Inq. Misc.* I, p. 416.
1247:
amongst the witnesses to charter 23.
1247:
amongst the witnesses to charter 22; one of those designated as 'stewards of the grantor'.
1247:
one of the witnesses to charter 24.
1258:
one of the parties to the Scotto-Welsh agreement. *Littere Wallie*, p. 185.

Tudur
1270:
rhingyll of Eiryoes. NLW Peniarth MS. no. 231, p. 79.

Yrewyn, Alanus (de)
1258:
acted as the envoy of the Scots (*sic*) in negotiating the Scotto-Welsh treaty. *Littere Wallie*, p. 186.
1271:
acted as an envoy of Llywelyn ap Gruffydd, handing money over to Henry III's receivers. Ibid., p. 150.

APPENDIX III
A BIOGRAPHICAL GAZETTEER OF CLERICAL SERVANTS OF THE THIRTEENTH-CENTURY PRINCES

The bishops of Bangor and St. Asaph frequently appeared in the service of the princes; they have been discussed in some detail in chapters III and IX, and are, therefore, excluded from the following gazetteer. The same criteria for inclusion have been adopted as apply to Appendix II.

Adam (Master Adam)
1221:
possibly the Master Adam *de Sancte Trinitate* who witnessed charter 9.
1225:
Master Adam *de Sancte Trinitate* headed the witness-list to charter 10.
1230:
Master Adam amongst the witnesses to charter 13.
1231:
amongst a group of envoys to Henry III from Llywelyn. *Patent Rolls, 1225–32*, p. 436.
1232:
amongst a group of envoys to Henry III from Llywelyn. *C. Pat. R., 1232–47*, pp. 3–4.

Anian, abbot of Aberconwy
1258 (April):
one of those who sealed the agreement between Llywelyn ap Gruffydd and Maredudd ap Rhys. *Littere Wallie*, p. 168.
1258 (May–June):
with Madog ap Philip (*q.v.*), appeared as Llywelyn's special proctor and messenger; agreed to a 100-mark payment by Llywelyn for a truce. Ibid., pp. 27–9.
1261:
with Richard of Bangor, acted as Llywelyn's envoy to Henry III; sealed, on Llywelyn's behalf, an agreement for a truce. *Foedera*, I, p. 404.
1262 (May–June):
acted as Llywelyn's envoy, with full powers, to Henry III, in negotiations for a further truce; sealed the truce *vice* Llywelyn and guaranteed to have Llywelyn's seal affixed. *Littere Wallie*, pp. 17–18.
1263:
witnessed the submission of Gruffydd ap Gwenwynwyn to Llywelyn; one of a large group chosen to provide for readjustments of territory between the two men. Ibid., p. 78.

David the clerk
1222:
brought word to Henry III of the truce made by his master, Llywelyn, with William Marshall. *Foedera*, I, p. 166.
1225:
brought word to Llywelyn that Henry III could not meet him on the appointed day at Shrewsbury. Ibid., I, p. 178.

APPENDIX III

1231:
amongst a group of envoys to Henry III from Llywelyn. *Patent Rolls, 1225–32*, p. 436.

1232:
amongst a group of envoys to Henry III from Llywelyn. *C. Pat. R., 1232–47*, pp. 3–4.

David, clerk of David ap Llywelyn
1241 (October):
received from Henry III an imprest of £20 to his master's use. *C. Lib. R., 1240–45*, p. 85.
Possibly David, archdeacon of St. Asaph (*q.v.*).

Master David, archdeacon of Bangor
1257:
together with Philip ab Ifor (*q.v.*), acted as an envoy from Llywelyn ap Gruffydd to Henry III. *C. Pat. R., 1247–58*, p. 573.

1259:
amongst the household of the bishop of Bangor, travelling to England. *C. Pat. R., 1258–66*, p. 57.

1260:
with the bishop of Bangor, acted as an envoy to Henry III. Ibid., p. 83.

Master David, archdeacon of St. Asaph
1231:
headed a group of envoys from Llywelyn to Henry III. *Patent Rolls, 1225–32*, p. 436.

1235:
amongst a group of 'correctors' of the truce between Llywelyn and Henry III. *Close Rolls, 1234–37*, p. 179.

1238 (February?):
sent by Llywelyn to treat for a peace with Henry III. Henry complained that David was *minus sufficienter instructus*. *Close Rolls, 1237–42*, p. 125.

1238 (March):
sent to Henry III by Llywelyn to complain of infractions of the truce. *C. Pat. R., 1232–47*, p. 212.

1238 (June):
one of a group of envoys who agreed to a year's extension of the truce with Henry III. Ibid., pp. 225, 237.

1240:
amongst the witnesses to the Treaty of Gloucester. *Littere Wallie*, p. 6.

1241 (Feb–March):
as David *cancellarius*, one of a group given power by David ap Llywelyn to conclude an agreement with English representatives. Ibid., p. 20.

1241 (March–April):
as David *cancellarius*, amongst a group of proctors sent by David ap Llywelyn to settle disputes with the marchers. Ibid., p. 18.

1241 (August):
probably the Master David, clerk of David ap Llywelyn, who came to talk to members of the king's household, with the bishop of St. Asaph. *C. Pat. R., 1232–47*, p. 257.

1241 (?late August):
as Master David *cancellarius*, one of a group of envoys sent by David ap Llywelyn to conclude an agreement of peace with Henry III. *Littere Wallie*, p. 153.

APPENDIX III

David ab Ithel, clerk
1272:
  possibly the David *clericus* amongst the witnesses to Rhodri ap Gruffydd's quitclaim of his lands in Wales. *Littere Wallie*, p. 85.
1274:
  one of the auditors of the account of the keeper of Dolforwyn. Ibid., p. 24.
1279:
  one of a group of envoys who handed over a payment from Llywelyn ap Gruffydd to representatives of Edward I. Ibid., p. 149.

David ap William, clerk
1247:
  amongst the witnesses to charter 23.
1256:
  cancelled from a list of envoys to Henry III. *C. Pat. R., 1247-58*, p. 470.
1260:
  Master David ap William headed a group of Llywelyn's envoys to a parliament. *C. Pat. R., 1258-66*, p. 81.
1263:
  as Official of Dyffryn Clwyd, appeared amongst those who witnessed Gruffydd ap Gwenwynwyn's submission to Llywelyn; also one of a group designated to provide for any future readjustment of territory between them. *Littere Wallie*, p. 78.

Einion ap Goronwy, rector of Dineirth
1268:
  one of a group of envoys who handed over money from Llywelyn to Henry III's receivers. *Littere Wallie*, p. 143.
1269:
  again, one of a group handing over money. Ibid., p. 148.
1270:
  as *rector ecclesie de Dinardh*, again one of a group handing over money. Ibid., p. 144. Cf. p. 150, where he is referred to in Henry de la Zuche's letter of quittance as Goronwy ab Einion.

Master Gervase (Iorwerth, Jervasius)
1259:
  possibly the Gervase of Llanfair who was a member of the bishop of Bangor's household on a visit to England. *C. Pat., R., 1258-66*, p. 57.
1267:
  possibly the Master Gervase, canon of Bangor, who came to Henry III seeking licence for the chapter to elect a bishop. *C. Pat. R., 1266-72*, p. 165.
1277:
  Master Gervase, Llywelyn's clerk and vice-chancellor, accompanied Anian of Bangor as an envoy to Edward I. *Cal. Anc. Corr.*, p. 87.
1281:
  Master Gervase, clerk of the prince, was one of the witnesses to an agreement between Llywelyn ap Gruffydd and the abbot of Cymer. *Littere Wallie*, p. 46. For a full discussion and references to Gervase's post-conquest career, see pp. 36-7 above.

Instructus (Ystrwyth, Ostrucius and variants)
Note: it is by no means certain how many individuals were referred to by this name. The time-span within which the various, but clearly related, forms appear is over thirty years, which suggests that more than one man may be involved.

APPENDIX III

1204:
Master Osturcius, clerk of Llywelyn, was granted 100s. by King John, to be paid annually until the king provided him with an ecclesiastical benefice. *Rot. Claus.*, I, p. 11; Cf. ibid., pp. 10, 43, 60; *Rot. Pat.*, I, pp. 89a (which has the form *Instructus*), p. 126; *Pipe Roll 7 John*, p. 160.

1209:
Osturcius, Llywelyn's clerk, was to receive rom King John £19 2s. 5d. in payment of his master's wages. *Rot. Mis. II Johann*, p. 125.

1209:
Master Strwyth amongst the witnesses to charter 3.

1221:
Ostricius, clerk of the prince, defended the title of Elena, daughter of Llywelyn ab Iorwerth, to an estate in Wellington, co. Salop, and called the king's council to warranty. Eyton, *Shropshire*, IX, p. 43, quoting Assize Roll, 6 Henry III m. 3d.

1221:
Henry III granted money to Ostricius *ad se in scolis sustentandum*. *Rot. Claus.*, I, p. 464.

1221:
Master Instructus is included amongst the witnesses to charter 9. It would seem unlikely that this is the man referred to in the entries immediately above and below.

1222:
grant of Henry III of money to Instructus, to keep him in the schools. *Rot. Claus.*, I, p. 511.

1223:
Ostricius, Llywelyn's clerk, acts as his messenger to Henry III. *Patent Rolls, 1216–25*, p. 383.

1225:
Master Instructus, archpriest of Caer Gybi, amongst the witnesses to charter 10.

1231:
Master Instructus was one, apparently the senior, of two envoys sent by Llywelyn to Henry III. *Patent Rolls, 1225–32*, pp. 452, 460.

Uncertain date:
In a letter to Henry III, Joan, wife of Llywelyn, defended Instructus, *vester et domini mei clericus*, from reports that he was disloyal to the king. *Royal letters ... Henry III*, II, pp. 487–8.

Note: the date of this letter is earlier than 1237, when Joan died, and probably before 1231, after which date Instructus no longer appeared, and seems to have been replaced by Master David, archdeacon of St. Asaph.

John

1237:
as notary of the donor, appeared in the witness-list of charter 16.

Madog Fychan

1279:
headed the list of envoys, all clerks of Llywelyn ap Gruffydd, who handed over a payment of £500 to representatives of Edward I. *Littere Wallie*, p. 149.

1284:
mentioned, as canon of Bangor, by Peckham, who described him as *incentor guerre*, who pulled a knight from his horse, killing them both. *Registrum ... Peckham*, III, p. 781.

226   APPENDIX III

Madog Goch
1243:
  described as 'our clerk', Madog Goch ended the witness-list to charter 21.
1247:
  possibly the Madog, clerk of the grantor, who witnessed charter 22.

Madog filius Magistri
1275:
  one of the sureties found by the prior and convent of Valle Crucis for a loan made to them by Llywelyn. *Littere Wallie*, p. 33.
1279:
  one of a group of clerical envoys who handed over payment from Llywelyn to Edward I's representatives. Ibid., p. 149.
1280:
  Llywelyn petitioned Archbishop Peckham that two of his clerks, apparently in minor orders, should be allowed to keep their benefices. Haddan and Stubbs, *Councils*, p. 527.
1281:
  as *notarius noster*, witnessed a charter of Llywelyn ap Gruffydd to Heilyn ap Tudur. *Rec. Caern.*, p. 211.

Madog ap Philip
1258:
  acted with Anian, abbot of Aberconwy, as the proctor and special messenger of Llywelyn in arranging a truce with Henry III. *Littere Wallie*, p. 27.
1260:
  Master Madog ap Philip was one of a group of envoys sent by Llywelyn to England. *C. Pat. R., 1258–66*, p. 81.
1261:
  probably the Master Mattheus sent to England as an envoy by Llywelyn. *Close Rolls, 1259–61*, p. 482.

Maredudd, abbot of Aberconwy
?1272:
  possibly the unnamed abbot of Aberconwy who sealed and witnessed the quitclaim by Rhodri ap Gruffydd of all his lands in Wales. *Littere Wallie*, p. 85.
1278:
  with David, dean of Arllechwedd, inspected the record of the 1274 *causa* against Gruffydd ap Gwenwynwyn. Ibid., p. 110.
1278 (Sept.):
  brought forward a deed sealed by Rhodri ap Gruffydd in the latter's case against Llywelyn ap Gruffydd before Edward I's court at Rhuddlan. *C. Close R., 1272–79*, p. 506.
1280:
  conveyed a request of Dafydd ap Gruffydd to the general chapter of Citeaux that he be included in the *missae* and *orationes* of that house. *Littere Wallie*, p. 153.
1280 (Nov.):
  handed over at the abbey 100 marks from Llywelyn to Rhodri ap Gruffydd. Ibid., p. 42.
1281:
  M. abbot and the convent of Aberconwy promised payment of £40 to Llywelyn to secure his benevolence and avoid his displeasure. Ibid., p. 25.

APPENDIX III 227

Philip ab Ifor
1225:
  probably the Master Philip who acted as envoy from Llywelyn to Henry III. *Rot. Claus.*, II, p. 18 (a).
1231:
  probably the Master Philip who acted as envoy from Llywelyn to Henry III. *Patent Rolls, 1225–32*, pp. 452, 460, 466.
1237:
  amongst the witnesses to chapter 16.
1238:
  one of a group of envoys who swore on Llywelyn's behalf to accept a one-year prolongation of the truce with Henry III. *C. Pat. R., 1232–47*, p. 225.
1240:
  amongst the witnesses to charter 19.
1241 (March/April):
  Master Philip, 'our clerk', was used to carry letters from David ap Llywelyn to Henry III. *Littere Wallie*, p. 18.
1257:
  one of a group of envoys from Llywelyn given safe-conduct by Henry III. *C. Pat. R., 1247–58*, p. 573.

Richard of Mold
1266:
  probably the 'Richard the Clerk, vice-chamberlain to the lord prince', who handed over a loan from Llywelyn to the dean and chapter of St. Asaph. *Littere Wallie*, p. 39.
1268:
  Richard the clerk of Mold was one of a group of Llywelyn's envoys who handed over money to Henry III's receivers. Ibid., p. 143.
1269:
  Richard the clerk of Mold was one of a group of Llywelyn's envoys who handed over money to Henry III's receivers. Ibid., p. 145.
1270:
  as 'treasurer of Llywelyn ap Gruffydd' (only so recorded in English letters o. quittance), Master Richard of Mold was one of a group of Llywelyn's envoys who handed over money to Henry III's receivers. Ibid., pp. 144, 150.

Richard ap Madog
1260:
  one of a group of clerical envoys sent by Llywelyn to England. *C. Pat. R., 1258–66*, p. 81.

Roger of Rhuddlan
1269:
  one of a group of envoys who handed over money from Llywelyn ap Gruffydd to Henry III's receivers. *Littere Wallie*, p. 145.
1270:
  described in letters issued by Henry III's receiver as *Rogero dicto Biscop tunc maiore de Rothelan*, he was one of a group of envoys handing over money from Llywelyn. Ibid., p. 151.
1271 (April):
  probably the Roger, clerk, who handed over money from Llywelyn ap Gruffydd to Henry III's receivers. Ibid., p. 150.

1271 (May):
   among a group of envoys handing over money from Llywelyn ap Gruffydd to Henry III's receivers. Ibid., p. 140.
1272:
   probably the Roger, clerk, who handed over money from Llywelyn to Henry III's receivers. Ibid., p. 143.

Simon
1237:
   designated as 'your clerk' he was sent by Henry III to Llywelyn ab Iorwerth in the course of negotiations. *Close Rolls, 1234–37*, p. 536.

Master William
1272 (Jan.):
   possibly the William, clerk, who was one of Llywelyn's envoys handing over money to Henry III's receivers. *Littere Wallie*, p. 143.
1272 (April):
   amongst the witnesses to Rhodri ap Gruffydd's quitclaim to Llywelyn of his lands in Wales. Ibid., p. 85.

Friar William of Llanfaes
1279:
   sent by Llywelyn ap Gruffydd as an envoy to Edward I. *Cal. Anc. Corr.*, p. 62.
1282:
   wrote a letter to Edward I in support of Llywelyn ap Gruffydd. Ibid., p. 99.

William ap Daniel
1280:
   one of two clerks on behalf of whom Llywelyn petitioned Archbishop Peckham that they be allowed to retain their benefices. Peckham referred to them as 'your clerks'; they were apparently in minor orders. Haddan and Stubbs, *Councils*, p. 527.
pre-1282:
   William ap Daniel granted thirty acres of land in Aberffraw by Llywelyn ap Gruffydd. Seebohm, *Tribal System*, Appendix, p. 22.
1282:
   William of Llanfaes, writing to Edward I, referred to the fact that Llywelyn felt that he should not have to return goods which he had taken as wreck from an English merchant, because no inquisition had yet been made in his lands, as William Daniel, who was entrusted with making the inquisition, would declare to the king, as indeed he was once ready to attest at Dunanmey. *Cal. Anc. Corr.*, p. 99.
Post-1283:
   received annual payments from Edward I. *B.B.C.S.*, XV (1953), p. 311.

William Rufus (possibly a layman)
1271:
   one of Llywelyn's envoys handing over money to Henry III's receivers. *Littere Wallie*, p. 140.

APPENDIX IV
LLYWELYN AP GRUFFYDD AND THE OPPOSITION TO DAVID AP LLYWELYN

It has long been recognized that at some time in the early 1240s Llywelyn ap Gruffydd, the future prince of Wales, established himself as ruler in part of the Perfeddwlad. The clearest evidence is provided by a charter of Llywelyn in 1243 in Dyffryn Clwyd, confirming to Einion ap Maredudd his lands and privileges in that *cantref*.[1] The nominal ruler of the Perfeddwlad in the early 1240s (with the exception, after 1241, of Tegeingl) was David ap Llywelyn, the half-brother of Llywelyn ap Gruffydd's ill-fated father. The question thus arises of Llywelyn's relations with Prince David in these years. The key to the situation lies in the strife between David and his half-brother, which flared up in the late 1230s and reached a climax in 1240–41, when David treacherously seized and imprisoned Gruffydd, an action which earned him the hostility of the bishop of Bangor and many of the magnates of Wales.[2] Henry III's campaign against David in 1241 thus met with considerable Welsh support, and one of the provisions of the Treaty of Gwern Eigron, which marked David's submission to Henry in August 1241, was that David should hand over Gruffydd, together with the latter's eldest son, Owain Goch, and others who had been imprisoned with them, to Henry III, whose court should decide upon Gruffydd's rights to a share of Gwynedd.[3] The prisoners were duly handed over, but Owain and Gruffydd remained captives in the king's hands, being lodged in the Tower of London. Gruffydd was held in the Tower until his death, while trying to escape, in March 1244.[4] Owain remained in London for some months more and was then moved, on Henry's orders, to Chester,[5] whence he escaped, or was released, to Gwynedd following David ap Llywelyn's death in 1246.[6]

Llywelyn ap Gruffydd did not suffer the same fate as his father and elder brother as his activity in the Perfeddwlad proves. He may, however, have shared the animosity which they may be assumed to have felt towards David ap Llywelyn. He seems, indeed, to have established himself in the Perfeddwlad against David, rather than under his protection or with his acquiescence. This conclusion is suggested first by the fact that the first name in the witness-list to Llywelyn's 1243 grant to Einion ap Maredudd is that of Richard, bishop of Bangor, whose early opposition to David was noted by Matthew Paris, who may have drawn much of his information about Gwynedd in this period from Bishop Richard himself.[7] More explicit evidence relating to Llywelyn's role in the early 1240s, though of a sort which must be treated with some caution, is to be found in

---

[1] J. C. Davies, 'A grant by Llywelyn ap Gruffydd', *N.L.W.J.*, III (1943) p. 158.
[2] For analysis of this and subsequent incidents, see G. A. Williams, 'The Succession to Gwynedd, 1238–47', *B.B.C.S.*, XX (1964), pp. 393–413.
[3] *Littere Wallie*, p. 9.
[4] *BT, R.B.H.*, pp. 236, 238.
[5] *C. Lib. R., 1240–45*, pp. 252–3. Cf. *C. Pat. R., 1232–47*, p. 462.
[6] See Lloyd, *Hist. Wales*, II, p. 707.
[7] Haddan and Stubbs, *Councils*, p. 475.

230 APPENDIX IV

Sir John Wynn's *History of the Gwydir Family*, written some three and a half centuries after the period under review. Sir John gives the following account:[8]

> Wee receive it by tradition from father to sonne in Evioneth, that david ap lle'n beinge prince by the ayde of his uncle the kinge came to the Towne of Pullhely in llyn to p'le with the bretheren Engian and gruffith [*sc.* the sons of Caradog and, according to Wynn, brothers of Senana, wife of Gruffydd ap Llywelyn] whome the bretheren mett with such a force at that meetinge or daye of truce that the prince tould them they weare two [*sic*] stronge to be subiects, whereof they answered that he was rather two weake to be a prince, and soe p'ted without anye conclusion of agreement. in thend they weare forced by longe warre to forgoe that countrey and to lose their land there, and to joyne themselves to their nephewe ll'in ap gruffith whoe then had his courte at Maesmynan in Flintshire and held as afore is mencioned the cantreds of Englefield dyffryn Clwyd Rose, and Rovoniog, agaynst his uncle david, haveinge warre one thone side with the kinge, one thother side with his uncle . . .

Prima facie, some elements in this account seem clearly to be wrong, such as the reference to David as 'prince by the ayde of his uncle the kinge'. But given David's weak position in Gwynedd in the early months of his principate, and the fact that he hastened to secure it by doing homage and making concessions to the king at Gloucester,[9] it may well have appeared that David only retained Gwynedd by Henry's aid. It should also be borne in mind that, with the exception of his efforts in the summer of 1241, Henry III apparently made no attempt to enforce Gruffydd's rights under Welsh law to a share of Gwynedd.[10]

The implication in Wynn's account that Llywelyn carried on hostilities with both David and Henry III at the same time may, however, be misleading. It is instructive at this point to consider another document issued by Llywelyn ap Gruffydd in the early 1240s. The document in question is a quitclaim[11] by Llywelyn of all his rights in Gwerthrynion and Maelienydd to Ralph Mortimer and his wife Gwladus, daughter of Llywelyn ab Iorwerth. The document is undated, but a rough date can be fixed with tolerable certainty. It was issued after Llywelyn ab Iorwerth's death in 1240, for the style used by his grandson is *Leulinus filius Griffini filii Leulini quondam principis Norwallie*. Again, it was issued before 1245, by which date Llywelyn ap Gruffydd had joined forces with Prince David in the struggle against Henry III and the marcher lords.[12] Still, the crucial question of the chronological relationship between the quitclaim and the 1243 charter remains open. The key to the problem is the fact that the quitclaim would appear to be closely related to a group of six undated charters in which nine Welshmen, amongst them descendants of the twelfth-century lords of Gwerthrynion, quitclaimed to Ralph Mortimer their rights in that territory. These quitclaims were almost certainly made, as Mr. Beverley Smith has indicated, in the aftermath of the war of August 1241, which revived Mortimer power in the

---

[8] Wynn, *Gwydir Family*, p. 11.
[9] *Littere Wallie*, pp. 5-6.
[10] Some of the witnesses appearing before the 1281 commission of Edward I into the operation of the law of Hywel Dda refer to a plea in England between David and Gruffydd ap Llywelyn, and some mention a judicial combat. But if there was a case, it had no effect on the tenurial situation. See *C. Chanc. R., Various*, pp. 195 (Cynfrig Sais), 198 (Dafydd ab Einion, Tudur ap Madog).
[11] The two copies of the quitclaim in the Mortimer cartulary are printed in J. B. Smith, 'The Middle March in the Thirteenth Century', *B.B.C.S.*, XXIV (1970), pp. 88-9, 92.
[12] Lloyd, *Hist. Wales*, II, p. 703.

middle march: the execution of the documents was probably not long delayed.[13] The presence in the witness-list to Llywelyn's quitclaim of the names of several men who were witnesses to the charters of the men of Gwerthrynion, including men such as John Lestrange and Thomas Corbet, who certainly did not constitute regular members of Mortimer's entourage, suggests that Llywelyn's document was executed at about the same time as the other six. It should probably be dated to the late summer of 1241. The establishment of its political context will thus prove extremely interesting.

In the summer of 1241, Mortimer had suffered the attacks of Welsh chiefs, backed by *senescalli* of David ap Llywelyn.[14] On 12 August, 1241, Mortimer stood as one of the sureties for a fine promised to Henry III by Senana, wife of Gruffydd, in return for which the king undertook to free Gruffydd and his son Owain from Prince David's prison.[15] Mortimer had much to gain by fomenting the ruinous conflict between David and Gruffydd: it would distract the prince of Gwynedd and allow Mortimer greater freedom to pursue his ambitions in the march. But if the quitclaim issued by Llywelyn ap Gruffydd does indeed come from the late summer of 1241, there would appear to be another dimension to Mortimer's policy: namely, the opening of a further conflict, between David and Llywelyn ap Gruffydd. The presence in Llywelyn's entourage, at the time of the quitclaim, of two men from Gwynedd Uwch Conwy is highly significant here: these two were Tudur ap Madog of the line of Iarddur, whose patrimonial lands were in Arllechwedd and Anglesey, and Einion ap Caradog, one of the brothers referred to in Sir John Wynn's account quoted above.[16] The presence of Einion ap Caradog goes far, in fact, to corroborate Wynn's account of the brothers' hostility to, and eventual flight from, David ap Llywelyn.

It would seem that dissident elements from David's dominions did indeed join Llywelyn ap Gruffydd—but not, at first perhaps, in the Perfeddwlad. On the basis of the evidence, it is more likely that they assembled in the lands of Ralph Mortimer, whose wife was Llywelyn's aunt, where they were given shelter. The fact that Mortimer troubled to take Llywelyn's quitclaim indicates that he took seriously the young man's political potential as the focus of internal opposition to David.

It is worth considering at this point the question of whether Henry III knew of Mortimer's manoeuvres. There are two copies of Llywelyn ap Gruffydd's quitclaim in the Mortimer cartulary. Both contain a clause by which Llywelyn promised to help Mortimer to keep his hold on Gwerthrynion and Maelienydd, aiding him against all men; but one of the copies[17] has the saving clause *salva fide domini regis Anglie*. If this was in the original, then it appears that Llywelyn was in the king's faith in the late summer of 1241. Noteworthy, too, is the fact that Llywelyn styled himself *filius Griffini filii Leulini quondam principis Norwallie* in the 1241 quitclaim. This reflects contemporary English chancery practice with respect to David, who is designated in English royal documents as *filius Lewelini quondam principis Norwallie*.[18] It is thus significant that in Henry's agreement of

---

[13] J. B. Smith, art. cit., pp. 83–4.
[14] *Close Rolls, 1237–42*, p. 359.
[15] *Littere Wallie*, p. 19.
[16] For Tudur ap Madog's career, see Appendix II *sub nomine;* for his lands, see above, p. 132. For Einion ap Caradog see Appendix II *sub nomine*, and above pp. 118–19, 133.
[17] See note 11 above; the quitclaim with the saving-clause is the first of the two.
[18] See *Littere Wallie*, pp. 9, 10, 12, 19, 22.

12 August with Senana, he stipulated[19] that two of her sons, Dafydd and Rhodri, should be handed over to him as hostages; her husband and Owain were, of course, to be taken into royal custody. Llywelyn is not mentioned. It is hard to resist the conclusion that Henry's silence betokens the king's awareness that Llywelyn was proving very useful as a thorn in David's side. Llywelyn remained useful for some years yet. The 1243 charter indicates that the grantee, Einion ap Maredudd, a man of Dyffryn Clwyd, was one of his adherents, while the witness-list of the same document reveals that Llywelyn had been joined by Iorwerth ap Gwrgunon of the line of Rhufon ap Nefydd Hardd, whose lands lay in the Conwy valley.[20] How Llywelyn ap Gruffydd was established in the Perfeddwlad is not clear, but once again there is more than a hint that Henry III knew of, and acquiesced in, his activities. The presence of Richard of Bangor amongst the witnesses to Llywelyn's 1243 charter has been noted above: it should be stressed in the present context that in the 1240s Richard was virtually a royal partisan, as his declaration of fealty to Henry III in April 1246 makes clear.[21] Again, two men associated with Llywelyn's entourage in the early 1240s were Cynfrig Sais (in 1241 and 1243), who received a royal pension for some years from June 1245,[22] and Gruffydd Gryg (in 1243), who appears as a royal official in the Perfeddwlad in the period 1247-56.[23] If Llywelyn ap Gruffydd was in conflict with Henry III in 1243, then the presence at his court of Richard of Bangor, Cynfrig Sais and Gruffydd Gryg is hard to explain.

It is difficult to establish even roughly the date at which the role attributed above to Llywelyn came to an end, but most probably his attitude changed when he heard of the death of his father in March 1244. The moving of Owain ap Gruffydd from London to Chester, together with a group of his adherents, in July 1244[24] may indicate that Llywelyn had already joined forces with David and that his role as a threat to that prince and a magnet for opposition to him was to be taken over by his older brother.

This analysis of Llywelyn ap Gruffydd's activities in the early 1240s serves to illustrate two aspects of the political life of Gwynedd. First, it reveals how rifts within the princely house might be exploited by English king and marcher lord alike. Secondly, it suggests that a critical element in the weakness of David ap Llywelyn was the alienation of members of the class of prominent freemen from whom were drawn the servants of princes, marcher lords and English kings, and whose growing political importance in the thirteenth century we are coming to appreciate.

---

[19] Ibid., 52-3.
[20] See above, pp. 104, 131.
[21] *Littere Wallie*, pp. 21-2.
[22] See *C. Lib. R., 1240-45*, p. 311; *C. Lib. R., 1245-51*, pp. 20, 57, 105.
[23] See Appendix II *sub* Gruffydd Gryg.
[24] *C. Lib. R., 1240-45*, pp. 252-3. Amongst Owain's companions was Bleddyn ap Meurig (for whom see Appendix II *sub nomine*), who had been in Gruffydd ap Llywelyn's entourage in 1226 and was probably put in the Tower with him in 1241.

APPENDIX V

THE ITINERANT COURT, JULY 1273–JANUARY 1277

The evidence for the location of the itinerant court is, at best, very thin and for long periods almost non-existent. For the years 1273–7, however, more references are available than for any other comparable period, and they are, perhaps, just numerous enough to enable some tentative conclusions about the prince's itinerary to be drawn. It should be recalled that these years saw the conspiracy of Gruffydd ap Gwenwynwyn, his son Owain and Dafydd ap Gruffydd, against Prince Llywelyn and the consequent political crisis of 1274, as well as the war of 1277 between Llywelyn and Edward I.[1] In the first case, the need to investigate the conspiracy clearly drew Llywelyn to the middle March, to the borders of Gruffydd ap Gwenwynwyn's territory, in April 1274. In the second case, the war, which was formally decided upon by Edward in November 1276, did not develop until mid-1277, and so the location of the court has been traced up to January of that year: thereafter, it is likely that it was determined by the exigencies of the military situation. There is a possibility, however, that preparation for military activity was already influencing the prince's movements. Bogo de Knovill reported to the king that in 1276 he had kept a garrison in Montgomery for fourteen weeks, during which time the prince of Wales was several times in the neighbourhood of Montgomery with his army.[2] Llywelyn's presence in that area in 1276 has not been recorded in the following itinerary but must be taken into account. All these factors should be borne in mind when the itinerary is examined.

July 11, 1272	:	Dinorben[3]
July 22, 1273	:	Mold[4]
September 3, 1273	:	Llanfair Rhyd Castell[5]
February 26, 1274	:	Cricieth[6]
March 26, 1274	:	Aber[7]
April 17/18, 1274	:	Bach yr Anneleu, Cydewain[8]
July 9, 1274	:	Penrhos[9]
December 20, 1274	:	Llanfair Rhyd Castell[10]
December ?, 1274	:	Pool[11]
May 22–26, 1275	:	Aberyddon (Talybont)[12]

---

[1] See J. G. Edwards' Introduction to *Littere Wallie*, liii–lx.
[2] A. J. Taylor, 'Montgomery Town Wall', *Arch. Camb.*, XCIX (1947), p. 282, quoting P.R.O., Liberate Rolls, C.62/52.
[3] *Cal. Anc. Corr.*, p. 86.
[4] Ibid., p. 94.
[5] Ibid., p. 161.
[6] Ibid., p. 92.
[7] Ibid., p. 163.
[8] *Littere Wallie*, pp. 99, 110.
[9] Ibid., p. 33.
[10] Ibid., p. 175.
[11] *BT, Pen. 20*, p. 221.
[12] *Cal. Anc. Corr.*, p. 28; Haddan and Stubbs, *Councils*, p. 505; *Littere Wallie*, p. 45.

APPENDIX V

August 9, 1275	:	Dolwyddelan[13]
August 27, 1275	:	Sechtone[14] ? Sychdyn, near Ewloe
September 11, 1275	:	Trefchyn[15]
October 6, 1275	:	Talybont[16]
May 14/17, 1276	:	Dinasteleri (Ardudwy)[17]
July 15, 1276	:	Llanfair Rhyd Castell[18]
December 16, 1276	:	Aber[19]
January (early), 1277	:	Llanfaes[20]
January 22, 1277	:	Aberalwen[21]

Perhaps the first point to emerge from this skeletal itinerary is that, although the lands under Llywelyn ap Gruffydd's direct control extended into Powys and the middle March in these years, his itinerary is mainly confined to Gwynedd. Within Gwynedd, there seems to be some concentration on sites in, or contiguous to, those upland commotes where, significantly, the level of commutation of renders was low: over half of the locations within Gwynedd come into this category.[22]

In the second place, the references do not reveal a set pattern of itineration, though such a pattern, consistently liable to disruption by the exigencies of the politico-military situation, may have existed in rough form. A degree of forward planning of the itinerary may be inferred from the conspiracy of 1274: Owain ap Gruffydd of Powys was to have led a small band to the court, where he was to be secretly admitted by Dafydd ap Gruffydd, in order to murder the prince.[23] The plan implies that the location of the court could be predicted with some precision, because the success of the plot clearly depended on Owain's being able to make a secret and rapid journey through Gwynedd to the court. In the event, bad weather forced the abandonment of the plan.

Finally, it is noteworthy that, while many of the locations are at old established *llysoedd* or newer stone castles, granges of the Cistercians figure prominently in the itinerary, further underlining the importance to the prince of close relations with that order: Aberyddon and Dinastcleri belonged to Cymer, and Llanfair Rhyd Castell to Aberconwy.

---

[13] *Littere Wallie*, p. 33.
[14] *The Register of Thomas de Cantilupe, bishop of Hereford*, transcribed by R. G. Griffiths, introduced by W. W. Capes (Canterbury and York Soc., 1906), p. 9. If the identification is correct, it is most interesting. In late August, Edward I arrived in Chester to take Llywelyn's homage, which was due to be performed at about the date at which the prince was at *Sechtone*: see *Littere Wallie*, lvi, and references there cited. *BT*, *R.B.H.*, p. 262, alleges that Llywelyn did not go to the king, on the advice of his barons, and subsequently 'returned to Wales'. This suggests that the prince did actually go very near to Chester. If he reached Sychdyn, then he and Edward were separated by only a dozen miles. An hour's ride could have altered the fate of the principality.
[15] Haddan and Stubbs, *Councils*, p. 508.
[16] Ibid.
[17] *Cal. Anc. Corr.*, p. 86.
[18] Ibid., p. 126.
[19] *Littere Wallie*, p. 43.
[20] Ibid., p. 172.
[21] *Cal. Anc. Corr.*, p. 87.
[22] See above, pp. 68–9. In this category are Llanfair Rhyd Castell, Aberyddon, Dolwyddelan, Talybont, Dinasteleri, Cricieth and Aberalwen.
[23] *Littere Wallie*, p. 136.

APPENDIX VI
TWO EDWARDIAN EXTENTS: DATING AND SIGNIFICANCE

(a) **The Extent of Anglesey**

The earliest surviving extent of Anglesey, which has been printed in Seebohm, *Tribal System*, as Appendix Aa,[1] has generally been mis-dated following an error in the record of the extent itself. The survey of Llanfaes which heads the extent is stated to have been made *die Lune in crastino sancti Gregorii Anno Regni Regis Edwardi vicesimo secundo*.[2] This has been taken as 13 March 1294, for St. Gregory's day fell on 12 March. But the morrow of St. Gregory in 1294 was not a Monday: it was a Saturday. In 1284, however, the year in which the extents of the counties of Caernarvon and Merioneth were made, the morrow of St. Gregory did fall upon a Monday.[3] Either, *die Lune* should read *die Sabbati*, or *vicesimo secundo* should read *duodecimo*.

That the latter alternative is the correct one, and that the extent cannot have been drawn up later than 1284, is proved by an entry made towards the end of the roll on which the extent is most fully preserved. The entry is one of a group, inserted after the *summa* for the whole county, relating to lands mentioned in the extent which had been granted out by royal charter since the extent was made, and for which the sheriff was not to be held accountable. One of the lands mentioned is the vill of Nantmawr, in Twrcelyn,[4] which had been granted out to Tudur Fychan for his life and that of his son Rhys. The grant had been made on 21 August 1284,[5] which thus provides a *terminus ante quem* for the making of the extent. March 1284, or a date close to that month, therefore, seems a likely date for the compilation of the extent.

It now becomes possible to explain one puzzling feature of the extent: a schedule sewn on to the end of the roll contains a survey of the demesne vill of Penrhos,[6] although Penrhos is also surveyed in the main body of the extent. The survey on the schedule is not a mere duplicate of that on the main roll, but is far more detailed, though it contains none of the cash valuation of customs and services which is a pronounced feature of the main document. The clue to the nature of this supplementary survey is given in the report of an inquisition set up to determine the changes incumbent upon the *villani* of Penrhos when the latter complained in 1322 that they were over-burdened.[7] The inquisition reported on a post-conquest extent of Anglesey which had been made by Richard Abingdon, chamberlain of north Wales from March 1284 to January 1286, and who was the extentor of Merioneth and, probably, of Caernarvon:[8] it can thus be assumed with some certainty that the main body of the Anglesey extent under discussion was the work of Richard Abingdon. The inquisition also noted that the king had associated

---

[1] Seebohm, *Tribal System*, Appendix A, pp. 3–25.
[2] Ibid., p. 3.
[3] C. R. Cheney, *Handbook of Dates for Students of English History* (London, 1961) pp. 120, 138.
[4] Seebohm, op. cit., Appendix A, p. 21.
[5] *C. Chanc. R. Various*, p. 288.
[6] Seebohm, op. cit., Appendix A, pp. 3–25; cf. pp. 13–14.
[7] Ibid., pp. 29–31.
[8] *Medieval Welsh Society*, pp. 107–8.

with Richard Abingdon, for the purpose of making the Penrhos section of the extent, Prior Llywelyn of the Dominican priory of Bangor. Richard, however, was unaware of this and made the extent alone. After Richard had left Penrhos, Prior Llywelyn arrived and proceeded to make another extent, which he subsequently caused to be enrolled along with the extent of the whole county. This second survey, carried out by Prior Llywelyn, is surely represented by the schedule sewn on to the end of the roll. The extent on the schedule is thus of very great, indeed unique, value: it was made by a native of Gwynedd, a grandson, indeed, of the great Ednyfed Fychan, for Mr. J. B. Smith has indicated that Prior Llywelyn is almost certainly to be identified as Llywelyn ap Gruffydd ab Ednyfed Fychan.[9] The Penrhos extent is thus the nearest thing which exists to an extent made under the thirteenth-century princes: its detailed description of the dairy due *maronia*[10] (Welsh *maeroniaeth*), its references to the *crannoca Lewelini* (apparently distinguished by its composition rather than its magnitude)[11] and its portrayal of a group of tenants corresponding in part to the *gwŷr mal* of the 1352 extent,[12] are amongst the data of interest to the student of governance.

(b) **The Extent of the Lands of the See of Bangor**
In the *Record of Caernarvon* there appears an extent of the lands of the bishopric of Bangor,[13] drawn up 'in the sixth year of the principate of prince Edward'. The headings to each of the sections of the extent reveal that it was made in late autumn, but give no information which can be used to fix the year. The extent has generally been ascribed to 1348, in the principate of the Black Prince.[14] As the document contains some interesting details of tenurial and personal obligation, it is desirable to fix the date of its compilation as accurately as possible. This may be done by the identification of persons mentioned in the extent.

In the course of the survey of lands in the commote of Twrcelyn, it is stated that Tudur Fychan owed the bishop five shillings per year for the lands which he held in Nantmawr.[15] Tudur Fychan was granted Nantmawr for life in 1284 for good service to Edward I.[16] By 1307, he had been succeeded as tenant of the vill by his son Rhys,[17] and by 1328 Nantmawr was in the hands of William

---

[9] J. B. Smith, 'Welsh Dominicans and the Crisis of 1277', *B.B.C.S.*, XXII (1968), p. 354.
[10] Seebohm, op. cit., Appendix A, p. 25: see above, p. 62.
[11] Seebohm, loc. cit. The *crannoca Lewelini* is glossed as follows: *videlicet, terciam partem frumenti et aliam terciam farine avenate et terciam partem farine ordeacee* ...
[12] Compare the named *gavelli*, ibid., pp. 24–5, with the *gafaelion gwŷr mal* in *Rec. Caern.*, p. 70. See above, p. 59
[13] *Rec. Caern.*, pp. 93–115. It is worth noting that the extent of the lands of the bishopric of Bangor, preserved in NLW B/Misc. Vols./27 (Welsh Church Commission MS. 1), an unpaginated manuscript which has frequently been regarded as a major untapped source, is simply a defective version of the extent under discussion here.
[14] See, for example, P. C. Bartrum, 'Pedigrees of the Welsh Tribal Patriarchs', *N.L.W.J.*, XIII, p. 139; A. D. Carr, 'The Extent of Anglesey, 1352', *Trans. Angl. Ant. Soc.*, 1971–2, p. 154. The lands of the see in Arwystli provide an exception to the general statement regarding the time of year when the extent was drawn up: they were surveyed in January: *Rec. Caern.*, p. 115.
[15] Ibid., p. 109.
[16] See note 5 above.
[17] J. Griffiths, 'Early Accounts relating to North Wales *temp.* Edward I', *B.B.C.S.*, XVI (1955) .p. 112.

APPENDIX VI

Shaldeford, who still held it in 1341.[18] By 1352, Edmund de Wauncey held two-thirds of the vill, the remaining third being held by Thomas of Bodenham and his wife Alicia.[19] Again, in the vill of Bodffordd in Malltraeth, the extent records that Madog ap Cynfrig Arch' held five bovates of land.[20] This man is certainly to be identified as Madog ap Cynfrig, archdeacon of Anglesey, who appears in records relating to 1284 and 1301.[21] Madog also styled himself Matheus in 1284[22] and is undoubtedly the Matheus, archdeacon of Anglesey, who petitioned Prince Edward in 1305.[23] By 1309, he had been succeeded by Einion Sais as archdeacon.[24]

The cases of Tudur Fychan and Madog ap Cynfrig make it evident that the extent was drawn up in the autumn of 1306, in the sixth year of the principate of Edward of Caernarvon, rather than in 1348.[25] Its value as evidence of conditions in the time of Llywelyn ap Gruffydd is, therefore, considerably enhanced.

Addendum

Since this book was in the Press, I have seen A. D. Carr's *Medieval Anglesey*, Llangefni, 1982. In this important book Dr. Carr now accepts (p. 270) a date of 1306 for the Extent of the lands of the Bishop of Bangor but points out that in the case of the post-conquest Extent of Anglesey '1294 is the date used in later accounts' (p. 51 n. 45). Dr. Carr does not, however, deal with the detailed arguments for a date of 1284 advanced above, and it may be suggested that the later accounts base their date on what I have argued is the erroneous date written at the head of the Extent. [Dr (later Professor) Carr later accepted the date of 1284 for the Extent of Anglesey.]

---

[18] *C. Fine R., 1327–37*, p. 91; *C. Pat. R., 1340–43*, p. 225.
[19] *Rec. Caern.*, p. 68.
[20] Ibid., p. 105.
[21] *C. Chanc. R., Various*, p. 284; *C. Pat. R., 1343–45*, p. 228.
[22] *Littere Wallie*, p. 135.
[23] *Rec. Caern.*, p. 206.
[24] *C. Pat. R., 1307–13*, p. 181.
[25] The survey of the Arwystli lands must, of course, have been made in January 1307.

APPENDIX VII

EIRYOES

In the early years of his episcopate, probably in 1270, Anian II, bishop of St. Asaph, caused to be drawn up a list of men pledged to answer to him for offences committed against the jurisdiction of his church, together with those standing surety for the accused. The document, which was copied into the Red Book of Asaph, contains a reference to the *ballivus* (*rhaglaw*) and *preco* (*rhingyll*) of Eiryoes.[1] It was common practice at this period for the clerks of St. Asaph to designate a *cantref* or commote official, such as the *rhaglaw*, by the name of the *llys* which constituted the centre of his operations: in the document under discussion, there are also references to officials of Dinorben and Denbigh, that is, of the *cantrefi* of Rhos and Rhufoniog. It is probable, therefore, that Eiryoes denotes such an administrative centre which has hitherto escaped attention.

Amongst those on the list of men accused are many known officials of Llywelyn ap Gruffydd from the Perfeddwlad, the area on which the bishop's campaigns against oppression by the prince or his ministers were centred. It is, thus, to the Perfeddwlad that one looks for the location of *Eiryoes*. A place bearing precisely that name has not been found, but a likely identification is provided by Eirias, a vill near the coast a little to the east of Llandrillo yn Rhos. Indeed, such an identification helps to explain a complex geo-political situation in that area.

Early in the fourteenth century, Madog Gloddaeth petitioned[2] the king for confirmation of his tenure of the office of *rhaglaw* of Creuddyn, with the bailiwick of Penmaen-Llysfaen and of Evyas, in the county of Caernarvon. Evyas would appear to be a possible rendering of Eirias, and certainly the location of the bailiwick suggests this, for Penmaen-Llysfaen was a tract of country immediately to the east of Eirias. The petition to the king makes it clear that the whole area mentioned was part of the post-conquest principality, even though it lay to the east of the Conwy and was geographically sited within Rhos.

The retention within the principality of the Eirias-Penmaen-Llysfaen area would seem to suggest that it had constituted all, or part, of an administrative entity, distinct from the *cantref* of Rhos, in the pre-conquest period. The antiquity of such an arrangement can only be the subject of guesswork. The name Llysfaen may denote an old-established *llys* in the area, yet even if this were the case, the existence of such a small administrative area in the Perfeddwlad, where in the thirteenth century *rhaglawiaid* normally controlled whole *cantrefi*, still presents a problem.[3] It is possible that the answer may lie in the strategic value of the Eirias-Penmaen-Llysfaen area, the most notable feature of which is a tract of high rugged land, Mynydd Marian, which dominates the route from the east to Conwy. This interpretation is supported by a mandate of Henry III to John Lestrange[4] on 2 April 1244 to strengthen the fortress of Degannwy and to put up a building with a good barrier in the pass of Penmaen to defend it. This prompts speculation as to whether or not the Penmaen area, including Eirias, may have

---

[1] NLW, Peniarth MS. no. 231, p. 79.
[2] *Cal. Anc. Pet.*, p. 209.
[3] See above, pp. 119–23.
[4] *C. Lib. R., 1240–45*, p. 225.

APPENDIX VII

been regarded as part of the land appurtenant to Degannwy, which David granted, together with the castle, to Henry III in 1241. In that case, the whole complex of Creuddyn, Eirias and Penmaen-Llysfaen may have formed a single administrative bloc.[5] Significantly, these were the areas to which Madog Gloddaeth referred in his petition of the early-fourteenth century.

---

[5] See also the grant by Edward I to Robert Despenser, in 1290, of the wardship of the lands of Michael de Sancto Edmundo, a deceased tenant-in-chief, of Ayros and Aber Conwy in Wales: *C. Chanc. R., Various*, p. 325.

BIBLIOGRAPHY
A. PRIMARY SOURCES

1. MANUSCRIPT SOURCES

British Library
Harleian Manuscript 1240.
National Library of Wales
Liber Antiquus of St. Asaph: SA/MB/22.
Peniarth Manuscripts 225, 231.
Welsh Church Commission MS. 1: B/Misc. Vols./27.
Wynnstay Manuscripts, Strata Marcella document 34.
Public Record Office
Ministers' Accounts: S.C.6/1171/7.
Rentals and Surveys: S.C.11/768.
Shrewsbury Public Library
Haughmond Abbey Cartulary: Shrewsbury Public Library MS. 1.

2. PRINTED SOURCES

(a) Calendars etc. published by the Public Record Office
Calendar of Chancery Warrants, 1244–1326 (1927).
Calendar of the Charter Rolls, 1226–1516 (6 vols., 1903–27).
Calendar of the Close Rolls, 1272–1500 (46 vols., 1900–55).
Calendar of the Fine Rolls, 1272–1471 (12 vols., 1911–49).
Calendar of Inquisitions, Miscellaneous, 1216–1377 (3 vols., 1916–37).
Calendar of Inquisitions Post Mortem, 1216–1307 (4 vols., 1898–1913).
Calendar of Liberate Rolls, 1226–1272 (6 vols., 1916–64).
Calendar of Patent Rolls, 1232–1509 (1906–16).
Calendar of Various Chancery Rolls: Supplementary Close Rolls, Welsh Rolls, Scutage Rolls, 1277–1326 (1912).
Close Rolls, 1227–1272 (4 vols., 1902–38).
Patent Rolls, 1216–1232 (2 vols., 1901–03).
Register of Edward the Black Prince (4 vols., 1903–33).

(b) Publications in the Rolls Series
Annales Cambriae, Ed. John Williams ab Ithel (London, 1860).
Annales Monastici, Ed. H. R. Luard, Vols. I and II (London, 1864–65).
Giraldi Cambrensis Opera, Eds. J. S. Brewer, J. F. Dimock and G. F. Warner (8 vols., London, 1861–91).
Matthaei Parisiensis, monachi Sancti Albani, Chornica Majora, Ed. H. R. Luard (7 vols., London, 1872–83).
Registrum epistolarum fratris Johannis Peckham archiepiscopi Cantuariensis, Ed. C. T. Martin (3 vols., London, 1882–85).
Royal and other historical letters illustrative of the reign of Henry III, Ed. W. W. Shirley (2 vols., London, 1862–66).

(c) Record Commission Publications
Ancient Laws and Institutes of Wales, Ed. Aneurin Owen (London, 1841).
Registrum vulgariter nuncupatum 'The Record of Caernarvon' e codice MS. Harleiano 696 descriptum, Ed. Sir Henry Ellis (London, 1838).

BIBLIOGRAPHY

Rotuli Chartarum in Turri Londinensi Asservati, 1199–1216, Ed. T. D. Hardy (1837).
Rotuli de Liberate ac de Misis et Praestitis, Regnante Johanne, Ed. T. D. Hardy (1844).
Rotuli Litterarum Clausarum in Turri Londinensi Asservati, 1204–27, Ed. T. D. Hardy (2 vols., London, 1833–44).
Rotuli Litterarum Patentium in Turri Londinensi Asservati, 1201–16, Ed. T. D. Hardy (London, 1835).
Rotuli de Oblatis et Finibus in Turri Londinensi Asservati tempore Regis Johannis, Ed. T. D. Hardy (London, 1835).
Rymer, Thomas, and Sanderson, Robert (compilers), *Foedera, conventiones, litterae, et cujuscunque generis acta publica*, Ed. A. Clarke and F. Holbrooke (4 vols. in 7) London, 1816–69).
Statutes of the Realm (9 vols. in 10, London, 1810–22).

(d) Publications in the History and Law Series of the Board of Celtic Studies of the University of Wales
Brut y Tywysogyon (Peniarth MS. 20), Gol. Thomas Jones (Caerdydd, 1941).
Brut y Tywysogyon, or the Chronicle of the Princes (Peniarth MS. 20 version), Trans. Thomas Jones (Cardiff, 1952).
Brut y Tywysogyon or the Chronicle of the Princes (Red Book of Hergest version), Ed. Thomas Jones (Cardiff, 1955).
Calendar of Ancient Correspondence concerning Wales, Ed. J. Goronwy Edwards (Cardiff, 1935).
Calendar of Ancient Petitions relating to Wales, Ed. William Rees (Cardiff, 1975).
The Latin Texts of the Welsh Laws, Ed. Hywel D. Emanuel (Cardiff, 1967).
List of the Welsh Entries in the Memoranda Rolls, 1282–1343, Ed. N. M. Fryde (Cardiff, 1974).
Llyfr Colan, Gol. Dafydd Jenkins (Caerdydd, 1963).
Llyfr Iorwerth, Ed. Aled Rhys William (Cardiff, 1960).
The Merioneth Lay Subsidy Roll, 1292–93, Ed. Keith Williams-Jones (Cardiff, 1976).
The Welsh Assize Roll (1277–1284), Ed. J. Conway Davies (Cardiff, 1940).

(e) Other printed sources
i. Books
Annales Cestrienses, Ed. R. C. Christie (Record Society of Lancashire and Cheshire, vol. 14, London, 1887).
Cartae et alia munimenta quae ad dominium de Glamorgan pertinent, Ed. G. T. Clark (6 vols., Cardiff, 1910).
A Catalogue of the manuscripts relating to Wales in the British Museum, Comp. Edward Owen (4 vols., London, 1900–02).
Councils and ecclesiastical documents relating to Great Britain and Ireland, Eds. A. W. Haddan and W. Stubbs, Vol. 1 (Oxford, 1869).
The Court Rolls of the lordship of Ruthin or Dyffryn Clwyd, of the reign of King Edward the First, Ed. R. A. Roberts (Cymmrodorion Record Series, II, London, 1893).
Cronica de Wallia and other Documents from Exeter Cathedral Library MS. 3514, Ed. Thomas Jones (n.d.).
Cyfreithiau Hywel Dda yn ol Llyfr Blegywryd, Gol. Stephen J. Williams a J. Enoch Powell (Caerdydd, 1942).
Cyfreithjeu Hywel Dda ac eraill, seu Leges Wallicae, Ed. William Wotton (1730).
William Dugdale, *Monasticon Anglicanum*, Eds. J. Cayley, H. Ellis, B. Bandinel (8 parts, London, 1817–30).
Early Welsh Genealogical Tracts, Ed. P. C. Bartrum (Cardiff, 1966).
Flintshire ministers' accounts, 1301–28, Ed. A. Jones (Flintshire Historical Society Publications, iii, 1913).

BIBLIOGRAPHY 243

Heraldic Visitations of Wales, by Lewys Dwnn, Ed. S. R. Meyrick (2 vols., Llandovery, 1846).
History of Gruffydd ap Cynan (1054–1137), Ed. A. Jones (Manchester, 1910).
Llawysgrif Hendregadredd, Gol. John Morris-Jones a T. H. Parry-Williams (Caerdydd, 1971).
Ministers' Accounts for West Wales, 1277–1306, Ed. Myvanwy Rhys (Cymmrodorion Record Series, XIII, London, 1936).
Register and Chronicle of the Abbey of Aberconway, Ed. Sir Henry Ellis, in Vol. 1 of *Camden Miscellany* (London, Camden Society, 1843).
Report on manuscripts in the Welsh language to the Historical Manuscripts Commission, Comp. J. Gwenogvryn Evans (2 parts, London, 1898–1910).
Rotuli Parliamentorum, 1278–1503 (6 vols., published by order of the House of Lords).
The Statutes of Wales, Ed. Ivor Bowen (London, 1908).
Survey of the Honour of Denbigh, 1334, Eds. Paul Vinogradoff and Frank Morgan (British Academy Records of the Social and Economic History of England and Wales, Vol. 1, London, 1914).
Survey of Penmaenmawr, Ed. J. O. Halliwell (1857).
Welsh Medieval Law, Ed. A. W. Wade-Evans (Oxford, 1909).
Sir John Wynn, *The History of the Gwydir Family,* Ed. J. Ballinger (Cardiff, 1927).

ii. Articles devoted largely to the publication of primary sources

J. Griffiths, 'Early accounts relating to North Wales *temp.* Edward I', *Bulletin of the Board of Celtic Studies,* XIV (1952), pp. 235–41, 302–12; XV (1954), pp. 126–56; XVI (1955), pp. 109–34.
Idem, 'Two early ministers' accounts for North Wales', *Bulletin of the Board of Celtic Studies,* IX (1939), pp. 50–70.
R. I. Jack, 'Records of Denbighshire Lordships, II, The Lordship of Dyffryn Clwyd in 1324', *Transactions of the Denbighshire Historical Society,* XVII (1968), pp. 7–53.
E. D. Jones, N. G. Davies and B. F. Roberts, 'Five Strata Marcella Charters', *National Library of Wales Journal,* V (1947–48), pp. 50–5.
M. C. J. (ed.), 'Extent of Merionethshire *temp.* Edward I', *Archaeologia Cambrensis,* 3rd Series, XIII (1867), pp. 184–92.
E. A. Lewis, 'Rolls of the Small Hundred Court of Ardudwy, 1325-26', *Bulletin of the Board of Celtic Studies,* IV (1928), pp. 153–66.
T. Jones Pierce and J. Griffiths, 'Documents relating to the early history of the borough of Caernarvon', *Bulletin of the Board of Celtic Studies,* IX (1939), pp. 236–46.
T. Jones Pierce, 'A Lleyn Lay Subsidy Account', *Bulletin of the Board of Celtic Studies,* V (1931), pp. 54–71.
Idem, 'Two Early Caernarvonshire Accounts', *Bulletin of the Board of Celtic Studies,* V (1931), pp. 142–55.
Idem, 'Lleyn Ministers' Accounts, 1350–51', *Bulletin of the Board of Celtic Studies,* VI (1933), pp. 255–75.
W. H. Waters, 'The Account of the Sheriff of Caernarvon for 1303–04', *Bulletin of the Board of Celtic Studies,* VII (1935), pp. 143–53.

B. SECONDARY SOURCES

(Note: many of the works listed below as secondary sources contain much primary material.)

i. *Books*

P. C. Bartrum, *Welsh Genealogies, c. 300–1400* (8 vols., Cardiff, 1974).
D. A. Binchy, *Celtic and Anglo-Saxon Kingship* (Oxford, 1970).

BIBLIOGRAPHY

J. A. Bradney, *A History of Monmouthshire* (4 vols., London, 1904–33).
C. R. Cheney, *English Bishops' Chanceries, 1100–1250* (Manchester, 1950).
H. R. Davies, *A Review of the Records of the Conway and the Menai Ferries* (Board of Celtic Studies, History and Law Series, Cardiff, 1924).
N. Denholm-Young, *Seignorial Administration in England* (London, 1937).
Dictionary of Welsh Biography down to 1940, Eds. Sir John Edward Lloyd, R. T. Jenkins, Sir William Llewelyn Davies and Margaret Beatrice Davies (London, 1959).
D. L. Douie, *Archbishop Pecham* (Oxford, 1952).
C. du F. Du Cange, *Glossarium Mediae et Infimae Latinitatis*. Ed. L. Favre (Niort, 1884–87).
J. G. Edwards, *Edward I's Castle-Building in Wales* (British Academy Sir John Rhys Memorial Lecture, London, 1944).
Idem, Hywel Dda and the Welsh Law Books (Bangor, 1929).
Idem, The Normans and the Welsh March (British Academy Raleigh Lecture, London, 1956).
T. P. Ellis, *Welsh Tribal Law and Custom in the Middle Ages* (2 vols, Oxford, 1926).
R. W. Eyton, *Antiquities of Shropshire* (12 vols., 1854–60).
Richard Fenton, *Tours in Wales (1804–1813)* (Cambrian Archaeological Association, 1917).
Geiriadur Prifysgol Cymru, Gol. R. J. Thomas (Caerdydd, 1950–   ).
Colin Gresham, *Eifionydd, a study in landownership from the Medieval Period to the Present Day* (Cardiff, 1973).
Lord Harlech, *North Wales*: Volume 5 of *Illustrated regional guides to ancient monuments under the ownership or guardianship of the Ministry of Works* (London, 1948).
Rhys W. Hays, *The History of the Abbey of Aberconway, 1186–1537* (Cardiff, 1963).
H. J. Hewitt, *The Organization of War under Edward III, 1338–62* (Manchester, 1966).
Dafydd Jenkins, *Cyfraith Hywel* (Llandyssul, 1970).
J. E. A. Jolliffe, *Angevin Kingship* (London, 1963).
R. E. Latham, *Revised Medieval Latin Word-List* (1965).
E. A. Lewis, *The Medieval Boroughs of Snowdonia* (London, 1912).
J. E. Lloyd, *A History of Wales from the Earliest Times to the Edwardian Conquest* (2 vols., 3rd ed. London, 1939).
Idem, The Welsh Chronicles (British Academy Sir John Rhys Memorial Lecture, London, 1928).
J. Morris-Jones, *A Welsh Grammar, Historical and Comparative* (Oxford, 1913).
T. Jones Pierce, *Medieval Welsh Society: Selected Essays*, Ed. J. Beverley Smith (Cardiff, 1972).
Thomas Pennant, *Tours in Wales*, Ed. John Rhys (3 vols., Caernarvon, 1883).
F. M. Powicke, *Henry III and the Lord Edward* (Single volume ed. Oxford, 1966).
Idem, The Thirteenth Century (2nd ed., Oxford, 1962).
William Rees, *An Historical Atlas of Wales* (Cardiff, 1951).
Idem, South Wales and the March, 1284–1415: a social and agrarian study (Oxford, 1924).
Melville Richards, *Welsh Administrative and Territorial Units* (Cardiff, 1969).
Michael Richter, *Giraldus Cambrensis. The Growth of the Welsh Nation* (Aberystwyth, 1972).
Glyn Roberts, *Aspects of Welsh History: Selected Papers* (Cardiff, 1969).
A. J. Roderick (ed.), *Wales through the Ages* (Llandybie, 1959).
Royal Commission on ancient monuments in Wales and Monmouthshire:
   Inventory of the monuments of Anglesey (London, 1937).
   Inventory of the monuments of Caernarvonshire (3 vols., 1956–64).
   Inventory of the monuments of Merioneth (1921).

BIBLIOGRAPHY 245

Frederic Seebohm, *The Tribal System in Wales* (2nd ed., London, 1904).
F. M. Stenton, *The First Century of English Feudalism* (2nd ed., Oxford, 1961).
R. Stewart-Brown, *The Serjeants of the Peace in Medieval England and Wales* (Manchester, 1936).
D. R. Thomas, *Esgobaeth Llanelwy: The History of the Diocese of St. Asaph* (3 vols., Oswestry, 1908–13).
D. S. Thomson, *Branwen verch Lyr* (Dublin, 1961).
W. H. Waters, *The Edwardian Settlement of North Wales in its Administrative and Legal Aspects, 1284–1343* (Cardiff, 1935).
S. W. Williams, *The Cistercian Abbey of Strata Florida* (London, 1889).

ii. *Articles*

P. C. Bartrum, 'Notes on the Welsh Geneaological Manuscripts', *Transactions of the Honourable Society of Cymmrodorion*, 1968, pp. 63–98.
L. A. S. Butler, 'Medieval Finds fron Castell y Bere, Merioneth', *Archaeologia Cambrensis*, CXXIII (1974), pp. 78–112.
A. D. Carr, 'The Barons of Edeyrnion, 1282–1485', *Journal of the Merioneth Historical and Record Society*, IV, iii (1963), pp. 187–93; iv (1964), pp. 289–301.
Idem, 'Some Edeyrnion and Dinmael Documents'. *Bulletin of the Board of Celtic Studies*, XXI (1965), pp. 242–49.
T. M. Charles-Edwards, 'The Heir-Apparent in Irish and Welsh Law', *Celtica*, IX, pp. 180–90.
J. Conway Davies, 'A grant by David ap Gruffydd', *National Library of Wales Journal*, III (1943), pp. 29–32.
Idem, 'A grant by Llywelyn ap Gruffydd', *National Library of Wales Journal*, III (1943), pp. 158–62.
R. R. Davies, 'Colonial Wales', *Past and Present*, LXV (1974), pp. 3–23.
Idem, 'The Survival of the Bloodfeud in Medieval Wales', *History*, LIV (1969), pp. 338–57.
Idem, 'The Twilight of Welsh Law, 1284–1536', *History*, LI (1966), pp. 143–64.
J. G. Edwards, 'The Historical Study of the Welsh Lawbooks', *Transactions of the Royal Historical Society*, 5th Series, XII (1962), pp. 141–55.
Idem 'Madog ap Llywelyn, the Welsh Leader in 1294–95', *Bulletin of the Board of Celtic Studies*, XIII (1950), pp. 207–10.
Idem, 'The Royal Household and the Welsh Lawbooks', *Transactions of the Royal Historical Society*, 5th Series, XIII (1963), pp. 163–76.
Idem, 'Sir Gruffydd Llwyd', *English Historical Review*, XXX (1915), pp. 589–601.
D. L. Evans, 'Some notes on the history of the principality of Wales in the time of the Black Prince', *Transactions of the Honourable Society of Cymmrodorion*, 1925–6, pp. 25–110.
E. D. Evans, 'Castell y Bere', *Journal of the Merioneth Historical and Record Society*, III (1957), pp. 31–44.
Colin Gresham, 'The Aberconwy Charter', *Archaeologia Cambrensis*, XCIV (1939), pp. 123–62.
John Griffiths, 'The Revolt of Madog ap Llywelyn in 1294–95', *Transactions of the Caernarvonshire Historical Society*, 1955, pp. 12–24.
A. H. A. Hogg and D. J. C. King, 'Masonry Castles in Wales and the Marches: a List', *Archaeologia Cambrensis*, CXVI (1967), pp. 71–132.
Margaret Howell, 'Regalian Right in Wales and the March: the Relation of Theory to Practice', *Welsh History Review*, VII (1975), pp. 269–88.
Daniel Huws, 'Leges Howelda at Canterbury', *National Library of Wales Journal*, XIX (1975–76), pp. 340–44.
Dafydd Jenkins, '*Cynghellor* and Chancellor', *Bulletin of the Board of Celtic Studies*, XXVII (1976), pp. 115–18.

Idem, 'Iorwerth ap Madog', *National Library of Wales Journal*, VIII (1953), pp. 164-70.
Idem, 'Kings, Lords and Princes: the Nomenclature of Authority in Thirteenth-Century Wales', *Bulletin of the Board of Celtic Studies*, XXVI (1976), pp. 451-62.
Idem, 'A Lawyer Looks at Welsh Land Law', *Transactions of the Honourable Society of Cymmrodorion*, 1967, pp. 220-47.
Idem, 'Legal and Comparative Aspects of the Welsh Laws', *Welsh History Review, Special Welsh Laws Number*, 1963, pp. 51-9.
Idem, 'Yr Ynad Coch', *Bulletin of the Board of Celtic Studies*, XXII (1968), pp. 345-46.
Francis Jones, 'The Heraldry of Gwynedd', *Transactions of the Caernarvonshire Historical Society*, 1963, pp. 38-59.
Idem, 'Welsh Bonds for keeping the peace, 1283 and 1295', *Bulletin of the Board of Celtic Studies*, XIII (1950), pp. 142-4.
G. P. Jones, 'Rhos and Rhufoniog Pedigrees', *Archaeologia Cambrensis*, LXXX (1925), pp. 289-306.
Glanville R. J. Jones, 'The Defences of Gwynedd in the Thirteenth Century', *Transactions of the Caernarvonshire Historical Society*, 1969, pp. 29-43.
Idem, 'The Distribution of Medieval Settlement in Anglesey', *Transactions of the Anglesey Antiquarian Society and Field Club*, 1955, pp. 27-96.
Idem, 'The Site of Llys Aberffraw', *Transactions of the Anglesey Antiquarian Society and Field Club*, 1957, pp. 5-7.
Ceri W. Lewis, 'The Treaty of Woodstock, 1247: its background and significance', *Welsh History Review*, II (1964), pp. 37-65.
E. A. Lewis, 'The Decay of Tribalism in North Wales', *Transactions of the Honourable Society of Cymmrodorion*, 1902-03, pp. 1-75.
Ralph Maud, 'David, the Last Prince of Wales', *Transactions of the Honourable Society of Cymmrodorion*, 1968, pp. 43-62.
D. Huw Owen, 'Tenurial and Economic Developments in North Wales in the Twelfth and Thirteenth Centuries', *Welsh History Review*, VI (1972), pp. 117-35.
Idem, '*Treth* and *Ardreth*: some aspects of commutation in North Wales in the Thirteenth Century', *Bulletin of the Board of Celtic Studies*, XXV (1974), pp. 446-53.
T. Jones Pierce, 'Aber Gwyn Gregin', *Transactions of the Caernarvonshire Historical Society*, 1962, pp. 37-43.
Idem, 'Ancient Meirionydd', *Journal of the Merioneth Historical and Record Society*, I (1949-51), pp. 12-20.
Idem, 'Einion ap Ynyr (Anian II), bishop of St. Asaph', *Flintshire Historical Society Publications*, XVII (1957), pp. 16-33.
Idem, 'The Old Borough of Nefyn, 1355-1882', *Transactions of the Caernarvonshire Historical Society*, 1957, pp. 36-53.
Michael Richter, 'David ap Llywelyn, the first Prince of Wales', *Welsh History Review*, V (1971), pp. 205-19.
Idem, 'The Political and Institutional Background to National Consciousness in Medieval Wales', in T. W. Moody (ed.), *Nationality and the Pursuit of National Independence* (Belfast, 1978), pp. 37-55.
Glyn Roberts, 'Biographical Notes: Madog ap Llywelyn', *Bulletin of the Board of Celtic Studies*, XVII (1956), pp. 41-2.
A. J. Roderick, 'The Feudal Relations Between the English Crown and the Welsh Princes', *History*, XXXVII (1952), pp. 201-12.
Idem, 'The Four Cantreds: a study in administration (to 1282)', *Bulletin of the Board of Celtic Studies*, X (1939-41), pp. 246-56.
Idem, 'Marriage and Politics in Wales, 1066-1282', *Welsh History Review*, IV (1968-69), pp. 1-20.

Joy Russell-Smith, 'Keys in Sawles Warde', *Medium Aevum*, XXII (1953), pp. 104–10.
J. Beverley Smith, 'The "Cronica de Wallia" and the Dynasty of Dinefwr: A textual and historical study', *Bulletin of the Board of Celtic Studies*, XX (1963), pp. 261–82.
Idem, 'Crown and Community in the Principality of North Wales in the Reign of Henry Tudor', *Welsh History Review*, III (1966), pp. 145–71.
Idem, 'The Middle March in the Thirteenth Century', *Bulletin of the Board of Celtic Studies*, XXIV (1970), pp. 77–92.
Idem, 'Offra Principis Wallie Domino Regi', *Bulletin of the Board of Celtic Studies*, XXIV (1966), pp. 362–7.
Idem, 'Owain Gwynedd', *Transactions of the Caernarvonshire Historical Society*, 1971, pp. 8–17.
Idem, 'Welsh Dominicans and the Crisis of 1277', *Bulletin of the Board of Celtic Studies*, XXII (1968), pp. 353–7.
Llinos Beverley Smith, 'The Gage and the Land market in Late Medieval Wales', *Economic History Review*, 2nd Series, XXIX (1976), pp. 537–50.
A. J. Taylor, 'Montgomery Town Wall', *Archaeologia Cambrensis*, XCIX (1947), pp. 281–83.
C. Thomas, 'Thirteenth-Century Farm Economies in North Wales', *Agricultural History Review*, XVI (1968), pp. 1–14.
R. F. Treharne, 'The Franco-Welsh treaty of alliance in 1212', *Bulletin of the Board of Celtic Studies*, XVIII (1958), pp. 60–75.
R. F. Walker, 'Hubert de Burgh and Wales, 1218–1232', *English Historical Review*, LXXXVII (1972), pp. 465–94.
R. B. White, 'Sculptured Stone Heads from Aberffraw, Anglesey', *Archaeologia Cambrensis*, CXXVI (1977), pp. 140–9.
Gwyn A. Williams, 'The Succession to Gwynedd, 1238–1247', *Bulletin of the Board of Celtic Studies*, XX (1962–64), pp. 393–413.
Keith Williams-Jones, 'Llywelyn's Charter to Cymer Abbey in 1209', *Journal of the Merioneth Historical and Record Society*, III (1957), pp. 45–78.

iii. *Unpublished theses*

Glanville R. J. Jones, 'The Military Geography of Gwynedd in the Thirteenth Century' (University of Wales M.A. thesis, 1949).
O. E. Jones, 'Llyfr Coch Asaph: A Textual and Historical Study' (University of Wales M.A. thesis, 1968).
R. F. Walker, 'The Anglo-Welsh Wars, 1216–1267' (University of Oxford D.Phil. thesis, 1954).

INDEX

Aber, 4, 80, 104, 126, 130, 205, 233, 234
Aberalwen, 234
Aberconwy, 239
Aberconwy, abbey of, 33, 34, 38, 48, 49, 80, 99, 100, 151, 152, 163, 166, 181-3, 199, 200, 204, 215, 234
Aberconwy, abbot of, 5, 32-4, 37, 39, 78, 83
Aberdyfi, xx, 202
Aberffraw, xv, xxi, 4, 38, 42, 60, 61, 85, 105, 109, 139, 156, 158, 167, 168, 185, 197, 218, 228
Abermaw, 79
Abermenai, 78
Aberyddon, 34, 233, 234
Aberystwyth, xix
Abingdon, Richard, 235, 236
Abraham, bishop of St. Asaph, 35, 84, 169
Adam (Master), 26, 31, 222
Adam ab Iorwerth, 20
Aher, Robert fitz, 201
Anglesey, xiv, xv, xviii, xxi, xxx, xxxvii, 46, 59, 61, 65, 68, 77, 79, 97, 102, 107-10, 112, 113, 128, 130, 131, 139-47, 156-8, 180, 192, 195, 200, 214, 231, 235, 237
Anian, abbot of Aberconwy, 222, 226
Anian, bishop of Bangor, 36, 173-5, 179-81, 224
Anian I, bishop of St. Asaph, 172, 173, 181
Anian II, bishop of St. Asaph, 69, 70, 166, 173-82, 184, 185
Ardudwy, xiv, xviii, xxiv, 2, 36, 37, 44, 47, 90, 93, 142, 152, 153, 158
Arddau, 33
Arfon, 52, 79, 142, 147, 157, 158, 195, 200
Arllechwedd, 79, 99, 100, 123, 124, 128, 130, 132, 142, 147, 158, 195, 216, 231
Arllechwedd, dean of, 33, 52, 226
Arwystli, xxvi, xxix, 6, 236, 237
Ayros, 239

Bach yr Anneleu, 22, 233
Bancenyn, 203

Bangor, xiv, 37, 157, 203
Bangor, bishop of, 3, 8, 9, 32, 36, 42, 43, 92, 97, 107, 168, 169, 182, 183, 192, 209, 211, 213, 216, 220, 222, 223
Bangor, friars of, 79, 181, 214, 236
Bangor, see of, xxxvii, 34, 38, 39, 81, 93, 134, 166, 173, 179, 180, 224, 225, 236
Bardsey, abbey of, 52, 56, 65, 71-3
Basingwerk, abbey of, xv, 5, 18, 28, 55, 67, 157, 182, 183, 201, 203, 204
Beaumaris, 98
Beddgelert, 99, 132, 156, 157, 204
Bellward, Alice, wife of William le, 221
Berwyn, xiii, xvi, 53
Bigod, Hugh, 89
Bigod, Roger, 15
Bleddyn ap Llywelyn, 205
Bleddyn ap Madog, 120, 134, 205
Bleddyn ap Madog, gwely, 120
Bleddyn ap Meurig, 205, 232
Bleddyn Fardd, 15
Bleddyn Fychan, 106
Bodellog, 171, 209, 211, 213
Bodenham, Thomas and Alicia of, 237
Bodfeio, 124
Bodffordd, 132, 237
Bodhunod, 114
Bodlennyn, 103
Bodlew, 140
Bodorfach, 130
Bodwrdyn, 112, 133, 156
Bodwrog, 132
Bohun, Humphrey de, xxvii, xxxiv
Boniface of Savoy, archbishop of Canterbury, 166
Botandreg, 132
Braose, Isabella de, xxi
Braose, William de, xxi, xxxi, 211
Brecon, xxvi, xxvii, 5
Bromfield and Yale, lordship of, 43
Brycheiniog, xxx, 15, 89
Bryn Derwin, xxiv, 158
Bryncelyn, 118
Brynffanugl, 103
Builth, xxvi, xxx, 5, 89
Burgh, Hubert de, xx, xxi, xxxi

250 INDEX

Burnell, William, 107

Cadwaladr ap Gruffydd, xvii, 148, 149, 151
Cadwaladr ap Hywel, 28
Cadwgan, bishop of Bangor, 169
Caeo, 218
Caernarfon, xiv, xv, xvi, 4, 80, 202, 204
Caernarvonshire, xxxvi, 110, 130, 218, 235
Caerphilly, xxvii
Cafflogion, 98, 132
Calxston, Philip de, 212
Canterbury, archbishop of, 33
Caradog ap Thomas, 117, 205
Cardigan, xx, xxi
Carmarthen, xx
Carn Dochan, 197
Carn Fadryn, 4
Carnan, 121
Castell y Bere, 4, 143, 194, 197
Cefnllys, 16
Cefnyfynydd, 204
Cegidfa, 192
Ceinmeirch, 58, 66, 72, 122
Cemais, 42, 59, 61, 200, 204
Ceredigion, xiii, xiv, xix, xxix, 151
Ceri, xxxi
Cerrigtegfan, 121
Chester, xiii, xv, xxiii, 47, 69, 79, 81, 106, 155, 205, 209, 212, 213, 219, 229, 232, 234
Cîteaux, 226
Clare, Gilbert de, xxvii, xxxiv, 207, 213
Clegyrog, 111, 112, 133
Clun, xxiv
Clwyd, xiii, xvi
Clynnog Fawr, 157
Coedanau, 200
Colan, xl
Coleshill, xvi, 203
Collwyn ap Tango, 17
Conwy, river, xiv, xv, xvi, xxiii, xxiv, 79, 84, 114, 116, 123, 128, 131, 200, 238
Conwy, treaty of, xxix, xxxiv, 9, 105, 161, 207, 218, 220, 232
Corbet, Thomas, 231
Cororion, 130
Creuddyn, 52, 79, 97, 130, 131, 238, 239
Cricieth, 51, 197, 233, 234
Crogen, 57, 78
Crugeny, 91

Crymlyn, 132
Cwmllannerch, 91
Cydewain, 233
Cyfeiliog, xxix, 36
Cyfnerth ap Morgenau, xl
Cyfnerth ap Rhufon, 131
Cyfnerth ap Rhufon, gwely, 115
Cymer, abbey of, 28, 34, 80, 151, 163, 166, 181, 182, 207, 234
Cymer, abbot of, 33, 34, 36, 39, 182, 207, 217, 224
Cymydmaen, xxiv, 56, 73, 156–8
Cynan ab Owain Gwynedd, 141, 152
Cynfrig ap Carwed, 42
Cynfrig ab Ednyfed, 22, 104, 206
Cynfrig ap Goronwy, 103, 120, 122, 134, 206
Cynfrig ab Iorwerth, 97, 102–4, 108, 121, 123, 125, 126, 128, 130, 187, 188
Cynfrig ab Iowerth, gwely, 103
Cynfrig ap Madog, 206
Cynfrig Sais, 14, 210, 232
Cynfrig Sais, 230
Cynfrig Wenkwys, 206

Dafydd ab Einion, 230
Dafydd ab Einion (Eiryoes), 206
Dafydd ab Einion Fychan, 9, 17, 106–9, 123, 129, 187, 206, 207, 209, 213
Dafydd ap Gruffydd, 207
Dafydd ap Gruffydd ap Dafydd Fychan, 109
Dafydd ap Gruffydd, xxiv, xxv, xxvii, xxviii, xxix, xxx, xxxii, xxxiv, 3, 7–9, 16, 17, 28, 72, 104, 152, 156–62, 170, 174, 175, 178, 204, 216, 220, 226, 232–4
Dafydd ap Mabon, 120, 121
Dafydd ap Mabon, gwely, 131
Dafydd ab Owain, xviii, 116, 141, 142, 147, 148, 200
Dafydd Fychan, 107–10
Dafydd Gethin ap Dafydd, 109, 110
Dafydd Goch ab Iorwerth, 210
David, archdeacon of Bangor, 32, 35, 223
David, archdeacon of St. Asaph (the chancellor), 31, 34, 35, 223, 225
David, the clerk, 26, 31, 222, 223
David, Master, 183
David ab Ithel, 23, 224

INDEX

David ap Llywelyn (Meirionydd), 144–7
David ap Llywelyn, xiii, xxi, xxii, xxiii, xxxii, 1–6, 11, 13, 18, 26, 27, 31, 33, 35, 51, 67, 84, 99, 102–6, 112, 117, 118, 122, 132, 143, 150, 152–5, 166, 168–70, 182, 183, 201–4, 208, 209, 211–13, 215, 217, 219, 221, 223, 227, 229–31
David ap William, 26, 32, 35, 224
Daykin Grach, 113
Degannwy, xxiii, xxiv, xxv, 79, 197, 200, 209, 221, 238, 239
Deheubarth, xvii, xx, xxvi, 139, 163, 164, 167
Denbigh, 7, 84, 134, 209, 216, 218, 220, 238
Denbigh, Honour of, xxxvii, 49, 51, 66, 70–3, 75, 93, 101–3, 109, 118, 120–2, 133
Despenser, Robert, 239
Dinas Emrys, 4
Dinasteleri, 234
Dincadfael, 71
Dindaethwy, 77, 98, 99, 107–9, 121, 130–2, 156
Dindryfwl, 130
Dinefwr, xxvi, 139
Dinllaen, 43, 104, 149, 162, 202, 217, 218
Dinorben, 84, 85, 109, 119–23, 134, 188, 200, 205, 206, 209, 214, 215, 217, 218, 220, 233, 238
Dinsylwy Rys, 130
Diserth, xxv
Dolbadarn, 4, 197
Dolforwyn, xxxiv, 22, 23, 177, 194, 205, 210, 224
Dolgellau, 59, 60
Dolgynwal, hospital of St. John, 6, 27, 202
Dolwyddelan, 4, 51, 113, 197, 234
Dunanmey, 38, 228
Dunoding, 200
Dyfed, xxv
Dyfi, river, xvi, 79, 151
Dyffryn Clwyd, xxxvi, xxxvii, 74, 114, 122, 130–4, 154, 160, 161, 203, 214, 229, 230, 232

Edeirnion, 145
Ednyfed (Dinorben), 209

Ednyfed Fychan, 11–15, 17–19, 35, 80, 90, 97, 102–6, 108, 120, 123, 125, 126, 129, 130, 166, 188, 202, 207–10, 236
Ednyfed Fychan, gafael, 130
Edrud ap Marchudd, 17, 130
Edward I, xxiv, xxviii, xxix, xxx, xxxiv, 3, 7, 8, 33, 36, 47, 69, 81, 82, 104, 105, 107, 110, 112, 113, 115, 118, 121–3, 127, 143, 144, 146, 161, 162, 176, 177, 179, 180, 183, 192, 196, 197, 206, 207, 209, 210, 213, 214, 216–18, 220, 224–6, 228, 230, 233, 234, 236, 239
Edward II (of Caernarvon), 47, 70, 123, 124, 145, 188, 192, 205, 236, 237
Eifionydd, xiv, xviii, 118, 122, 133, 141, 142, 157, 230
Einion (Crogen), 78
Einion (Denbigh), 209
Einion ap Caradog, 23, 24, 117–19, 122, 126, 129, 133, 207, 209, 210, 220, 230, 231
Einion ap Goronwy, 22, 224
Einion ap Gwalchmai, 14, 98, 109, 110, 131, 132, 202, 210
Einion ap Gwalchmai, gwelyau, 98, 109, 132
Einion ap Llywarch, 210
Einion ap Maredudd, 28, 90, 203, 229, 232
Einion ap Nest, 82
Einion ab Owain, 107
Einion ap Rhodri, 116, 117
Einion ap Rhodri, gwely, 141
Einion Ddu, 123
Einion Fychan, 106–10, 129, 208, 210–12, 217
Einion Sais, archdeacon of Anglesey, 237
Eiryoes (Eirias?), 123, 206, 238–9
Elfael, xxi, xxvi, 5, 220
Elias, 84
Elise ab Iorwerth, 145
Elise ap Madog, xviii
Ellesmere, 201
Erddreiniog, 90, 130
Ewloe, 4, 194, 197, 216, 234

Flintshire, 75, 230
Fremingham, Ralph de, 221

Gelleiniog, 141, 152

INDEX

Gerald of Wales (Giraldus Cambrensis, xiv, xv, xvi, xviii, 46, 163, 166, 199, 200
Gervase (pencenedl), 192
Gervase, Master, 32, 36, 37, 224
Gervase of Llanfair, 36, 37
Glamorgan, xxv
Gloddaeth, 120, 121
Gloucester, treaty of, xxii, 3, 117, 169, 208, 211, 215, 223, 230
Goronwy ap Cynfrig, 103, 104, 106, 129, 212, 213, 217
Goronwy ab Ednyfed, 12, 15–19, 104, 213
Goronwy ap Heilyn, 9, 17, 42, 104, 106, 120, 122, 129, 134, 207, 213, 214, 220
Goronwy ap Seisyll, 85, 134, 214
Goronwy Fychan, 106
Goronwy Grach, 124, 188
Gregory of Bangor, 180
Gregory of Basingwerk, 183
Gregory X, Pope, 175, 176, 182
Grey, John de, 47, 106
Grey, Reginald de, 8
Gruffydd ap Caradog, 117, 122, 133, 230
Gruffydd ap Cynan (d. 1137), 78, 93, 110
Gruffydd ap Cynan ab Owain, xviii, 115, 141, 142, 152, 199, 200, 215
Gruffydd ab Ednyfed, 18, 104, 105, 118, 124, 214, 215
Gruffydd ap Gruffydd Maelor II, 162
Gruffydd ap Gwenwynwyn, xxiv, xxv, xxvi, xxviii, xxiv, xxx, xxxiv, 23, 33, 34, 174, 177, 182, 192, 206, 207, 210, 213, 214, 216, 218–20, 222, 224, 226, 233
Gruffydd ab Iorwerth, 105, 146
Gruffydd ab Iorwerth (Powys), 145
Gruffydd ap Llywelyn, xxi, xxii, xxiii, xxxi, 2, 51, 105, 142, 151-5, 169, 202, 203, 209, 229–32
Gruffyd ap Madog, xxiii, xxv, 13, 159
Gruffydd ap Madog Gloddaeth, 121
Gruffydd ap Maredudd, 111, 126, 156
Gruffydd ap Maredudd, gwely, 111
Gruffydd ap Meurig, 192
Gruffydd ap Rhys, 106
Gruffydd ap Rhodri, 116, 117, 147, 148, 215
Gruffydd ap Tudur, 99, 113, 131, 132
Gruffydd Fychan, 7, 23

Gruffydd Gryg, 50, 122, 134, 214, 232
Gruffydd Hiraethog, 114
Gruffydd Llwyd (Sir), 106
Gwalchmai ap Meilir, 14, 17, 109, 110, 125, 128
Gwenllian, wife of Ednyfed Fychan, 19
Gwent, 15, 89, 213
Gwenwynwyn, xix, xx, xxxi, 14, 153, 200, 210
Gwern Eigron, treaty of, xxii, 170, 209, 229
Gwerthrynion, 5, 203, 204, 230, 231
Gwilym ap Cadwgan, 84
Gwion of Bangor, 35
Gwion, bishop of Bangor, xviii
Gwion ap Madog, 120
Gwion ap Madog (Tegeingl), 6
Gwladus Ddu, 230

Haughmond, abbey of, 43, 149, 150, 197, 201-3
Hawarden, xxx
Hawise (Lestrange), wife of Gruffydd ap Gwenwynwyn, xxviii
Heilyn ap Cynfrig, 103, 119, 134, 215
Heilyn ab Iddig, 261
Heilyn ap Roger, 78
Heilyn ap Tudur, 97, 104, 131, 162, 204, 220
Helen (Elena), daughter of Llywelyn ab Iorwerth, xx, 207, 225
Henllan, 172
Henry II, xvi, 6, 196
Henry III, xx, xxii–xxvi, xxxi, xxxii, 3, 7, 11, 18, 19, 31, 33, 36, 38, 43, 69, 70, 79, 84, 89, 103, 106, 122, 123, 130, 143, 145, 146, 148, 150, 153–6, 158–61, 167, 169, 170, 182, 183, 194, 202, 205, 206, 208, 210–17, 219–32, 238, 239
Honorius III (Pope), 153
Hopton, Walter of, 82, 221
Hwfa ap Cynddelw, 101, 191, 192
Hywel I, bishop of St. Asaph, 169
Hywel ap Cynfrig (or Cynddelw), 123, 124, 126, 216
Hywel ap Cynfrig, 212
Hywel ab Ednyfed, bishop of St. Asaph, 35, 166, 169, 170, 183, 209
Hywel ap Goronwy, 105
Hywel ap Gruffydd, xviii, 105, 134, 152, 218
Hywel ab Iorwerth of Gwynllwg, 20
Hywel ap Llywelyn, 140

INDEX

Hywel ap Madog, 145, 146
Hywel ap Rhys, 211, 218
Hywel Dda, xxxix, 6, 13, 14, 38, 114, 209, 210, 230
Hywel 'de Sochlac', 209

Iarddur, gafael, 100
Iarddur ap Cynddelw, 99, 100, 112, 124–6, 128, 132, 231
Ieuaf ap Cadwgan, 86
Ieuaf ap Cynan, gafael, 71
Ieuaf ap Ll[ywelyn], 216
Ieuan ap Hywel, 114
Ieuan Wyddel, 111
Iorwerth ap Caradog of Gwynllŵg, 10
Iorwerth ap Gwrgunon, 18, 24, 98, 100, 114, 115, 125, 131, 156, 207, 216, 232
Iorwerth ap Gwrgunon, gwely, 100, 114, 128
Iorwerth ap Hoidelw, 78
Iorwerth ap Hywel ap Tudur, 111
Iorwerth ab Iarddur, 100
Iorwerth ap Llywarch, gwely, 111
Iorwerth ap Madog (jurist), xl
Iorwerth ap Madog, gwely, 120
Iorwerth ap Madog Foelgoch, 84
Iorwerth ap Maredudd, 101
Iorwerth ap Philip, 75–7
Iorwerth Drwyndwn, xviii, 152
Iorwerth Foel, 146
Iorwerth Fychan and Einion Mon, gwely, 109
Iorwerth Fychan ab Iorwerth ap Tudur, 111
Iorwerth Goch, 75, 76
Ireland, 105, 214
Irfon Bridge, battle of, xxx
Ithel ap Bleddyn, 261
Ithel ap Dafydd, 157
Ithel ap Philip, 6
Ithel ap Tegwared, 216

Joan, daughter of King John, wife of Llywelyn ab Iorwerth, xix, xxi, 86, 105, 208, 210, 214, 225
John (king), xix, xx, xxiii, xxxi, 116, 147, 148, 215, 225
John, bishop of St. Asaph, 174
John, notary, 225
John the Scot of Chester, 207

Kilwardby, Robert, archbishop of Canterbury, 5, 35
Knovill, Bogo de, 233

La Mare, 212
Leominster, 94
Leicester, Robert of, 38, 81
Lestrange, John, 212, 219, 231, 238
Lestrange, Roger, 34
London, 33, 107, 208, 219, 232
London, Tower of, xxiii, 143, 155, 219, 229, 232

Llanberis, 204
Llandaff, bishop of, 169
Llanfaes, 57, 58, 61, 79, 80, 181, 203, 234, 235
Llangollen, 13, 208
Llanrwst, 71
Llechog, 75, 76
Lledwigan Llan, 140, 143, 145–7
Lledwigan Llys, 98
Llifon, 130, 156
Llygad Gwr, 4
Llŷn, xiv, xvi, xviii, xxiv, xxv, 62, 68, 72, 73, 76, 93, 118, 122, 128, 131, 133, 142, 147–50, 152, 153, 156–8, 162, 195, 200, 230
Llysaled, 90, 130
Llysfaen, 52, 238
Llyslew, 112, 133, 156
Llywarch, 'treasurer' to Gruffydd ap Llywelyn, 20
Llywarch ap Bran, 101, 110, 125, 126, 128, 132, 156
Llywelyn ap Dafydd Gethin, 109
Llywelyn ap Gruffydd, xiii, xxiii, xxv–xxx, xxxxii–xxxv, xli, xlii, 2–8, 10, 15, 16, 18, 19, 22, 26–8, 31–7, 42, 43, 51, 53, 55, 58, 60, 62, 67, 69, 70, 75–8, 81–3, 85, 87, 89, 91–4, 97, 99–102, 104–8, 111–14, 117, 118, 121–3, 126–8, 131–3, 138, 141, 143, 144, 146–50, 152, 155–62, 166, 168–84, 192–6, 203–7, 210, 211, 213, 214, 216–18, 220–34, 236, 237
Llywelyn ap Gruffydd (friar), 59, 62, 105, 118, 218, 236
Llywelyn ap Gruffydd ab Iorwerth 191, 192
Llywelyn ab Ednyfed, 132

254 INDEX

Llywelyn ab Iorwerth, xiii, xviii–xxii, xxx–xxxii, xl, xli, 1, 2, 5–8, 11, 13, 14, 26, 27, 31, 34, 35, 43, 48, 61, 67, 70, 78, 80, 81, 86, 94, 97–106, 109, 110, 114–17, 122, 128, 139, 141, 142, 147–54, 163, 166–9, 181–3, 193, 199–205, 207, 208, 210, 211, 212, 214–16, 222, 223, 225, 227, 228, 230
Llywelyn ap Llywelyn ap Maredudd, 144
Llywelyn ap Maredudd ap Llywelyn Fawr, 143, 146
Llywelyn ab Owain, 140
Llywelyn ab Owain, gwely, 140
Llywelyn Fawr ap Maredudd, 142, 143, 145
Llywelyn Fychan ap Maredudd, 142, 143, 144

Mabon Glochydd, 79, 120, 121, 131, 188
Madog ap Bleddyn ap Meurig, 216
Madog ap Cynfrig, archdeacon of Anglesey, 237
Madog ab Einion, 28, 204
Madog ap Gruffydd (Cydewain), 7, 82
Madog ap Gruffydd Maelor, 13, 167, 202
Madog ab Iarddur, 100, 112, 125
Madog ab Iorwerth Goch, 120, 121, 134, 217
Madog ap Llywelyn, 76, 106, 113, 143–7
Madog ap Mabon, 121, 131
Madog ap Magister, 26, 38, 39, 226
Madog ap Maredudd, 50, 123
Madog ap Maredudd ap Dafydd, 123, 134
Madog ab Owain, 140
Madog ab Owain, gwely, 140
Madog ap Philip (Master), 32, 33, 222, 226
Madog ap Rhirid, 202
Madog Fugail, 84
Madog Fychan, 36, 225
Madog Fychan of Bromfield, 180, 219
Madog Gloddaeth, 238, 239
Madog Goch, bailiff, 216
Madog Goch, clerk, 226
Madog Goch ab Iorwerth, 114
Maelgwn ap Rhys of Deheubarth, 15, 202

Maelienydd, xxvi, 5, 16, 203, 231
Maenan, 130, 131, 220
Maesgwyn, 103
Maesmynan, 230
Malltraeth, 98, 130–3, 156, 237
Mansel, John, 219
Marchros, 132
Marchudd, 97
Maredudd, abbot of Aberconwy, 226
Maredudd ap Cadwgan, 111
Maredudd ap Cynan, xviii, xxiii, 142, 143, 152, 197, 199, 200
Maredudd ap Gruffydd, 112
Maredudd ab Ieuaf, 134, 216
Maredudd ab Iorwerth, 98, 110–12, 125, 132, 133, 217
Maredudd ab Iorwerth, gwelyau, 98, 110, 111
Maredudd ap Llywelyn, 144
Maredudd ap Llywelyn Fawr, 143
Maredudd ap Madog, 144
Maredudd ab Owain, 15, 16
Maredudd ap Rhicert, 148–51, 158, 217
Maredudd ap Rhotpert of Cydewain, 6, 202
Maredudd ap Rhys, xxvi, xxvii, xxxii, xxxiii, 7, 10, 15, 51, 177, 222
Maredudd Fychan, 151
Margam, abbey of, 94
Margaret of Bromfield, 7
Margaret, daughter of Madog ap Maredudd, xviii
Marshall, William, 222
Matusalem ap Hwfa, 101
Matusalem ap Hwfa, gwely, 101
Mawddach, xvi
Mechain, 209
Meilir, 109, 110
Meirionydd, xiv, xv, xviii, xxii, xxiv, xxv, 2, 44, 47, 49, 142–7, 151–3, 158, 178, 182, 200
Menai, xvi, xxx, 79, 105, 121, 124, 130, 132, 133, 157, 188, 200
Menteith, earl of, xxv
Merionethshire, xxxvii, 34, 36, 61, 62, 65, 68, 78, 90, 133, 235
Meurig ap Gruffydd, 220
Middle, pact of, xxii
Mochdref, 120
Mold, 233
Montfort, Eleanor de, xxviii, xxix, xxxiv, 177, 214
Montfort, Peter de, 15

INDEX

Montfort, Simon de, xxvi, xxxii
Montgomery, xx, 233
Montgomery, treaty of, xxvii, xxviii, xxxii, xxxiii, xxxv, 8, 21, 69, 161, 177, 207, 209, 213, 220
Mordic Ddu, 23
Morgan ap Hywel of Gwynllŵg, 20
Morton, 218
Mortimer, Ralph, 118, 154, 203, 230, 231
Mortimer, Roger, xxvi, 16, 204
'Moston', 214
Mynydd Marian, 238

Nant, 131
Nant Conwy, xviii, 115
Nantfychan, 121
Nantmawr, 113, 235, 236
Nefyn, xiv, xv, xviii, 4, 43, 73, 80, 149, 197, 202
Neigwl, 57, 216
Neville, Ralph, 7

Oswestry, 7, 216, 221
Owain, the chamberlain, 23, 217
Owain ap Dafydd, 116, 142, 147, 148, 201
Owain ap Gruffydd, xxiii, xxv, xxix, xxxii, xxxiv, 16, 18, 19, 51, 98, 107, 110–12, 148, 151, 155, 157–62, 168, 170, 203, 204, 229, 231–3
Owain ap Gruffydd Maelor II, 162
Owain ap Gruffydd ap Gwenwynwyn, xxviii, 206, 207, 210, 220, 234
Owain Brogyntyn, 145
Owain Gwynedd, xvi–xviii, 14, 100, 101, 110, 114, 116, 117, 140, 141, 147–9, 156, 192
Oxford, 170, 219

Painscastle, xxi
Pandulf, papal legate, 153
Paris, Matthew, xxxviii, 229
Pateshull, Simon, 208
Peckham, John, archbishop of Canterbury, xxxiv, xxxvi, 8, 36, 39, 160, 180, 225, 228
Pembroke, earl of, xx, xxi
Penhwnllys, 113, 132
Penllyn, xiii, xviii, 5, 55, 57, 67, 114, 131, 157, 216, 217
Penmaen-Llysfaen, 52, 238, 239
Penmynydd, 90, 130

Pennant, 141, 204
Pennant, Gwernogof, 99, 132, 221
Pennardd, 157, 204
Pennarfynydd, 118
Penrhos, xxxvii, 59, 61, 62, 233, 236
Penrhyn, 91, 130
Penyberth, 118
Penychen, 118
Philip, king of France, xix, 7
Philip, father of Iorwerth, 76
Philip ap Gilbert, 43, 149, 150, 217
Philip ab Ifor, 26, 31, 34, 35, 227
Philip ab Owain, 140
Philip ab Owain, gwely, 140, 141
Pipton, treaty of, xxvi
Pool (Welshpool), 233
Porthaethwy, 56, 79, 121, 200
Porthaml, 132
Powys, xiii, xviii–xx, xxiii–xxv, xxvii, xxviii, 139, 152, 153, 163, 164, 167, 177, 191, 192, 203, 210
Prydydd y Moch, 199, 200
Pwllheli, 57, 80, 230
Pyll ap Cynfrig, 84
Pyll Goch, 23

Radnor, 204
Ranulf of Chester, xx, 15, 207, 213, 215, 216
Ratlingcope, priory of, 3
Reiner, bishop of St. Asaph, 169
Richard, bishop of Bangor, 36, 168–73, 203, 222, 229, 232
Richard of Mold, clerk, 21–3, 227
Richard ap Cadwaladr (Rhicert ap Cadwaladr), 43
Richard ap Madog, 227
Rivaux, Peter de, xxi, xxii
Robert, bishop of Bangor, 168
Robert of Nefyn, 197
Roger, clerk of Rhuddlan, 22, 227, 228
Ruthin, xxxvi, 202
Rhicert ap Cadwaladr, 149, 150, 202, 218
Rhicert Goch, 84
Rhirid ap Cadwgan, 57
Rhirid ap Madog, 217
Rhodri ap Gruffydd, xxiv, xxxiv, 33, 34, 156, 159, 160, 162, 177, 195, 206, 207, 210, 218, 220, 224, 226, 228, 232
Rhodri ab Owain, xviii, 46, 115, 119, 125, 141, 142, 148, 200

INDEX

Rhos, 40, 42, 52, 69, 70, 78, 84, 85, 97, 119, 120, 122, 123, 128, 130, 131, 134, 210, 214, 216, 217, 230, 238
Rhos Fyneich, 32, 80
Rhosfair, 61, 124, 203
Rhuddlan, xv, 7, 33, 47, 82, 103, 120, 122, 134, 181, 183, 206, 214, 217, 218, 226
Rhuddlan, statute of, 145
Rhufon ap Nefydd Hardd, 71, 114, 213
Rhufoniog, 42, 58, 69–72, 93, 130, 134, 160, 191, 230, 238
Rhwng Dwyfor a Dwyfach, 61
Rhys ab Ednyfed, 104, 105, 120–2, 134, 206, 217, 218
Rhys ap Gruffydd (d. 1356), 106
Rhys ap Gruffydd (the Lord Rhys), xx, 1, 6, 18
Rhys ap Gruffydd ab Ednyfed, 85, 104, 106, 129, 218
Rhys ap Gruffydd ap Rhys, 202
Rhys ap Maredudd, xxvi, xxvii, xxix, xxx, xxxiv
Rhys ap Tudur, 235, 236, 218
Rhys Fychan, xxix, 15, 16, 204
Rhys Gryg, 202

St. Asaph, xv, 34, 42, 44, 75, 83–87, 92, 97, 119, 134, 138, 166, 168, 169, 173, 176–80, 182, 184, 204
St. Asaph, bishop of, 208, 210, 223, 227
St. David's, bishop of, 169
St. Edmundo, Michael de, 239
Salop (Shropshire), xx, 211
Sechtone (Sychdyn), 234
Senena, wife of Gruffydd ap Llywelyn, xxxi, xxxii, 230–2
Shaldeford, William, 237
Shrewsbury, 208, 211, 212, 222
Simon, clerk, 228
Snowdonia, xv, 51, 100
Stafford, 211
Stephen of Nefyn, 197
Strata Florida, 2, 33
Strata Marcella, 28, 152, 200–2, 204
Swydd Llannerch Hudol, 192

Talyboleon, 42, 132, 133
Talybont, 60, 61, 68, 78, 101, 234
Tangwystl Goch, xxi
Tegeingl (Englefield), xxiii, 42, 43, 47, 50, 69, 113, 119, 122, 123, 130, 131, 134, 214, 229, 230
Tegwared ab Ithel, 134, 218

Tegwared ap John, 82
Tegwared, the deacon's son, 84
Tewkesbury, 94
Thomas ap Rhodri, 116, 117, 133
'Toronyth', 103
Trecastell, 90, 130
Tref Madrun, 93
Trefan, 157
Trefchyn, 234
Trefddisteiniaid, 98, 109, 132
Trefeglwys, 203
Trefor Fychan, 109, 132
Trefraint, 132
Tregarnedd, 124, 130
Trelywarch, 111, 132
Tre'r beirdd, 204
Trewalchmai, 132
Trysglwyn, 130
Tudur, rhingyll of Eiryoes, 221
Tudur ab Ednyfed, 11–13, 17–19, 24, 84, 104, 106, 108, 121, 122, 129–31, 134, 210, 213, 218–21
Tudur ab Einion, 118
Tudur ap Goronwy, 47, 104, 106, 126
Tudur ap Gruffydd, 111, 112
Tudur ap Gruffydd, gwely, 111, 112
Tudur ap Madog, 18, 24, 98–100, 112, 113, 125, 126, 131, 132, 155, 207, 221, 231
Tudur ap Madog, gwelyau, 99, 100, 113
Tudur ap Madog, 120
Tudur Fychan, 113, 131, 235–7
Twrcelyn, 75, 100, 114, 121, 130, 131, 156, 235
Twrgarw, 132
Twynnan, 103
Tywyn, xiv, 78

Valle Crucis, 13, 226
Vaudey, abbot of, 7
Vere, Geoffrey de, 201

Wauncey, Edmund de, 237
Wellington, 225
Westminster, 210
William, Master, 228
William ap Daniel, 38, 39, 228
William of Llanfaes, 38, 228
William Rufus, 228
Windsor, 214
Woodstock, treaty of, xxiv, 170
Worcester, xxix, 208

INDEX

Worcester, treaty of, xx, 207, 210
Wyrion ap Cynddelw, gwely, 99, 100
Wyrion Cynan, gwely, 141
Wyrion Eden, 90, 91, 102–4, 106, 125, 164
Wyrion Einion ap Gwalchmai, gwely, 98
Wyrion Iarddur, gwely, 99, 100
Wyrion Mabon, gwely, 121
Wyrion Utot, gwely, 61

Ynys Lannog, 107, 156, 158, 202, 203

York, archbishop of, 33
Yrewyn, Alan de, 221
Ysgeibion, 122
Ysgeifiog, 98, 110, 111, 138
Ystrad-geirch, 90
Ystrad Tywi, xxv–xxvii, 152
Ystrwyth (Ostrucius, Instructus, etc.) Master, 31, 32, 38, 201, 215, 224, 225
Ystumanner, 68, 144

Zuche, Henry de la, 224